THE Hits JUST KEEP ON COMING

THE HISTORY OF TOP 40 RADIO

BY BEN FONG-TORRES

MF Miller Freeman Books

San Francisco

Published by Miller Freeman Books
600 Harrison Street, San Francisco, CA 94107

un Miller Freeman
A United News & Media publication

Published in association with GAVIN, "The Most Trusted Name in Radio"
Gavin is published weekly by the Miller Freeman Entertainment Group
For subscription information, call (415) 495-1990.

GAVIN

Distributed to the book trade in the U.S. and Canada by
Publishers Group West, P.O. Box 8843, Emeryville, CA 94662

Distributed to the music trade in the U.S. and Canada by Hal Leonard
Publishing, P.O. Box 13819, Milwaukee, WI 53213

Design and Typesetting: Dodie Shoemaker and Peter Grame

Fong–Torres, Ben.
    The hits just keep on coming : the history of top 40 radio / Ben
    Fong-Torres.
            p. cm.
    Includes bibliographical references.
    ISBN 0-87930-547-9
    1. Popular music radio stations—History.   2. Popular music—
    History and criticism. I. Title.
    ML68.F68 1998
    791.44'6—DC21   98-41412
                                                       CIP
                                                       MN

Printed in the United States of America
98 99 00 01 02 03   5 4 3 2 1

THE *Hits* JUST KEEP ON COMING

THE HISTORY OF TOP 40 RADIO

Contents

Preface

IN THE STILL OF THE NIGHT

What was it about the radio? Why do so many people recall, so easily, those many teenage nights when they'd feign sleep while they listened to a favorite DJ or music show on a transistor radio hidden under their pillow?

For many American kids, that portable radio signified independence, an escape from the standard entertainment: the huge console radio or television set in the living room, whose programming was controlled by their parents. The music coming out of that miraculously small radio—especially the rock and roll and the jumpy country music and the fluid harmonies of doo-wop—differed enough from the pop crooners adults listened to that teenagers could embrace it as their own. And the disc jockey, with his energy, his jive lingo, his knowledge of the latest goings-on, was an entertainer in his own right, a star, reachable by a phone call or a visit to a sock hop.

For most kids, then, it was liberation and entertainment. Especially for me. I was raised in Chinatown restaurants in and around Oakland, California, and doomed to a young life of chores and schoolwork, a combination that left little time for hobbies or friends. In what time there was between school and work, there was the radio.

Before the transistor miniaturized the radio, I heard whatever was on the big Zenith console. Aside from the comedy and crime series, I'd hear an endless stream of ballads aimed at adults. "Why Don't You Believe Me?" by Joni James, "Don't Let the Stars Get in Your Eyes" by Perry Como, and "How Much Is That Doggie in the Window?" by Doris Day were the first hits I remember.

And, I admit, I loved it. I was not aware, at age ten, of rhythm and blues, whose artists paved the way for rock and roll. I knew R&B and country tunes only as they were covered by pop artists. "Your Cheatin' Heart," for me, was Joni James, not Hank Williams, and "Sh-Boom" was by the Crew Cuts and not by the Chords.

4

With Elvis and rock and roll, that all changed. As I wrote in my book, *The Rice Room:*

"At night, when we were supposed to be asleep, [my brother] Barry and I read our comics by flashlight under the covers. When transistor radios were first sold, we treasured the one we got. But I also managed to get a pocket radio, in the shape of a rocket, that required clipping a wired antenna to an outside line. I'd string it out our second floor bedroom window to the clothesline and listen to music through a plastic earpiece. It was barely low-fi, but I didn't care."

The music came by way of nightly shows called *The Burgie Music Box* and *Lucky Lager Dance Time.* Although I was only ten or eleven, I knew both sponsors, since I helped lug cases of their empty beer bottles to the storage room at our restaurant. I remember the sometimes clumsy mix of middle-of-the-road pop and teen hits in the Lucky Lager Top Ten countdowns…"Young Love" by Tab Hunter followed by "Canadian Sunset" by Hugo Winterhalter; then the Platters…then Guy Mitchell with "Singing the Blues." I had no idea, of course, that in time—say, fifteen or twenty-five years—I'd meet the man who programmed the music for those shows and write about him, and, eventually, become the editor of the magazine he would found.

When, in the fall of 1956, the Bay Area got its first Top 40 station, "Wonderful KOBY," my sister Sarah brought home their Top 40 surveys, and I found a new hobby.

Before I could even accumulate a short stack of surveys, however, I had to leave town. In the summer of 1957, my father, who'd operated small restaurants in Chinatown, became a partner in a fancier place on Route 66, in Amarillo, Texas, and took me along. There, without the rest of our family, I turned even more to the radio. In the Panhandle, the first station to go the Top 40 route, KFDA, played equal parts country and rock and roll. I heard as much Marty Robbins and Marvin Rainwater as I did Chuck Berry and Buddy Holly. I didn't know it then, but Top 40 meant democracy in radio.

The author as radio groupie, 1960, with Gary Owens.

I was in it for the music and the disc jockeys. And, soon after getting back to Oakland, I caught onto a new station, KEWB, and, in particular, to its morning DJ, Gary Owens. The station called itself "Color Radio, Channel 91," a takeoff on color television at a time—in 1959—when it was still a novelty.

I don't recall how I did it—it may have been from writing sophomoric fan letters to Owens—but I got a job there in the fall of 1960 as a Saturday assistant to one of the newscasters. I'd pull college football scores off the wire machine and relay them to the newsman. Every Saturday morning, I floated to the KEWB studios in downtown Oakland. I don't remember how much I made, but just getting past the guard—because I was, after all, an employee—was payment enough for me.

By now, I was a confirmed radio nut, and, in high school, I only got worse. Inspired in equal measure by Top 40 radio and Steve Allen, I worked (as much as I could in the context of being a Chinese restaurant slave) to do anything even approximating that of a broadcaster. At Oakland High, I wrote a humor column for the school paper, then won office as Commissioner of Assemblies. That meant that I could open the weekly gatherings of the student body with comedy monologues. And, given the most minute of openings, I'd book KEWB disc jockeys for guest appearances. In the cafeteria, I sometimes set up a sound system and spun records, and began getting hired to be a DJ at dances for various youth groups. Being a Chinese restaurant geek, committed to working every evening, I couldn't be among the social elite. But, on occasion, I could be the guy playing the records for them. And that was good enough for me.

Well, almost. Being a Chinese-American kid in the early sixties, I knew it was a pipe dream, but I fantasized about someday becoming a disc jockey. I dared not express my fantasies aloud, having been plopped dead center into a culture that expected all its children to grow up to be doctors and lawyers.

I wasn't exactly furtive. I didn't hide the KEWB Fabulous 40 surveys I so loyally collected each week from local record shops. My best friends in high school knew about my passion; even played along with me as I set up an embarrassingly cheap faux radio studio at home.

We didn't have the money to buy a record player, so our first phonograph was one that Barry had patched together. He got a children's 78 rpm model at a thrift shop and honed the capstan down until the speed decreased to 45, then mounted it onto a cigar box. We had a few records, but I sometimes resorted to cut-rate albums of hit singles as sung by sound-alike artists.

But, no matter how funky the hardware, I loved acting out my fantasy. I had a knack for mimicking voices and DJ patter; I learned the rhythms of Top 40 radio; and I mastered the art of the talk-up—that is, talking over the instrumental beginning of a song, concluding the micro-second before the vocal begins. Years later, I would hear radio pros call it "hitting the post." On songs like Gene McDaniel's "A Hundred Pounds of Clay," I was a cinch to nail the post. But it would be many years before I'd have a chance to hit the post on a Top 40 station.

As I would learn while researching this book, I was only one of many thousands who fantasized about being a DJ—setting up rinky-dink record players, taping commercials and jingles off the radio to insert between records, hanging out wherever we might be able to meet an actual disc jockey. That was the plan, Stan: Meet one, then be one.

You might think that I was an unemployable nut. But in and around that time, I was a hyperactive editor and writer at my college daily and then, just a couple of years after graduation, an editor at *Rolling Stone*, the rock publication out of San Francisco that, soon enough, became the arbiter of all that was hip and countercultural. To our way of group thinking, what was groovy was on the emerging FM dial—the free-form stations sprouting in our hometown, as well as Los Angeles, New York, Boston, Detroit, and maybe a pirate operation off the coast of Britain. What was square? Top 40.

I was torn. But, invariably, under my bylines on stories about media, I was a traitor to my first love, and I turned my coat so effectively that, three decades later, when I finally met Robert W. Morgan, he greeted me as, "Ah, yes—the *Rolling Stone* anti-Top 40-christ!" I could only hang my head. I had been a true fan of the format—and, in particular, of Morgan and the Real Don Steele when they arrived in Oakland to shore up a faltering KEWB in 1964—but he was right. I'd taken to looking down on a genre that I thought had outlived its usefulness, that was a dinosaur, little more than an outpost for teenybopper music and manic, hopelessly outdated disc jockeys.

But, now and again, I let my true sentiments show. For example, my review of a Jackson 5 concert in 1974 went exactly like this:

"I remember the day my voice changed. I was at my after-school job at Moon's Chinese Kitchen in Emeryville, California, taking take-out orders over the phone. In the middle of confirming a shrimp fried rice and prawns, the 13-year-old pipes gave out a pre-plunge squeak, and suddenly I was within reach of my lifetime ambition, to replace one of the Seven Swingin' Gentlemen on Color Radio, KEWB, Channel 91. I felt an ecstasy I would not feel again for, oh, too many years."

In *Rolling Stone*'s first years, Bill Drake's formattics on such stations as KHJ ("Boss Radio") in Los Angeles and KFRC ("The Big 6-10") in San Francisco ruled. Soon, stations around the country were copping his style, down to the jingles and the placement of newscasts at twenty minutes past or before the hour—"20/20 News."

And in "Random Notes," which it was one of my jobs to collect and write, how did I invariably introduce a long paragraph of short items? "20/20 News."

Top 40, Baby!

This Is Dedicated...

This is a book of love. And, as with any book requiring research and interviews, it could not have happened without the support of many people, both friends and people who once were strangers.

My first call was to Bonnie Simmons, a longtime radio and music buddy. I'd connected her years ago with the Rock and Roll Hall of Fame and Museum, and she put together its impressive radio exhibit of biographies and air checks. She made tapes of those air checks available to me, getting me off to an informed (and well-entertained) start.

After making up an initial wish list, I was fortunate to come across Don Barrett's *Los Angeles Radio People*, an A to Z listing of just about anyone who's ever set mouth before a microphone in Southern California. Don connected me with some key figures early on.

Los Angeles is the historical home of such powerhouse Top 40 stations as KFWB, KRLA, and KHJ, better remembered as "Boss Radio." Ron Jacobs, its first program director, lent immediate support with his vivid memories of everything from Bill Gavin's influence on him to his own influence on radio broadcasting.

Tragically, only a few months before I began work on the book, radio lost its quintessential Top 40 disc jockey, the Real Don Steele. I learned that I would have to rely, in great part, on his widow, Shaune McNamara Steele. She turned out to be a blessing, as she shared transcripts of the only in-depth interviews her husband ever gave, as well as air checks and video-tapes of his work. She even found a clipping of the first newspaper mention Don got when he arrived in Oakland, California, in 1963 to work at KEWB. It was in a column written by a college kid who, some thirty-five years later, would be writing about him again—in a book on the history of Top 40 radio.

As I dove into research, I learned of the wealth of air checks and jingles available on the Internet. But I far preferred the samplings of great Top 40 radio that fans and students of radio, as well as disc jockeys and other industry pros, sent me. Chief among them are Ron Lyons, a former KEWB DJ who, years ago, sent a tape of the classic jingles from my beloved "Color Radio"; Roger Steffens, an expert on Alan Freed and Bob Marley (how's that for range?); Steve Rood; Norman Davis; Liz Salazar; Bobby Ocean; Don Worsham; Rick Scilleppi; Kevin Gershan; and Art Vuolo, known and loved in the business as "Radio's Best Friend." Art has been videotaping disc jockeys at work for more than twenty years; besides letting me see some legendary DJs at work, he provided a wonderful set of air checks of Joey Reynolds and several New York radio greats.

Some other passionate keepers of the rock and roll flame who helped me were John Goddard of the Village Music record store in Mill Valley, California, who lent me a copy of the extremely hard-to-find movie *American Hot Wax* (naturally, it aired on cable about a month later); Joel Selvin of the *San Francisco Chronicle*, whose latest book is on Sly Stone—who spent a couple of years as a DJ while assembling the Family Stone; Steve Resnik, one of the all-time collectors of music and radio treasures; and Woody Goulart, editor of the on-line tribute to KHJ, the Boss Radio Forever web site (*http://www.bossradioforever.com*).

For research assistance, I called on a delightful young journalism student from San Francisco State University who had served an internship at *Gavin* magazine. Laura Swezey is well on her way to success as a writer. For editorial assistance, I thank Lori Cooper, Ken Cooper, and Kathryn Gallagher. Kathryn also supplemented the fine work of photo researcher Erica Ackerberg. For their help in the research process, I also want to thank the Museum of Television & Radio; Claude Hall, whose "Vox Jox" column in *Billboard* magazine was one of my must-reads in the early sixties; Jack Raymond of WEIM in Leominster, Massachusetts; John Hart; Larry Kent; Ian Whitcomb; Al Kostors, and three of my best friends in and out of radio: Gary Owens, Russ "the Moose" Syracuse, and Tommy Saunders.

As was the case with my previous books, research and writing left little time for a normal life. On my rare trips out of my office to the rest of the house—and the world—it was always good to see my wife, Dianne, and our little boy, Buster. Dianne gave unstinting support and loving encouragement; Buster mostly barked. Thanks to our friends who kept Dianne company, along with television shows like *Ally McBeal, The Practice*, and *Law and Order*. Oh—did I mention that Dianne was a probation officer?

For general good cheer and support, I thank my in-laws, Robin and Chuck Ward and Eileen and Richard Powers, and outlaws—that is, my sisters Sarah and Shirley, brother Burton, and mother Mom. And I thank Tom

Gericke; Bob Barnes; Catherine Baron; Holly George-Warren and her boys, Robert and Jack; Peter "Dr. Evil" Dmytryk and his girls, Nancy and Emily; Quincy McCoy, Dave Sholin and Annette M. Lai at *Gavin* magazine; and Louis and Nancy Chan at the Yet Wah, where I escaped for karaoke breaks.

I am grateful to Miller Freeman Books for welcoming the idea of a new line of books under the *Gavin* imprint, for agreeing to this one as the inaugural title, for providing Matt Kelsey as my editor, and for blessing me with a superb copy editor, Carolyn Keating.

Thanks, and more, to David Dalton, the CEO of *Gavin*, for making it possible for me to take leave of the magazine, where I had been managing editor for four years, for this project. *Gavin* is a trade magazine, long known as "The Most Trusted Name in Radio." Although available by subscription only, and tailored for industry professionals, its news and feature articles, along with record reviews covering a wide range of radio music formats, make interesting reading for all followers of radio and music.

The publication of this book coincides with the fortieth anniversary of Bill Gavin's founding of the publication. His love of good radio—radio that informs, reflects, and serves its listeners—and his personal integrity inspired many, many people in the broadcasting and music industries. He is still missed by thousands of colleagues and friends. With hope that it does justice to the man and his work, and with thanks and appreciation to his family, I dedicate this book to Bill Gavin.

Introduction:
Radio Ga Ga

"God, disc jockeys, then parents."
—*KHJ Boss Jock Robert W. Morgan reporting the results of a poll at a teen fair in Hollywood in 1966, asking who is the biggest influence on your life?*

How do you write a book about a forty-five-year-old phenomenon that, like the records it used to spin, has gone through forty-five revolutions per minute?

I've chosen to do it like a radio show. And so, heeding the advice of programmers from the earliest to the latest stations, I've prepped, researching the history not only of Top 40, but also of what set the stage for it, and interviewing as many of the main players as I could find. Given that many of these people span three or four decades in radio, and have jumped from town to town—and even from format to format—I've forsaken the idea of a strict, chronological narrative. Instead, like a variety show, there'll be spotlights on singular performers and programmers, based on interviews with, among others, Dick Clark, Casey Kasem, Bill Drake, Robert W. Morgan, "Cousin Brucie" Morrow, and Joe "Rockin' Bird" Niagara. A personal fab four—Gary Owens, Bobby Dale, Scott Shannon, and Rick Dees—are featured in question-and-answer sessions. And, like jingles and commercials, there'll be sidelights—sound bites, excerpts, and anecdotes from here and there, "there" often being *Gavin*, the radio magazine (and Bill Gavin, its founder).

Finally, like any right-thinking radio announcer should, I'll billboard—that is, say what's coming up.

This is a book about the most dynamic of all radio formats, and about the disc jockeys—or DJs—who drove it.

Dick Clark, the first national DJ, with Fabian.

Unless you were cruelly sheltered, or simply had taste buds that led you away from the pop culture mainstream of the fifties and the sixties, you grew up with Top 40. You heard your first rock and roll on Top 40 stations, and learned about its artists from men who, although many of them were just a few years older than you, seemed to inhabit another world. They had nicknames: "Woo Woo"…"Moondog"…"Weird Beard" …"Cousin." They had a group identity. "The Good Guys." "The Seven Swingin' Gentlemen." "The All-Americans." "The Boss Jocks." They gave away cash and prizes on the air, and they presided over sock hops and *Bandstand*-type shows on local television. They were like Dick Clark. Only they lived in your town.

They also got in trouble for taking payola, or for chasing underage girls, or for being drunk or on drugs. They got fired, hired, and fired again, and they committed suicide or died in automobile wrecks. But those things always happened off the air. True radio fans noticed when a DJ dropped out of sight, off his show and off the weekly "Fab 40" or "Swingin' 60" or "Tunedex" survey. But many listeners never noticed the personnel shifts, as their favorite stations never missed a beat. There was always something going on, between the music, the jingles, the commercials, the news and …sports and weather reports, and the platter chatter and contests and dedications. There was never a second of dead air.

Top 40 evolved into a tight format, but, compared with the orderly programs of the networks and with the announcers of what was called middle-of-the-road (MOR) music—pop music for the "then" people—Top 40 sounded like absolute chaos.

It would be designed to draw adults as well as teenagers, but on the surface, it was a hyped-up soundtrack for that other cold war of the fifties and early sixties: the one between adults and kids.

As they always seem to do, youth won out. Station owners who derided Top 40 were forced to adopt the format. Disc jockeys raised on "good music," or who liked jazz, R&B, and other roots music, sniffed at the pablum they were sometimes forced to play, then considered their employment options and cozied up to its performers at record hops and station-sponsored concerts. Advertisers did similar cheek-turning, or complete about-faces.

Together, they created a new national jukebox, one whose concept of mainstream included many strains of music, and one that, despite the tumultuous social, political, musical and business changes over the decades, endures as a symbol of musical democracy. The everlasting mantra of the format is: "Play the hits." That is, what the people want to hear. That was what Top 40's founding fathers—Todd Storz, Gordon McLendon, and Bill Stewart—had discovered in the early fifties, and that's been the programmer's cry ever since.

Each time there's been a dip in the format's collective ratings—a new competitor, a new crisis, a call for its collective head—some consultant or PD (Program Director) comes along and, like a John Wayne pushing his troops through a muddy jungle, implores: "Play the hits."

But, as the music—and its listeners—change, is it still a democracy? Can it even consider being one? Early on, Top 40 played whatever was popular. Besides the twin cores of leftover pop and the still infant rebel, rock and roll, stations found room for country (Johnny Cash, Sonny James, Johnny Horton, Marty Robbins, Ferlin Husky, Patsy Cline), blues (Bobby Blue Bland, Ray Charles, and Etta James were early chart-toppers), novelty tunes (The Chipmunks, Stan Freberg, "Mr. Custer," "Ahab the Arab"), jazz (Dave Brubeck's "Take Five," Vince Guaraldi, Astrid Gilberto), and even soundtracks ("Theme From *A Summer Place*," "Moon River").

Nowadays, each of those categories either has its own format or no radio home at all, except for the odd specialty show, usually on weekends, late at night, on a non-commercial station.

Funny thing. That's where some of the music that formed rock and roll got its first exposure. It was that music, presented the right way, in the right place, at the right time, that gave birth to Top 40 radio, and a rebirth to radio itself.

Chapter

Video Killed the Radio Star

O n the eve of rock and roll, radio was being read its last rites. Or so it seemed, as, in living room after living room, families were carting in this long-delayed invention called television, and pushing the console radio out of the center of their evening lives. Given how enormous a presence television became, it's amazing how faltering its early steps were.

Television had been around for almost as long as radio. Commercial radio began in the early twenties, and by that time, scientists, engineers, and other seers had been talking about the wireless transmission of visual images for two decades. In 1923, David Sarnoff, the general manager at RCA, sent a memo to the corporation's senior executives, predicting that "television will make it possible for those at home to see as well as hear what is going on at the broadcast station."

Postwar Radio Wars

Veterans of radio's Golden Age had little use for pop music's intrusion—in any form. Here's how humorist Henry Morgan, in 1972, concluded his introduction to *THE BIG BROADCAST*, a wonderful encyclopedia of radio programs from 1920 to 1950:

> Television warmed up after World War II, and radio started its dive somewhere around 1951 or 1952. Radio actually died when *Stop the Music* got higher ratings than Fred Allen. Bert Parks went on from *Music* to become the celebrated singer on the Miss America pageants, which are still thrilling people who get thrilled by things like that, but all that's left of radio is in the pages that follow.

Stop the Music, a quiz show that randomly called contestants at home, began on the ABC network in 1948. According to *The Big Broadcast*, it was "an immediate success; so much so that Fred Allen, who was on at the same time, announced a bond guaranteeing $5,000 to anyone who was called by *Stop the Music* while listening to *The Fred Allen Show*."

In 1946, ten thousand TV sets were in use in American homes. Six years later, the number had grown to twenty-seven million.

But while radio consoles quickly found homes throughout the country, television went through two decades of experimentation—slowed considerably by the stock market crash of 1929 and the resulting Great Depression—before NBC received the first commercial television license from the Federal Communications Commission in 1941. Then, the fledgling industry—only a hundred or so TV sets existed—ran straight into World War II. Development and production efforts came to a standstill, as manpower, raw materials, and money went to the war effort.

At war's end in the mid-forties, television and its backers were ready to roll again, and it found a public eager for a new entertainment medium—a medium whose first stars were familiar to them from network radio. Between 1947 and 1948, television took a small but significant leap: the number of cities with television stations tripled, from eight to twenty-three, and there were forty-one stations on the air, up from just seventeen. By the end of 1954, 354 TV stations were operating. The radio networks, urged on by Sarnoff and anxious to be part of this promising new media, drove the growth, but in late 1948, the FCC, wanting to study the potential impact of television, froze all pending licenses. The delay continued through the Korean War.

Stations that were on the air stayed on however, and people continued to purchase TV sets. In 1946, there were only ten thousand sets in American homes. Three years later, there were a million, and by 1952, some twenty-seven million receivers were aglow.

Network radio didn't need any FCC study to tell them about the impact. Advertising revenue began to dip, plunging from $134 million in 1948 to $103 million in 1952. Meanwhile, network television ad dollars exploded from $2.5 million in 1948 to $172 million in 1952, which was the year the FCC finally allowed the frozen license applications to go forward. By then, television had replaced radio as the country's favorite evening entertainment, and network radio, although anxious to reap the benefits of the new industry, instead saw a massive exodus of talent—both in front of the microphone and behind the scenes.

But that was radio on the network level. Independent stations, which made up the majority of licensees, had started aggressively pursuing local advertisers. In fact, local and regional ad revenues rose from $417 million in 1948 to $473 million in 1952.

The radio networks fought television first by continuing the kinds of

Cheer Up, Bunky...

Radio got a booster shot in 1953 when, in the midst of all the doomsday talk about the industry, a study by the Arthur Politz research firm showed that, despite television, radio was in good health.

Among its findings:

- There was at least one radio in 43 million homes, accounting for 96 percent of American families. Television sets were in 19 million homes (or 42 percent).
- Some 13 million people owned portable radios, and 26.5 million automobiles had radios (71 percent).
- Two-thirds of those surveyed said they listened to radio every day, and 88 percent said they listened at least once a week.

Politz asked radio listeners to tell what times of the day they used the radio. The highest numbers went to early morning ("between waking and breakfast") and late evening (between supper and bed-time), each scoring 29 percent of the listeners' responses. Mid-mornings (between breakfast and lunch) and late afternoons were also strong. The bottom line was that television had not made the dramatic dent in prime-time radio listening that the older industry had feared. And while the infant tube was drawing its greatest audience in the evening, radio was being used throughout the day.

Radio, the research reminded, could be used in tandem with other activities—driving, working, doing homework—without interfering with those activities. That was one feature television could not boast.

Radio would survive.

programs that had previously brought them success, then by cutting corners, trimming the live bands and orchestras that had been staples of the format, converting comedians into quiz show hosts, and broadcasting the audio portions of their television sibling's shows. They even cut their advertising rates, only to see their numbers—audiences and dollars—continue to fall.

The indies, many of them operated by owners and managers who were free of network constraints, improvised. As Bill Gavin wrote, "In the early fifties, television had started the destruction of big time, big name network radio by luring away those big name shows to the magic TV tube. Much of radio's audience went with them. Those of us who had made our careers in network radio felt that it was the end of the world—our world. There were, however, many hundreds of radio stations that had been making handsome profits without a network, simply by identifying with the preferences and concerns of their local listeners. In doing so, radio spawned a new breed of broadcast entertainer, the disc jockey."

Chapter

The First Time...

L egend has it that the first DJ ever on radio was Martin Block of WNEW in New York, who played records and announced them as if they were bands and singers performing in a "Make Believe Ballroom." So much for legend. Block began his show in 1935, and when *Make Believe Ballroom* became a huge success, the idea of an announcer spinning records spread quickly, with all credit to Block. But it was Al Jarvis who originated the concept and, in fact, who came up with the original *Make Believe Ballroom.*

Jarvis, who died of a heart attack in 1970 at age sixty, wasn't really the first DJ, either, despite putting in a claim for himself. A native of Canada who was raised in Los Angeles, Jarvis joined KFWB in 1932 (it was KELW at the time). As he told his story to the *Orange County Register:*

> A few weeks after I got the job...I was hounding the owner-manager to let me air pop records instead of those electrical transcriptions. By using commercial records, I figured, I would not only have a more diversified program, but I could present some of the world's great stars. It was the first time on radio, it was the first time any records were played. That's how the *Make Believe Ballroom* was born.

That's how *Ballroom* was born, but radio announcers had been playing records on Los Angeles stations as early as 1926. Jarvis, however, was recognized as the first to inject his own personality into his show. Before him, announcers did what Gary Owens would parody decades later. They stood, they enunciated, they spoke with formality, and they mostly recited copy written by others.

As for Block, he'd worked at a number of stations in Southern California and was at KELW in an off-the-air staff position when he observed Jarvis's takeoff with *Ballroom.* Soon, he himself took off for New York, where he landed an announcer's job at WNEW. When the station launched live coverage of the trial of Bruno Hauptmann, who was accused

Martin Block plays make-believe.

THE HEP PARADE OF '49...

with a rousing line-up of top rhythm stars setting the downbeat for love!

See and Hear

MAKE BELIEVE BALLROOM

FRANKIE LAINE
KING COLE TRIO
TONI HARPER
JACK SMITH
KAY STARR
THE SPORTSMEN
CHARLIE BARNET
JIMMY DORSEY
JAN GARBER
PEE WEE HUNT
GENE KRUPA
RAY McKINLEY

with JEROME COURTLAND
RUTH WARRICK
RON RANDELL
VIRGINIA WELLES
AL JARVIS

Screen Play by Albert Duffy and Karen DeWolf
Story by Albert Duffy
Directed by Joseph SANTLEY
Produced by Ted RICHMOND
A COLUMBIA PICTURE

Based on the radio programs of
AL JARVIS and MARTIN BLOCK

Block becomes the first disc jockey to cross over into movies. Alan Freed would not appear on film until 1956, with *Rock Around the Clock*.

of kidnapping the infant son of the Lindberghs, it soon found itself with long gaps between bulletins. That's when young Block suggested playing records. He dashed off to a nearby music store, purchased six records, and had himself a DJ show—"recorded and transcribed with your favorite bands and singers, old and new."

Like Jarvis, Block spoke in a natural tone, and he was an instant hit. Management soon expanded his show from fifteen to ninety minutes a day. Each featured band got fifteen minutes on an imaginary revolving stage, and Block talked about them as if they were performing live, in a ballroom.

It was Block, according to the author of a book commemorating WNEW's fiftieth anniversary, who inspired Walter Winchell to coin the term "disc jockey." Yet Bill Randle, one of the deans of the profession, has traced the term to the late Jack Kapp, a record executive who called DJs "record jockeys" in 1940—possibly because their job often included controlling the sound volume, or "riding the gain," on their records. However they got their tag, the radio field was soon filled with disc jockeys.

This is your daddio of the raddio, the platter-pushing papa, Pork the tork, the boss man, porkolating and getting you porkified with my groove porkology!

—Porky Chedwick, WAMO-Pittsburgh

Jarvis and Block, the two pioneer announcers, soon found fame and outrageous fortune. In fact, one wound up enriching the other in an early version of radio wars. Jarvis, who'd parlayed his popularity into various concert and record deals, left KFWB in 1946 to join crosstown KLAC for an astounding seven-year contract worth $1.7 million—nearly $250,000 a year. KFWB then contracted Martin Block to come home to Los Angeles. He could still do a recorded show for WNEW—he'd make believe he was in New York—and continue with a syndicated show he was already doing. All together, Block could pull in $2 million for a year of record-spinning.

As things turned out, Block failed to win over Los Angeles and returned to Manhattan, and Jarvis returned to KFWB. They would shortly be rendered obsolete by the changes sweeping through society, pop culture, and radio, becoming that most dreaded of all things in show business: the flip side of hip.

On the "A" side were Alan Freed and a wave of disc jockeys, both old and young, black and white, who were playing music—created largely by blacks—that was reaching an eager new audience outside the black community.

Since this is not a history of rock and roll, suffice it to say that, in the aftermath of World War II, America went through a seismic retrofitting. The big bands that had come into fashion in the thirties were no more, and the vocalists who took stage front—as well as the people who wrote and arranged their music—intent on keeping things light, romantic, cute, and not very danceable, were being upstaged by black musicians, who—rooted in jazz, gospel, folk and the blues—were making music that swung.

With racial barriers just beginning to come down (school segregation was ruled illegal in 1954) black music began to cross over. Often, it was established (white) companies assigning their pop stars to record cover versions of songs composed and originally performed by black artists; other times, it was the real thing getting rare exposure, either on a nighttime radio show, or on a black-oriented station that non-black listeners had heard about.

Teenagers led the way across racial lines. Bored to death by pop music aimed squarely at adults, they ached for music that could make them feel some kind of emotion; music that could inspire them to *dance*, "slow 'n' dreamy" or "hot 'n' steamy."

That music had always been there. What was rockabilly but a hopped up form of country and western swing, with a nod to the rawness that was Hank Williams? What was R&B but the blues, blended with variations of doo-wop, gospel music, jazz and swing? What was rock and roll but a wedding of the two?

Rock and roll was also attitude and style. It coalesced in one human being, an impossible package named Elvis. It was also ushered in by a movie, *Blackboard Jungle*, in which teenage rebellion got its first theme song: "Rock Around the Clock." And it pulsed on a foundation of artists and songs that exemplified both its wide range and cohesiveness: Chuck Berry, Buddy Holly, Little Richard, Fats Domino, LaVern Baker, Jerry Lee Lewis, Bo Diddley, Sam Cooke, Elvis Presley, the Moonglows; the city, the country, the world.

Al Jarvis claimed that he created the first *Make Believe Ballroom.*

It was not a singular sound, any more than jazz or classical music could be pinned down to one prototypical representative. But its common denominator was this: You could dance to it. You could *feel* to it.

This new music also had a common town crier: the disc jockey—the guy who played the music on the radio, who rode the gain, who jockeyed the discs into the national consciousness.

And—surprise—these were not the DJs of Top 40 radio. They were the

Top 40 Time Line

1935: *Your Hit Parade* debuts on the NBC Radio network, with live performances of the most popular songs of the week, as determined by sales of sheet music, records, jukeboxes, and radio airplay. Among the singers through the years: Frank Sinatra and Doris Day.

July 23, 1941: The term "disc jockey" appears in *Variety,* replacing "record jockey."

August 1, 1941: *Lucky Lager Dance Time* debuts on KFAC in Los Angeles, offering a nightly program of hit records and a "Lucky Ten" countdown show on Saturdays.

1949: KOWH, in Omaha, Nebraska, introduces a playlist format of popular records.

1951: Alan Freed joins WJW in Cleveland and, after noticing a number of white teenagers buying R&B records in a local shop, begins his late-night *Moondog Rock n' Roll Party,* bringing black music to a largely white audience.

1953: Bob Howard of WDSU in New Orleans plays *The Top 20 at 1280.*

1954: WINS in New York lures Freed out of Cleveland, where he'd been staging wildly popular R&B concerts. Freed takes WINS to the top of the ratings and sets up shop at the Paramount Theater in Brooklyn.

January 1955: Freed's first New York shows are called *Alan Freed's Rock 'n' Roll Party.* Freed claims to have coined the term to describe the music he was playing, although

precursers of Top 40, the ones who, along with Alan Freed, made up the first wave, who played the music out of a passion for it; out of a sense for what their listeners might want to hear; out of a desire for mutual discovery.

Before the music had even been named "rock and roll," these were the people who put it on the air:

"Symphony Sid" Torin, WHOM and WOV, New York: Torin got his nickname from a fellow disc jockey who knew that he was moonlighting at a record store called the Symphony Shop in New York. Torin's main gig was a half-hour show, the *After School Swing Session* on WBNX in 1937, on which he played gospel, jazz, and race records. Three years later, the gravelly voiced announcer was on WHOM, where he settled into the all-night shift. He also did the graveyard shift at WMCA and WJZ, then moved to Boston (and WBMS) in 1951. A few years later, he was back in New York, hosting the *Birdland Jazz Show* on WOV ("First in the Negro Community"). Among his listeners was Dick Clark, who names Symphony Sid and fellow WOV DJ Freddie Robbins, along with Martin Block and Art Ford of WNEW, as early radio influences. In the sixties, Torin's palette extended to Latin music. He promoted shows at the Royal Roost, where, ever the DJ, he spun records between sets.

John R., WLAC, Nashville: John Richbourg had a direct impact on a teenaged Robert Smith, who picked up the 50,000-watt Music City station from his home in Brooklyn. Smith, the future Wolfman Jack, wrote a memoir, *Have Mercy!,* in which he recalled John R.'s theme, comprised of a chorus chanting, "Hey, John R., whatcha gonna do? C'mon, John R., man, and play me some rhythm and blues." To which Richbourg would roar out his response: "Yeah! It's the big John R., the blues man. Whoa! Have mercy, honey, have mercy, have mercy. John R., 'way down south in the middle of Dixie. I'm gonna spread a little joy. You stand still now and take it like a man, you hear me?"

Gene Nobles, WLAC, Nashville: Nobles, who joined WLAC in 1943, was all over the place, hosting three shows, including *The Midnight Special* and *Gene's Record Highlites.* WLAC itself was all over the place, as Wolfman Jack explained in his autobiography: "The Nashville station had a signal strong enough to reach Brooklyn because they appealed to the FCC with the idea that black people in some rural areas around the South didn't have any stations in their own area with the kind of programming that they wanted to hear. So WLAC got permission to have one of the most powerful signals in the country, so long as they carried rhythm and blues." Thanks to Nobles, John R., and others, they did. Nobles, a native of Hot Springs, Arkansas, and a former carnival barker (his specialty was bingo), was outrageous for his

Hunter Hancock

time, insulting his audience and dealing out double-entendres. He came close to getting fired when, after a spot for a petroleum jelly, he advised listeners to keep some in their cars "for whatever might come up."

Hunter Hancock, KFVD, KGFJ, Los Angeles: "I was a little nervous when I started," Hancock says, and he had good reason to be. Born in Texas in 1915 and steeped in Southern traditions, he loved jazz and played it when he went on the air in L.A. in 1943. It was when a friend hipped him to "race records," and he gained listeners in droves, that he got a bit shaky. "Some folks," he said, "called me a 'nigger-lover.'" But he continued into the mid-sixties with his show, *Huntin' With Hunter*, also known as *Harlematinee*, promising records "from bebop to

"rocking and rolling" was known in R&B records to mean having sex.

1955: Todd Storz purchases KOWH. While at a previous station, WTIX in New Orleans, he'd heard Bob Howard, and came up with his own program, *Top 40 at 1450*. Now, in Omaha, he and his assistant, Bill Stewart, turn the show into a format.

Gordon McLendon, owner of KLIF-Dallas and a friend of Storz's, builds on the idea, adding zany promotional stunts and emphasizing local news and sports. Along with music director Bill Meeks, McLendon introduces station call letter jingles at KLIF.

AIR CHECK

Huntin' with Hunter

Here's Hunter Hancock at work, joking his way out of the Crests' "Sixteen Candles":

"They don't call me *Old* HH for nothin'…Sixteen candles would only fill up one side of my cake! There's the other side and both ends yet to go! But I can tell you one thing. Old Hunter Hancock has sure had his fun, he-he-he-he. Maybe I should write a book. Uh, maybe I'd better not. Those were the Crests singing 'Sixteen Candles.' And you know something else: They say you have to be born with it in order to have it. Well, in that case, Lloyd Price should've been twins, because he's got enough for two! Here is Lloyd Price now with 'Personality!'"
Song ends.

"…That was Lloyd Price, puttin' out on 'Personality.' And if you dig these sounds, make it to Dolphin's of Hollywood, 1065 East Vernon, for the lowest prices on records anywhere in Los Angeles! Any 45 r.p.m. record is only 88 cents, any $3.98 monaural LP is only $2.98, and any $4.98 stereo LP is only $3.98. Get your records at Dolphin's at Hollywood and you won't have to listen to my program to hear your favorite records. And they've got everything: rhythm and blues, jazz, spirituals, a tremendous stock of oldies, and they even have a few 78 r.p.m. records still available. So, if it goes around to make a sound, you'll find it at Dolphin's. You can get that great record by Big Jay McNeely, 'There's Something on Your Mind,' the Drifters' 'There Goes My Baby,' the Coasters' 'Charlie Brown,' Fats Domino's 'I'm Ready,' and all the rest of the big hits that you're hearing here on "Huntin' with Hunter" on KGFJ. Dolphin's is open weekdays till 4 A.M. and Sundays from 10 to 10. Be sure to tell 'em that 'ol H.H. sent you down to 1065 East Vernon, to Dolphin's of Hollywood!"

1955: Bill Gavin, previously programmer of the *Burgie Music Box* on KNBC in San Francisco, begins programming *Lucky Lager Dance Time,* now being heard on forty-eight stations in eleven western states.
1956: With McLendon, Storz, and Gerald Bartell (operating out of WOKY in Milwaukee) leading the way, and with Elvis Presley having made his explosive series of appearances on television, Top 40 becomes a popular format.
1958: Bill Gavin combines information from his *Lucky Lager Dance Time* and other radio sources and creates *Bill Gavin's Record Report.*
1958:
At the first Todd Storz DJ convention in Kansas City, Mitch Miller, Columbia Records' head of A&R, an inventive but conservative producer, vilifies rock and roll and castigates Top 40 stations for surrendering their air time to "bobby soxers and

ballad, swing to sweet, and blues to boogie…some of the very best in rhythm and blues records, featuring some of the greatest and most popular Negro singers, musicians, and entertainers in the world."

George "Hound Dog" Lorenz, WKBW, Buffalo: While Alan Freed spread the sounds to his legion of Moondoggers in Ohio, listeners in Buffalo—and in more than a dozen states along the Eastern Seaboard—got "the Sound of the Hound" from Lorenz, who blasted out from a 50,000-watt powerhouse of a station. The Hound Dog jumped around—he'd been in Buffalo in the early fifties, then invaded Cleveland, pitting his "hound-doggers" against the Moondoggers before hitting it big on the big KB. Lorenz often did his show from a black nightclub, the Club Zanzibar, and he hosted Little Richard, Elvis, Chuck, and Fats, among others. He truly loved his music. "I feel I'm taking part in the dawn of a new era in our great American music," he said.

"Jumpin'" George Oxford, KSAN, KDIA, San Francisco / Oakland: Oxford began at KFRC in 1945 with a poetry program. He wanted to be a newscaster; if he had to play records, he'd prefer classical music. But, when he joined KWBR in Oakland in 1947 and began to spin some R&B, his show took off, and Oxford stayed on board for a career that lasted into the seventies. At one point, in 1952, he was on KSAN ten hours a day, with the help of tape recording. In 1955, *Billboard,* not yet convinced that rock and roll was more than a fad, urged the industry to "Keep Pop Alive in '55." Ol' Jumpin' gave his answer on the air: "Be alive in '55!"

Porky Chedwick, WAMO, Pittsburgh: WAMO, where Porky began working

Carrying the Soul

Record Exchanger, a California-based magazine devoted to the early history of rock and roll, captured a chat between George "Hound Dog" Lorenz and Little Richard in 1970.

Richard: I was really glad to see you're still carrying the soul, and you were when nobody else was. You were one of the first white cats to really carry soul all over the country, though a lot of them tried to take credit.

Lorenz: I keep doing my thing…What was your biggest seller on Specialty?

Richard: "Long Tall Sally" [released in late 1955]. It sold over five million, and "Tutti Frutti" [issued early in 1956] sold over a million, but it sold two million for Pat Boone because black entertainers hadn't broken across the line for Top 40 play.

Lorenz: If you remember, that's how we met. You came to see me because you weren't getting exposure. It was at that time we started to beat the drums for Little Richard.

Richard: I don't know how you did it, but every other record was me. You were playing me like they did the Beatles.

in 1949, is actually in Homestead, just outside Pittsburgh. But then "Pork the Tork" was just outside normality, telling anyone who was listening—and many were, in Pittsburgh and the tri-state area—that he kept a grape in his ear "to make my head ferment," and that he'd graduated from the University of Spinner Sanctum with a doctorate in insanity. Chedwick was quite alone as a white man playing black music and spouting jive, much of it rhymed, in a blue-collar town. But the kids lapped it up. As for adults: "I was probably ridiculed and laughed at even by my close associates, neighbors, and friends," he told *Goldmine* magazine in 1980. "I knew I didn't have a dream here. I knew the music was going to be the music of tomorrow."

Pete "Mad Daddy" Myers, WHK, Cleveland; WINS, New York: "Jocko" Henderson did it in Philadelphia and New York, Joe Niagara did a light version of it at WIBG in Philly, and others had that skill to rhyme at will. But "Mad Daddy" may have been the sharpest of the improv rock and roll poets. "Everything was in rhyme," says Neil McIntyre, who began his radio career as a gofer for Myers in Cleveland. "While a record was on, he would rewrite a commercial to make it rhyme." He also used the tape machines to add a maniacal reverb to his laugh. And yet, in the early years, when his station was still an assortment of programs, Myers did double-identity duty. As McIntyre recalls, "He was this nice, smooth-talking fellow in the afternoon, and then, at night, he was this wacko 'Mad Daddy'." After some headline-grabbing stunts, including a parachute dive into Lake Erie, he invaded New York in 1963, where neither his "Mad Daddy" routine (on WINS) nor his laid-back persona (on WNEW) really clicked. Soon after he was told that he was being shifted from middays (1 to 4 P.M.) to late evenings (8 to midnight), Myers committed suicide with a shotgun. *The New York Times* reported that he left a note that "indicated that Mr. Myers had been despondent over a plan to shift the time of his radio show." He was forty years old.

Dewey Phillips, WHBQ and WDIA, Memphis: A good ole boy straight out of the old "Li'l Abner" comic strips of Al

baby sitters." After the bearded Miller, who'd just issued his first sing-along albums, takes his seat, Chuck Blore, another pioneer of Top 40 (he created the widely imitated "Color Radio" sound at KFWB-Los Angeles in 1958) rises to the defense of those in radio who choose to play what people want to hear, no matter "the prophets of doom, bearded or otherwise."

1959: The second Storz DJ gathering, in Miami Beach, includes a sizeable representation from record companies and promoters. Taking note, a local newspaper headlines its coverage "Booze, Broads and Bribes."

1960: Payola, long suspected in the radio industry, is investi-

AIR CHECK

Jumpin' with George

On his show on KSAN in San Francisco, Jumpin' George plays "Annie Had a Baby," in which Hank Ballard laments that the new mom "can't work no more." "Work," George knows, is street slang for sex. He doesn't reveal this to his listeners. Instead, he fashions the smoothest of setups for his next record:

"You know, in teen jive talk, the phrases come and go. I've been hearing 'cool' or 'cool it' for the past couple of years. It might catch on! Then there's 'groove it,' 'in the groove.' Now I'm hearing 'super.' I asked some kids over at McClymond's High School the meaning of 'super'—superior, supreme, a guy who eats a lot of soup? They said, 'No, Jumpin', it's just crazy: super.' Well, whatever the case, here's one that's cool, crazy, in the groove, super, and…'Sincerely Yours,' by the Moonglows…"

Dewey Phillips, proprietor of *Pop Shop*.

gated by Congress by the House Legislative Oversight Subcommittee.

1961: WABC, with consultant Mike Joseph having laid the groundwork, and with Sam Holman in place as program director, begins battle with WINS, home of Murray the K and a Top 40 station since 1957; WMCA, home of the "Good Guys", and WMGM, where Peter Tripp ruled until the payola hearings sent him packing. WABC, later programmed by Rick Sklar, will take Manhattan by the mid-sixties and become one of the most powerful stations in the country. Meanwhile, ABC's Chicago station becomes a powerhouse, with Dick "the Screamer" Biondi ruling from 9 P.M. to midnight. By 1965, the station's star is Larry Lujack.

Capp, Phillips was a cotton-pickin' picker of hits and hitmakers, including Jerry Lee Lewis and local boy Elvis Presley. When Sun Records' Sam Phillips (no cotton-pickin' relation) gave Dewey a pre-release copy of "That's All Right" in 1954, the DJ flipped and played it thirty times in a row. On the air, he invited the singer to the studio for an interview. Elvis, who'd heard that his record might be played, was at the movies and had to be dragged out by his father and taken to the WHBQ studios. Phillips fooled the shy and nervous Presley into an interview by chatting with him informally—as if he were just getting to know him—and leaving the microphone on. Around the country, few disc jockeys heard what Phillips heard in the R&B number, but "That's All Right" hit the top of the country charts. Phillips also hosted a TV show, *Pop Shop*, in 1956, and it was so popular that it kept *American Bandstand* out of Memphis for six months.

Georgie Woods, WDAS, Philadelphia: The Georgia-born Georgie was "The Guy with the Goods." Moving from a New York DJ job to WHAT in Philadelphia in 1953, Woods jumped to WDAS in '56 and made his name breaking records and staging concerts at the Uptown Theater that were studded with Motown stars, provided gratis by Berry Gordy, Jr., for, as they say, "promotional considerations." In tandem with Dick Clark, he not only helped propel Jerry Butler's "For Your Precious Love" into the charts in 1958, he came up with a nickname for the singer: "Iceman." Clark counts Woods as one of the best among a crop of "very good, influential disc jockeys" in Philadelphia, including Hy Lit, Joe Niagara, and "Jocko" Henderson. "I always found out about black kids and what they were listening to through Georgie," says Clark. Woods got close to the black community, and it was no radio act. In October, 1963, Bill Gavin reported: "One night last week, as he was driving home from work, Georgie noticed a disturbance and stopped to investigate. As he later told friends, he found a police office roughly treating a Negro youth. Georgie identified himself to the officer and protested what was going on. He was immediately arrested, held in jail for two hours, and then released when charges were withdrawn." In fact, Gavin noted, "the chief of police has commended Georgie's good work."

26

Zenas "Daddy" Sears, WGST and WAOK, Atlanta: Many moviegoers received a series of shocks when they saw the rock and roll film *Jamboree* in 1957. The movie worked in cameos from nineteen DJs of the day, including Joe Finan of Cleveland, "Jocko" Henderson of New York, Howard Miller of Chicago, Joe ("Jose") Smith of Boston, Robin Seymour of Detroit, and "Daddy" Sears of Atlanta. Linda J. Sandahl, in the *Encyclopedia of Rock Music on Film*, notes, "It was a big shock to some parents to find that a couple of them were black." Likewise, it must've been a stunner for many in the Atlanta area to discover that "Daddy" was an erudite-looking white guy. Sears worked in Armed Forces Radio, playing to largely black troops. Later, on radio in Atlanta, he took it upon himself to locate R&B records and include them in his show. "I just liked black music, and that's what I played," he told Wes Smith, a writer in Chicago. Sears would go on to become a strong supporter of the Civil Rights Movement.

There were many others, of course, including New Orleans' Clarence "Poppa Stoppa" Hamman, Jr., and Ken "Jack the Cat" Elliott; San Francisco's Phil McKernan, whose son would grow up to be a musician—"Pig Pen" of the Grateful Dead; Memphis's Bill Gordon, who prides himself as one of radio's first "screamers"; Nashville's Hoss Allen, who worked alongside John R. and Gene Nobles; and all those who glided from R&B into Top 40 DJs. Some of them, including Buddy Deane, Tom "Big Daddy" Donahue, Joe Niagara, and Arnie "Woo Woo" Ginsburg, are elsewhere in this book.

Now how did black listeners feel about white DJs? If measured only by the numbers—the audience ratings of their shows and the turnouts at personal appearances—blacks seemed to accept the white disc jockeys as friendly purveyors of the music they loved. But, of course, it wasn't that simple. Chuck Leonard, who would become the first African American DJ on New York City's Top 40 powerhouse, WABC, has a deep appreciation of black pioneer disc jockeys. Born in Chicago, Leonard didn't consider himself a radio nut as a kid, but certain disc jockeys—black and white—stood out.

"R&B radio, up until a certain point, had a role that was very heavy on personality, and the personality jocks ruled the roost," he says. By the time he got into radio, in the early sixties, "straight men" were outnumbering the personalities. "But you did have like Cousin Brucie and Dick Biondi and 'The Geator with the Heater' [Jerry Blavat], but these were almost parodies of black jocks, I thought. I got the feeling they were trying to do jive talk, and they were trying to be the black jock in whiteface.

"Of course, the original would have been John R. I used to get that kind of stuff on the radio, when I was in high school, or grade school, even. I remember hearing about a guy named Jack L. Cooper, a black jock

1965: A disc jockey and program director, Bill Drake, succeeds with his programming ideas at California stations in Fresno (KYNO) and San Diego (KGB), and is hired by RKO General to transform KHJ-Los Angeles into a Top 40 station. He and program director Ron Jacobs produce "Boss Radio." The formula is replicated at KFRC in San Francisco, WRKO in Boston, CKLW in Windsor, Ontario (also serving Detroit), and WHBQ in Memphis, and competing stations are soon copying the Drake format.

1967: Free-form is born on the FM dial, on KMPX in San Francisco, WOR-FM in New York, and at such college stations as WTBS in Cambridge, Massachusetts, and WFUV at Fordham University in New York.

1968: While free-form, later called "progressive rock radio," spreads and causes consternation to Top 40, it's shut down on WOR-FM, which RKO turns over to Bill Drake, who installs an oldies format. Meanwhile, a format originally called "chicken rock," later renamed by Gavin as "adult contemporary," begins to take away more of Top 40's listeners.

1970: Advertisers are falling in love with the baby boomer generation, and 25-49 becomes the most sought-after demo (short for "demographic"). Through much of the seventies, Top 40 has to fight for its share of the advertising revenue pie. "Progressive rock" on FM matures into AOR ("album-oriented rock").

By 1956, Freed could combine his New York stage shows with his own movies.

1972: Buzz Bennett, highly regarded programmer, takes over KCBQ in San Diego and takes on Drake's KGB and combines extra-short jingles ("shotgun jingles"), endless contests, and in-depth research of listeners to beat Drake at his own game. Bennett calls his formula "Money, music, and magic." Throughout the decade, Top 40 increases its presence on the FM band, where, increasingly, the younger demos are to be found.

1978: Disco music is the rage, and when some stations, beginning with WKTU in New York, switch to dance music as a format, radio is further fragmented, as disco leads to a mix of Urban and Top 40.

1983: Top 40 comes back. The AOR format gives way to corporate rock, disco dies, and MTV recharges pop music by showcasing whoever gives the channel videos; many are

out of Gary, and he was the stuff that legends were made of. And when I was in high school, I worked for Al Benson, 'Yo Ol' Swingmaster.' So I studied at the feet of a master. He had been around forever."

Cooper was the first master— the first black DJ ever. He'd been on radio since 1924, doing comedy on a station in Washington, D.C. In Chicago in the early thirties, he was hired by a bakery, Ward's Tip-Top Bread, to do a show on WSBC, a station geared to minority audiences. Working out of the station's studios in a furniture store on the South Side, Cooper not only hosted a late-night show of race records, but, like Jumpin' George in San Francisco and others, found himself doing multiple shows, including *Jump, Jive, and Jam, Rug Cutters' Special,* and *Gloom Chasers.* Cooper was getting the job done—within a few months, the Tip-Top Bread people reported solid sales increases on the South Side—and was off to a long career in radio. Chief among his achievements: opening the doors for others.

One of the first ones through the doors was Al Benson, who worked at several Chicago stations beginning in the mid-forties. If Leonard studied at his feet, it's to his credit that he didn't choose to emulate Benson's speech, which, by most accounts, was unintelligible, partly because he liked to practice what he called "native talk" and partly because he liked to drink while on the radio. He fell asleep on the air more than once. "Al Benson," said Jerry Butler, "was the most illiterate, uncouth…why, he fell asleep during his own television show. You couldn't understand a thing he said most of the time." But he was voted the most popular DJ in Chicago in a 1948 poll by the *Chicago Tribune.* John Hardy, a former gospel DJ who became a staple of R&B radio in the San Francisco Bay Area in the fifties and sixties recalled simply: "Al Benson was *the* man."

In Memphis, meanwhile, Nat D. Williams was Al Benson turned inside out. When he joined WDIA as a DJ in 1948, he brought along a background as a schoolteacher (he taught history), journalist, and lover of blues music. Because WDIA knew nothing about the blues, Williams brought in his own records. Far from trying to be a hipster—even though he was a regular on Beale Street—Williams acted as a cultural historian. A class act,

Williams helped open WDIA's doors to more black performers. B.B. King would deejay—and sing commercial jingles—on the station, and a former student of Williams, Rufus Thomas, joined in 1950. With three formidable talents on staff, WDIA became the first black-oriented radio station in the South.

One of the most powerful of the black DJs of the fifties, Tommy "Dr. Jive" Smalls, gave Alan Freed his toughest competition when he arrived in New York City in 1954. Stationed at WWRL, Smalls had a reputation as the most powerful hitmaker among R&B disc jockeys, and he was staging big R&B concerts at the Paramount and the Apollo, the kinds of shows Freed had so successfully produced in Cleveland. In 1955 he hosted a report on R&B on *Toast of the Town*, Ed Sullivan's show on CBS-TV. In Freed's years in town, the two men held their own.

Unfortunately, they had more than radio and concerts in common. Like Freed, Smalls was caught in the payola dragnet. In fact, in May of 1960, the two were among eight men arrested in New York and charged with commercial bribery. Smalls was immediately fired by WWRL. He later pled guilty and paid a $250 fine. At age thirty-four, his radio career was effectively over.

It wasn't only Freed and Dr. Jive who were mounting all-star weekend shows in New York. Douglas "Jocko" Henderson, a Philly DJ who commuted to Harlem nightly to do a show on New York's WOV, staged R&B revues at Loew's State Theater. Henderson may have been the most futuristic guy on R&B radio. He made his two-hour late-evening show into a rocket ship ride—"Hey, mommio, hey, daddio, this is your spaceman Jocko, three, two, one: blast-off time!" While some R&B station owners urged black disc jockeys to scream and shout, Jocko laid out gentle, finger-snapping rhymes, just like one of his idols, "Hot Rod" Hulbert. A multifaceted performer who worked alongside Nat D. Williams at WDIA in Memphis, where he ranged from gospel in the morning to madcap mania at night, Hulbert had worked in Henderson's home town, Baltimore, and showed a flair for fast-talking rhyming and nonsense, "gugga-mooga" lines.

By the time Hulbert himself reached New York and WOV, Henderson was producing the shows at Loew's. Like his fellow DJ-entrepreneurs, Freed and Dr. Jive, Jocko always had his name first—and biggest—on the theater marquees, over any of the performing headliners. That was, of course, no accident. Beyond the fact of competing DJs, a case could be made for the announcers being substantially bigger stars than the musicians. The singing stars and bands appeared on the radio, or on stage, and

newer artists from overseas. Another factor: Mike Joseph's "Hot Hits" format, a reworking of Drake's dictum of playing the hits, relying not on call-outs but retail sales and requests. Morning shows, especially the "zoos" pioneered at KKBQ-Houston and WRBQ-Tampa, lead Top 40's return to ratings respectability, as Scott Shannon moves from Florida to New York City and, with Ross Brittain, make Z-100 king of the heap, A-Number One, while, in Los Angeles, Rick Dees takes KIIS-FM to double-digit ratings.

October 1984: The "P" word surfaces again in a *Los Angeles Times* report on payola and independent record promotion. And again in 1986…

1993: Top 40 is hyphenated with Rock, Alternative, Pirate, and other tags. Mainstream Top 40 is declared dead, as the industry notes a steep decline in the number of stations identifying themselves as Top 40. In 1992, 578 stations had employed the label. Now, only 441 do.

1997: Like a radio version of some teen scream-flick monster, Top 40 is b-a-a-a-a-c-k. Propelled by a new wave of pop artists, chief among them Spice Girls and Hanson, the format regains its health. As consultant Guy Zapoleon notes, through all the changes over four decades, "Top 40 is the only format that I know of that reflects the best of all the genres of music today. It's the ultimate variety format, plus all the basics of the great radio of the past."

then were gone. The deejay was there, day after day. A song was two or three minutes. The deejay stayed with his listener for three or more hours, in the background accompanying homework, or in the foreground providing gossip, information, and contest prizes. Hyped up and corny or warm and comforting, the deejay amounted to a friendly adult voice. They were accessible by phone, at local hops, and at big concerts. And, til they were fired or transferred, they were always on the radio.

The King of the Old Moondoggers

A lan Freed needed no Top 40. He rolled into prominence in radio, going from Akron, Ohio, to Cleveland in 1951, where he made up his own rules and created the rock and roll foundation for Top 40.

That freewheeling trait would lead to a downfall as tragic as any that beset a rock and roll star.

Freed, of course, *was* a rock and roll star—who happened to do his performing between the songs, when he was often inspired to exclaim, shout, sing, moan, and pound on a thick telephone book, purposely leaving the microphone on.

A dog bays. A chugga-chugga rhythm begins. The dog howls again. A liquid metronome begins ticking…From the near distance, a voice, casual, conversational, materializes. The volume increases as it asks, "All ready to rock? Atta boy. We're gonna have a ball. Saturday night again…"

Then, facing the microphone full-on, with the rhythm and the dog still going behind him, Freed speaks, at a quickening clip, to his unseen audience:

"Hello, everybody. How y'all? This is Alan Freed, the old King of the Moondoggers, and a hearty welcome to all our thousands of friends in northern Ohio, Ontario, Canada, western New York, western Pennsylvania, West Virginia. Along about eleven-thirty, fifteen minutes from now, we'll be joining the Moondog network…Good old Erin Brew, formula ten-oh-two, northern Ohio's largest-selling beer, makes it possible for us to be with you a whole extra half hour on Saturday nights. We'll be here until two-thirty in the morning, and operator 210 is at the WJW switchboard to

Freed in Akron.

Polished in the Big Apple.

take your telephone requests. When you're calling in play it cool when you call, we'll get to your requests as soon as we can. Pop the cap, have a good ball. Enjoy Erin brew, ten-oh-two, and *The Moondog Show!*"

He introduces a jumping jazz tune, "C-Jam Blues," and, immediately, he's adding his own lines, some sung, some scatted, over the horns and xylophone. "Aw, go!" he exclaims, just before the sax solo. "Ho, now!" He guides the Duke Ellington tune to its end. "That goes back a good many years; a good many tunes have been written 'round that riff." Freed then slides into a sincere pitch for good old Erin Brew, his sponsor since he moved from Akron to Cleveland three years before, in 1950.

We will not, here, try to tell the entire story of Alan Freed, except to the extent of his impact on Top 40 radio. The details of his mercurial career and sad destruction have been chronicled quite well in books—most notably John A. Jackson's *Big Beat Heat*—and less well in films. Those have ranged from the fifties rock and roll movies in which Freed played versions of himself—a powerful DJ who sided with the kids in defending rock and roll—to *American Hot Wax*, which condensed numerous key incidents in Freed's career into one made-for-Hollywood day and night. The

AIR CHECK

"The Big Beat"

Soon after arriving in New York in mid-1954, Alan Freed was forced to drop his "Moondog" tag. A street musician who wore a Viking getup and performed in front of Carnegie Hall had established himself under that name and sued the disc jockey. Freed, who in Cleveland had taken to calling his show the "Moondog Rock 'n' Roll Party," dropped the dog and, instead, emphasized "rock 'n' roll." And, as evidenced by an air check from early 1955, he poured it on:

"Hello, everybody! Yours truly, Alan Freed, the ol' King of the Rock 'n' Rollers, all ready for another big night of rock and rolling.

Rock 'n' roll records are the big beat in popular music in America today. Let her go!"—*(the engineer rolls the theme music)*—"and we'll be here til nine o'clock, reviewing the Top 25 rock and roll favorites of the week. So welcome to Rock 'n' Roll Party Number One!"

The instrumental theme is established, then fades under Freed.

"Yeah! Top 25 rock 'n' roll favorites, everybody, according to your mail requests, your telegrams and your record purchases all over the rock and roll record kingdom. We're gonna get off and running, warm up with Red Prysock on Mercury, 'Rock and *Roll!*'"

movie did convey Freed's genuine affection for both the music he played and his young listeners.

One of them—in real life—was Roger Steffens, a rock and reggae writer and historian who not only listened to Freed over WINS in New York in the early fifties, but taped him, so that he could hear him again and again.

"I used to have an old Pentron reel-to-reel," Steffens recalls, "and I put my mike in front of my '48 Bendix table model. Alan Freed was like the uncle I never had." In the midst of adult caterwauling about rock and roll, says Steffens, "He was our champion. He really understood kids, and he seemed like a real decent person."

Freed's *Big Beat* aired in New York City, first on WABC-TV; then, in 1959, on WNEW.

That, one fellow DJ agreed, was Freed's most tangible quality. Joe Smith, who would go on from radio work in Boston to become one of the recording industry's top executives at Warner Bros. Records, lists Freed as one of the outstanding radio personalities of all time, primarily on the strength of his charisma.

Freed, he said, had "a terrible voice, no style, but a sense of…" Smith took a second to gather his thoughts, conjuring those times. "You know," he continued, "Gillette used to spend tons of money in Top 40. They'd survey high school boys who were just going to start shaving and ask who their favorite disc jockeys were. It was almost always the nighttime jocks. At night, in the East, you could establish a very close relationship to some kid who's lying in bed with his radio. On the West Coast, it's la-la land and people with convertibles with their tops down at night, but in the East, when the weather got bad, that radio was your thing. So it was always nighttime disc jockeys. And Alan could present a sense of danger out there. He was like an on-the-edge kind of guy."

Actually, he was a hearty, partying kind of guy—at least on the evidence of his air checks. Invariably, he's cheering songs along. Like a hyped-up version of a jazz disc jockey, he made certain to name the musicians whose work he played. He put his heart into his commercials, but put equal energy into his readings of the endless dedications. He may have been intoxicated by the music—an engineer at WINS said Freed always had his headphone volume turned as high as it could go—or alcohol,

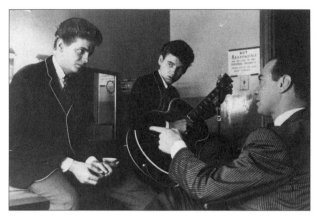

Freed in harmony with the Everly Brothers.

which the DJ was said to have, on occasion, in the studio, but he did not sound dangerous.

If there was danger, it must've been in the music. All around him, rock and roll and R&B were under attack—by parents' groups, church leaders, the press, and, most vocally, by those who believed the music posed an insidious threat to civilized society, something even more dangerous than Communism: racial equality.

No video history of rock and roll is complete without these two images: first, the chairman of the Alabama White Citizens Council, in white shirt and slacks, standing by a car with a sign reading "We Serve White Customers Only." He tells the newsreel camera, "We've put up a twenty-man committee to do away with this vulgar, animalistic rock and roll bop." Second, we get a look at the organization's executive secretary, who sits

A Sample Hour of Alan Freed

Early on, in Cleveland and New York, Alan Freed stuck with R&B, the blues, and jump music. A typical quarter-hour would include Dakota Staton, the Charms, B.B. King, and LaVern Baker. By 1957, with Top 40 the dominant format, Freed's playlist expanded, as he found room for pop and country as well as gospel and his favorite, R&B. Freed fan Roger Steffens logged the music from a "Rock 'n' Roll Party" on WINS in 1957:

Hard Headed Woman - Elvis Presley
Over the Mountain, Across the Sea - Johnny and Joe
Poor Little Fool - Ricky Nelson
Sunglasses - The Shades
Harvey's Got a Girl Friend - Royal Teens
Guess Things Happen That Way - Johnny Cash
C.C. Rider - Chuck Willis
Little Star - The Elegants
It's My Heart - Stix and Brix
Tuxedo Junction - Alan Freed Band
Padre - Toni Arden
Gas Money - Jan and Arnie
Little Serenade - Teddy Randazzo
Hootchy Kootch - Larry Williams
Shang Lang a Ding Dong - The Charades
To Prove My Love to You - Joe Jones

What Shall I Do - Ed Townsend
Fever - Peggy Lee
I'm Sorry I Did You Wrong - The Royal Holidays
Shut Up - The Wildtones
For Your Precious Love - Jerry Butler
Tomfoolery - The Monotones
Western Movies - The Olympics
Tears on My Pillow - Little Anthony & the Imperials
I Love You So - The Chantells
Devoted to You - The Everly Brothers
Itchy Twitchy Feeling - Bobby Hendricks
Still As the Night - Sanford Clark
Butterfly - Charlie Gracie
Treasure of Love - Clyde McPhatter
Sapphire - Big Danny Oliver

behind a typewriter. "The obscenity and vulgarity of rock and roll music," he says, "is obviously a means by which the white man and his children can be driven to a level with the nigger."

Others connected the music with Communism, saying it was a tool of the Red Menace for subverting the youth of America; or that, whatever forces held the strings to it, rock and roll was corrupting the morals of young people and leading to race-mixing. Whatever the merits of any such argument, one thing

Freed appeared with Little Richard and Bill Haley in several films, including *Rock Around the Clock* and *Don't Knock the Rock* in 1956, and *Mister Rock and Roll* in 1957.

was undeniable. By its sheer novelty, and by the force of its acceptance by the younger generation, it *was* scary.

Blackboard Jungle threw juvenile delinquency and rebellion against authority onto the big screen, bow-tied with an upbeat theme song that got the kids out on the dance floor. *Rebel without a Cause*, starring James Dean, and *The Wild One*, with Marlon Brando, provided a left-right follow-up.

R&B hits like the Dominoes' "60 Minute Man" and Hank Ballard and the Midnighters' "Work with Me Annie" upset more people, especially when they heard that "work"—not to mention "rock and roll," a phrase Freed had popularized on the radio—were euphemisms for sex.

Speaking of which, for wary parents, what more frightening vision could there be than the likes of Little Richard pounding on a piano, singing about a girl who "sure likes to ball" or, especially, Elvis Presley, whose handsome leer and nonchalant, sexual body language sprang out from once-safe television variety shows, triggering a national debate about rock and roll and youth?

The *New York Daily News* called the music "an inciter of juvenile delinquency" and pointed to Freed as a chief offender. Freed, after all, was staging concerts featuring mostly rhythm and blues artists and drawing both black and white music fans. (One of them, in 1954, was a Brooklyn teenager who'd grow up to be Wolfman Jack. The young man worked his way backstage at the Paramount Theater and talked his way into a job as gofer.)

The Freed concerts had created near riots in Cleveland and New York.

Despite pressure from law enforcement agencies, the disc jockey only expanded his territory, mounting a concert tour that arrived in Boston in March of 1958. Joe Smith, a popular disc jockey there, promoted the concert with Freed. "That," he recalls, "was with Chuck [Berry] and Jerry Lee Lewis and a cast of thousands, but there was a little to-do afterwards, and Alan made a mistake." Smith explains: "Boston was a very jumpy town; very strict and Catholic and church-managed. And him just bringing the show pissed off a lot of people anyhow. We hired extra cops, and at some point the cops said, 'You gotta turn the lights on, they're getting crazy here,' and so they turned the lights on, and Alan said, 'It looks like the police don't want you to have a good time here. Come on, let's have a party.' And kids started coming out of the seats and surged toward the stage. It was a kind of a messy evening."

It was enough that Freed had angered the police by showing them up. "Outside afterwards, there were some fights in the subway, so Alan got busted." He was indicted on charges of "inciting unlawful destruction of real and personal property" and "inciting to riot during a rock and roll show."

"That," says Smith, "was the start of his downfall."

The Boston troubles triggered cancellations of the rest of Freed's tour. Back in New York, Freed and WINS, unhappy with each other over various issues, parted ways. He would soon resurface on WABC, but, for the moment, the anti-rock forces savored a victory.

And those forces included a few disc jockeys. Another familiar piece of footage in rock and roll history documentaries is that of a DJ at WHK smashing a 78 r.p.m. record against the edge of his turntable and declaring: "Rock and roll has got to go!" While most disc jockeys either liked the music or were doing their job, playing what their listeners wanted to hear, some announcers agreed with critics that the music was mediocre at best, obscene and vulgar at worst. One group of R&B disc jockeys on the East Coast declared a ban on songs that promoted vices or degraded black people. Entire stations, including R&B pioneer WDIA in Memphis, announced bans on all suggestive songs.

The response from the youth of America was predictable. The more the authority figures ranted and raved, the more they flocked to the record shops and record hops, to the rock and roll movies and concerts, and to the disc jockeys who tied it all together, right on their own personal transistor radios.

Chapter

The Founding
Daddy-os

*A*ll right baby, this is Russ Knight, the Weird Beard, the savior of Dallas radio, *let me save you with music until midnight! Well I tell you, somebody's gotta come up here before midnight, honey, one of those Dallas good-lookin' girls and pull my Weird Beard tambourine. We got Billy, Roy, Dale, Trigger, the Dallas Salvation Army, ha! From 11-90 at the harmonic tone. (Quack!) A little music from Big D, a lot of Weird Beard dances goin' around, the Blackbottom, we got a brand-new dance from Joey Dee and the Peppermint Twist and it goes like this!*

The exact origins of Top 40 radio are in debate. Some say it was born in a bar in Omaha, Nebraska, or at a station in New Orleans. Others say it was born in Texas, where Gordon McLendon brought the format, with splashy promotional pizzazz, to his stations in Dallas, San Antonio, and Houston. Still others maintain it was created by radio programming consultant Bill Gavin, who weaved playlist reports from stations around the country into a chart.

Most radio and pop historians, however, point to that bar in Omaha, on the Missouri River along the eastern edge of Nebraska, as the birthplace of Top 40. Here, between 1953 and 1955—the exact year is uncertain—Todd Storz, the operator of KOWH, a daytime AM station, discovered the concept that would be known as Top 40.

Storz was sitting with his program director, Bill Stewart, in a tavern on 16th Street, across from the station. According to Stewart, they were talking about the impact of television on radio and about what they might do to improve KOWH's ratings. In the fashion of the day, KOWH tried to be all things to all people, airing a wide range of specialty music shows. Having been Number 1 for several years, the station now faced a stiff challenge from KOIL, whose owner, Don Burden, had an ear for talent. His disc jockeys

Robert Todd Storz is widely considered the inventor of Top 40 radio.

over the years would include Gary Owens, Bobby Dale, Dr. Don Rose, and the Real Don Steele.

While the men were waiting for one of the waitresses, a girlfriend of Storz's, to get off work, they noticed that customers had been playing the same few songs repeatedly over the course of four or five hours. Even after most of the customers had left, they saw a waitress punching up the same songs yet again. When they asked why, she replied, simply: "I like 'em."

The jukebox activity triggered an idea. Stewart went to the box and, with the waitress's help, wrote down the titles of the records they'd been hearing all evening. Since the less popular records, although available in the box, had received nary a nickel, the size of the playlist would be trimmed—to about thirty records. The most popular songs would get more repeated plays. With Storz's blessing, Stewart applied the jukebox theory to KOWH. Storz knocked off the classical, country, and other programs the station had been airing and focused on pop tunes aimed at homemakers. The ratings soared. "We got the station turned around."

Storz had been a disc jockey—legend has it that he was fired for responding to a complaint about his music selection by telling the listener, on the air: "Ma'am, on your radio you will find a switch which will easily turn the set off." He subsequently worked in sales before he and his father bought KOWH, along with an FM station, for $75,000 in 1949. Todd paid $20,000, Dad chipped in $30,000; and the remainder came from loans. By 1956, the Storz's Mid-Continent Company had collected four other stations: WTIX in New Orleans ($25,000), WHB in Kansas City ($400,000), WDGY in Minneapolis ($334,000), and WQAM in Miami ($850,000). Storz and his father could afford the steeper prices because KOWH had shot from last to first place among Omaha's seven radio stations within two years.

Success, propelled by the numerous contests and promotions concocted by Storz and his programming lieutenants, came before rock and roll. In the beginning, what became Top 40 had little to do with teens and pop music. It was simply disc jockeys following a playlist, doing what would be called "formula radio." When Gordon McLendon, operating three powerful stations in Texas, picked up the formula and according to some reports gave it the "Top 40" handle, radio had its first and most enduring music format.

There are variations on the Storz story. According to Stewart, the historic jukebox brainstorm happened in 1955. However, Storz is known to have come up with a program called *Top 40 at 1450* at his New Orleans stations, WTIX, shortly after acquiring it in 1953. George W. "Bud" Armstrong, who

38

was hired to manage the station, said he encountered a music show called *The Top 20 at 1280* at rival station WDSU, with Bob Howard as disc jockey. "I simply thought that if 20 was good, 40 was better." Richard Fatherly, another former Storz programmer, says that WTIX decided to "upstage" WDSU by starting its show an hour earlier and extending it an hour past the competition's show. With the extended record list, the program got the title, *Top 40 at 1450.*

"Top 40," said Armstrong, "was not a blinding revelation in a bar. "

A less arguable account of Top 40 dates it back to Storz and his father's first programming changes at KOWH, when, after research showed that music was a major reason people listened to the radio, dropped network and transcribed programming to make more room for the popular records of the day. Storz, in 1950, was simply extending programs like *Your Hit Parade* and *Lucky Lager Dance Time* which had been around since 1935 and 1941, respectively to the full broadcast day, with disc jockeys and local promotions.

Todd Storz, who suffered a fatal stroke in 1964, at age thirty-nine, added further intrigue to the Omaha tavern story when he spoke with *Television* magazine in 1957. Explaining his format, he said: "I became convinced that people demand their favorites over and over while in the army during the Second World War. I remember vividly what used to happen in restaurants here in the States. The customers would throw their nickels into the juke box and come up repeatedly with the same tune. Let's say it was 'The Music Goes Round and Round.' [Note: A tune called "And the Music Goes Round and Round" was a hit, by several bands, in 1936 and 1938.] After they'd all gone, the waitress would put her own tip money into the juke box. After eight hours of listening to the same number, what number would she select? Something she hadn't heard all day? No invariably she'd pick 'The Music Goes Round and Round.' Why this should be, I don't know. But I saw waitresses do this time after time."

Bill Stewart toiled for both of Top 40's chief architects, Gordon McLendon and Todd Storz.

Sound familiar?

Frankly, it appears that, whatever happened at KOWH, Bill Stewart, and possibly others, borrowed Storz's wartime experiences and transplanted them to that bar in Omaha. Gordon McLendon was reported to also have been toying with variations of Top 40 in 1953, when, according to a 1962 *Sponsor* magazine article, KLIF "burst into national prominence with its formula of music and news plus razzle-dazzle promotion." (Storz

An early KLIF Top 40 survey.

loyalists, including Fatherley, say that McLendon learned about the format from WHB, a Kansas City station bought by Storz in 1954. In an audio documentary about the Storz Broadcasting Company, Fatherley quotes WHB program director Johne Pearson: "We'd have people come in to visit us to see how we did it. Only one guy…took it home. Gordon McLendon came in and sat on my wastebasket and listened, and listened, and he went back to Dallas and picked it up."

By 1954, KLIF's lineup included one Bill Stewart, who, fellow DJ Don Keyes recalled, "really tightened the playlist. That's when we really went Top 40—hard Top 40." Before Stewart's arrival, Keyes said, "it was kinda loosey-goosey." Disc jockeys played what they wanted. "And Bill came in and firmed up that music policy, and away we went." And where had Stewart come from? Omaha. It's likely that the Storz-Stewart discovery of jukebox plays took place early in 1953, and that, no matter the actual date, the first station owner to greenlight Top 40 was Storz.

Dick Clark also thinks of Storz as the inventor of Top 40. "Todd Storz was the genius behind it, saying, 'Hey, people go into a saloon and they play the same forty records over and over again,'" Clark relates. "Alan Freed at the same time was discovering in Cleveland that they liked black-oriented records. So it was all seat-of-the-pants knowledge, grapevine knowledge. You picked what you thought was going to be a hit."

Disc jockey Lan Roberts worked at McLendon's KLIF in Dallas, and then for Todd Storz at WTIX in New Orleans. "As far as the Top 40 playlist is concerned, Storz was a little more innovative than McLendon was," he says. "McLendon relied more on personalities than music."

Gordon McLendon, Top 40's other great pioneer, apparently had no knowledge of—or perceptible interest in—rock and roll. Even worse, as his biographer, Ronald Garay, wrote, "Gordon's son Bart even said that his father 'knew nothing at all about music and cared nothing at all about music.' And there is no record of Gordon ever speaking favorably about rock and roll."

But Top 40 never had a more effective champion.

Gordon McLendon was eighty-three years old when he burst onto the …radio scene in Dallas. Or so he said. In 1947, when he began doing recreations of football games on the station he owned, KLIF, he introduced himself to listeners as "Gordon McLendon, the Old Scotchman, eighty-three years old this very day!" Actually, that very day, he was twenty-six. The nickname was, in part, a nod to his sportscasting idol, Red Barber ("the Old Redhead") and a way to be popular with as many people as possible. "I tried to think of some nickname that everyone would like, and I *am* Scottish," he told the *Los Angeles Times*. "I thought: Which of the races have no enemies? The Scots don't!"

When he began getting marriage proposals from seventy-five- year-old women, and, more importantly, when his vivid recreations of football and baseball games led to the creation of his own radio network, McLendon knew that, in radio, creativity ruled.

He'd been kick-started in the industry by his father, a real estate magnate who helped him acquire his first station, in Palestine, Texas, in 1946, and who would work alongside him in what became the McLendon Corporation, handling business details. But it was Gordon who was the undisputed front man, who worked the floor.

Gordon McLendon: Gary Owens calls him "the Orson Welles of radio."

"Gordon," disc jockey Gary Owens has said, "was the Orson Welles of radio." "Everybody thought he had the best ideas," says veteran programmer Neil McIntyre. "McLendon," says former employee Lan Roberts, "was the genius of the whole thing, and everybody had respect for him."

"Very few things that Gordon McLendon would do or attempt to do ever would be considered ordinary," wrote Garay, who studied a massive collection of papers McLendon left to Texas Tech University for his book, *Gordon McLendon: The Maverick of Radio.* "His greatest joy would come from charting new territory, in doing what others had not done, and in challenging what most thought to be impossible."

But for all his experimentations and risk-taking, McLendon had the basics of radio down pat. His formula for success was simplicity itself, and

Preparation, Please . . .

From the memos of Gordon McLendon comes this model for many program directors. The Old Scotsman wrote this in 1959:

A KLIF disc jockey is: informative, or humorous, or he merely introduces the records. He prepares his show—and he prepares the material for his show.

The KLIF disc jockey is a personality disc jockey—an entertaining disc jockey—because he is not mechanical, he does have something to say, he has prepared, he is conscious of what the tradition of KLIF disc jockeys has been.

A KLIF disc jockey prepares—he reads the morning and afternoon newspapers, some magazines and books, comments briefly upon what he's reading and seen, or has something amusing to say—in short, he is interesting to listen to.

was by no means exclusive to his chosen profession: "Give the people what they want." It would be echoed through the years, by station owners and managers, consultants and programmers. As McLendon put it, in a memo:

> Time and again—without exception—successful broadcast operators have proved that in order to survive and prosper financially, any radio station must provide a programming service of utility to a meaningful segment of the potential listening audience. Neither sales nor general administration nor engineering comes first. Programming does.

Years after he'd established his stations as among the nation's most influential, he noted: "The music and news format we use is much like soap. We all can buy the same records, play them on the same type of turntable, and we can all hire someone to talk. The difference in radio is like the difference in soap—it depends on who puts on the best wrapper."

Despite his obvious genius and talent, and perhaps because of his guts, McLendon sometimes failed to fit the right "programming service" to the audience. That was the case with his all-news experiment, WNUS, in Chicago, and with his all-want ads format, on an L.A. station, KADS. And while he had a resounding success with KABL, a cleverly marketed "beautiful music" station in Oakland (which he successfully put across as a San Francisco station), he could not duplicate the format in the slightly different market of Buffalo.

But McLendon's work in Top 40 radio secured his permanent position among the giants of the radio industry. Michael Spears, who was DJ Hal Martin at KLIF in the sixties, recalls a sign on the station's front door reading, "America's Most Imitated Radio Station." Gordon could have hung a sign around his neck proclaiming himself the country's most imitated radio executive.

Todd Storz is often cited as the more promotion-minded; that may be because of a 1956 *Time* magazine article that tore into Storz for his penchant for contests and stunts. *Time* said that Storz's "low estimate of listeners' intelligence is tempered only by his high regard for their cupidity." And that was only the first sentence. While grudgingly noting the financial success of the Storz's stations—in six years, a $50,000 investment had become a network worth $2.5 million—the unbylined *Time* reporter scoffed at the Top 40 format and the way "Storz shovels out jackpots in a succession of quizzes, guessing games and treasure hunts that occasionally tie up traffic when the search is on."

McLendon was left untrashed. But the Texan could concoct giveaways and marathons with the best of them. He once told an interviewer from his own station, KLIF, that he learned the value of promotion from C.E.

Hooper, who operated the dominant audience rating service of the time. "He said, 'Gordon, I've listened to it, and you're doing everything right but one thing…you've got to promote. You've got to have a lot of promotions on the air.'"

To revisit a few of McLendon's programming and promotional innovations is to discover ideas that would surface again and again, in the sixties, seventies, and later—sometimes credited to whichever radio professional had been smart enough to study the Old Scotsman.

There is the simple matter of aggressive, high-quality local news coverage and the clever placement of newscasts at twenty minutes past or before the hour, to counter those stations that place their news on the hour and/or half-hour. Bill Drake and Gene Chenault did it at their RKO stations in the mid-sixties, and they called it "20/20 News." McLendon, however, came up with those concepts at KLIF in the late fifties.

There is the promotional stunt called "the millionaire," often with a station's call letter attached—e.g. the famous "KYNO Millionaire" introduced by—once again—Drake, at his stepping-stone station in Fresno, California. The apparently wealthy person would simply hand out cash on the streets on behalf of the station being promoted. McLendon, it turns out, came up with the stunt in Dallas. A man would stand on a street corner and hand out as much as $20 to passersby and draw newspaper and television coverage—only to reveal, live on TV, that he was the new morning DJ on KLIF.

And then there's the device that centers on the idea, "Did you hear what

Adding Insult to Flattery…

When Gordon McLendon moved beyond Top 40, he didn't abandon the format's dependence on promotional flair. At his "beautiful music" station, KABL, he began airing announcements that broke an unspoken rule, that a station never mentions the competition. He did it in a series of cleverly worded promotions that clumped rival stations and announcers together, thereby setting KABL apart from the pack and positioning it as the station for "good music." Here, from memos and papers left behind by McLendon, is an example:

Moods and tempos change, and so do one's desires in radio fare. KABL points out to listeners who may be in the mood for popular or Top 40 music, the listenable pop music programming on radio stations KSJO, KOBY, KJBS, KDIA, KEWB, KSAN, KSFO, KEEN, KYA, and KFRC. Nowhere can one find more attractive popular-music radio entertainment than on the San Francisco dial. KABL hopes you will enjoy these stations, and invites you always to good music on KABL.

In one gentle swoop, McLendon had clustered Top 40, country, R&B, and middle-of-the-road stations into an amorphous ball. And he couldn't have done it more nicely.

...said this morning?" The DJ says something that gets him in trouble; he may even be suspended or fined. "I don't know what he said, but I'm going to tune in tomorrow."

That concept can also be traced to McLendon. When a news crew covering an armed robbery one night in 1954 interviewed the victim, he forgot to edit himself, and a few four-letter words hit the air. KLIF got all of six phone calls, but that was enough to give Bill Stewart, McLendon's right-hand programming man, an idea. Soon, KLIF had an ad in the local papers:

OOPS, SORRY

KLIF wishes to offer this apology for the unfortunate language used on an interview during an on-the-scene broadcast of an armed robbery Friday night at 8:44 P.M. To all of the many people who called the station, KLIF would like to say that we're sorry. But in covering news on the scene as we do, the remarks of a witness, who may be in a highly emotional state, can not be governed. However, in all humility—KLIF tenders this apology.

"All of the many people..."..."...covering news on the scene as we do..." It was brilliant advertising, it was effective, and, by sheer coincidence, over the next few weeks, on-air boo-boos took place at other McLendon stations, and they, too, found the need to offer sincere and public apologies.

Bill Stewart has been mentioned as an integral part of both McLendon's and Storz's operations, but, in the view of some industry veterans, he hasn't been mentioned enough. "It's debatable that Top 40 radio would have become the viable medium that it is without his contribution to it," says Claude Hall, the former *Billboard* radio columnist. He notes that McLendon himself credited Stewart with the success of KLIF. "Stewart," Hall writes, "was the first real program director in modern radio as we know it."

When Ken Dowe, a longtime lieutenant of McLendon's, names his two main mentors, they are the Old Scotsman—and Bill Stewart. "Bill Stewart doesn't get nearly enough credit," he says, "simply because there were not enough people who knew how important he was in the background.

"Todd's real contribution was the music rotation," says Dowe, "and Bill Stewart was probably as responsible as Gordon for helping to invent a lot of the crazy promotions, and then Todd just picked up on what he had done."

Larry Kent worked under Stewart as program director at KTSA in San Antonio. "It was Bill," he says, "who gave some structure and sizzle to the first primitive Top 40 formats by creating rotations, consistent playlists, and promotions and contests, which added fun and excitement that matched the music." Stewart, says Kent, was a soft-spoken sort, but when it came to radio, he was intense. Once, Kent recalls, his phone rang at 3 A.M. It was Stewart, with a most logical question: "Did you just hear what the all-night guy said?"

By dint of his duties with both Storz and McLendon, Bill Stewart was the Johnny Appleseed of the Top 40 format. Between him, other pioneers—chief among them Storz managers like Armstrong and Jack Sandler, who ran the powerful WMAO in Miami—and all the copycats, the concept spread quickly.

Make no mistake: it was a concept. As loose as it may have sounded in the beginning, at certain stations, its original architects knew what Top 40 radio should be, beyond playing the hits.

Edd Routt was a journalist who went to work for McLendon soon after interviewing him about his first radio station, in Palestine, Texas. Routt has written several books about radio. In one, he listed the format's main ingredients. "Top 40," he wrote, "consisted principally of music, light chatter, and news. Promotions in which money, merchandise, and services were awarded listeners were a vital part of the overall plan. Disc jockeys were selected

Here Comes The Knight

Russ Knight of KLIF in Dallas (named for the city's Oak Cliff district), sounded devilish. And that was before he put his voice through the echo machine. He delighted in skewering fellow stations and toying with his chosen medium:

…This is the Weird Beard, and I believe in doing my show under a handicap, friends. I'm in my Weird Beard strait jacket, got my hands tied behind my back, sure got my tongue locked here in my throat. Got my head on backwards, and those other stations said: *A singing jingle begins: "They said it couldn't be done…"* It's for L&M cigarettes.

After "Let Me In" by the Sensations, he returns:

…From KLIF, 1190, Russ Knight, the Weird Beard. Let's go to Channel 11-90 weather room, like the big boys do on television. Let's check the weather now. First of all, friends, around the country, these are indicative temperatures. We have a high mass of cumulus clouds *(taps pencil)*. Mark these little curlicues, friends. Just like birds; that's really clouds there, friends. High mass of clouds. In Boston we have 67 degrees. Hope I have time to give the Dallas-Fort Worth temperature. Mark that 67 degrees in Boston. In New Yawk City, 69 degrees. Sixty-nine for New York, and massive clouds there. In Miami, it's 73 degrees. In Oak Cliff, the weather bureau broke down, there you go. Whoops, we're just about out of time, friends. One more temperature here, from Butte, Montana, it's 78 degrees in Butte. That's kinda warm up there. You know, friends, that reminds me, I used to go with a girl from Butte. In fact, she had a couple of 'em…

for their sexiness, their voice, their ability to communicate excitement. Basic service consisted of time and temperature checks. Any idea of doing anything more than entertain the listener was out of the question."

Notice that nowhere in that description is there a mention of a target audience, or of young people, the first to attach themselves to Top 40 and make it a success.

As Bill Gavin wrote in 1967, "The advent of Top 40 in the early fifties didn't immediately orient itself to the teens. Perry Como and Patti Page had their regular share of hits. And, after the rock idiom became well-established for several years, the 18-to-24-year-old group still could dig the pop tunes."

Chapter

The Good Guys

I f Top 40 was designed to be ageless, so, too, are two of its early programming geniuses. Conveniently, each can represent a coast, although
each has overseen or influenced stations throughout the country.

Mike Joseph, who considers himself the first radio consultant in the history of the industry—he began advising stations in 1956—was affiliated
with WABC, the highly rated and regarded Top 40 powerhouse in New
York City. Through the years, he has continued to preach the simple sermon
"play the hits," even fashioning an eighties format, "Hot Hits," to pound
home his message.

Chuck Blore, to whom the word "genius" has been applied so often that
he could be mistaken for Ray Charles, worked for Gordon McLendon as a
disc jockey and program director. On his own, he
created the "Color Radio" format at KFWB in
Los Angeles (as well as two sister stations) that
swept the country beginning in 1958.

While Joseph has continued to consult for
radio stations, Blore got in and out, leaving
Crowell-Collier, the owner of the three stations he
programmed, in early 1963 to launch a successful
advertising business. His short time in the industry
(he returned briefly in the early seventies to program a Los Angeles adult-contemporary station)
may explain his popularity. He didn't stick around
long enough to get hated.

**Chuck Blore: He added
"color" to radio,
beginning at KFWB in
Los Angeles in 1958.**

But that's not really why he was so popular. "He's the best program director in the world," says Bill Ballance, who had been at KFWB for three years
when Blore blasted in to install the Top 40 format in late 1957.

47

With Bill Gavin cheering him on, Chuck Blore speaks at a Gavin Seminar.

Crowell-Collier, then best known as the publisher of encyclopedias and other educational books, purchased KFWB in 1956 and hired Bob Purcell to be general manager. Purcell, in turn, hired Blore, a young Los Angeles native who'd worked under McLendon and, as program director at his KELP in El Paso, achieved an astounding 74 percent share of the radio audience.

Before Blore, KFWB "was a mishmash," says John Hart, a broadcasting instructor who's writing a history of Crowell-Collier and its stations. "Everybody played their own records."

"Everybody" included some stellar talent. Besides Ballance, there were the pioneer DJs, Al Jarvis, B. Mitch Reed, and Joe Yocam. The music was pop, rock, and R&B, and Reed had an all-night jazz show.

Blore knew some of the names, but Ballance says, "there was no automatic continuing of our employment. We all had to go through a rigorous training process." Elliot Field, a McLendon veteran who came in from Houston, says Blore had to sell the format to various KFWB staffers. "Some of the old-timers, like Joe Yocam, went along; others needed convincing."

Blore, says Ballance, "laid out a marvelous format," first at KFWB beginning January 2, 1958—giving Los Angeles its first full-time Top 40 station, then at KEWB in Oakland and KDWB in Minneapolis. Field compares what he encountered in Los Angeles with the McLendon format he'd executed, since 1956, in Dallas, San Antonio, and Houston: "Similar, and better." Betty Breneman, whose future sister-in-law worked for Blore, is a little more dramatic. "When that hit the fan," she says, "it was like an earthquake."

"Chuck was a Vince Lombardi kind of guy," says Gary Owens. "His greatest quality was putting everybody together as a team. A memo would read, 'Hey, guys, we're Number One; we're going to be a bigger Number One. Keep it fresh, be brisk, be on top of it. You're the greatest,' signed Chuck."

Blore was blessed, early on, with self-knowledge. Although he badly wanted to be an on-air personality, he knew that his voice was, shall we say, stuck on the high wire, and would never be mistaken for that of Gary Owens or most any professional announcer. Yet he wouldn't give up. "And so I would create things to hide behind," he says. "I did voices, I did little skits. I would just constantly create things so that people would listen to my radio program in spite of the fact that I didn't have a pretty voice."

He impressed his boss, Gordon McLendon, with his creativity. In fact, the station owner took Blore's ideas and spread them around to his other stations. As Dr. Don Rose put it, "He did incredible things, but Chuck Blore was also blessed with a very poor voice, and that was his limitation." One day, Blore recalls, McLendon told him, "'You know, you're wasting your time as a DJ. You should be a program director.' And I said, 'No, no, no, no, no. I'm going to be the world's greatest disc jockey. You wait and see.' And he said, 'No, you're going to be a program director. And I think you've made a wise decision.'"

He had.

"Color Radio," says Blore, "was a culmination of lessons learned. I took Todd's musical approach and Gordon's local news approach. And what I added to that was the entertainment factor, which I always thought was a big deal."

"Entertainment" encompassed disc jockeys, a balance between a tight

The Care & Feeding of the Disc Jockey

After reading a Bill Gavin editorial in 1959 about how little attention some Top 40 stations were paying to their disc jockeys, a favorite programmer of Gavin's—Chuck Blore—wrote:

"I think your comments are directed to the run-of-the-mill radio stations. In market after market, stations try to emulate successful operations that they have heard elsewhere...They seem to [think] that the only factors in successful modern operation are (1) Top 40 records and (2) Go like Hell. You and I both know this is bad jazz, but unfortunately, if there is no similar operation in the area, these stations rocket to the top. These are the operators who hire high school kids to do the deejay work and pay them scale, or in many cases, below scale.

"The minute a good operator comes into the market, these stations have to go down the drain. By a good operator, I mean someone who gives a lot of thought and meticulous follow-through to the myriad things which go to make up the operation of a *good* modern radio station.

"One of the things that causes the most concern is the selection of top deejays. The good operator knows that because of the uniformity of sound necessary musically and otherwise, it is of prime importance that we have a distinct personality on the air at all times. It is imperative that every three or four hours the approach to the uniform sound be refreshed, and this refreshing is done by the DJ. At any top music and news station, you will find, the DJ is a highly talented, highly paid individual...

"Certainly there are policy restrictions, but to my mind, they have made him a better DJ. He no longer is permitted to run off at the mouth but he is encouraged to assert his personality. He may not be as free to inflict his musical tastes on the public, but now, and rightfully, I think, the public dictates the popular music of the day."

Blore as program director-turned advertising agency chief.

format and personality, promotions, and a revolutionary set of jingles (see Chapter 8). But there were also creative edges that only a Chuck Blore could bring to the table. For example, the phrase "Color Radio." That, Blore says, was simply a response to what was happening at the time. "Color television came along, and so we said, 'A-ha! Color radio! Let's call it Channel 98!'"

Blore had done something similar, and more dramatic, in El Paso. "When the phrase 'hi-fi' happened, over a period of time—about a month—I changed all the graphic equalizers and took them down just a fraction on our music, and what no one realized was that our music was getting a little duller and duller. And then the promotion was, 'Hi-fi is coming on'…and then I'd say, 'And now, Hi-fi is here. So that you can hear the dramatic difference, thirty seconds into this next record, we're going to flip the button…,'" And, sure enough, El Paso suddenly had "high fidelity" on their radio—at least on KELP. Or at least they thought so.

By maintaining several veteran KFWB voices while adding several McLendon-groomed personalities, including Bruce Hayes, Ted Quillin, and Elliot Field, Blore offered listeners a package both familiar and fresh. "The DJs were hired based on their ability to be entertainers," says Blore, "and to give the audience a different personality every three hours." While they were all proven talents, Blore took no chances. "We had such a rigid format," he explains. "We played this many records per hour, we had this many commercials per hour, we had whatever, and the time left in that hour was somewhere between six and eight minutes for a DJ to express his personality."

"One of the big differences between KFWB and the other stations," he continues, "was the preparation time I demanded from the DJs. They had to prepare an hour for every hour they were going to be on the air. What that means is about six minutes' worth of what they were going to say, which is about the time they had. They had to devote an hour to thinking it up."

For some, an hour wasn't enough. Blore hired Casey Kasem, a Storz DJ in Detroit and Cleveland, and, when a Crowell-Collier purchase of WMGM in New York fell through, placed Kasem in Oakland, at KEWB. Kasem, who used "wild tracks"—sound bites taken from comedy albums and other sources—was accustomed to asking his engineer to cue them up as he needed them. That wasn't the Blore way. "It almost put me in the hospital," says Kasem. After hearing Casey's show, one of Blore's programming assistants confronted the disc jockey and told him, "When you ask for all those wild tracks, that has to be written. Everything has to be scripted and handed to the engineer before you go on the air. Otherwise, the engineer does not have to give you anything that you call for." Kasem says he wound up spending ten hours a day writing out his show. "One day, my heart skipped a beat on a Friday, and I went to the Kaiser hospital. The doctor said, 'How hard have you been working?' I said, 'Real hard. From ten in the morning until midnight.'"

Demands for preparation aside, Blore agrees that he was not unlike a football coach, working to keep a team on the winning track. At KFWB, he recalls, "We had these DJ meetings every week, and a lot of it was just me picking on little things where we saw some cracks. And we'd kind of all figure out, 'How are we going to solve this problem, guys?' The only problem I couldn't solve was that Bill Ballance and Mitch Reed hated each other."

Ballance explained his side of their mutual enmity: "Mitch kept stealing stuff out of my mailbox. And I caught him several times. He would also steal my material, and not even rephrase it. But every one of the guys there detested Mitch. It's just that I was a little more verbal about it." According to John Hart, "Ballance caught [Reed] rummaging through his desk once and decked him." Ballance admits that he did. Reed, he claims, was disliked by many. As he sort of joked one night on the air, "I did not chop B.M.R. last night. I simply said that he has the type of personality that makes instant enemies at friendship clubs."

Chuck Blore wasn't in it just for the fun and camaraderie. The bottom-line color in "Color Radio" had to be green, and when rock—and its primary audience—was young, advertisers shied away. Kids, after all, had no

Off Ballance

Bill Ballance's columns in *Teen* and *Dig* magazines in the early sixties were comprised of one-liners he'd written and used on his show on KFWB. He never used jokes from gagwriters like Bob Orben, who made thousands of Top 40 disc jockeys sound witty. Over the years, Ballance has compiled enough material to fill forty-five four-drawer file cabinets. It's obvious, then, that he contributed to his official biography at KFWB, which began:

"Bill Ballance, KFWB Quip Jockey, master of instant wit, supple whimsey, observations on the half-skull and half aphorisms which are sharper than a hermit's toenails, was born in Peoria, Illinois. During his most recent visit there, the Mayor met him with a brass band...wrapped around his knuckles. Bill's theory is that a home town is where they always think a man is in some kind of trouble when he returns there for a visit."

spending power. And what respectable corporation wanted to be connected with that music, anyway? As Earl McDaniel, a former DJ at KFWB who went on to program KEWB in Oakland, noted, "There was no potential revenue for Top 40 then. You played rock and roll, you were demeaned. That's where KFWB really cracked it in Southern California. Chuck Blore, of course, is a genius. He came up with the idea of a child's voice saying, 'My mommy listens to KFWB,' which started to prove that it was the parents that were listening, and not just the teens. And then they did research to get advertisers like airlines and banks. It was a long time coming in that market."

Blore was not only resourceful with his own promotional ideas; he and his station could squelch those of competitors as well. In 1959, KFWB faced its first real rival, the Pasadena-based KRLA, which hit the air in September. One of its first contests invited listeners to try and find a DJ named Perry Allen. After giving a description of the new KRLA personality, the station promised a $10,000 cash prize to the first person who could locate him. While people began collaring strangers on the streets in hopes that they might be the mystery man, KFWB's general manager, Bob Purcell, knew that Allen was still finishing up his stint at WKBW in Buffalo. He dispatched two station staffers to Buffalo. Casey Kasem was working in Buffalo at the time. "I lived in the same apartment building where they found Perry Allen. They knocked on the door and said, 'Are you Perry Allen?' He said, 'Yes.'" The KFWB employees took Allen back to KRLA, confronted the station, and demanded the prize money. KFWB donated the cash to charity, while KRLA got in trouble with the FCC, which would ultimately order the owner to sell the station license. "It was the dumbest trick anybody could have pulled," says Kasem. "Everybody knew Perry Allen was still in Buffalo."

With KFWB and KRLA going Top 40 in 1958 and 1959, respectively, Los Angeles was late in getting a full-time Top 40 station. (KDAY and KPOP played the music, but were daytime outlets.) The Midwest and the South, where Storz and McLendon operated, along with broadcast groups like Plough, Balaban, Churchill, and Bartell, were well into "formula radio," as were stations in Buffalo and New York. Even San Francisco had "Wonderful KOBY" going since the Fall of 1956.

But, Storz and McLendon aside, few of the early Top 40 stations were memorable, according to Kent Burkhart, who worked for both of those pioneers and heard many of the others. "They weren't very good," he says. "The Balaban stations at one time were very well programmed. The Plough stations, other than the station in Baltimore, really never sounded too good."

Norman Davis worked weekends at KOBY in San Francisco, whose staff included classical announcers left over from the station's years as KEAR.

"KOBY had taken it right out of Todd Storz's book, and they were the first to try it in San Francisco," he says. "They weren't very good, but because they were the first, they were pretty successful for awhile." Davis moved to KYA, which had been acquired by the Bartell group, in 1959.

"It was really a drastic shock when they started doing this high-intensity rock and roll format," Davis says. "I remember how difficult it was to get through an hour. Bartell's whole idea was to put as much stuff on the air as you possibly could. The log sheet was about seventeen inches long, and it was full, single-spaced, with things you had to put on the air. There would be a spot and then some kind of break, or a little jingle, a public service feature, temperatures, and then there would be another spot, and a breaker, and there would be another spot. I remember one hour that I played four records, and they were all two minutes, because we had two five-minute newscasts an hour. *They* were both jammed with spots. We had eleven contests running. Bartell had this really bad series of jingles, and one of the features we had on the air was the Mayor's Report, and we'd have a one-minute jingle to introduce it. We were so concerned with getting all this crap on the air, the music was incidental. We made special short versions of the pop songs, which would cut one whole chorus or a bridge. We'd have Fats Domino do 'I'm Gonna Be a Wheel Someday,' and it would be forty-five seconds."

Because many commercials came on ETs (electronically transcribed discs), the engineers, Davis says, sometimes juggled ten or eleven discs on three turntables for each break. "Those guys would leave like they'd finished their shifts in a coal mine."

KYA ultimately got streamlined and knocked off KOBY. It would be the "Boss of the Bay" until KEWB—and Chuck Blore—invaded the territory.

While programmers fought radio wars with relish, some of the nation's top radio broadcasters actually conspired to stay out of each other's way. Todd Storz and Gordon McLendon, says Kent Burkhart, were members of the AIMS Group. "It was 'American Independent Market Stations,' or something like that," says Burkhart. "They belonged to the group, along with four or five other broadcasters, including, I believe, the Plough group. It was a group that exchanged information once a month by mail as to what they were doing—different promotions, sales techniques, disc jockeys, whatever. They would also meet twice a year and bring all their paraphernalia, with all their promotional activities on tape, and they would spend two or three days together, listening to tapes and exchanging ideas. And they agreed not to compete against each other, and not buy into markets the other guys were in—or else they got thrown out of the group.

"Well, the information was so vital at that time because it was a growing format, that nobody violated that code."

Maybe. Chuck Blore says he believed that "Todd and Gordon were spying on each other…they'd send their people into the other's market and bring back ideas about what the other was doing." Copying became part of the Top 40 tradition, and Blore believes that he was one of the most copied of all programmers.

Everybody, he says, was lifting his ideas. "There was a recording studio set up by Western Recorders to do nothing but tape-record KFWB and sell it to radio stations all over the country—all over the world, for that matter. It was an amazing time. I would go into these other cities and hear my ideas being mirrored back on the radio. I'd say, 'Oh, man. Shit, am I something or what?'"

At one point, he says, he decided to go through a rating period with no special promotions, just as an experiment. "And there was a program director in Philadelphia who called me and said, 'Man, what are you doing out there?' I said, 'What do you mean?' He said, 'Well, you're not putting anything on. Unless you put something new on, I'm going to lose my job.'"

Blore includes fellow pioneer programmer Mike Joseph among the copiers. "Mike Joseph had a big tape machine, and he was tape-recording KFWB, and he was basically basing everything that he did on what we were doing. I'm not kidding." Did he ever call Joseph on it? "I think one time,

Going Places and Kissing Things

Three months into his morning shift at the brand-new KEWB in Oakland, California, Gary Owens was polished and ready for Los Angeles. His humor ranged from non sequiturs to sly showbiz references, all delivered in a friendly, booming bass voice; the prototypical radio announcer. Randy Wood, mentioned below, was the president of Dot Records, home of Pat Boone and one-hit artist Wink Martindale, who'd find greater fortune as a television game show host.

"This is a Tues sort of day, the 29th of September. Here we go now, another recent graduate from Randy Wood High School, lovable little Wink Martindale…"

"Deck of Cards" plays.

"Time to Wink Martindale on KEWB, the song that ranks number eight on the rank of songs this week on the KEWB Fabulous Forty survey. How-doodle-you-do, G.O. back again, going places and losing things from now until nine, and the Ted Randal scandal…"

(Switches to the voice of an old man.)

"Ehh…this portion of the Garish Owens Show is brought to you by frozen chocolate things on a stick with sweet gooey stuff inside we met at a convention, and he didn't deny it." "Oh, like hell!" Joseph exclaims. "Like hell. I had never even heard of L.A. I always did my own thing. Anybody and everybody that knew me and worked for me in the late fifties knew that. And the guys from Storz and McLendon knew it, too. Any time I came into one of the Storz markets, Bill Stewart went crazy. "Do you know why Blore is pissed off?" Joseph asked. "Because at the time that Crowell-Collier bought MGM (WMGM) in New York, I was taking WABC Top 40 and I blew them out, because I did Blore's thing before he got there. Bill Purcell, who Blore worked for, told me that I ruined it for Chuck Blore."

(Actually, it was the FCC that "blew them out"—that is, kept Crowell-Collier from completing its purchase of WMGM in 1960. And although Joseph installed a Top 40 format and DJ staff in 1960 that would take WABC to market dominance, it wasn't until Joseph had departed that the station adopted the tag "The Good Guys" for its disc jockeys. As Rick Sklar, who was doing promotions at WABC, noted in his book *Rockin' America,* station manager Hal Neal "heard about the phrase from his sales reps, who picked it up in Los Angeles, where it had been used by program director Chuck Blore on KFWB." Amazingly, crosstown rival WMCA also began using the "Good Guys" slogan, even used it more often, made up "Good Guys" jingles and merchandise, and took possession of the identification. As it turns out, two New York stations—but not Joseph—stole from Blore,

that melts when it gets too hot."

KEWB jingle plays.

"In the Still of the Night" by the Five Satins plays.

(*In a character voice:*) Get your sho-be-doo out of here and don't ever come back." (*In his regular voice:*) "The Five Satins on KEWB, where it's the trend, friends, the thing to do. In the Still of My Basement here, it's 65 degrees in San Francisco downtown, East Bay 66 degrees, on the Peninsula 55, and Marin, 61 degrees from the movie of the same name."

(*Owens reads copy for a commercial for Skippy dog food, concluding:*) "And remember, gang, all of the KEWB DJs have Skippy every day."

A few songs and features later:

"And now, if you'll get close to your radio there, it's time for Gary Owens's Good Morning Kiss. As you know by now, gang, we have our osculatory overtones every morning about this same time. Our mistletoe's getting a little creepy-looking here. I'll tack some new up one of these days. But now (*his voice gets as low as it goes—almost as low as Barry White's*)...it's time for me to hold you in my strong, Crowell-Collier hairy-like arms and kiss you!"

We hear three or four seconds of muffled sounds, followed by a sprightly jingle, over which Owens exclaims:

"Wow!"

despite Joseph's statement that "I did Blore's thing before he got there.")

Ain't radio fun?

Despite the occasional sniping, it has been fun for Joseph, who still recalls the days when stations he worked with got seventy-five shares in the ratings—three out of every four radios that were on were tuned into his station. In New Orleans, he says, "In one book, I knocked off WTIX, and that made a hell of a lot of noise and scared the hell out of Todd Storz and Bill Stewart."

His secret? "Play the hits."

But all stations have done that. What Joseph added were a few new touches—playing album cuts in the mid-fifties, even while espousing a tight playlist of about thirty songs; and "very tight presentation; production techniques; very strong personalities—sooner or later, most of them became superstars. We emphasized personalities, but the station came first."

Joseph, a native of Youngstown, Ohio, broke into radio as a disc jockey at various stations in Cleveland in the mid-forties, when he was still in college. He got his programming start in Flint, Michigan, at WTAC, an NBC-affiliated station where he had to choose between going the NBC network way, with block programming, or Top 40, then in its infancy. He chose Top 40 and, within one rating period, scored a 75 share and found a career.

Joseph's travels took him to Buffalo, where he worked on the WKBW that produced Dick Biondi, Art Roberts, and other announcers who went on to prominence. After a couple of other successes, Joseph was ready for New York, where, as a consultant for WABC, he hired "Morning Mayor" Herb Oscar Anderson, Dan Ingram, and "Cousin Brucie" Morrow, along with an attorney-turned-sportscaster, Howard Cosell.

While he maintains that he has never copied anyone else, Joseph says that he's seen and heard his own ideas used by others. Bill Drake's short jingles? "I always used short jingles—most of them were three, five, seven seconds."

"And another thing they took from me was 'More Music.' I used 'More Music' way back in 1960, '62..."

The list goes on.

While it may be argued that others besides Joseph promised "more music" and kept their playlists short early on (Todd Storz is said to have wanted a rotation of only ten songs at KOWH before he was brought to his senses), Joseph has gone further. From the beginning, he says, he has conducted in-depth research of the music. "When I first go into a market," he says, "I go into every record store personally. I'll spend up to three weeks doing interviews, with an average of forty-five minutes each. And I get every single thing I can get: the sales on every configuration, every demo[graphic] for every single, the gender of every buyer, the race of every buyer. And one of the things I've always done is dayparts [limiting certain songs to specific parts of the day]. You see, this is one of the reasons I can't copy Storz or McLendon or Chuck Blore. They don't know my internal secrets, because I never told anybody. I follow the audience flow of the market around the clock. The type of listener, the age, the nationality of every single person in the market, around the clock. And I program my music accordingly. So every one of my formats is different, twenty-four hours a day, seven days a week, because the music in every market is different."

Bill Ballance became a regular in magazines and newspapers.

In the service of the station, then, music comes first—even at the expense, sometimes, of famed personalities. Joseph was thinking back to 1956, which he considers the first year of Top 40, if only because that's when he got into programming it. "Prior to that time, it was popular music," he argues. "But remember, Martin Block did a popular music show. In fact, I fired him at WABC. (Block had moved from WNEW to the ABC affiliate in 1954.) And he was my hero. But I had to fire him, obviously, because he was fifty-eight years old. And I will never forget. I was talking about the new and different sounds, and he looked at me and said, 'Mike, I was playing Top 30 in 1933.' And it's true. But the music was different."

Martin Block, by 1958, had been on the record with his views on rock and roll. He didn't like it, and it didn't help that he was sharing a frequency with Alan Freed. He spoke about the "decline" in pop music. In February, while his station was moving toward a Top 40 format, he declared that his show would "cover all musical preferences," based on a "Teenage Survey" of some sixty thousand listeners. This, he said, would result in a more personalized show, at a time when Top 40 disc jockeys were beginning to be perceived as time-and-temp-spouting robots.

Block's long-time rival, Al Jarvis, agreed. In 1958, he was back on KFWB, playing pretty much what he pleased, when Blore breezed in with his new format. He stuck it out, but he was lukewarm, at best, about the format. "Top 40 programming," he allowed grudgingly, "has apparently satisfied the needs of a majority of the music- and record-conscious audience."

Jarvis, according to Bill Ballance, never caught on or up to the format's pace, its requirement for what Blore called "the imperceptible overlap"—fancy language for no dead air between program elements. "Al," he says, "refused to get into the hurried, urgent pace of the Fabulous Forty Channel 98 format. He either couldn't do it, or he wouldn't't."

Jarvis was by no means alone in his wariness over what the new age had wrought. As Top 40 came to emphasize the "list" in playlist, a number of disc jockeys balked at being stripped of their personalities. Soon after KFWB pulled the big switch, KLAC—a crosstown pop and jazz station which prided itself on its deejay staff, "the Big Five" (Dick Haynes, Peter Potter, Bob McLaughlin, Alex Cooper, Gene Norman)—followed KFWB's lead. Potter left before the format flip, and Haynes, Norman, and three other staffers quit afterwards. None too subtle, KLAC called its new sound "Formula Radio." It was tantamount to a cigarette company coming up with the brand name "Death Sticks." In Detroit, Ed McKenzie, who had attained stardom as "Jack the Bellboy" on WJBK and WXYZ, quit the latter when it went Top 40 in 1959. "I would sooner dig ditches or sell hot dogs," he said.

Dick Biondi, working in Buffalo at WKBW, was not about to do either. He believed that there was room for personality—and opportunities for creative freedom—within the format. "The greatest DJ," he said, "is the one who can live within the formula...and make it sound not only happy and interesting, but as if he is producing and pulling the music all by himself."

Chapter

Bill Gavin: Let's Work Together

When I did a story on Bill Gavin for *Rolling Stone* in 1972, two radio people made it clear just whom I was profiling:

Elma Greer, music director of KSFO in San Francisco, called him "the most powerful man in the business." Every record company subscribed to and quoted the *Gavin Report*, she said. "Everybody's copied him, but he originated the thing. He's the only one who's really popular and respected, because it's an honest sheet."

Bob Harvey, then program director at KQV in Pittsburgh, added: "Bill Gavin is an incredibly honest man. I only wonder what he's doing in this business."

What he was doing was what he'd been doing since 1958: compiling and sending out facts and figures on record popularity, based on radio airplay reports, to radio stations and record companies. The goal was to help stations program their music; to be a conduit between radio and records.

In the beginning, Greer remembers, "He was just putting out little lists of records." This was before rock and roll, and his reports consisted of groups of pop records listed under "A through G," and "X through Z," the letters reflecting his recommendations for when and how often they should be played. "He was doing rotations then," says Greer, "before people knew what rotations were."

Correspondent stations and other subscribers received single type-written sheets mimeographed on blue paper, and the person who typed the early reports was Anita Rodenbaeck. She shared an office with Gavin and remembered him auditioning music as it slid from the middle of the road to some younger, more disheveled-looking hitchhikers. "Every now and then I'd say to Bill, 'Could we please not play any more of that Elvis? Could we listen to some good music today?' And he'd put on Beethoven."

Bill Gavin

59

LUCKY LAGER
DANCE TIME
ON REVIEW

Kim Fowley, the rock artist and producer, was raised on *Lucky Lager Dance Time*, which, he says, "was the event. As important as *American Bandstand*."

How was it that Gavin, who was already fifty-one when he started the report thirty-five years ago, would be open to rock and roll, a music that seemed designed to irritate adults? The answer is simple: Bill Gavin was a musician. He was a singer and pianist who gave up a teaching career for the stage. He was born in 1907 in Chetek, Wisconsin, just north of Eau Claire. By age nineteen, he was already a high school teacher. His subjects were history and music. Within a few years, music began to dominate his life. In 1929, he moved with his family to Berkeley. He attended the University of California, but also got a job singing and playing piano on KPO, a San Francisco station affiliated with NBC. (In later years, the station became KNBR.) In 1932, Gavin traveled with a musical comedy troupe to Milwaukee, where he ran into Janet Breed, whom he'd met in his high school days. They would marry in 1935.

Working with a traveling male quartet, The Blenders, Gavin wound up in Seattle in 1936. There, he was hired as an announcer on KOMO and KJR, joint NBC stations. By 1942, he was back in San Francisco, singing and playing piano on KQW (which became KCBS) and working as a producer for the Office of War Information (now the Voice of America). It was that experience, he said, that allowed him to develop radio programming skills.

At NBC radio in 1951, he started a nightly half-hour show of pop records, *The Burgie Music Box*, featuring the top thirty hits of the day, according to *Billboard* magazine's sales charts. The show ended in 1953, but within two years, another beer company came into Gavin's life. McCann-Erickson, an ad agency, had Lucky Lager as a client and needed help programming its *Lucky Lager Dance Time*, which broadcast nightly on forty-eight stations in eleven western states. Saturday nights, each affiliate featured its own Top Ten countdown, based on local record sales. Gavin decided to get information from all the stations and issue a combined report, all in the interest of learning "the overall average."

He began sending out his reports, says Greer, who would later work with Gavin, "because of his love of the business. Going from being talent to programming records to this was a natural step for him." At that time, the only popularity charts available were in *Billboard* and *Cash Box*, and they covered only sales, not requests and airplay. With Gavin as the conduit, *Dance Time* stations began exchanging information in 1957, and some station managers

WHAT'D YOU SAY?

pop ◆ Mitch Reed, WMCA-New York, is reported to be building his show entirely of alternate hits and oldies. Some listeners comment that they'd like Mitch better if he didn't talk so fast. —*Gavin Report,* March 1, 1963 ◆ pop turned to Gavin for help programming their music outside the Lucky Lager hours. Gavin became a consultant and began to diversify, offering his *Record Report* to stations outside the western region. In return, all he asked was that participating stations inform him of how new records were doing in their areas. He got affirmative responses from a dozen cities, including New York, Philadelphia, Boston, Cleveland, Chicago, Detroit, and Miami. Their reports made up the first *Bill Gavin's Record Report*, which he saw as a service to radio. And, he said, when record companies began asking to see his *Report*, "I got real stingy and said, 'No.' If they want it, they can pay for it." He suddenly had a side business.

Buck to the future: Buckminster Fuller spoke at the 1973 Gavin Seminar.

It was a good thing that he did. Rock was on a roll in the late fifties, and in 1960, when *Lucky Lager Dance Time* was playing more and more of the music, parents objected to a beer company sponsoring a show for teenagers. At the beer company's request, the show advised minors not to buy its product, making clear that beer was for adults only. But, as the changing music drew a younger listenership, protests increased, and the show was canceled.

Gavin now concentrated on his *Report*, and his timing was perfect. His compilations became a major force in the budding Top 40 format. "This was something new in our industry," says Elma Greer. "We always went by the trades, and suddenly we had this, giving us information faster."

The first subscriber from the record side was Sol Handwenger of MGM, and, from radio, it was Paul Drew, a disc jockey in Atlanta when he became one of Gavin's first correspondents. Drew rose to become vice president of programming for RKO Radio. "You came to rely on the information that you got from Bill Gavin as a way to determine, with all these choices, which records to play," he says. In college, when Drew, a native of Detroit, worked part time as a record promotion man, he'd come to rely on reports from record distributors to know what was selling. Now, he had Gavin's newsletter—soon referred to as a tipsheet in the industry—as well, and he trusted Gavin and his distributors, he says, more than the existing music trade magazines, *Billboard* and *Cash Box*.

Along with many other radio professionals, Drew liked the attention Gavin paid to smaller markets. "Bill told me that his report wasn't about New York,

AND THE STATS JUST KEEP ON COMING

pop ▶ A good description of some "Top 40" lists: "Half statistics and half helium."—Pete "Mad Daddy" Myers, *Gavin Report*, November 17, 1958 ◀ pop

An emotional Gavin, accepting a surprise "Man of the Decade" award at the 1973 Gavin conference, is comforted by wife Janet.

Los Angeles, and the other big markets," says Drew. "It was about what was going on in all the small markets. Nobody makes a record to be a regional hit, but it's lost on most of the people in record companies, and a lot of people in radio, that this country is made up of the northeast, the south, the southeast—and tastes are different. By getting all of the information from these little markets, Bill could show you on the front page, with his 'Sleeper of the Week,' that there was something here—not just for these three little out-of-the-way markets—but something that you people in the next level markets ought to be taking a look at."

The Gavin Report, as Bill edited his tipsheet's name, grew to several pages, stapled and sent out each Thursday. Each issue offered a "Smash of the Week," a "Sleeper of the Week," a "Hot Shot," a "Top Tip," and a "Record to Watch," along with regional and local prospects based on sales, requests, and airplay. A recommended playlist ranged from twenty to fifty or more records, with the fastest-moving titles underlined. "When a record was a Bill Gavin pick," says Elma Greer, "everybody listened to it again."

Another young disc jockey who watched Gavin carefully was Buddy Deane, who'd parlayed success at WITH in Baltimore into a popular afternoon dance show on WJZ-TV. Like so many DJs of that era, he predated Top 40 and chose his own music. Early on, he says, he did it the textbook way. "I just thought that first you play an uptempo number, then you play an instrumental, then you play a girl singer, then a boy singer, then another instrumental, then a group vocal. That's the way we programmed in those days. And this record promotion guy said, 'You know, Buddy, you need to play the records that people want to hear,' and I said, 'What do you mean?' And he said, 'Well, you know, the records you're playing are not what people are buying. And they've got to like them to buy them, don't they?' And he started making sense to me.

"And I started paying attention to this and listening to people. I took a lot of phone calls, and I'd listen to people talk about the records they liked, and then I started surveying record stores. I got a feel for what was going on, and then I followed the *Billboard* reports. They used to have reports from each city, and I'd pick up a record from, say, Cleveland or Chicago, St. Louis, someplace, and

ILLUMINATION

Research Report: The lyrics of "Midnite Special"—Paul Evans (Guaranteed Records)—stem from the superstition of Negro prisoners in the Southern jails that if the light of a passing train shines through their cell bars, they would receive a pardon in the morning. Hence, "Midnite Special, shine your everlovin' light on me." —*Gavin Report*, January 22, 1960

I would play it and see if I would get a reaction off of it.

"And in those days, you got a lot of telephone reaction. I remember that I played 'Memories Are

Made of This' by Dean Martin, and there was a cop that handled the traffic at the corner right up from the radio station, and he came up and said, 'What was that record you played by Dean Martin?' And I made a habit of going on those kind of records, because these are not people who are going to hype you, these are people that are just curious."

Impatient with *Billboard's* regional reports, which were issued monthly, Buddy Deane greeted Bill Gavin's newsletter with enthusiasm. "I got a copy of it and I learned fast that what Bill Gavin said—he had a little phrase that he used—that you could take that record and run with it, you could count on it. Bill Gavin said, 'Smash of the Week,' and he would capitalize and underline it, and boy, I got a hold of *that* record, because Bill was very reliable. He was very, very, very honest for his records, and I always tried to be honest with him if I told him a record was a hit."

Deane once told Gavin about a record he thought would be big—"and I found out I'd been hyped. Very often you hyped yourself, you know. And I called him and said, 'Bill, I'm sorry, that record…I made a bad mistake, it's a dud.' This was about three days after I told him it was a hit. 'I played this, there's no reaction, the kids don't seem to respond, I'm not getting phone calls on it, the kids dancing on the show stand around looking like, 'What is this?' So we became good friends and trusted each other."

Gavin did not mind that record industry people found his reports to be of interest, but his heart belonged to radio. In 1960, he began issuing a single-page supplement, mailed for arrival at stations on Wednesdays and Fridays, and labeled *CONFIDENTIAL!* It was for radio only, and, to many programmers, it was invaluable. Pat O'Day, program director of KJR in Seattle, says he based his station's playlist and the survey it published for listeners in part on the *Confidentials*.

"The *Confidential* was like bread to a hungry person," Paul Drew recalls. "If it didn't come on Friday, that was really a bit of insecurity because you really relied on that information. In those days, information didn't travel that fast. Those *Confidentials* were everything."

What Bill Gavin offered were tips on potential hits based not only on his ears and intuition, but also on exchanges of hard information—airplay, requests and sales—with his correspondents. Then he'd go to his typewriter and take his cuts.

Bill Gavin

Sometimes, he connected. In late 1958, he wrote, "A smash in Los Angeles [where it was first played] is 'Donna'–Ritchie Valens (Del Fi). Should be one of the first big records of 1959." In the spring of 1961, he wrote, "So far—in the S.F. area, at least—I seem to be a minority of one in picking the 'Travelin' Man' side of the new Ricky Nelson release. I'm skeptical of the ability of 'Hello, Mary Lou' to attract heavy sales, but I could be very wrong." He wasn't. "Mary Lou" made it into the *Billboard* Top Ten; "Travelin' Man" hit Number One.

Beyond songs, he could look past the horizon and hit a long ball. "It is entirely possible," he wrote in March 1963, "if singles sales continue to decline, that stations will continue to shrink their playlists, until by the year 1965, 'Top 40' will be replaced by 'Top 20.'" (FM, anyone?)

In 1965, Bill Drake split the difference and inaugurated a Top 30 format at KHJ. And, two years after that, FM rock was born.

Gavin could also be very wrong. In mid-1962, he told his readers, "I still can't hear a hit in Dion's 'Little Diane.' Hostile songs, putting somebody down, never did appeal. The flip, 'Lost for Sure,' may have some possibilities. Anyhow, I prefer it." "Diane" hit the Top Ten; "Lost" got lost.

He would sometimes remind readers of his own musical background by sending out a mild jeer: "Why did the producer of Teddy Randazzo's 'It's Magic' clutter up a brilliant arrangement by introducing a shrill-sounding gal's trio in the middle of the song?" he asked in late 1958. "Oh well, the flip is the side, anyhow." And when the Rolling Stones' "Tell Me" gave them their first American hit single in 1964, Gavin didn't try to hide his distaste. "I hate to admit that this hunk of garbage is selling, but it is. I still can't believe that it will achieve any notable success."

This kind of candor was unheard of in the trade industry, in which reviewers followed the rule of etiquette of saying nothing if they didn't have something nice to say, and it endeared Gavin to his readers.

Aware of his growing stature, he began writing editorials early on. In the fall of 1958, he offered this reminder:

"Sometimes some of us may get so involved in the record business that we forget that our job is to provide radio entertainment—to attract and please an audience. Record sales are not the only criterion of a record's entertainment potential. This is simply the easiest of all data to obtain. The radio stations that conscientiously keep in touch with the tastes and preferences of their listeners will always have a more vital 'sound'—as well as higher ratings."

KEEP-A-KNOCKIN'

pop ▶ If man bites dog, it's news. So it's news that KIOA-Des Moines edited the Bob Dylan single ["Knockin' on Heaven's Door"?] to make it longer. Was 2:28, now is 4:00. ◀ pop
— *Gavin Report*, August 24, 1973

Chapter

Hey, Mr. Deejay, I: The Initial Buzz

"Back in the sixties, DJs weren't always treated as celebrities; they were 'friends of the public.' At record hops the deejay was the liaison between the real celebrity and the fan. They were role models for kids."—*Gary Owens*

"DJs used to be American heroes. No more. Today, being a disc jockey is generally regarded as being slightly more respectable than snatching purses for a living, or robbing graves."

—*Larry Lujack, in his 1975 book,* Super Jock

The truth lies somewhere in-between. Disc jockeys, back in the day and through today, are correctly perceived both as talented broadcast professionals with a special knowledge of their music and their community, and as lazy sleazebags who see radio work as no work at all.

Although, as in any profession, there were many in radio who took the easy way out—they did their shows on cruise control, they drank, they womanized, they took payola—the ones who succeeded saw radio work as exactly that: Work. They got to know their music, their audience, their community, their station's philosophy. They followed the program director's orders and did their prep, they dissected their work and tried to do better.

Most of the radio people interviewed or profiled in this book are successes by almost any measure, but some of them acknowledge mistakes, misfortune, and lost opportunities. Many had a passion for the music, the medium, or both, from a very early age. That's the way it was with Charlie Tuna and Scott Shannon, Robert W. Morgan and Dick Clark, and—speaking of Clark—with Jerry "The Geator with the Heater" Blavat and Buzz Bennett, who got their starts as dancers on teen dance shows on television.

BUZZ BENNETT: "I FOLLOW UNTIL I'M A LEADER"

We begin our first visit with the dancer whose story reads like a movie pro-

Bennett: "I wanted to be Al Capone."

posal. In fact, Buzz Bennett claimed, *Hairspray*, John Waters' campy 1988 movie centered on a Baltimore girl (played by Ricki Lake) who became a star on the local bandstand show, was based on him.

At thirteen, Buzz (that's his real name) became a regular on Baltimore's highly successful TV dance program, *The Buddy Deane Show*, and began helping the host pick records. By sixteen, he was a disc jockey and a program director. As a programmer, he would be a pioneer in the field of research, win industry awards, and become a respected consultant.

But while the Ricki Lake character was a chubby adolescent being watched by her mother (played by Divine), Bennett, at thirteen, was a self-described gangster.

"So when I was real young in Baltimore, a friend of mine loved this girl, Helen, that danced on TV. To meet her, he decided to audition for the show." All he needed was a way to get from where he and Buzz lived, in Glen Vern, to WJZ-TV in Baltimore, twenty-five miles away. The buddy, Al, came up with a sensible idea.

"He said to me, 'Buzz, we need to swipe a car. You're good at that.' I was in gangs. I wanted to be Al Capone. I said, 'Well, why?' So he says, 'I'm in love with this girl.' So I rip off a car, and I take him up there so his dream can come true.

"They have two phases to getting onto the show. Number one, you had to dance, and they go around and tap you and eliminate you, and they end up with so many people they want to keep to dance on the show. Well, Al's got his partner and he's out there and he's ready to rock, and he's a great dancer." Spotting a girl who had no partner, Buzz approached her. Soon, they, too, were on the floor. Neither Al nor Buzz got the dreaded tap. They and their partners had survived.

"After you dance," Bennett recounted, "you have to go before what they call the Teen Committee, and that was like twelve people, six girls and six guys. These guys were sitting there in judgment of who got on and who didn't. They would ask you questions, to see if you had a personality and where you were coming from. And I remember somebody asked me a question, and the question was, 'Do you consider yourself a leader or a follower?' And my answer was, 'I follow until I'm a leader.' There are a bunch of other questions, too. But this is what got me on the show."

Bennett with Elton John.

Al didn't make it past his session with the Teen Committee. Meanwhile, Bennett not only joined the show, he was elected to the committee, he began dating Helen—so much for his best friend—and helping Deane. "I used to pick the music because my mother owned record shops and would make me work in them. Then when I went on the *Buddy Deane Show*, he would make me listen to all the records with him." He helped Deane put together his reports for Bill Gavin's *Report*, and, given the title "teen assistant," he earned $35 a week.

At age fourteen, Bennett recalled, "Alan Freed was a friend of mine. All the jocks, man, Murray the K, and all those guys and Buddy Deane were like a little pack on the East Coast."

On Deane's show, however, the stars were the best dancers. Said Bennett: "I got so popular on that TV show that everywhere I went in the city, if I walked in a restaurant it would silence, and people would whisper to each other when [I came] in the door. I would get three or four thousand pieces of mail a week. "I will never, ever, no matter what happens, be a bigger star than I was on the *Buddy Deane Show*.

"My first job in radio was at WWIN in Baltimore, at 50 cents an hour.

It was the *Don McNeil Breakfast Club*, and all you would do is on the hour and half hours say, 'WWIN Baltimore.'"

Through Deane, whose hometown was Pine Bluff, Arkansas, a teenaged Bennett got a job at KOTN—several jobs, actually. "I did two shifts, I did 10 to 2 in the morning, I did 3 to 7 in the afternoon, and I was the program director, and I did sales, and I was the assistant manager."

By 1962, he'd helped lead the station to astronomical ratings, and warranted his own mentions in the *Gavin Report*—as a nominee for Music Director of the Year honors.

Buddy Deane ruled Baltimore airwaves.

"When I was sixteen years old, guys that were forty-five were working for me," Bennett said. "Buddy Deane always called me the 'teenage monster' because I knew Einstein's theory of relativity, and I was reading *Brave New World*, and he said, 'You don't know how smart you are.' I *didn't* know. I thought I was dumb."

Bennett's radio road took him home—to Baltimore and to "The Big WITH," a Top 40 station with a mixed staff. "We were like two black guys, and George Wilson, the program director who hired me, did the morning show." Buzz did the afternoon shift, handled the music, and assisted Wilson. "In those days they made you do so much work and paid you nothing."

Bennett was earning $75 a week—a steep drop from his Program Director/DJ salary in Arkansas. He did record hops for supplemental income, but thought of money as secondary. "I wanted to be in radio," he said. "That was my passion. I would go down and hang out with the program directors in Baltimore, and I'd get them to give me a bunch of news copy out of the trash can, and I'd go read it on a little recorder that Buddy had given me."

Now, he had his own show, in his hometown.

One afternoon, he answered the request line. It was Al—his former best buddy. "You talk too fast," he told Bennett, then hung up.

It was good to be home.

HE KEPT REACHING FOR THE STARS

When I first heard Casey Kasem, he wasn't doing any countdowns, and he wasn't telling little stories about the musicians whose records he was play-

ing. He was, like so many Top 40 nighttime disc jockeys, talking fast, spinning the hits, reading dedications, and goofing around with characters and wild tracks, some of them taken from Stan Freberg albums—a shrill "That's *right!*" and "You catch on *fast!*"—the voice of the exasperated record producer in the comedian's takeoff on the Platters' "The Great Pretender."

That was at KEWB in Oakland, and, although Casey was doing fine with his routine, he learned one day that the general manager of the station wasn't among his admirers. One afternoon early in 1962, Kasem relates, the boss called him into his office. "'Casey,'" he said, 'we're going to change your show.' And I said, 'Well, what do you mean, John? I'm number one. I even beat baseball.' He said, 'I know. We just want

Casey: Beating baseball ratings wasn't enough.

to change it. We had a couple other wild trackers here and they're not here any more, and you're wild tracking.'" He meant Don MacKinnon and Don Bowman, two of radio's more creative, comic disc jockeys.

Kasem repeated the fact that his show was on top of the ratings.

"'I know, but I want you to change.'

"I said, 'Well, what do you want me to do?' He said, 'I want you to be a disc jockey. Talk about the artists, talk about the music.'"

Kasem, who doubled as music director at KEWB, had an ear for music—in fact, he says, he and Bill Gavin often talked about the latest releases—but he'd never given much thought to details beyond the song title, the artist's name, and the record label.

"All right, John, when do you want me to start?" Kasem asked.

Kasem at WJBK in Detroit, where he thought he'd break Elvis records.

"When you go on the air tonight," his boss replied.

Kasem thought his nights at KEWB were numbered. When he returned to the station in the evening, he thought to himself, "Well, I'll do the time, the temperature, the weather forecast, and introduce the records, and tomorrow I'll be fired."

At the studio, he began what had become his pre-show ritual: cleaning up the mess that "Emperor" Bob Hudson had left behind.

"I'd go in there and I'd be picking this paper up, and that cigarette up and cleaning out the ashtrays and everything. Well, as I was going in, wedged in the door to this little studio was a big trash barrel about five feet high with reams of news copy in it. And on top of that news copy was a magazine, *Who's Who in Pop Music 1962*. I think *Record World* put it out as a supplement. And I started looking through it."

Kasem was astounded at his find. "They listed the hits, they listed where the artists were born, where they went to school, some of their hobbies— real rudimentary stuff—nothing you could get excited about, but enough for me to get a show on that night. And I always teased anything I did. Even when I was doing Happy and the Little Girl Without a Name, I always said, 'Coming up next…' So I continued the drama, except it wasn't comedy and it wasn't wild tracks—and it caught on instantly."

A year or so later, Kasem, whose overriding ambition was to be an actor, moved to Los Angeles, where Emperor Hudson had found a new home, at KRLA, and encouraged Casey to join him. At KRLA in 1964, Kasem continued to offer mini-biographies and anecdotes of the artists he played, and he enjoyed high ratings. Always looking for more, he got a tele-

JUST A THOUGHT:

Casey Kasem, now at KRLA-Pasadena, continues his popular feature of thumbnail bio sketches of record artists. Like, "In a moment, we'll hear a song by a former truck driver who parlayed an accident into a million bucks." I've suggested to the Caser that he make his bio feature files available for national syndication. — *Gavin's Gab*, June 21, 1963

vision gig, hosting a *Bandstand*-styled show, *Shebang*, and found his first work doing voice-overs for commercials.

Casey, says Ron Jacobs, program director at rival KHJ "Boss Radio," was an atypical disc jockey. Jacobs recalls the glory years of KHJ in the late sixties, and his deejay staff, and how, for an appearance at a Rose Parade, they demanded individual motor homes. "They were fucking stars. They would laugh at KRLA and Casey Kasem. Well, who's laughing at who now? Casey was busting his butt doing voice-over work, and I told these guys, 'You work three hours a day. You got twenty-one hours a day. You can either sit at Nickodell's and have some record promo man jerk you around, or you should be working on something.'"

Kasem seemed to be working twenty-one hours a day—especially after he successfully pitched an idea for a national radio show in which he'd combine his mini-bios with the kind of Top 40 countdown that stations had been doing for years. The takers? None other than Jacobs, who in 1970 co-founded Watermark Productions with fellow PD Tom Rounds.

American Top 40 hit the air in mid-1970 on seven stations. Within ten years, it would grow to more than nine hundred stations around the world and cross over to television. Casey Kasem became a bona fide star, and his voice, laden with gravel and sincerity, was popping up regularly on commercials.

All because of a general manager tired of wild tracks in 1962.

It's Kasem's drive that has kept him on top, but he acknowledges the help he's received along the way. At his first Top 40 station—WJBK in Detroit—he heard the early Elvis Presley, and he had a brilliant idea. "I thought I'd make a name for myself by breaking Elvis's records on the air—literally." But his program director advised against it. "I think he's going to be around for awhile," he told Casey. "I think you should go with the trend."

Kasem also thanks fate for his very occupation. After a couple of stints in Buffalo radio, he'd joined the Detroit station as a summer relief newscaster. As WJBK disc jockeys went on vacation, he was asked to do some additional fill-in work. When the ratings shot up after he'd subbed for a two-DJ team, the station hired Casey as a full-time DJ. "Otherwise," he figures, "I'd have been a newsman."

Knowing him, he'd have turned a weekly countdown of news stories into a top-rated show.

A CONVERSATION WITH GARY OWENS

You know Gary Owens as the ear-cupped announcer on Laugh-In. *I know him as a guy I used to idolize—and still do, in many ways. I grew up in Oakland, where Gary stopped for two years, beginning in 1959, on his way to Los Angeles. As he does now, he combined a smooth, friendly, bass-based Voice of Authority with a penchant for silly words, gags, and non sequiturs. I joined his Complete Failures Club and bought his single "What Is a Freem?" He signed my Oakland High yearbook, advising, "Stifling a child's extraovertentualities tends to subjunctuate his biophysical transmogrifications."*

In Hollywood, Owens went beyond radio renown and became a multimedia star. (Besides Laugh-In *and numerous variety and game shows, he's been on twenty-seven albums, and he's voiced a thousand cartoons and even more commercials. In a poll conducted by the publisher of the book,* Los Angeles Radio People *to determine "The Top 10 Los Angeles Disc Jockeys Between 1957-1997," Owens finished Number One.*

You could knock out the words "Los Angeles," and the result could well be the same.

Gary takes success in stride, and he doesn't take it for granted. In his sixties, he continues to work in voice-overs, in cartoons, and on his first love: radio.

Gary Owens, DJ and emcee.

My first Top 40 was KOIL in Omaha. I got into it in a strange, almost surreptitious way. I was the teenage news director, so to speak. So my job was to give the newscasts all during the morning show from 6 until noon, and so one day, I can't remember the guy's name, but he was a good disc jockey. He didn't like Don Burden at all, because Burden would give him a bad time, quit in the middle of the show. And I'm the only one there, in addition to the chief engineer. So he says, "I'm out of here. Goodbye." And this is about 6:30 in the morning. So George Dunleavy, who was the program director, said "Gary, take over." I said, "I've never run a turntable." I didn't know anything about them. We had six turntables, three on one side, three on the other. They ran commercials and 45s. They had two Magnacorders that were reel to reel, and I didn't know how to run those either, and I had a lavaliere microphone, which I knew how to run, because it was around my neck, so I had to stand during the show.

Here I'm thrown into this, and I'm goosing every record. "And now, the lovely Patience and Prudence, 'Going to Get Along without You Now' on the lovely KOIL Omaha," and *waaaah*…of course, there would be a bad cue. And then I'd put myself down and say, "All those darned elves are here. It's Elves Presley." Then I'd find something on there to cue up Elvis saying, "Heartbreak Hotel" or whatever it was to try and tie it in, and so, even though word plays had always been part of me, that's where they started jumping out, as a protection device.

The program director liked me. But Don Burden said, in his own romantic way, "You're one of the worst I've ever heard."

He was probably critiquing your technical work.

He didn't like my "imperceptible overlap." I believe Chuck Blore may have created that phrase—or Don Keyes or Gordon McLendon—but the imperceptible overlap meant there was just a fraction of a space in between the end of a record and the beginning of a jingle or a commercial.

But I didn't know what that meant. Here's a whole new career for me and I felt so bad. I was really depressed because I wanted to do well, but I just was not schooled technically.

So I came home that day and Arleta met me at the door of our apartment. And I just stood at the door for a while with a tear, I could only afford one tear, but with two…a portable one, a plastic tear which I put under each eye alternately, and she said, "What's the matter?" And I said I

Gary Owens (standing left) is among a group of DJs and wives visiting singer Maurice Chevalier. KYA's Norman Davis (wearing eyeglasses) is seated.

was filling in as a disc jockey and I was just terrible, just terrible. And I said, "I don't want to do this. Let's go back to South Dakota," where we were from. And she said, "No, no. Give it a chance." And I said, "I don't like not being good at whatever I'm doing." She said, "Well, give it thirty days. If you don't feel you're good at that point, then we'll go back." And it was the best advice in the world, because within thirty days, I learned how to do it very well, and my skills came about rapidly once I learned how to segue and do all these things.

The rhythm of my voice at that time was pretty fast, because rock and roll was pretty fast. Most of it was, "Number three this week, from the KOIL survey" or whatever it would be. You could put one-liners in. There were a lot of one-liners and of course it is a world of one-liners for the most part. You tried to sum up as quickly as you could, so if you were talking about Elvis or talking about Buddy Holly or whoever it might be, "The Crickets will be here, putting their hind legs together and making a funny noise with Buddy Holly in just a moment, right here on KTSA, on KLIF, on WNOE," and just fill in the call letters, wherever I was doing Top 40.

I worked for all the McLendon stations except KELP in El Paso. But you know what Gordon and Don Keyes, who was the vice president of programming for the McLendon chain, and who hired me, would do. They would send you around if you were a little different as a disc jockey, and I was different—I would do strange things like the Complete Failure Club. If anyone had ever failed, they could send for the little card which officially made them a failure. I would spend a couple of months at KTSA San Antonio, KILT Houston, KLIF Dallas, WNOE New Orleans.

Then I went to a Balaban station, WIL in St. Louis. I wanted to get into a bigger city. I wanted to move up in market size, and St. Louis is a huge city with a great eastern sort of feeling to it. At WIL, there were three peo-

Happy Th—Oops!

WKRP in Cincinnati, a situation comedy that had a four-season run on CBS beginning in 1978, once depicted a station promotion, a Thanksgiving turkey giveaway, in which WKRP staffers let the birds out of their office windows, to disastrous results. Gary Owens knows something about the actual bird dropping.

"Well, it really happened—in Louisville, I believe," he said. "It was a real contest, and the guy didn't know that turkeys couldn't fly, dropped them out of the air and killed the poor things. It was a giveaway and they had bands on the feet, and if you found the call letters of the station you'd win a prize if you brought that turkey in. It may have been WAKY, but it was a Top 40 station, and it actually had happened either in the late fifties or early sixties."

ple to play the records, so I would cue the musician, the musician would cue the engineer, and then the engineer would cue another guy who would play the record. It was a union city, and they had staff musicians from the older days who were still there, so it would be like, "And now, Laurie London and 'He's Got the Whole World in His Hands.'" You would cue three or four people along the way.

You were married to Arleta. How was it for her, with your moving from market to market?

She was very, very good in coming along with it. She never complained, never once complained, because the moves were paid for, of course, but we were uprooted all the time. You'd meet someone that you'd like, a couple next door or whatever it might be, and eight months later we're in another city. It was a difficult time. There were a lot of lateral arabesques as they say in the wonderful Peter Principle, sideway moves that maybe were unnecessary. She never complained about it. Weighing 90 pounds, she has a good right hook. I would make a sound like a duck.

And Chuck Blore brought me out from St. Louis to KEWB in Oakland-San Francisco.

At KEWB, you did very well. But you were moved from mornings to other shifts before you left in the spring of '61.

I had made my feelings known to Bob Purcell and Chuck Blore that I was not happy. I loved San Francisco and I loved Oakland, but basically the reason I came to the West Coast was to be in Hollywood. When I accepted the job from WIL I wanted to come to Hollywood and to KFWB. At that point, Chuck said, "Well, we don't have any openings at KFWB, but we're starting our new station in Oakland." And it was great. We became number one, and in fact I was the first disc jockey to beat Don Sherwood [of market leader KSFO] in San Francisco by one point.

It was interesting because Don used to phone me on the air and usually he would talk with what was at the time a prototypical feeling for a rock and roll disc jockey. "What's Number Four this week?" I'd give him some dumb answer, of course, and he'd put me on the air and actually helped me build my rating as much as anything. And Herb Caen was very nice to me. At least once or twice a week he would put in one bad joke I would do on the air, and referred to me as the "'cubist' Gary Owens."

I told management, unless I can go down to Hollywood I probably will accept a job with another station down there. I love it here, but in my heart, I want to do cartoons—and there were no cartoons in San Francisco at the time—I want to do movies, I want to do all the things I've actually done. So at this point, they were buying WMGM in New York and that's where the transition started. So they put me on shifts that were less spotlighted. Remember him, Les Spotlighted?

More than anything, it was, "Let's keep Gary out of our hair until he can go down to Los Angeles."

So they were probably trying to avoid a dramatic exit.

I think that was it. It was a transitional exit. It wasn't that long, it was '59 to '61. I was impatient. Youth and impatience go together a lot.

I never really went berserk that I can recall. I would be angry a lot and it would take the form of humor many times. I always had some running joke about management, whatever it would be. It would be a Stan Freberg sort of satire where the boss was an unnamed sort of individual who was sort of like Gordon Jump of WKRP who wasn't quite sure of what he was doing.

Chuck Blore was a very good friend. He just knows the business so very well and he knows what people like.

Chuck never bothered us when we were on the air. Jim Hawthorne, who's one of my best friends, was program director at KFWB when I was there, and we had a red line—a hotline—and I hated it because it was like Pavlovian dog time. You hear the bell and you salivate. It always bothered me because it set off my pacing. You'd worry because you'd see the red light, and it was only if something was wrong that they would phone on that. Sometimes it would be "Okay, remember you've got to be at the boat show this afternoon," but usually that would wait until the show was over, so I didn't want any negatives bringing me down while the show was on the air. So Jim phoned me a couple of times, and one morning and I got angry, and I ripped the phone off the wall and I put it in front of his door with some note, saying, "Don't do this when I'm on the air, please," or something to that effect.

You've got a classic announcer's voice. I imagine a lot of people can't believe you really speak that way.

The *Laugh-In* thing was kind of a satire of the Westbrook Van Voorhees kind of announcers, although I actually speak that way most of the time. It wasn't that much different from my normal conversation. We're having a normal conversation now and I'm still projecting, because I learned to project. When I began, I loved Paul Harvey very much, because he was totally different. "*Good* day!" So when I became a newscaster, it was kind of a combination of maybe Lowell Thomas, Edward R. Murrow, and Paul Harvey. So I always projected from that time on. I started at sixteen doing part-time radio, so you are influenced by people.

Of course I was influenced by Steve Allen. I loved his ad-libbing. I

Owens went from radio to TV cartoons—and even became a cartoon.

thought he was wonderful, and I also loved Robert Benchley's and Frank Sullivan's work as writers. I never analyzed it. It just happened. My conversation as a kid was always that way, whatever it would be. We would listen to Spike Jones records.

The metamorphoses for me was I wanted to do things on the outside, I wanted to do cartoons, I wanted to do movies, I wanted to do television. It wasn't happening very much unless you were doing an extenuation of what you were doing in rock and roll. Either you did a blemish commercial or a dance hop for KPOP, which was all fun, but I wanted to go into the Xerox and the automobiles and all those sort of things.

I imagine being connected with Top 40 or rock and roll for years would stereotype a DJ.

Pat O'Day

Sure, it would. And Dick Clark was very successful and still is with it. My total feeling, the overview for me, was I wanted to be sort of a kaleidoscope so where if I wanted to do some animated cartoons I could do that or do a TV show, or a series, or host a show. They weren't choosing many people from rock and roll at that time, other than making it a direct lineage between rock and roll and what you did on the outside. So in other words, if you wanted to play a psychiatrist in a television show in the early sixties, it was pretty hard for you to get cast that way, because they'd be thinking of Elvis and you together or you and Roy Orbison, or whoever it might be.

I liked a lot of the rock and roll. I found joy in almost every record. I never was a member of a caste system saying, "This is good, and I'm above all of this." Rock and roll—it was such a good time. I went into it at the best time in the world to go into rock and roll.

PAT O'DAY: LOCAL BOY MAKES GOOD

Disc jockeys are an itinerant lot; while many in the industry wax rhapsodic about the importance of radio connecting with the local community, they skip town the moment a bigger market beckons. Then, there's Pat O'Day.

Look over the roll call of stations for a DJ like, say, Lee "Baby" Simms or Joey Reynolds, and you can count between twenty-five and thirty stations in about as many years.

Look at O'Day's resume: He begins in 1957 with tiny stations in Astoria, Oregon; then makes as short stop at KLOG in Kelso, Washington in 1959 before moving on to KJR in Seattle.

And there he stayed, for some fourteen years, by which time he had established himself not only as a disc jockey and the program director of the most powerful radio station in the Pacific Northwest, but was ready to own and operate his own station in Honolulu.

O'Day had the simplest of formulas for success. As a programmer, he decreed that the foremost purpose of radio was to entertain, and that, no matter the format, a station should strive, as it had since the first dramas and comedies, to help listeners create a "theater of the mind." On the air himself, handling afternoon drives, he exuded the good cheer of a friendly neighbor, blending down-home humor with an obvious knowledge of the territory, of local names and events. And he built smooth bridges between song, patter, and commercials.

"Soul and Inspiration" by the Righteous Brothers is fading, and O'Day comes on. The voice is strong, measured, medium-tempo:

"Number One in Seattle, this is KJR, and is that great? 'Soul and Inspiration,' the Righteous Brothers, 75 degrees from All-American, All-Request Radio. My soul and inspiration is Jerry Kaye, who, on a warm day like today, he's in the news room, he's taken all of his clothes off. He's sitting on the teletype, and the machine is printing the farm news on his behind. Let's see if I can read it. It says: There's a difference between fryers, and that's why Washington Fryers are easily the freshest of all chickens."

And there it was: his preaching put into practice. In thirty seconds, he'd done an outro that identified the record, plugged his station, gave the most basic weather, tied into a mention of a fellow DJ, as well as got off a joke that triggered a silly visual image and that led seamlessly into a piece of live commercial copy.

O'Day was an unabashed fan and emulator of pioneers like Chuck Blore. "Chuck," he says, "felt pretty much the same about broadcast as I did. I carefully hired my jocks. They had to be real communicators and entertainers. We had a goal, and that is that every thirty minutes, we want to make people laugh, or cry, or do *something*."

Among O'Day's hires was Mike Phillips, who calls KJR one of the great experiences of his life. "What made KJR a great station," he says, "was Pat O'Day and his dedication to hiring and developing jocks that were very creative. To inspire creativity, I remember one week when O'Day told all of us to get on the air for an entire week, and when we opened the mike, we had to say something we had never said on the air before. Naturally, that resulted in a lot of dumb things being said, but it also gave us the freedom to expand our creativity."

Phillips well remembers the Blore connection. "Because O'Day was such a giant fan of Chuck Blore and of Gary Owens, in particular, all of us ended

"Woo Woo:" They named a sandwich after him.

up emulating Gary Owens to a fairly great degree. We liked his sense of humor, we liked his voice and his inflection, and we got our hands on as many Owens air checks as possible, so KJR pretty much sounded like a mini Gary Owens station."

Other KJR alumni include Larry Lujack, who moved on to a long run in Chicago radio [at WLS and WCFL] and Lan Roberts, who'd worked for McLendon and Storz at KLIF-Dallas and WTIX-New Orleans, respectively, before settling into Seattle as a morning personality on both KJR and crosstown rival KOL from 1961 through 1974.

By then, O'Day had been general manager for several years, and was soon to get into station ownership. Also by then, all of radio had felt the impact of Bill Drake. O'Day saw Drake as the flip side of Blore, and he'd have none of it—not the short a capella jingles, not the stripped-down deejay patter, and certainly not the tightened music playlist.

"I felt that our real security was in the broader playlist," he says, "because of the greater variety and the greater demographics I could get. As long as my disc jockeys offered a level of entertainment that people couldn't find anywhere else, then I had the perfect balance.

"A new station would come in with their tight playlist, and to this audience in this town, that enormous redundancy was bad news, not good news. They would come in and advertise their 'more music.' They'd go six months commercial-free, and sit down and say, 'What in the hell is wrong?' because they hadn't been able to get close to us."

KJR got strong competition over the years from KOL (in fact, O'Day lured Lan Roberts away from KOL), but remained strong until the late seventies, when a Top 40 FM station, KYYX, came onto the scene.

The station was owned by one Patrick O'Day.

"WOO WOO" GINSBURG: "I STARTED AS A JOKE"

He was not, especially by his own admission, the world's greatest DJ. But he had that definable something, that everyteen quality about him, that propelled him to the top of the Boston radio scene.

His name is Arnie Ginsburg, and that's about how he sounded. Joe Smith, the record executive who made his name as a Boston DJ, and who, in fact, was replaced at WMEX by Ginsburg, is trying to pay him a compliment. Asked to name outstanding DJs through the ages of Top 40, he comes up with Alan Freed, the Real Don Steele, Joe Niagara of Philadelphia, Buddy Deane of Baltimore, Bill Randle of Cleveland, Howard Miller of Chicago, the R&B jocks Georgie Woods and Symphony Sid...and one more:

"Arnie Ginsburg was very unusual...if you ever heard Arnie, this was one of the worst voices and styles, and he copied the tooting the horns and the ringing the bells, and he did it very well, for a lot of years."

Ginsburg accepts the compliment buried in there somewhere, but, he notes, he already had his show name—*Night Train*—set; it was based, he says, on an R&B song of the same name, and he was already making the noise—primarily to distract from what he knew was a weak, young-sounding voice, one that even occasionally cracked, like a preadolescent's. Whether it was the sound of a choo-choo train or the horns and kazoos he played to punctuate his words, he adopted the nickname "Woo Woo." And, oh—by the way—he'd already been established on crosstown WBOS for four years before he was called over to WMEX.

WBOS was one of those stations at the upper end of the dial, tough to pull in and, for most Boston teenagers, tougher to have a reason to try and locate.

"BOS was a combination of foreign languages and music," says Ginsburg. "In fact, I started right after the Arabic hour. I started on the air as a joke." Already in his mid-twenties, he was more interested in the technical and business sides of radio than in performing. Thus, he brought with him a devil-may-care attitude.

"I threw out the whole format that other stations had," he says. "We eliminated news. All the other stations had news on the hour or five minutes of the hour. We just went straight-ahead music, non-stop. I played pop, rock and roll, and I added the horns, the bells, and whistles."

The 3-D's "Arnie Ginsburg Theme," over which Arnie has played his various noisemakers, concludes, and he begins:

"...And a frantic, friendly Friday night in Boston town; old aching adenoids, Arnie Ginsburg, "Woo Woo" *(train whistle sounds twice)* for you-you on the "Night Train" show, all set with all the tops *(cork popping sound effect)* in pops; brand-new Wimmex Tunedex Top 20 coming your way. Number seven sound this week, the Marcels and 'Blue Moon'!"

Unimpressive though his voice might have been, Ginsburg hosted wildly successful record hops and had a sandwich named after him—the

Ginsburger—at a sponsoring restaurant, the Adventure Car Hop. And he stayed on top of the radio ratings for more than a decade.

As pop journalist Pete Johnson noted in the liner notes for the album *Cruisin' 1961*, featuring a Ginsburg recreation of his *Night Train* show: "He transformed adolescent insecurities into a triumph. His voice…combined with the constant clatter of kazoo, cowbell, buzzer, Bermuda bell, car horn, *oogah* and train whistle, epitomized the noisy awkwardness of teenagery, but Arnie managed to bring it all off with a humorous grace."

Chapter

You Turn Me On, I'm a Radio

BEAT THE CLOCK

Yes, the star of any radio show is…No, not the music. No, not the disc jockey. The music delivers the audience, and the DJ delivers the music. The real star is the *station*. And everything is geared toward getting the listener to remember the call letters—especially if and when a rating service comes calling. That explains the jingles, the contests and other promotions, the strategically placed mentions of the station—before a *song,* never before a commercial.

And that explains the "hot clock." The clock, notes Earl McDaniel, the KFWB DJ and KEWB programmer, did not come to the fore until personality-based Top 40 gave way to the tighter Drake format. "You knew you had a certain number of records to play, and you said your name or the call letters a certain amount of times, but after that, you were on your own."

However, as the following sidebar illustration, based on the recollection of Bill Angel, KFWB's longtime director of music, shows, Chuck Blore did have a breakdown for news, sports, and other elements at KFWB. Also, program director Ron Jacobs, whose station was KHJ, the epitome of the Drake format, shows in another illustration, a version of the "hot clock".

Typically, this meticulously detailed breakdown of each hour guided the DJ through every element of every sixty minutes. Although the clock was different for various dayparts, there are several constants: Commercials and other elements of a break—known as a stopset—were carefully constructed and placed. A basic rule of early Top 40—no longer obeyed—required some programming element between commercials. It didn't matter if it was a jingle, a quick one-liner, a time check, or a billboard of an upcoming feature, as long as commercials didn't segue into each other. Finally, the clock enforced the station's music rotation policy. Depending on their popularity, songs might be placed as often as once an hour (in the early years of Top 40) to once every six hours. The allotments for "extras," "hitbounds," oldies, and recurrents (recent hits) were also controlled by the hot clock.

The disc jockeys were expected to follow the clock to a tick—or wedge them into whatever time was left. They still are. Only today, the "clock" is in the form of a computer readout, down to scripted liners.

Hot, Hot, Hot

Hot clocks are the grandfather clocks of radio. Nowadays, to guide them through their hours, announcers refer to computer screens or printouts. There, he or she finds every song or musical option, every commercial, and every element of each stopset—the break between music clusters, including jingles and recorded liners.

But, back in the day, the hot clock, usually hand-drawn by the program director and tacked onto a wall or placed in a binder, did the trick. Here are two examples. The first is from the memory bank of Bill Angel, who handled music at KFWB when Chuck Blore turned it into "Color Radio" in 1958; the second is from the files of Ron Jacobs, pioneer programmer of "Boss Radio" on KHJ in the mid-sixties.

The KFWB hour was simplicity itself. Blore's strategy, much like Gordon McLendon's, was to counter-program against network affiliates and other stations' news, which aired at the beginning of the hour, by concluding his newscasts a minute before. While others were in news, KFWB would have music.

The KHJ clock was far more complicated and precise. Set up for a year-end countdown of the "Big 93" hits of 1967, it helps explain why the Drake system overwhelmed the likes of such Top 40 veterans as Dave Diamond and Bobby Dale. Jacobs offers a guided tour:

At 3. "M.O.T." was a contest, "March of Time."

At 11. "CAP" was how we referred to tape cartridges. P was a promo. This note also indicates more than one subject, rotating, and the standard end cue of L-23, "Happy New Year—from 93 KHJ."

At 18 or 20. Apparently there were intros into various months of the year, to tie

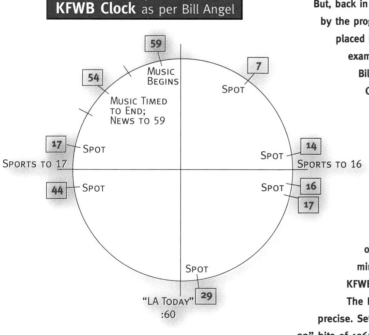

KFWB Clock as per Bill Angel

59 — MUSIC BEGINS
54 — MUSIC TIMED TO END; NEWS TO 59
7 — SPOT
17 — SPOT — SPORTS TO 17
14 — SPOT — SPORTS TO 16
44 — SPOT
16 — SPOT
17
29 — SPOT
"LA TODAY" :60

in with the month the song was a hit.

At 23. Facts about the month featured in the previous record.

At 30 would be produced ID, sandwiched between two records.

At 37. The "Big 93 Book" was a listing we published of the Top 93 songs of the year.

From 37 to News Ending, we see one of the keys to KHJ's success: a long "more music" sweep, followed by finishing our news before the competition started theirs. The news ended with a production lead-in to the next song. "...64 degrees in Hollywood. This is J. Paul Huddleston." FX (Sound effect): *Boom.* Morgan or Drake's voice: "February...nineteen sixty-seven." Record. *Clean.*

51 or 55. Same as 23.

"Time sig" indicates we went from "KHJ Big 93 Time" to "KHJ Happy New Year Time."

"Tymp X-5:" "X" series cartridges were production. ("L" were logos. The famous Johnny Mann "93 KHJ" was—what else—L-1.) This note refers to a contingency if the song opened cold (no instrumental intro), then the X-5 (with tympani) would replace an L series component. That's all well-programmed radio really is—particularly Top 40—a sequence of events, totally linear, which, by themselves, would have little or no impact.

"Horn" is a Happy New Year horn, apparently to be played whenever the jock wanted (within our basic rules). once an hour.

A KHJ Format Clock

Starts: Sat 12/30 @ 6PM

Stops: Mon 1/1 @ 6PM (May be sooner or later, per R.J. fone call)

10-18 (10-17 @ 6PM Sat, 9AM Sun Only)

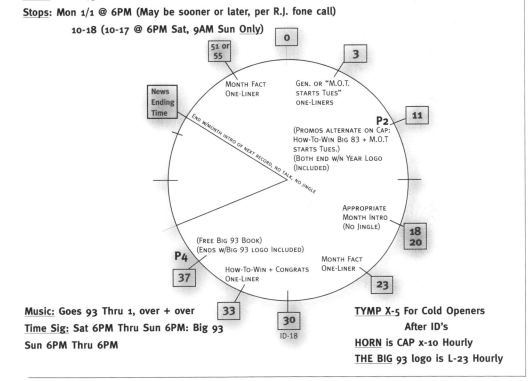

51 or 55

0

3

GEN. OR "M.O.T. STARTS TUES" ONE-LINERS

MONTH FACT ONE-LINER

News Ending Time

END W/MONTH INTRO OF NEXT RECORD, NO TALK, NO JINGLE

P2
11
(PROMOS ALTERNATE ON CAP: HOW-TO-WIN BIG 83 + M.O.T STARTS TUES.)
(BOTH END W/N YEAR LOGO (INCLUDED))

APPROPRIATE MONTH INTRO (NO JINGLE)

18
20

MONTH FACT ONE-LINER

23

(FREE BIG 93 BOOK) (ENDS W/BIG 93 LOGO INCLUDED)

P4
37

HOW-TO-WIN + CONGRATS ONE-LINER

33

30
ID-18

Music: Goes 93 Thru 1, over + over
Time Sig: Sat 6PM Thru Sun 6PM: Big 93
Sun 6PM Thru 6PM

<u>TYMP X-5</u> For Cold Openers
After ID's
<u>HORN</u> is CAP x-10 Hourly
<u>THE BIG</u> 93 logo is L-23 Hourly

JINGLES: 'THE HITS BETWEEN THE HITS'

Several stations are high on Pam's (PAMS') new A-Go-Go jingle package. KJR-Seattle had 50,000 KJR Go-Go buttons made up, and they're the hottest item in town (Well…almost).

—*Gavin Report, May 21, 1965*

Some people whistle; some hum. I sing. Can't help it. A tune pops into my consciousness, and suddenly I'm doing a snatch of the Beach Boys' "Sloop John B.," or "I Remember You" by Frank Ifield, or the theme from *WKRP in Cincinnati*, or—here's where it gets *really* strange—some radio jingle I've heard somewhere. Not just teenaged favorites from KEWB ("Color Radio, Channel 91") or, later, KFRC ("The Big Six-Ten…Golden!"), but jingles I've caught once or twice: "KLEA…Country Sunshine!" or "77…WABC!"

What is *that*?

It's exactly what the radio industry wants to be happening.

Jingles, more than any single song or, in some cases, more than any single DJ or show, are the most important element in a radio station's strategy for being remembered when listeners are asked—say, by a ratings company—what stations they've listened to recently.

Jingles were a part of radio long before Top 40. In fact, soon after businesses began sponsoring programs—*The Eveready Hour*, a variety show on WEAF in New York, dates back to 1923—they learned that sung commercials are more memorable than those that are simply read. The first known singing jingle, according to the album *The Years to Remember: Those Great Moments in Radio*, was heard around 1926, when Ernie Hare and Billy Jones, known as "The Happiness Boys," sang pitches for various products, including Interwoven Socks and Best Foods.

By the late thirties, advertisers were producing slick singing jingles in the style of big band vocal ensembles. Radio listeners knew them as well as they knew the hit songs of the day:

Pepsi Cola hits the spot,
Twelve full ounces, that's a lot!

By the forties, radio had figured out that singing jingles could be applied to stations as well as to products. In New York, WNEW asked pop artists to do short numbers incorporating its call letters. The musicians, of course, were happy to cooperate. Also in New York, at WJZ, a pair of musicians, Ginger Johnson and Eric Siday, produced theme songs—akin to jingles—that incorporated the call letters, but didn't focus on them.

But the radio jingle as it sounded in the Top 40 era can be traced to Gordon McLendon. He'd acquired KLIF in Dallas in 1947 and, looking to put some local, live music shows on the air, he hired Bill Meeks as music director. Soon after Meeks put together a vocal group, he found the need to have them record what would become known as jingles.

Bill Meeks turned a house band into an ensemble of jingles singers.

"We needed time to switch musicians and set up for the next program," Meeks told Don Worsham of the Media Preservation Foundation, who is working on a book on the history of radio jingles. "The limited space at KLIF did not permit two programs to be prepared for air at once." The jingles, then, were a stalling device.

The first one was heard in November 1947. It didn't take long for McLendon to see the short songs touting KLIF as more than something to play while singers and technicians set up a show. In the ratings, he knew that the network stations had the upper hand, since most listeners recalled the names of programs more readily than station call letters. Unable to afford newspaper and billboard advertising, McLendon decided to use his own airwaves to promote his station.

In 1951, Bill Meeks set up his own shop to produce jingles for both commercials and radio stations. He called his company PAMS, which stood for Production Advertising Marketing Service.

While PAMS got rolling, McLendon didn't stand still. He hired another music wizard, Tom Merriman, as KLIF's music director. Under Merriman, the station jingles became more elaborate, and as stations around the country heard about them, they asked for customized sets for themselves. Suddenly, McLendon was in the jingles business.

And, soon, so were others. Merriman left KLIF in 1955 to form a partnership in CRC (Commercial Recording Corporation), which would produce some of the first jingles designed specifically for Top 40 radio.

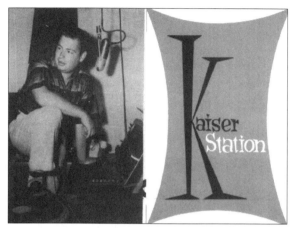

Ron Jacobs: At KPOI, he traded pesticide commercials for jingle packages.

With PAMS leading the way, jingles became a perfect partner in the evolution of the format. At its best, Top 40 was a non-stop whirlwind: the most popular records of the day, upbeat, often funny disc jockeys; commercials; contests; news; weather; sports; time checks; requests and dedications. Jingles bridged the elements, and they repeated the station call letters and frequency…well, frequently.

Depending on where a radio fan grew up, the all-time classic jingles were used by WABC in New York…or by its rival, WMCA, whose IDs were based on "I'll Take Manhattan"…or by KFWB, "Color Radio, Channel 98" in Los Angeles…or were the WLS jingles by the Anita Kerr Singers, circa 1960, when the Chicago giant went Top 40.

Chances are, they were not the ones heard on KPOI in Hawaii. There, Ron Jacobs, the twenty-year-old program director, knew all about the big-name jingles producers. A native Hawaiian, Jacobs had heard stations operated by Storz, McLendon, and Blore on trips to Michigan and Los Angeles. But, as with many smaller stations, he couldn't afford to pay for them, and had to resort to bartering.

"We used this odd fellow named Gaston Johnson, who sold a product, Johnson's No-Roach," Jacobs relates. "He would come through town every year and give us the commercials, and then he'd go off to somewhere in Europe where there were no big musicians' fees, and produce these commercials. And we'd get our KPOI jingles from Gaston, and we'd play a year's worth of No-Roach commercials."

Meanwhile, at KFWB in Los Angeles, one of three stations owned by the educational publishing company Crowell-Collier, Chuck Blore could have pretty much whatever jingles he could conjure. In 1958, Blore had just seen *West Side Story*, and the music, composed by Leonard Bernstein, stayed with him. When he began working with the production team of Bob Sande and Larry Green on a package of jingles, he mentioned the Broadway play. And he had what he believes to be an original idea. "Until that time," said Blore, "there had never been a station musical logo"—that is, the call letters matched to one, consistent set of musical notes (think "N-B-C"). "There had been jingles before, but wherever the music line took the call letters is how they came out. And I had in my mind the advertising success of Lucky

Strike—'L.S.M.F.T.,' and that sort of thing—always repeating the same thing and the same melody. So when we did our first jingle package, I said, 'Every time we do the call letters, it has to have the same melody.'"

The idea spread quickly. But, according to jingles historian Don Worsham, Ginger Johnson and Eric Siday had come up with that concept for WWSW in Pittsburgh, and did the same for WHDH in Boston and WFBR in Baltimore. However, Worsham added, Blore's package at KFWB "is the preeminent example of using a musical logo in association with a call letter."

Bill Meeks

The package did connote *West Side Story*. The voices—the Johnny Mann Singers—sounded young; the arrangements were bright and jazzy, by turns swinging and lush. Whether touting the "Seven Swingin' Gentlemen," the news, sports, weather, time of day ("Have a good good good good morning, get up as bright as the sun"), or good ratings ("Hooper rated; super rated!"), a KFWB jingle stood out from the pop, rock, country, and R&B music Channel 98 was playing, but worked in concert with all the other jingles to emblazon the station image into the listener's mind. They ranged from ten-second instrumental stingers to productions that stretched out to a minute and a half, serving as entertainment on their own—as "hits between the hits," as Worsham puts it.

As with so much of Blore's work, the KFWB jingles were soon echoed around the country. Pat O'Day, whose KJR modeled itself on Blore and his star disc jockeys, went to PAMS and had them do new jingles modeled on Blore's. "But how can you beat what's great, right? Why reinvent the wheel?" he says.

Chuck Blore cycled his sound around to his own stations, and that's how I came to know, and sing along to, the KEWB package. The jingles were just too darned clever. For drive time, for example, the gang did a mid-tempo mini-tune, in the style of the Modernaires, say, with a Sinatra, "Witchcraft" swing to it:

Keep listening and driving wherever you happen to be
Just driving and listening to KEWB
All this music you've been hearing
Should have kept your mind from veering
Keep your hand up on the steering…wheel
We'll see that you're knowing where traffic is slowing
Even driving is fun with Channel 91!

And, as if the rhymes and the "wheel" to "we'll" transition weren't enough, the last line was sung to the musical logo for "KEWB, Channel 91." Perfecto.

"That melody," Blore notes with pride, "is still used at KFWB, which is an all-news station. But it's the same melody, although it's forty years later."

Meantime, up in Washington state, Pat O'Day is talking about the jingle that went, "KJR Seattle, Channel 95": "You talk to anybody in Seattle, they can still sing the logo after forty years of brainwashing."

THANKS FOR THE JOB: WHAT'S MY NAME?

Beau Weaver (not his real name) is back at KFRC in San Francisco for the station's twentieth anniversary as a Top 40 station:

"You know, there are a lot of disc jockeys who don't use their real name," he says. "And I am prepared, at this moment, to reveal some of the real names of the disc jockeys who were legends on KFRC:

Norman Davis as Lucky Logan, with a fan.

"Charlie Van Dyke? That isn't his real name. *(Drum roll.)* His name is Chuck Steinle.

"Hal Martin: his real name is Michael Spears.

"Eric Chase: his real name: Paul Stelgis.

"Kevin McCarthy's real name: Danny Corey…

"And then, of course, the one everybody knows. I mean, 'Bobby Ocean,' right? Give me a break. *Bobby Ocean*. Nobody's name is Bobby Ocean, is it? I'm going to reveal Bobby Ocean's real name, ladies and gentlemen…*(Drum roll)* Bobby Ocean's real name is…*Johnny* Ocean!"

Some disc jockeys actually did use their own names. I'd wager that Joe Yocam, Dick Biondi, Ted Quillan, Robin Seymour, John Landecker, Tom Maule, Jerry Blavat, and Herb Oscar Anderson were not dreamt up in various program directors' offices. And some names that seemed to have been inventions were real: Dick Clark, Buzz Bennett, Bill Ballance, Johnny Holliday. (Actually, it's Johnny Holliday Bobbitt, and I will refrain from the obvious punch line.)

But then, there were Johnny Dark, Johnny Rabbitt, Jimmie Rabbitt, Pete Bunny, Peter Tripp, Bobby Tripp (who was also Bobby Mitchell, but really was Michael Guerra), Lucky Logan, Jack Hammar, Dick Sainte, Don Sainte-John, Mark St. John, Gina St. John, Scott St. James, Johnny St. Thomas, and all those guys whose names featured two first names: Bobby Dale, Art Nelson, Jim Wayne, Frank Terry, Howard Clark, Gary Stevens, and Jay Stevens.

Not to mention those who didn't bother to get different first and last names, like Dan Daniels, Harry Harrison, and William F. Williams.

It is no surprise that most of the above are fake names, designed to sound slick, friendly, All-American, and, above all, memorable. What's strange is that, early in the history of Top 40, many DJs, entering a profession that would put their names in high profile, were given no choice in the matter of those names. They were issued, not unlike fatigues to an Army recruit or a number to a new prisoner, and accepted without debate, or even discussion.

Norman Davis (that's his real name) was Norm Davis at his first jobs, in Boise and Pocatello, Idaho, and in Spokane, Washington. But when he moved to San Francisco in the mid-fifties and got a job at KSAY, a middle-of-the-road music station, he learned that his name would depend on the time of day that he worked. "It was a

"The Geator with the Heater."

Turning On the Geator

Jerry Blavat was a kid in South Philadelphia when he got into showbiz. At twelve, he was dancing on the original, pre-"American" version of *Bandstand,* hosted by Bob Horn. He was head of the show's Committee, which screened new records for the show. Blavat's ears had been tuned toward R&B music from visits to the Sun Ray drugstore's record department, where he could listen to the latest sounds for hours. By age fifteen, he was road manager for Danny and the Juniors. At nineteen, he had a talk show on WCAM in Camden, New Jersey. One night, because of a snowstorm, he was forced to play records. He resorted to his own collection, playing R&B sounds then unheard on the radio. He was an immediate sensation, and he needed a nickname.

"I just can't be Jerry Blavat, everyone knows Jerry Blavat," he remembers thinking. "In town, there's Jocko, 'the Ace From Outer Space.' Lorenzo was 'Hound Dog.' There's 'Fat Daddy' in Baltimore. I gotta come up with a handle."

Somehow, he was inspired by the phones ringing in the studio—they reminded him of alligators, which he'd heard referred to as "geators." "The Geator," he felt however, wasn't quite enough. He needed a rhyme, and he thought, "When you're a kid on the corner, and you're hanging with the guys and it's 10 degrees out, you're shivering. I remember when a guy comes by in a car we all jump in the guy's car and go cruising, and we say, 'Turn the heater up, we're freezing.' I was so crazy. I was the 'Geator with the Hot Heater.'" He would slide the "hot" over to another nickname—"The Boss with the Hot Sauce"—and the Geator took hold of Philly.

Blavat is still on radio in Philadelphia, on WSSJ—the former WCAM, in fact—an oldies station that has adopted the nickname "Geator Gold Radio."

A happy-go-Lucky Logan takes a ride in San Francisco.

daytimer meaning it signed off at sundown, and there were three shows: morning, midday, and afternoon," Davis says. "The morning would be, say, the Ted Greene Show, and mid-day would be the Bob White Show, and they rotated so that every two weeks you did a different show, but it was always the Ted Greene and Bob White shows, regardless of who was doing it."

Davis next moved to the city's first Top 40 station, KOBY, where he received the stock name for the all-night DJ, Al Knight. Less than a year later, in 1959, he shifted to KYA, and, suddenly, he was Lucky Logan—no matter that it'd be his fourth name in the same city, in a short time span. It was the decision, Davis said, of the station's owner, Bartell Broadcasting. "They had a couple of guys working for them who became so popular that they moved on to other stations under their own name, and the station didn't like that much, so they gave everybody a name, and usually, the jocks at all their stations had the same names, so there was somebody in Milwaukee doing Lucky Logan, so they said, 'That's going to be you.'"

As Lucky Logan, Davis established a popular requests and dedications show in the evenings. Less than a year later, a new program director, Les Stein, joined the station. Besides bringing in several new disc jockeys and cutting down on-air clutter, he told Davis to drop the phony name. "Just don't use any name for a couple of weeks," he suggested.

Just as stations, in the days before disc jockeys, originated programs of their own and claimed ownership to the shows (and their titles), so also they considered fabricated DJ names to be theirs. In the twenties, a comedy duo, Sam and Henry, left WGN in Chicago for rival WMAQ. WGN wouldn't let them keep their names, and the pair thus became Amos 'n Andy.

George Oxford, the pioneer R&B DJ known as "Jumpin' George," had to leave his name behind when he jumped from KSAN-San Francisco across the bay to Oakland's KDIA in 1959. While a string of announcers became "Jumpin'," Oxford renamed himself "G.O. George." More than

twenty years later, Oxford, then 70, helped emcee a music festival in
Oakland for KSOL, a descendant of KSAN. "KSOL," he reported, "gave me
back my name of Jumpin' George…all rather
beautiful."

In Buffalo in the fifties, WNIA had a stable of
conveniently alliterative names—Mike Melody,
Tommy Thomas, Jerry Jack, Bob Bell—as did
WINE, where Mark Hall could be anybody—
including, for a moment, one Roger Okincella,
who later became Roger Christian, a success as
both a DJ and a songwriter (for the Beach Boys
and others) in Los Angeles. WWOL, another Top
40 contender in Buffalo, gave the name Guy King
to several guys, including a young man who eventually reached greater heights as Tom Clay.

Bobby Ocean remembers working as Johnny
Scott on KYNO in Fresno, California—where

"Your name will be
Bobby Ocean." His
heart sank.

Bill Drake first experimented with his "Boss Radio" format—when he got
the call he'd been hoping for. "The program director wants to see me. And
immediately all the adrenaline shoots through your body. And he said that
the Drake organization was on the phone. So I pick up the phone, and this
guy says, very curtly, 'Johnny Scott?' 'Yes.' He says, 'Bill Drake.' I said, 'I know
who you are, sir.' He says, 'You still want to go to San Diego?' 'Oh, yes, sir.'
'You start Monday.' Whew! My heart went up like that! And he said, 'And
your name will be Bobby Ocean.'" Even as his heart sank, he knew better
than to argue. "They had too many people who would go."

If there's such a thing as mildly racist, a good example would be the DJ
name Rick Shaw. It's been used by a number of announcers, including one,
in San Francisco, whose real name was Hugh Silvis. Silvis, who suffered a
heart attack and died in June, 1998, worked with various McLendon stations
in Texas, at KIMN in Denver, and at WOR in New York before landing in
the Bay Area, on KFRC, in 1975. By then he'd gone through a few names.
At a coffee shop next door to his last station, K101, he recited his air names:
"Charlie Knox, Bob Baker, Mike Morgan," he says. "Sometimes you go to
a station and they had extra jingles, and that's what you get. So I got to
Houston and I'm ready to go on the air, and they say, 'Well, we're in a big
battle. Maybe a trick name would give us an extra edge over the competition,' and so I go on the air, and there's no name. If you're used to shtick,
what do you do if you can't say your name? So, about 3:15, I'm saying, 'And
I'm…glad to be here!' Around 4:00, they got hold of Bill Stewart, who was

McLendon's National PD, and was allegedly imbibing a few in a bar in Cleveland. 'Aw, name the sucker "Rick Shaw"; I named the first Rick Shaw, and it's not copyrighted.' That's how I became Rick Shaw."

Even when a disc jockey leaves a station and could, ostensibly, relieve himself of a laughingstock name, it's sometimes not quite so simple. Take Charlie Tuna. That's the *nom de mike* for Art Ferguson, who tells how he got the name in his interview in Chapter 14. After joining KHJ in Los Angeles in 1967 and establishing himself in the market, he moved to KTNQ around 1980 and thought about reverting to his real name. He decided to take a vote of listeners. Should he take back his own name, or continue as Charlie Tuna? "Ninety percent said, 'You gotta be Charlie Tuna.'"

Oh, yes—Bobby Ocean's real name is...*(Drum roll)* Ernest Raymond Lenhart.

Oh.

Chapter

Busted

Payola is many things to many prosecutors. It was—at least until new laws were passed—legal. It was a form of lobbying, a means of saying thank you for favors done, a way to establish and maintain a friendship. It was direct pay-for-play—cash or other forms of reward in exchange for putting a specific record on the air, or for fraudulently reporting airplay to the trade magazines in hopes of getting the record on the charts. That, the law says, amounts to commercial bribery.

Whatever it was, most agreed, it was nothing new. "Beginning at the turn of the century," wrote the late WABC–New York programmer Rick Sklar, "song pluggers had played the piano in the sheet music store windows, then had manned the front lines for the music business the way salespeople do in other industries. Like most other purveyors of products, they entertain, they cajole, they sell—and some of them bribe."

Juggy Gayles, who actually was a song plugger for a publishing company in the late thirties, concurred. "There was always payola, even in the days of swing," he told *Rolling Stone* magazine in 1994. "It changed from one thing to another. First it was grass, then it was coke. From coke it went to everything else." And, working for a major label in the sixties, "I had to go out and pay off the disc jockeys with cash."

On the other side of the payola coin was Bill Gavin. Paul Drew loved Bill Gavin. As a DJ on WGST in Atlanta, he was the first radio person to subscribe to what became the *Gavin Report*. Exchanging information with Gavin, Drew came to see him as much more than the publisher of a radio tipsheet. Gavin became a friend, a mentor, a father figure. Drew emulated Gavin, publishing his own tipsheet out of Atlanta, the *Southern Music Survey*. He also took to heart Gavin's calls for professionalism, high standards, and integrity. He believes that, over the years, he earned Gavin's own trust and

Paul Drew

respect. In fact, he confides, when Gavin, then seventy-five years old, wanted to sell his publication in 1982, Drew was on top of a short list of people he contacted. They did not reach an agreement, but the two remained close to the end, when Bill Gavin died in early 1985 of lung cancer. In 1993, when the publication he'd founded instituted a Bill Gavin Heritage Award to be presented at its annual seminar, Paul Drew was the first recipient.

Now, toying with a tuna salad at Greenblatt's deli on Sunset Boulevard in Hollywood, Drew allows an observation—apparently held privately for many years—to be expressed.

"The thing I always [noticed] about Bill," he says, "is that he had a certain naivete about him. Here's this business which I'd describe as…I think people in the record business would rather make one dishonest dollar than two honest dollars—but Bill seemed to be oblivious. It was almost as though it didn't go on."

A case in point: In March of 1959, Gavin noted a newspaper article about Nat "King" Cole, one of the many pop performers being bypassed by Top 40 radio in favor of rock and roll. Cole, Gavin reported, said that success depended on "connections" and "influence" more than talent, that "the rackets probably have an influence on breaking hit records, as indicated by recent Congressional hearings," and that "disc jockeys must be taking payola, because…they can't be programming as they do just because they like the records they're playing." Gavin expressed astonishment at Cole's remarks, which he said were the type normally made by "disgruntled failures" rather than by a proven star. A Congressional committee, he reminded, had found "only one record pushed on operators by coercion," and that the single in question never achieved success. Finally, said Gavin, Cole's comments about DJs and payola were "naive." Radio people get their greatest rewards, he said, "from playing what most of the listeners want to hear, thereby getting higher ratings and increased revenue."

Gavin, however, was neither blind nor naive. "In a few stinking instances," he wrote the in spring of 1959, "record companies and publishers are victims of a venal squeeze from top-rated shows. I refer to cases, well known in the industry, where it is necessary to make profit-sharing 'deals' with the producers or jocks in order to get any new record

NO, NOT ME

pop "In a recent issue of *Billboard*, reporter June Bundy erroneously referred to me as a 'record promoter.' Now Ira Cook has picked it up, and is also calling me a 'noted record promoter.' Now—wait a minute. Please—the record industry has enough problems as it is without assigning me to their ranks as a promoter. All I do is try to help stations program more effectively. I thought everybody understood that when I tell you a record is a hit, it's because it's so—not because somebody pays me to try to get it played." —Bill Gavin, June 22, 1960 pop played....Fortunately this practice is not widespread. I am hopeful that before too long, it will consume itself in its own greed and disappear."

In fact, the month before his citation of the Nat Cole comments, Gavin wrote about how radio station management "is moving in with rigid control policies. Why? One reason might be that too many jocks have gone into the publishing, management, and/or record production businesses as sidelines, and are so concerned with plugging their own products on the air that they forget their listening audience."

And, the previous fall, Gavin had signaled that he knew about shady dealings at record stores. "Cheers," he wrote, "for the retailers who refuse to make phony listings in their sales reports to radio stations in exchange for free records and a 100 percent guarantee on returns. Some stations are alertly spotting such practices and throwing out the loaded reports. I am now discounting sales reports on two items being promoted in this manner. Please let me know if you hear of any such maneuvers in your area."

Gavin had apparently heard from Buddy Deane. By the late fifties, Deane, a former DJ whose TV dance show was so popular that it effectively kept *American Bandstand* out of Baltimore—*Bandstand* was an ABC network show, but the *Buddy Deane Show* was on the ABC affiliate—decided to return to radio as well. He wanted to be able to spin records, get direct audience responses, and predict hits. He also put out *Deane's Disc Digest*, an early version of the Top 40 survey, and distributed it through record shops.

Deane learned quickly about record promotion, and he wrote to Gavin to suggest a meeting of radio people "to discuss the hype issue with label distributors and reps."

His *Disc Digest*, he says, "became so prominent, record stores started ordering off of it, and I felt a responsibility. If I said, 'This record is going to be a hit,' boy, I was *sure* it was going to be a hit. And I had a very effective young lady who went to work for me who had worked for a one-stop— like a soda fountain juke box—and she was very familiar with the record business and knew how the hype worked. Usually, they would give them free records to make sure that the record got on the juke box.

"So we found that they were giving boxes of free records to some of the record stores to report certain records. I had a few guys come in and slip $300 in a record jacket, and I said, 'Thanks, and I appreciate you thinking of me, but I can't use this.' So they went around me and went to the record stores, and when we called the record stores, these records that we didn't think were that strong would suddenly show up in the Top Ten. And we would find that, indeed, they had gotten a free couple of boxes of records just to report that tune to me, so I'd play it on television and radio.

"You learned who to trust and who not to."

The payola scandal of 1959 was not a simple matter of politicians versus disc jockeys, or, more specifically, a Congressional subcommittee versus Alan Freed, King of the Moondoggers—or, as various Freed-centered films depicted it, law and order against him and rock and roll. It was payback time for ASCAP.

The American Society of Composers, Authors and Publishers is a music licensing organization that was founded in 1914, back in the day when its members earned most of their royalties through sales of sheet music and phonograph records. ASCAP, along with record companies and musicians' unions, saw radio as a threat. If radio allowed listeners to hear records for free, why would they want to buy them? The more recordings radio played, the less need the medium would have for live orchestras, bands, and other musicians—and the less use there would be for sheet music.

In response to what they felt were exorbitant licensing fees being set by ASCAP, broadcasters, who originally refused to pay royalties for playing ASCAP music, announced a boycott of ASCAP in 1939 and helped created a competitor, Broadcast Music Inc. (BMI).

A laughing Freed is booked, along with (left to right) Mel Leeds, program director of WINS, and Peter Tripp, the WMGM disc jockey, at a New York police station in May, 1960.

While ASCAP was the proverbial overweight gorilla, with Tin Pan Alley tunesmiths as part of its foundation, and maintained stringent membership requirements, BMI opened its doors to all songwriters, and quickly drew musicians on the fringes—country and western, rhythm and blues, and, later, rock and roll. By offering a payment system based totally on the success of a song (ASCAP's system favored the more established composers), BMI also attracted some ASCAP members.

The old guard at ASCAP sneered at BMI's licensed music as "obscene junk." The two rivals were constantly at each other's throats, especially as changing tastes and technology (transistor radios, long-playing albums, 45 r.p.m. singles) combined with rock and roll and Top 40 radio to shift the balance of music power to forces more closely aligned with BMI.

Caught in the middle of this battle, which included various lawsuits, were the disc jockeys who played R&B and rock and roll. According to

Dick Clark, ASCAP equated the eradication of rock and roll with its main goal: the demise of BMI.

In 1958, the nation was abuzz with talk about how such popular television quiz shows as *The $64,000 Question* and *Twenty-One* might be rigged. The talk, and resulting press, led to an investigation in the House of Representatives by the Special Subcommittee on Legislative Oversight. The 1959 hearings, resulting in the collapse of the game shows, were a media sensation. Facing an election year, congressmen and other public servants were all ears when they heard from ASCAP, charging commercial bribery in the broadcasting and music industries. ASCAP clumped BMI into its list of parties that it said conspired "to suppress genuine talent and to foist mediocre music upon the public."

In a way, disc jockeys had been asking for it. For years, it was general knowledge in the music biz that DJs, especially in the years before they were given more rigid playlists, were open to payola—especially since Dick Clark, for one, knew it to be a legal practice. "It was not against the law," he wrote in his memoirs, *Rock, Roll & Remember*. "A record company could give a disc jockey $100,000, a list of records with how often to play each one, and it wasn't illegal."

Said Joe Smith of WMEX in Boston: "You declared it, which I did. I can never, ever remember having somebody give me a record with a fifty-dollar bill and saying, 'Play this record.' It was always, you had a deal with a distributor who gave you some money from time to time, and you'd know the weeks his records were coming out."

But the givers and takers were flagrant about it. Clark quoted a friend, a promotion man for a major record label, telling how he'd take a briefcase loaded with $25,000 out on tour once or twice a year. "In each city we rented a suite of rooms at a hotel and invited all the local disc jockeys over for a party." One by one, they'd be called into another room and handed between $100 and $500, depending on their stature.

"I accepted payola once," "Cousin Brucie" Morrow admits, thinking back to the late fifties. "It was two cherry pies. The promotion man at that time delivered records to us personally in those days. His mother owned a company that was a bakery and he brought me two cherry pies. I liked the record and was going to play it anyhow, so I took the cherry pies."

Beyond those pies, Morrow says, he never took a bite from the record biz. "I was very lucky," he says. "Not that I wouldn't have been tempted. I got in there as a kid and I didn't understand what was going on. I witnessed things in program directors' offices. I used to sit in the office because I was trusted and I really didn't know what was happening. I saw exchanges of money, gifts, booze, cartons. I even knew a program director who had his wedding paid for and a trip to Paris and [was] given a car. I saw big RCA 21-inch color TVs."

Once, Morrow recalls, "I got cornered by some guy who wanted to pay me X amount of dollars, and by this time I knew what was going on, so I looked at him straight in the eye, and I said, 'If you're talking under $250,000 cash, stop.' In other words, everybody has their plateau, and of course that's a ridiculous number because you know they're passing out $100 bills, $500 for a station like our size, and guys were walking away with pretty big gifts."

Russ Regan, a popular promotion man in the sixties in Los Angeles, is now a record executive. "I'm not trying to pretend like I didn't do anything," he says. "You know, you have to be in the mix, to be out there and do the dinners and the parties and the gifts or whatever. But those are all legitimate things to do."

Joey Reynolds has 'fessed up to accepting payola. (See his profile in Chapter Ten.) But, he suggests, "Let's use another word. Let's use 'lobbying.' 'Payola' really doesn't mean anything to anybody. Lobbying does. It means getting your own way by bribing people or seducing them emotionally." To some, it means paying for airplay. "Well," Reynolds responds, "I really don't know that anybody really had an arrangement to pay for play, until the pigs and the greed set in."

Whatever arrangements they had, Congress, nudged along by rock and roll—and radio's—various enemies, would soon be interested.

MIAMI VICE

The lords of the music biz work in mysterious ways. Here in Miami in 1959, all eyes are on rock and roll disc jockeys and how, despite all the talk about sales charts and tabulations of requests, hits are being paid for by promotion men representing the record labels.

Swelled by media attention into the biggest, fattest target this side of the McCarthy and quiz show hearings, what does the biz do? It convenes in Miami Beach on a holiday weekend—Memorial Day—and proceeds to rub the press and public's faces in the dirt of payola.

The occasion was the second annual International Radio Programming Seminar and Pop Music Disk Jockey Convention, hosted by Todd Storz and his chain of stations. Storz didn't create the problem, merely the stage for it. Some 2,500 people—mostly DJs and the people who wanted to influence them—attended. The organizers put together an actual seminar, with a keynote speech from the president of the National Association of

Broadcasters and an array of well-intentioned panel discussions about news reporting, ratings, and commercials.

But was anybody listening? Not according to the local papers. The *Miami Herald's* headline on its story about the weekend read, "Booze, Broads and Bribes." According to *Time* magazine, "everywhere a DJ went, record company promoters kept telling him: 'Without you, we're dead, boy.'"

To show the platter-spinners just how important they were, the promotion people and labels—fifty were represented in Miami Beach—reportedly lavished them with the aforementioned three B's.

Despite a *Life* magazine photograph showing disc jockeys in a hotel lobby tossing dollar bills in the air, the B's did not include bucks—at least, not literally. On arrival, the announcers had been given play money by RCA Victor. The bills, though phony, could be used in a convention-closing auction, where the highest bids would win valuable items and vacation trips. Guests could add to their bankroll by gambling and visiting hospitality suites, where they could listen to music, have a drink, and, perhaps, hook up with the second of the three B's. Or, as *Time* put it: "Squads of local beach girls in bikinis were relieved by company-strength detachments flown in from New York." Some disc jockeys, whether out of generosity or drunkenness, gave their play dough to the "beach girls," who wound up with many of the auction prizes.

Joe Smith, a recent bridegroom, brought his wife with him from Boston. He did not cavort with any beach girls. But, he recalls, "They'd give you like a thousand dollars of play money, and I would gamble, and lose, and they'd still pay me, and they'd give me a prize. My wife said, 'Is *this* the music business?'"

Paul Drew also missed out on the bikini brigade, but he almost had a date with Anita Bryant. Just the year before, she had been second runner-up for Miss America, and she'd just begun recording for Carlton Records. Juggy Gayles, longtime promo man, made the arrangement. "It may have been for Saturday night," Drew recalls. "Then [Gayles] came to me and said, 'Could I switch you to Sunday night, because Bob Green [a disc jockey on WFUN in Miami] wants to date her, and he works on Sunday, so could I switch the two of you?' I said, 'Sure.' And they went out and fell in love, so I didn't take her out. He became her husband." But yes, Drew says, "I can remember there were a lot of women who could have been hookers around the hotel."

The press reports on the convention horrified the public. But insiders had a different perspective. As Rick Sklar wrote in his memoirs, "The convention simply brought together under one roof scenes that were going on regularly in every large American city. The 'normal' business entertainment for a DJ or a greedy program director was only just getting started when the music publisher or record plugger picked up the dinner check. From there it moved to a private suite where call girls, cash, expensive gifts, and drugs were available for the taking. For some, it became a way of life." Or, as Stan Richards, of WILD in Boston, said in 1959, "This seems to be the American way of life, which is a wonderful way of life. It is primarily built on romance. 'I'll do for you. What will you do for me?'"

In the immediate aftermath of Miami Beach, Bill Gavin was restrained. Reporting that at least fifty DJs and music directors actually did some business at the convention—they volunteered to take part in a planning committee for a national DJ association (which he referred to as the Disc Jockey Association, which might meet in Minneapolis)—he said such an organization could work with Storz for the next convention, "but only if we have the decisive voice in planning the agenda and conducting the meetings, and only if record company promotion activities are restricted and controlled." Storz apparently agreed. Saying that he thought record companies had spent some $250,000 to keep the DJs spinning in Miami Beach, Storz admitted that "there was too much swinging." The next gathering, he hoped, would be a "shirt-sleeve working session." But there would not be a third convention—at least not one sponsored by Storz. An ad hoc group of disc jockeys tried to hold an image-saving meeting in Chicago the following fall, but, faced with newspaper reporters at every turn, adjourned early and scattered.

THE HEARINGS: SEE DICK RUN

In late 1959, the payola dragnet began. The pressure came from all sides, and disc jockeys were not the only targets. The Federal Trade Commission went after record companies and distributors, charging that the use of payola amounted to unfair competition. Many labels promised to stop the payments. The New York district attorney's office announced grand jury hearings on misdemeanor commercial bribery charges against disc jockeys, resulting in pressure on their employers, whose operating licenses were suddenly in jeopardy. ABC—television and radio—was among the first to act, asking on-air employees to sign an affidavit denying any involvement in payola. The responses of two of the industry's biggest stars led them down two opposite roads.

Dick Clark, the clean-cut young host of *American Bandstand*, was up to his necktie in arrangements with record companies, publishers, and other music-related businesses, and was clearly a high-profile target. He had an attorney draft a personal affidavit, in which the definition of payola was narrowed to a direct pay-for-play situation, signed it, and agreed to divest himself of his interests in any various music concerns. With Clark's hit television shows intact, ABC expressed its confidence in his integrity.

Alan Freed, who had moved his radio show to WABC in March 1959, refused to sign the ABC affidavit, telling the station manager that he, like Clark, was "in the music business" and had received various gifts. "I can't sign this because I am going to perjure myself," he said. He later said he would sign "when I see Martin Block's signature and Dick Clark's signature." Freed was not aware that Clark had signed a custom-tailored statement. By the time he was ready to consider giving in, he learned that the network would be dismissing him, regardless, and that the loss of that job would only be the beginning of his problems.

The Congressional subcommittee hearings began in early 1960. Before Freed or Clark took the stand, several disc jockeys confessed to taking money and gifts for promoting records. Joe Finan, who, along with Bill Randle and Alan Freed, was one of Cleveland's biggest radio names, said he'd accepted consulting fees from record distributors. Joe Smith, from Boston, said he'd profited by about $9,000 in three years, giving his $18,000 salary (for all three years) a substantial boost. Arnie "Woo Woo" Ginsburg admitted to receiving some $4,400 in "goodwill" money from distributors over two-and-a-half years.

Dick Clark followed Alan Freed to the witness stand.

The hearings took an ironic detour in March, when John Doerfer, chairman of the FCC, was revealed to have taken a vacation in Bimini paid for by the Storer Broadcasting Company, owner of several Top 40 stations. He resigned within a week.

In late April, Freed and Clark appeared before the subcommittee. Although carefully prepared by his attorney, and aware that his testimony might be used against him in criminal cases being pursued by the New York district attorney, Freed gave the congressmen a detailed accounting of his connections with record distributors, his deal with WABC, and named record companies that paid him for "consultation." But he also replied "yes" when asked: "You were receiving this money from the record companies to plug their records on the air. Is that not true?" Freed recanted his statement, and then, under tougher questioning, held his ground. By then, it may have been too little, too late.

A few days and witnesses after Freed, Dick Clark took his seat at the witness stand. He, too, was well prepared. He went on the offensive, telling the congressmen that, with the media having coined the word "Clarkola," he had already been "convicted, condemned and denounced." Clark brought along statistics (for which he paid some $6,000) that he hoped would prove that, while he did have an interest in a good number of artists and their labels, and that their music accounted for 27 percent of the records played on *American Bandstand,* that those records did not reach an inordinate level of popularity.

You Never Forget Your First Jock

When word first leaked out that Joe Eszterhas had written a screenplay about a disc jockey in Cleveland in the fifties, the assumption was that it'd be based on Alan Freed. Surprise.

Soon after *Telling Lies in America,* an evocative little film about...well, about lying, came out, Johnny Holliday, who lives and works in Washington, D.C., got a clipping of the *New York Times'* review from a friend, who jotted a note: "The only thing he didn't do is mention you by name."

Holliday, who specialized in spouting alliterative clichés in a happy, hyped-up, harefooted style, worked at WHK in Cleveland from 1959 to 1964, then moved on to WINS in New York and KYA in San Francisco before fleeing back East to join ABC Sports (where he is today). He is so immersed in jock-dom (of the sporting kind) that he didn't even know who Joe Eszterhas was.

After seeing the clipping, Holliday recalled that a public radio special on the 75th anniversary of WHK had included Eszterhas, "who told about how he raced home every day to listen to me, and what an influence I was on his childhood."

Intrigued, Holliday tracked Eszterhas down. "His manager sends word: 'Well, fax me your name, your phone number, what questions you'd like to ask Mr. Eszterhas. I can't promise he'll get back to you, but we'll do our best.' So I fax him this letter. I say, 'Dear Joe. I am still every teen queen's dream. I'm still serving up the cream of the top pop crop. I'm elbow deep in the ballad bowl. Fender bender, bumper jumpin', chrome-cracking my way home every day in the boulevard of broken tail-lights.'

"Four days later, I'm at ABC, and I've got a call. It's Joe Eszterhas. So I pick up the phone and Joe says, 'I cannot believe I'm talking to you.' We talked for forty minutes."

The *Cleveland Plain Dealer* reporter turned *Rolling Stone* writer turned notorious Hollywood scriptwriter told Holliday, "You came to my school, you had a record hop. I came that close to actually reaching out and touching you."

Eszterhas remembered Holliday's WHK basketball team, the Radio Wonders, which played games to raise money for charities. (Holliday would organize a similar team at KYA.) "I think the night you played, you got a brain concussion," said Joe. "You got hit in the head."

The writer asked an amazed Holliday whether he'd seen *Telling Lies in America.* Like most Americans, Holliday hadn't. Within days, he received a tape.

"So I watched the movie," the disc jockey reported, "and I was dying, laughing with my wife. I said, 'Man, this is exactly like it was.'"

The congressmen, by and large, accepted Clark's show and tell, and his testimony that he'd done nothing "illegal or immoral"; that he'd gotten into the music business only to take advantage of tax laws. Although, as Clark notes in the interview that follows, he did not emerge unscathed, he was dismissed with his dignity—and his television shows—intact.

Soon after the hearings, the subcommittee suggested that payola be declared officially illegal, by way of amendments to the Federal Communications Act. None of the disc jockeys who testified were arrested, but the investigation frightened enough stations and disc jockeys that a westward rush ensued. Many of them would deny that it had anything to do with payola, but, whatever the reason, cities within reach of Washington, D.C., began to lose radio announcers, among them Peter Tripp, Joe Niagara, Tom Donahue, Bobby Mitchell, Robin Seymour, Joe Smith, Stan Richards, and Tom Clay. "A lot of people left in the middle of the night," says Dick Clark. "It was a good idea to get away from the pressure. They didn't have enough money for the investigative committee to go west of the Mississippi, so everybody ran."

Freed himself moved from New York to Los Angeles, where his friend, former WINS program director Mel Leeds, had landed a job as program director of KDAY, which positioned itself as an R&B station. The gig paid only $25,000—good money for 1960, but nothing compared to the kind of money Freed had been making in New York. But Freed was down, out, and under legal assault.

In fact, just days after starting on KDAY, he would have to return to New York, where, on May 10, 1960, District Attorney Joseph Stone's grand jury had handed down what amounted to indictments for misdemeanor commercial bribery charges that, investigators claimed, dated back at least ten years. On May 19th, Freed and seven others were arrested and booked at a police station in Manhattan and charged with receiving a total of $116,850 in payola. Freed, who had refused to testify before the grand jury, was charged with twenty-nine counts. Mel Leeds was also charged (with forty counts), along with disc jockeys Tommy "Dr. Jive" Smalls of WWRL (forty-eight counts), Hal Jackson (thirty-nine counts) and Jack Walker of WLIB (thirty-three), Peter Tripp of WMGM (twenty-nine counts), and two record librarians, WINS' Ron Granger and WMGM's Joseph Saccone.

Today, Alan Freed is remembered in an exhibit at the Rock and Roll Hall of Fame and Museum in Cleveland.

Despite his legal woes, Freed, back in Los Angeles, sounded as energetic as ever. Having signed an agreement with KDAY to steer clear of anything close to payola, he pushed records strictly out of passion, and helped break several sides, including Kathy Young's "A Thousand Stars" and the Shells' "Baby Oh Baby."

Kim Fowley worked as a "food runner" for the disc jockey for a couple of months in 1960. Fowley, who would attain fame as a songwriter and record producer, called Freed a "gentleman," adding, "He genuinely loved the music and the kids." The 1976 film *American Hot Wax* may have simplified Freed's story, but, Fowley says, "it was close in terms of him talking to kids and listening to demos. Like Rosie and the Originals—a guy brought an acetate to [Alan of 'Lonely Blue Nights'], he played it, and twenty-five thousand records were ordered. The kids went wild."

Freed's daughter, Alana, told John A. Jackson, the author of a Freed biography, that her father "was really plugging along. He had a great show." But the show closed after KDAY refused to allow Freed to promote a Hollywood Bowl concert he was staging. Fired by KDAY, Freed next had to cope with his trial on the commercial bribery charges. Coincidentally, he hooked up with a Miami Top 40 station, WQAM, but lasted only three months. He was said to be drinking heavily, and he was increasingly difficult to deal with.

Things didn't get any easier as his trial approached. Wary and weary, Freed agreed to plead guilty to two of twenty-nine counts, and, in the spring of 1963, paid a fine of $300. Behind that, however, were insurmountable legal bills and, just around the corner, Federal charges of income tax evasion. By the time those hit, in the spring of 1964, Freed was too weak to fight. Living in Palm Springs, he entered a local hospital in December 1964 for uremia poisoning resulting from kidney failure. A month later, he was dead. He was forty-three.

He seemed to have lived for music. Now, people said, it was music—or his involvement with the music business—that killed him. "Alan was the Oliver North for that whole thing," says Kim Fowley. "He was the scapegoat. There were others involved, and he got it, the theory being that he did race-mixing."

In his short time with Freed, Fowley says he never saw the disc jockey take a dime. A man much more experienced with payola, Juggy Gayles, said much the same. "To me, Alan Freed was a phenomenal man—and he never took a dime from me," he asserted. Before the scandal, he said, "We'd go out, and Alan used to pick up the tab. Alan loved to blow money; he spent more money than he could make, and he died broke."

Ernie Farrell, a veteran promotion man out of Cleveland, knew Freed well, and he echoes Gayles. "Alan Freed," he roars, "took about as much payola as Bill Gavin! For every $1,000 you spent on Alan, he spent $2,000 on you. That's why he went broke."

DICK CLARK'S BANDSTAND

I've always been ambivalent about Dick Clark. He was never a Top 40 disc jockey (good thing, too; that would've given him gray hair and wrinkles long before his time) as we've come to understand the term. But, with his daily afternoon *American Bandstand* on ABC-TV and, for several years, his Saturday night *Dick Clark Show* on the same network, he had the kind of impact on pop radio in the late fifties that MTV would in the early eighties. More than any single disc jockey on any radio station, he dictated what songs and artists would hit, and top, the charts.

**Dick Clark hosting
American Bandstand.**

I dug Dick Clark as a smooth liaison 'twixt teens and grownups. He slipped rock and roll right past wary parents into teenaged minds. Sure, he seemed to promote some questionable talent, like Fabian, Frankie Avalon, and Bobby Rydell. But he also gave many, many worthy artists their first national television exposure, among them Chuck Berry, Johnny Cash, Sam Cooke, Buddy Holly and the Crickets, Jerry Lee Lewis, Jackie Wilson, James Brown, the Four Tops, Marvin Gaye, the Beach Boys, Aretha Franklin, the Doors, Linda Ronstadt, and Stevie Wonder. And he got the country dancing.

As I went through college in the mid-sixties, however, I fell into the mindset that placed Dick Clark into the enemy camp. From the so-called "hip" perspective, he was a capitalist, an exploiter of pop culture. As much as I'd enjoyed his work in previous years, I now scoffed at his money-grubbing ways. It was ironic, but ah, such sweet irony, that the very first story I ever published in *Rolling Stone*—just an item for its "Flashes" column, actually—was about Clark promoting a movie he'd made about the Haight-Ashbury scene. That was in 1968. Five years later, on the occasion of the twentieth anniversary of his stewardship of *American Bandstand*, I met him for something more than an item in *Rolling Stone*. It was a page one story, entitled "Dick Clark: Twenty Years of Clearasil Rock."

Clark has never gotten over that article. Two years later, when I was in Las Vegas on assignment, and he was hosting an oldies revue in town, he could not have been more charming, taking my wife, Dianne, and I out on the town with his future wife Kari. In recent years, he's agreed to interviews, usually timed with his production company's projects, including the

American Music Awards. Now, twenty-five years since that *Rolling Stone* piece, he kicks off our conversation with a rather provocative remark: "The writings you laid down still come back to haunt me." Really? "Oh, people come back and dig that old shit up. Now that we've got computers, you can pump up anything that anybody ever uttered."

In the quarter century since those utterances, Clark has said his piece, in two memoirs, video retrospectives, and countless newspaper and magazine interviews. But the following piece, which has been edited for space, is what he remembers.

Dick Clark has few frustrations. But the man who's had things go his way for twenty years—who fell into the *Bandstand* job through other people's mistakes; who emerged from the central depths of the fifties payola scandal as the Clearasil-clean millionaire prince of rock and roll (while the King, Alan Freed, died penniless); who considers himself "just a bystander" in today's drugola mess; who's built an entertainment empire covering TV, radio, films, concert promotions and corporate consultant work in the field of youth—is upset.

Standing behind a bar in his Malibu beach house after barbecuing and eating a steak dinner, he gets mixed up with his Japanese dessert, and he dips his strawberry into the brown sugar instead of the sour cream first, and he makes a face. Wrinkles show around the eyes, and the forty-three-year-old who looks thirtyish suddenly looks fortyish.

The subject is a movie he badly wants to do, has spent four years trying to put together. Called *The Years of Rock*, it would be "the definitive study of what happened in twenty years of rock and roll." But more important, it would relieve Dick Clark of one of his other frustrations.

"I got to do this film," he said, "because I don't want to be remembered for doing a medley of my Clearasil commercials. My youngest kids say to me…'Tell me about the olden days.' And I want to be able to pull out a piece of film and say, 'That was what it was all about. That's why you are like you are today.' And right now, that film is nowhere, except for a thirteen-minute sampler financed by Warner Bros. which has since dropped out of the project. They got discouraged with the failure of all the *other* music films."…

But, of course, this episode in Dick Clark's career has an upbeat little twist. Even if the movie is in limbo, he's got this album out, timed with all the recent promotion of his televised celebration of *American Bandstand's* twentieth anniversary, an oldies package on Buddah Records called *Dick Clark: 20 Years of Rock and Roll*. It has just been certified gold—"A legitimate half-million seller," he said proudly.

It is not Clark's first record, and, as for the word "legitimate"—well, he brought it up.

As the man running the most influential record show in America in the late fifties, young Dick Clark, as one disc jockey working in Philadelphia at that time put it, "had a piece of everything." In the fifties, payola was not illegal; you broke the law only if you failed to pay taxes on such income. Clark, the Philly DJ was saying, had a price. "He really put them up against the wall, and he was never reasonable about how much…he always wanted half the publishing and three cents a record, and… "

And so, it is said, in the transcripts of the House Legislative Oversight Subcommittee hearings on payola in 1960, Dick Clark had some hits. He owned or part-owned thirty-three corporations in the music business—record companies, publishing firms and record pressing plants. He got the copyright on the Crests' "Sixteen Candles" and played it heavily on *Bandstand* and earned $12,000 in royalties. All together, he got the copyrights to 160 songs, 143 of them as "gifts." Clark explained: "If you were a songwriter then and you had a song, you'd want me to own it because I could do the best by it. That's just good business."

Philadelphia, home of *Bandstand*, was riddled with payola. As "Cousin Brucie" noted, New York City, where he worked, "was not a testing area. We were a Broadway. In other words, before a show or record came into New York, it had to go out of town. Philadelphia was the spot. Philadelphia, as far as I was concerned, was really the major influence." Joe Niagara, who was working in town at WIBG, said the city was "a red hot spot. You couldn't help it because of the impact of *Bandstand*. The acts were here, and the people who wrote songs, the people who published songs, the promoters. They were all in and out of town constantly. There was no other place that kept this kind of action."

And the action, insiders said, centered on Dick Clark.

The *Bandstand* host, professing his innocence from the beginning, weathered a seven-month investigation and then sailed through the hearings as calmly as if they were just…TV shows. At the end of the sessions, the chairman of the committee called him "a fine young man."

How did he do it? Said Clark: "I had done nothing illegal or immoral. I had made a great deal of money and I was proud of it. I was a capitalist." No more, no less. Said the anonymous Philadelphia radio veteran: "Clark was no cleaner than anybody else. They never even got into half the shit that Clark did, because he was sitting before a committee that, when the cameras were shut off, all the Congressmen would rush up to ask for his autograph for their daughters. It was a total fucking joke." So how did he do it?

"The same way that all the bastards that are testifying in the Watergate thing will all end up running large corporations, they look so good."

Dick Clark hoped that the payola issue wouldn't dominate a piece on his twenty years in the business. He could even see the headline: "Old Payola King Talks About New Payola." And he didn't want that; didn't want to add to the gas.

"We're far removed from that mainstream of music commerce today," was about all he would say. The payola hearings of thirteen years ago followed government investigations of Jimmy Hoffa and TV quiz shows, and Clark has been quoted as calling the payola hearings "just politics. An election year and all; they were just looking for headlines." Did he feel the same about the "drugola" talk now getting senatorial attention? "I don't know if it was politically timed," he said, "but I know when it'll explode. When Watergate is over."

The story of how Dick Clark emerged out of those 1960 hearings look-ing so *ific*—as his finger-snapping, Beechnut-cracking, side-swaying teen galleries would have put it—is a large part of the story of Dick Clark.

Dick had wanted to be a disc jockey since age thirteen, after he saw Gary Moore and Jimmy Durante doing a radio program. He went to Syracuse University, and in his first year got a spot on the campus station. For his audition, he did an imitation of a radio announcer. He did impersonations in high school, he said, "to get over a terrible inferiority complex…I was not physically terribly attractive. I was skinny and I had a lot of pimples like everybody else did, and I was going through that teenage thing of 'I don't want to get involved with too many people.'" His mimicry was apparently enough to cover up some of the blemishes, and Clark got elected class pres-ident in his senior year.

At Syracuse, he studied business administration, majoring in advertising and minoring in radio. After college, he bounced around in DJ and news-caster jobs at radio and TV stations in Syracuse and Utica, New York, where he earned $52.50 a week.

In late 1951, he moved to Philadelphia. Clark skipped right into the story of how he was actually the third man to stand behind the podium of what was then *Philadelphia Bandstand;* how the two original hosts started the show in 1952, and how he got tapped as the solo host in August 1957.

But first things first.

Another radio announcer who was there recalled Clark's beginnings. "He was hired onto WFIL radio as a summer replacement. I think the manager and Dick Clark's father co-owned a TV station in Utica or Syracuse. Anyway, he was the second of two guys hired, and after the summer, they had to drop one of them. Normally, the first one would have stayed, but he used to do a network feed from the Epiphany Church, and every time he did it, he'd mispronounce it as the 'Epifanny Church.' So they fired him for that, and Dick got to stay."

The star of the station, longtime nighttime DJ Bob Horn, was teamed up with a rotund television pitchman, Lee Stewart, on WFIL-TV, Clark recounted—"almost like a disc jockey comedy-oriented team, because they had nothing to fill in the afternoon on the station.

Dick Clark on *Bandstand:* **"I was cast as an All-American boy."**

"I can remember those guys walking around the music library, practically saying, 'What the hell are we going to *do?*' And they had old musical films of people like George Shearing, Peggy Lee, and Nat Cole. They determined they would play some of those. They would make calls to viewers at home, and interview guests that came to the studio. They asked to have a studio audience. The studio was at 46th and Market Street in Philadelphia. It was out of the way. The only people in the area were the girls who went to West Catholic High School. So the only people that came by that first Monday or Tuesday were little girls in their Catholic school uniforms who sat in the studio bored to tears. And the music films came up, and they said, 'Could we dance?' So the two girls would dance together. A bright-eyed cameraman turned the camera on the girls, and the director said, 'That's interesting,' and punched it up. Couple of people called in and said, 'That's fun, let's watch the kids dance while the films or the records play.' By the end of the week, the response was overwhelming. And then they remembered that in the movies, people never really sang, they did a lip synchronization. So they brought artists in and they would mime their records. And the format never changed in twenty years.

"When I started, the big stars were Joni James, Patti Page, Eddie Fisher, the Four Aces. It had nothing to do with rock and roll music, because there wasn't any. There were also jazz and blues. Dizzy Gillespie had a song that played. LaVern Baker was there constantly. So, between Alan Freed in Cleveland and Bob Horn and Lee Stewart in Philadelphia and George 'Hound Dog' Lorenz in Buffalo, they began to find out that white kids liked black music. It's a very significant period of time, before I got there."

Philadelphia Bandstand sometimes drew 60 percent of the daytime audience, and the dance party format began spreading around the country. Rock and roll was beginning to pay off, and Bob Horn was one of the first ones paid. As Tom Donahue said in the book *The Deejays*, Horn was "the closest thing to a Roman Emperor I've ever known." Donahue worked at WIBG in Philadelphia through the fifties and saw a lot of payola money flying around. "Horn," he said, "was making a *lot* of money."

Horn was also forced to work with this skinny kid. "Bob Horn and I," said Clark, "did a radio DJ show in the afternoon the same time the TV show was on. He would come on and do the first fifteen or twenty minutes with me. He was the shill, the well-known disc jockey the station used so that they could sell it, and hopefully draw an audience. Then he'd split and do a TV show, and I did the rest of the show, and he would occasionally come in and do a fifteen-minute thing at the end. It was a bad setup. He was being used, and he didn't like it. He didn't like me. He made it abundantly apparent that he hated every minute of it, and I can see why, in retrospect."

Horn, who didn't like Lee Stewart much, either, did not have to share a studio with Clark for long. In 1956, as Donahue remembered, Horn was arrested for drunken driving. "He could not stop, getting busted driving a hundred miles an hour. Also, young girls…"

Horn was accused of statutory rape with a fourteen-year-old girl, herself alleged to be part of a teenage vice ring. Horn was also in trouble over charges of tax evasion on payola income. He was acquitted of rape, but the payola (he was the first DJ to be convicted) and the drunken driving did him in. WFIL's owners also owned the *Philadelphia Inquirer*, and the paper was conducting an anti-drunk driving campaign when Horn hit 100 on the speedometer. In July 1956, the station picked the clean cut 26 year-old Dick Clark to take over *Bandstand*.

Clark says he was still a naive young man. All he knew was that Horn didn't seem to like kids much, and so, if he were to succeed, he would have to get along with them. But not so well that he might be accused, as he so gingerly put it, of "jumping on one of those thirteen-year-olds in there." He eschewed the rocket powered, rhythm 'n' rhyming bebop talk prevalent among radio jocks in the fifties. He wore a coat and tie and kept his hair short and bear-greased.

"Pretty much what you saw was Dick Clark according to the mores of the times," he says. "I was cast as an All-American boy, and although I smoked and drank and swore and all of that in private life, that was not presentable on television. That was the myth that was built up. But other than that, that was pretty much me."

Clark got rich quick. In his first year, he says, he combined his still-pal-try WFIL salary with enough work at record hops to come out with "at least $50,000." When the station began plans to hook up as an affiliate of ABC-TV, and possibly replace *Bandstand* with whatever the network fed it, Clark scurried up to New York to pitch the network on his dance party. After much hounding, the heads of ABC began to seriously consider the show. Clark snuck a friend, a record promoter who pretended to be a sponsor, into a meeting and he reported back to Clark: They thought he had droopy eyes, and the show had a lousy set, but network quality lighting and staging could make it—and him—work.

They agreed to send *Bandstand* out to sixty-seven affiliated stations.

"And in order to show them that we had people watching, in the first three or four days we were on, we ran a contest on 'Why I'd Like a Date with Sal Mineo.' It drew forty thousand pieces of mail."

Bandstand—*American Bandstand*—was on its way, and when the show hit teenaged America, they...well, they caught the beat, and they could dance to it. Suddenly, along with *Dig* magazine, sock hops, soda shop jukeboxes, and drive-ins, they had their own TV show.

American Bandstand consistently presented the big artists, lip-synching them at the rate of two a day, ten a week. There inevitably arose the need for new artists, and—inevitably—they came from Philly.

"Man, everybody sang in South Philadelphia," said Jerry Stevens, who joined WIBG in 1960, after the payola rumble and the subsequent departure of several "Wibbage" big guns. "It was a third-class, hang-around-the-drug-store scene. People like Jimmy Darren, Fabian, and Frankie Avalon—they all lived in the same row of houses."

"Philadelphia," said Tom Donahue, "was always an incredibly good market in that you get a big record, you could sell a hundred thousand in town." And, of course, *Bandstand* attracted newly established artists for their first television appearances, and those included Johnny Mathis, Neil Diamond, Fats Domino, and a crew-cut duo called Tom and Jerry, who later changed their names to Simon and Garfunkel.

In 1958, Clark began commuting to New York. It was really the big time now, the *Dick Clark Show*, Saturday nights from the Little Theater. Here, pop stars performed to a seated, non-dancing audience and to another audience: in six million homes around the country watching Clark, the Royal Teens, Dion and the Belmonts, and Connie Francis, while the girls snapped the sponsor's gum and wore big green and white buttons reading "IFIC"—a slang word coined by the company.

Saturday night lasted two years, and Clark became a millionaire. He was getting smarter all the time, but on the air, he maintained himself as a straight, bland MC, smoothly leaning toward the camera to start each show, mastering the short, inoffensive interview, never outright defending either teenagers or rock and roll. He was the understanding older brother, and only once, in the trade papers, did he speak out, against Mitch Miller, the pop head at Columbia Records who railed against rock and roll at a DJ convention in Kansas City in 1958 and chastised radio for abdicating to "the preshave crowd that makes up twelve percent of the country's population and zero percent of its buying power, once you eliminate the ponytail ribbons, Popsicles, and peanut brittle."

"He was grinding his ax that was going dull at the time," said Clark, "and that's sheer business, man. When somebody jeopardizes your way of living, then you've got to quick run in there and take care of business."

Dick Clark sits back on his Malibu floor, against a fur-covered stool, and shakes his head. I am railing at a buddy of his, a record company president who purged "drug-oriented" groups off his label, then released Grateful Dead material months later, when the Dead were high on the charts. He re-released ten R&B stiffs under the title *The History of Soul* when black music began to dominate pop charts. Clark reasons that, in business, anything goes, "as long as you can sleep with yourself at night." I shake my head, slowly.

"The problem," says Clark, "is that you're an idealist, and I'm a fucking whore."

When they hauled Dick Clark before the House Subcommittee, he showed them just how much he slept, and how wide awake he could be. Accused of favoring records in which he had a financial interest, he hired Computek, a firm that did consulting for the U.S. government, to check his records.

"I'll show you how fucking innocent I was," said Clark. "They [the government] went to one of the biggest broadcasting chains in the world that was riddled with payola. They arrived on a Thursday night, said, 'We'll be back tomorrow to examine the logs.' When they went back on Friday, there weren't any logs. They had disappeared...and it all went, *zappo*, to Dick Clark, twenty-seven-year-old cat in Philadelphia. 'You want the records? Here they are! Look at them!' I could've burned those motherfuckers in two minutes. I had them examined; the examiner said, 'You're right, you're straight.' They thought, 'How could a kid in Philadelphia make that much money?' They thought people came in with bag loads of cash and put it in my office. I found a better way to do it: to be in the music business. It was offensive to me, they thought I was that ignorant."

And the fact that one of his labels admitted paying people to play records—"that blew their minds, but that's not what they were after. They wanted to prove I was the taker of bribes."

Clark ended up dumping his corporations. "It was called 'with a shotgun to your head.' Which would you like to be, in the music business or the television business?" Clark scratched lightly at his hair. "Do you have any idea what those would be worth now? Who could predict that in another dozen years the industry would be a $2 billion a year business? I made the wrong choice!"

In the end, said Clark, "the Chairman, Oren Harris, said something about the fact that you're a bright young man, and I hope we haven't inconvenienced you. 'Inconvenienced'? Hell, they took my right testicle and almost my left!"

He still did better than most. There were those that were forced out of town —and there was Alan Freed.

With the payola hearings ahead of him, he lost both his radio and TV jobs; the next year, after the hearings, he was indicted again on payola charges in Los Angeles. Later, shortly before his death in 1965, he was indicted for evading $47,920 in income taxes. The first case was finally dumped in 1964, and Freed was fined $300. But he was dying, by then.

"I was the last friend Alan had," says Clark, "and I don't want to say what he did wrong. He made a lot of mistakes. I never met the man in my heyday, when I was king and he started it all. I met him afterwards, and he was groveling around, and I tried to get him a job, and two days before he died, I was called to contribute to keep him in the hospital, and it was just one of those terrible…bad scenes. You don't want to know about it."

But I did, and, interestingly enough, Lance Freed, Alan's son, could not recall such a closeness between his dad and Dick Clark.

"There was a cordial, professional relationship before the hearings," he said, "but there wasn't a lot of contact afterwards." With his dying father in a Palm Springs hospital, Lance remembered people calling and bringing food. "But I never recall Dick Clark calling or coming down."

Later, on the phone, Clark corrected himself. "It was not an intimate friendship; I was one of several trying to get him back going again…Alan was the king; he found it, he had the gut reaction. He wasn't bright enough."

While Dick Clark, from Syracuse University, in business administration, was bright enough?

"What you're intimating now," he said, "—and you're right: I had a little more education. Alan had raw emotions; I knew the game."

"Big Daddy" Tom Donahue.

TOM DONAHUE: MORE MONEY, LESS WORK

Tom Donahue is in the Rock and Roll Hall of Fame as the godfather of free-form FM rock radio, beginning in 1967 in San Francisco.

But he was also "Big Daddy" Tom Donahue, a pioneer R&B and rock and roll jock at WIBG in Philadelphia in the fifties, and a kingpin deejay-concert promoter and tipsheet publisher while at KYA in San Francisco, where he worked alongside Bill Drake.

Donahue would come to disdain Top 40 radio, but, as a young man in Washington, D.C., it was his ticket out of a possible career as a butcher.

He was splitting his time between college and butchery and wondering

AIR CHECK

Here's Johnny

Toss hyper and happy into a ballad bowl, rev it up to warp speed, and you've got the Johnny Holliday style. Here he goes:

"Hello, everybody, good afternoon, welcome into the Johnny Holliday glass cage with the old refugee from the Sunshine State to serve up our cream of the pop crop, here's Bob and Earl!"

"Harlem Shuffle" plays.

"Hey, that's Bob and Earl, shakin' a tail feather, doin' the Monkey time with the 'Harlem Shuffle' on WHK and the Fabulous 50 Tunedex tune spot Number 22 with Johnny Holliday. Twenty-eight degrees our street-level temperature outside in Cleveland…"

After a station promotion, "Dang Me" plays.

"Hey, that's Roger Miller's 'Dang Me' on our Wednesday afternoon platter patrol from WHK, Color Channel 14, your little old Cleveland host who loves you the most, Johnny

Holliday till seven o'clock tonight…"

"(Remember) Walking in the Sand" plays.

"From the WHK funderful 50 Tunedex on the Johnny Holliday shenanigans, that's the Shangri-Las and '(Remember) Walking in the Sand.' Remember, this coming Sunday afternoon at two o'clock, our WHK Wonders basketball team, with a record of fourteen wins against only two defeats, will take on the Cleveland Browns basketball team, led by the great Jimmy Brown. The Radio Wonders, you know, have raised over $15,000 thus far this year and I sure hope you're going to be there Sunday afternoon because every dime goes to the Greater Cleveland CYO. All the Swinging Seven DJs are gonna be there, including Carl Race and Scott Burton and Keith Morris, and of course your Buckeye Buddy, Johnny Holliday…"

about what to do for a living, his first wife Grace recalled. "He wanted to think of a profession where he could make the greatest amount of money with the least amount of work." Although his first radio job, at a station in Charleston, West Virginia, did entail labor—Donahue had to clean the bathroom as well as host a show for $50 a

Johnny Holliday, "your little old Cleveland host who loves you the most," hangs out with the Four Seasons.

week—he stuck with radio. Soon, he applied for a DJ slot at WIBG and won it, over a hundred other applicants.

Along with Joe Niagara and, later, Bobby Mitchell, Donahue began injecting black music into WIBG's early fifties menu of pop tunes. For this, Donahue became a black sheep in his family.

Donahue, his widow, Raechel, says, was descended from Martha Ball—as in the wife of George Washington—and his parents were journalists in the nation's capital. "And they about had a fuckin' heart attack when he became a disc jockey in what were called race and blues stations."

At "Wibbage," Donahue parlayed a commanding bass voice, a deep love of gospel, blues, and R&B music, and sayings like his opening line "I'm here to clear up your face and mess up your mind," into high ratings.

With the heating up of the Congressional payola hearings, however, he, along with Mitchell, Niagara, and numerous others, left town. "It was move or be prosecuted," says Raechel.

Donahue and Mitchell ultimately landed at the same station, KYA in San Francisco. If the City of Brotherly Love had been dominated by Clark, San Francisco, the pair soon learned, was ripe for the picking. It was Donahue who was "400 pounds of Solid Sounds," but both he and Mitchell became heavies in the music scene. They set up firms covering booking, management, and publishing. They started a record label and nightclub, they groomed racing horses, and they operated a music tipsheet/radio consultation service. *Tempo*, their tipsheet, was known in the industry more for being funny than helpful.

They'd handicap new records the way *The Racing Form* dissected horses, with one-liners, many of them putdowns. Raechel recalls the line on the Supremes' "Where Did Our Love Go?": "All over the floor." When the

Everly Brothers released a song called "Ferris Wheel," *Tempo*, aware of one of the pair's bouts with alcoholism, commented: "One of them fell off his last week."

Mitchell and Donahue also found time to do their shifts at KYA. At the station, they were the lords. "They were seen as big operators; they all had Cadillacs," says Tommy Saunders, who, with fellow Buffalo emigré Russ "The Moose" Syracuse, joined the station in the fall of 1962. "We'd drive into the parking lot behind the Mark Hopkins, and it looked like a Cadillac dealership. Every single one of those guys had a Cadillac. We had these used '59 VW Beetles."

Saunders and Syracuse reported to a young program director, Bill Drake, who'd arrived in December 1961.

Tom Donahue, it was widely assumed, had little use for Drake. After all, they became polar opposites in the industry, Donahue championing total freedom from formats and debunking Top 40 in particular, Drake reinventing that format by tightening it up.

The truth, says Raechel, is that "they were pretty tight." In fact, one reason given for Drake's departure from KYA in 1963 was his unwillingness to fire Donahue. The general manager's reported reason for wanting the dee-jay dismissed: "He looks at me funny."

"Well," says Drake, "you have to realize that Big Daddy was a very personable, imposing man, with the beard and the size, and a very brilliant guy. He was everything that Clint wasn't. Tom had a dominating personality, and I think that's what Clint didn't like. I told him, 'I'll bet you when the [ratings] book comes out, he'll probably have the highest ratings on the station. If you want him fired, you fire him. I'm leaving.'"

According to Drake, Donahue did notch the highest numbers of all KYA DJs, but, by the next year, he, too, was gone. Big Daddy stayed in San Francisco, tending to his music mini-empire, enjoying a couple of hit records on Autumn Records, producing what turned out to be the last-ever Beatles concert, at Candlestick Park in August of 1966, and keeping himself on the alert for the next radio revolution.

Chapter

Hey, Mr. Deejay, II: I'm Sorry

DICK BIONDI: THE ORIGINAL SCREAM

He called himself "the ugliest and skinniest disc jockey in the world," "The Big Noise from Buffalo," "The Big Mouth," "The Screamer," "The Wild Eye-tralian," "The Supersonic Spaghetti Slurper."

He was Dick Biondi, one of the all-time great Top 40 disc jockeys. In fact, longtime radio consultant Mike Joseph considers him the single best DJ in rock radio history. He

Dick Biondi in concert.

listed a few attributes: "His energy...his presentation, his appeal to the younger generation. He had absolute magnetism in the markets where I worked with him and saw him operate, like Youngstown, Pennsylvania, Buffalo, and Chicago. He fit with the format. He sounds and sounded like a rock jock should."

That is to say that Biondi didn't sound like a schooled radio announcer. Possessed of a high, slightly scratchy voice and an excited delivery, he was a kid having fun. In that way, other kids, tuning in to him, could identify closely with him.

As self-deprecating as he was with the labels he put on himself, Biondi spread the insults around. On WKBW in Buffalo, where he had a sensational two years, he joked about his fellow DJs and put the knock on his boss. The last time (that is, he was fired for this stunt), he was annoyed that the manager was in the studio one night after getting back from his honeymoon,

117

Biondi, borrowing from Dean Martin and Jerry Lewis, called himself "The Wild Eye-tralian."

telling him to "straighten up." As soon as he left, Biondi opened his microphone. "Hey, my boss just left the studio. Can you imagine him coming in here the day after his honeymoon? He's driving down Main Street in a gray Impala, so if you see it, throw rocks at it…it'll serve him right!" Someone saw and threw, says Biondi. "So I got fired."

By then, he knew he could afford to lose a job. It was only 1960, but Biondi, a native of Endicott, New York, had been on the radio since 1951, and he understood the value of controversy.

He was an early champion of R&B music and of rock and roll's early pioneers. Once, when he began playing a Little Richard record, the station manager rushed into the studio, ripped the tone arm off the disc, and threw it across the room, telling Biondi, "We don't play that kind of crap here."

Ultimately, that kind of crap prevailed, and Biondi befriended, among others, Buddy Holly, Jerry Lee Lewis, and Elvis Presley.

At one Presley show, he told the *Chicago Tribune*, "I asked him to autograph my T-shirt. And he said to me, 'What are you going to do with it?' I said, 'I'm going to jump into the crowd and see what happens.' Unfortunately, that's exactly what I did, and all these screaming young girls started tearing at me like crazy. They all wanted a piece of that shirt,

Gardening at Graceland

Yes, he was a screamer, and, no, he wasn't chock full of one-liners or character voices. What Dick Biondi offered was enthusiasm and sincerity, whether about his pride in his Italian heritage or about the smooth shave of a Gillette blade. For his stint on the Cruisin' *series of DJ albums, Biondi recalled two of his career highlights: Getting in trouble for playing an Elvis Presley record, and taking leaves from Graceland to give away to listeners.*

Biondi comes on as "Running Bear" by Johnny Preston fades out.

"Ooh, I love those Indians' songs. Dick Biondi on KB in Buffalo, last week in February 1960, and gee, who woulda thought I would've lasted this long, right? Remember last year? Ha! Just about this time? Presley record? Remember what the Hound was say-

ing? Good old George, making fun of me, all that sort of stuff, said he'd get the record first? That's pretty good.

"By the way, I gotta tell you something. Remember last November when we went down to Nashville, and to Memphis, to Graceland, to Elvis' mansion, and we sent out all those leaves from Elvis' front lawn? Somebody called up the other day and wanted to know if we had any more of the leaves left. I said no, but I want to apologize to the young lady in Branford, Pennsylvania, who called. I did find a couple more leaves, believe it or not, in my suitcase, so young lady, if you're listening tonight, all you've got to do is write Dick Biondi, WKBW, Buffalo, New York."

and no one got a piece bigger than a quarter. I wound up in the hospital emergency room with cuts and scratches." And, no doubt, a bit of ink from the newspapers.

A combination of success and controversies kept Biondi on the move. When WLS in Chicago went to Top 40 in 1960, he was its first late evening DJ, helping carry the station banner for three years. From there, it was on to Los Angeles, where, at KRLA, he helped present the Beatles and the Rolling Stones in concert. He returned to Chicago when WCFL joined the rock radio wars in the late sixties and won over the Windy City again.

Dick Biondi: Still playing the oldies.

After a good, six-year run at 'CFL, Biondi was booted, he says, by a station manager who thought him too abrasive on the air. After a short stop in Cincinnati in 1973, he gave up radio. Or so he thought.

Settling into Myrtle Beach, South Carolina, for a long vacation, he found himself itchy for a microphone and visited the local station. The manager, who had no idea he was talking with a legend, offered Biondi about $100 a week. The Screamer could have used a heftier paycheck, but he took the offer. "The important thing," he said, "was that I was still on the radio."

PAL JOEY REYNOLDS HITS THE POST

The song, "Exodus," ends, and Joey Reynolds begins: "That was done by Ferrante and Teicher. I remember that was Number One for about eighteen weeks in Miami, I was working there at the time, you know why [when] disc jockeys play oldies they always refer to the city they were in rather than the year? They say, 'Oh, that was popular when I was in such-and-such.' That's the way it is, we're a bunch of gypsy savages."

Joey Reynolds

Reynolds was in Detroit in late 1966 when he made that observation (and made it just that way: with non-stop commas that gave way to periods only because even he needed an occasional breath of air). He'd just come in from Cleveland, where he'd been on two stations that same year. And between WXYZ in Detroit and his most recent job, he logged another 18 stations in ten cities.

Gypsy savage that he was, he was also the king of nighttime radio at "KB"—short for WKBW—a 50,000-watt station out of Buffalo that reached far beyond the Empire State. Try two-thirds of the mainland. He introduced listeners to characters like the Count, Esquire Yawl, his wife Margie, and his dog named Pet. He won two DJ of the Year honors from *Gavin* before moving on to Cleveland, Detroit, Miami, and, most recently, New York, where he hosts a nationally syndicated all-night talk show.

Joey Reynolds: An early bridge to Howard Stern's style of radio.

Joey Reynolds, I've been told, was *the* wild man of evening radio; a Howard Stern, a dozen years before Stern came along, who actually spun records. Reynolds himself volunteers that the late Robert W. Morgan, who was a keen assessor of broadcasters, dubbed his show "the *Rocky Horror Show* of radio."

But, having grown up in San Francisco, out of the reach of KB Radio, I had no idea what the Reynolds rap was—until I heard an aircheck. (Courtesy of "Radio's Best Friend," videographer Art Vuolo, who apparently stalked Reynolds—at least by way of tape recorders—as a kid in Michigan.)

He was wild. He anticipated free-form radio, with his unadulterated raps. He paved the way for shock, with his blistering candor, if not his language.

One night, he'd apparently barely survived an MC stint in which fans had pelted him with candy. "Ladies and gentlemen," he announced loudly, "I've got jelly beans today, emceeing the Beatles concert, and I left orders with Oliver [apparently his engineer]. Hey, kids: I hate kids and grownups. Any kids come to the station tonight, Oliver, here's a bag of jelly beans. Give it to 'em! And you'd better not come to the station tonight. This audience was ridiculous! Where do you get the nerve to throw stuff at a *star?* Shame on you! Would I go to your house and say, 'HIII!' and throw jelly beans at you? You came to my house—the theater—I was on stage, and the lights were on me. And you throw things at me!"

As for free-form: Reynolds excelled at all the typical Top 40 formattics, playing with sound effects, drop-ins, pre-recorded one liners; ad-libbing smart-ass remarks following commercials; and talking up the records, hitting the post, and even squeezing in phrases between the first lines of a song.

But, once, when he messed up, he immediately turned it into a bit. The song was Brenda Lee's "I'm Sorry," and Joey spoke over its languid opening, ending just a beat before Brenda began singing. That wasn't good enough. "Think we can hit the cue a little better than that," he said, signaling the engineer to restart the cartridge. He did, and Joey tried again:

"Hitting a cue meaning I talk over the instrumental portion of the song until the vocalist begins, and, uh, by the time she starts singing, I should have shut up with what I have to say, and the closer you are, the better a disc jockey you are, and now, ladies and gentlemen, Brenda Lee sings 'I'm…"

I'm sorry…

"*Agggh!* Two tries! I'm gonna try it again, pal!"

The record begins again.

"I can do it!" Reynolds shouts, but you know he's not sure. He raves for a second or two, catches the rhythm, and intones, "twenty-six after nine o'clock and this is a million-dollar sound from Brenda Lee. You and me, "I'm Sorry."

The song begins *half* a beat later. "Am I close enough?" Reynolds interrupts. "Gotta get it closer? That was just a hair of a pause there. All right."

The engineer punches the button once more. "I don't make it this time, I'll hang up my disc jockey strap and leave." He pauses to let the strings build. "This is Brenda Lee to sing her million-dollar sound on WYXZ "I'm Sorry"!

He rushed it, but he hit the post. "That's so much better, I'm so glad!" he exults, and finally lets the song run its length.

Listening to this aircheck three decades later, I can only laugh and cheer him on, and imagine how it would have been to have been able to hear this when it was actually happening. And I want to know how this young man with an unremarkable voice and a lightning wit broke through.

"I didn't have any fear," he said. "Fearlessness is a really good motivator. I was screwed up as a kid, and I brought it out on the air." Reynolds recalled a recent chat with a comedian. The subject was Howard Stern, who, it could be argued, borrowed a bit of 'tude from Joey.

"I think Howard was a kind of ignored kid in school," Reynolds said, noting what Stern has said and acted out in his movie, *Private Parts*. "He is not the most attractive guy, and he has a lot of issues. And when you tell somebody like that that they can't do it, that's like putting a red flag in front of a bull. And I had a similar background."

Now a talk show host on the WOR Radio Network, with a hundred stations hooked up to his all-night talk show, Reynolds remains unique. For one thing, he is one of the few disc jockeys from the early years who 'fesses up to having taken payola, and for getting into radio for more than fame, fortune, and the love of music by the likes of Bobby Goldsboro.

"When I started in radio," he told *Gavin* in 1997, "I wanted to collect records and get laid. I wanted to get out of the poor neighborhood we lived in, and I wanted to be somebody. I already was somebody, but I just didn't know it." Propelled into the fast lane, he said, he couldn't control himself. "I wouldn't stop drinking or doing cocaine till I hit rock bottom. There wasn't enough of anything, including pussy when you wanted it. They didn't make enough of it. And they didn't make enough records when I was doing payola, either. But I can't be beating anyone up with that. I'm suggesting that I've gotten a little more comfortable in my own skin."

BILL BALLANCE AND HIS STALLION GANGLIA

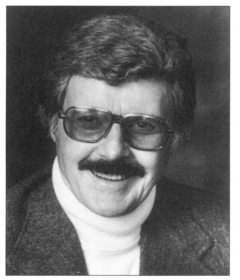

Ballance: Master of the "insinuendo."

Bill Ballance had two radio careers. Top 40 fans remember him as one of Chuck Blore's original crew of disc jockeys when KFWB became "Color Radio" in 1958. Ballance, a master of one-liners, many of them double-entendres, attained national popularity through his columns in *Teen* and *Dig* magazines—collections, essentially, of the jokes he'd told on his show. After leaving KFWB in 1965 and working at various stations in Hawaii and San Diego, he came up with *Feminine Forum*, a call-in talk show on KGBS in 1970 that featured sex as the main subject. The show sailed to Number One in the ratings, got syndicated, and inspired a flock of similar shows around the country.

It was a long way from the fifteen-minute newscasts Ballance did when he began in radio on a college station in 1936 while attending the University of Illinois. After serving in the U.S. Marines, he worked as an NBC staff announcer at KOA in Denver, a switching point for the network's Blue and Red Networks. (The Blue Network was later sold, and became ABC.)

"I would do cut-ins on *Pepper Young's Family*," Ballance recalled. Once, he stumbled: Pitching Lizard Glass Wax, he said: "Today, ladies, buy your jar of Glizard Ass Wax." "And it went to all of the NBC stations west of Denver, and got not one complaint, because everybody thought, 'Oh, he couldn't have said that.'"

In 1955, he was at KFWB, where disc jockeys brought in their own records. The station floundered and changed hands the following year. Crowell-Collier, the new owner, brought in Robert M. Purcell as manager. Well aware of radio trends, Purcell began steering the music toward R&B and rock and roll, leaving only B. Mitch Reed's all-night jazz show alone. And he brought in Chuck Blore as program director. Soon, KFWB would be full-time Top 40. For some of the announcers, accustomed to the freedom of saying and playing what they pleased, "Color Radio" was a challenge.

Ballance met it. "My style always included humor, one-liners. So I would merely inject my one-liners over the instrumental openings and closings and segues and in the middle of commercial clusters. At the pre-Blore KFWB, Ballance had already been playing R&B and become a fan of Ray Charles, LaVern Baker, and others, and he was comfortable with its off-spring, rock and roll. "I loved the records of that particular era."

One fellow disc jockey, he said, had a tougher time. It was one of the pioneers of pop music radio, Al Jarvis. "Al Jarvis was and regarded himself as an icon," said Ballance. "Whether because of old habits or out of defiance," he continued, "Jarvis would never use the overlapping tight cue method required by the Fabulous Forty format." At that time, Ballance explained, "the engineer actually played records, and we would poke a buzzer in our announce studio. And the engineer would let the next record fly. Jarvis paid lip service to the overlapping and the tight cues, but he continued to play records as he had for years. At the end of a record he would say, 'And that was a recording by Jo Stafford. *(pause)* Jo, of course, has recorded other'… I mean, no preparation. Just sort of leisurely. Al refused to get into the urgent pace of the Fabulous Forty."

Ballance, meantime, built a following—and a reputation for getting into trouble with his suggestive language. Said John Hart, a childhood fan of KFWB who is working on a history of Crowell-Collier: "Some of his words sounded like they had a sexual connotation. One of his favorite expressions was 'stallion ganglia.'"

"I used to call them 'insinuendos,'" said Ballance, chuckling. "I would say, 'I'm sitting here stroking my Stallion Ganglia, and wondering about this or that,' to lead into a commercial or a record. A ganglia is merely a nerve in your wrist. But it sounded lewd. And Chuck used to roar with laughter. I never had any complaints except from some little old ladies out in the San Fernando ravine."

Ballance stayed at KFWB until 1965. By then, some of the color had left the station. Blore was gone, KRLA and KHJ offered tough competition, and KFWB had nearly been torn apart by a strike. The station's news staff walked out in July 1961, and, along with disc jockeys, stayed out until November. Management brought in announcers from sister stations and published an advertisement in the *Los Angeles Times*. The strikers, the station said, were seeking a salary of $200 a week, up from the AFTRA scale of $155. KFWB also published salary figures for its announcers, ranging from newscasters ($173) to star disc jockeys like Ballance ($432.70) and Elliot Field ($480.76).

…"I was astonished to see that run," said Ballance. "I think it's pretty transparent, that it was run so that the public would say to themselves, 'Gosh. Look at all the money these guys are making. Why should they be on strike?' I thought it was a very foolish thing to do. And I thought it also was an outrageous invasion of privacy.

"The strike was just horrendous, and it was totally unnecessary," Ballance concluded. "I said, 'This is going to kill us.' And it was caused by one of the newsmen. And it was a matter of like a dollar more an hour, or something like that. And Purcell was back in New York for Crowell-Collier in the process of buying a station, and his substitute just let things get worse and worse, and the first thing you know, we were picketing in front of the station we loved. And they flew in these other people from out of town and it created bad blood. A lot of the spirit evaporated."

AIR CHECK

Fats Domino Sings Mozart

Besides talking at an almost unfathomably rapid pace, B. Mitch Reed put his voice through echo chambers and filters and added honking horns. He also interrupted himself with drop-ins (recorded sound bites) to add to the frenzy. At WMCA, in late 1963, B.M.R. sounded like this:

As "Rumble" by Jack Nitzsche ends, Reed comes in over the last notes, singing "Ba-ba-ba!" Then, barely taking a breath, he yells:

"Oh, I wish I could've been the bell-ringer! Yeah, it still is, it's 'Rumble,' Jack 'Specs' Nitzsche on WMCA, Scooters, does your school have a blackboard, sure it does, but there are plenty of countries where the kids don't even have a school and you can help them with Dollars to Teenagers, CARE, New York 16, and Scooters, the Wide Wide Weird World will pick up on that, here's a suggestion from Bush, now at Bush you can purchase a famous-name TV set for that low, low price of only $99.95 and—ha!—carry it with you and go over to a friend's house, fifteen miles out-side the New York [area] and plug in and watch the Giants play tomorrow *(Woman's voice, breathy: 'Where's it located?')*—well, honey, as long as I was...fifteen miles outside the New York area's where you can watch the game, otherwise you gotta spend the bread and go see 'em over there at Yankee Stadium...I don't know who you are, honey, but you ask the most ridiculous questions— and best of all at Bush you only pay five dollars down and $2.50 weekly for this TV set...get your TV set right now at Bush for the lowest TV prices in town *(honk)* with me B. Mitch Reed, twenty-two in front of the hour of eight at WMCA 60 beautiful degrees tonight we will review the brand new albums, *Fats Domino Sings Mozart, Mozart Sings Fats Domino* and *Fats Domino Plays Dominoes."* *(Woman's voice: "Believe me, you'll enjoy it!").* *Over the beginning of a WMCA jingle, Reed mutters an unintelligible response, including the words "jazz" and "sugar."*

B. MITCH REED: BOY ON A COUCH

Considering how well-traveled a lot they are, it's amazing how few disc jockeys can claim substantial success in a major market on both coasts of the United States. East Coast legends like Cousin Brucie, Murray the K, Hy Lit, Joe Niagara, Arnie Ginsburg, Joey Reynolds, Dan Ingram, Ron Lundy, and Harry Harrison never made a big splash on the Pacific Coast. Los Angeles and San Francisco giants like Gary Owens, Bill Ballance, Emperor Bob Hudson, Robert W. Morgan, The Real Don Steele, Charlie Tuna, Sam Riddle, Dave "The Hullabalooer" Hull, and Don MacKinnon were never heard of—or at least, never heard on the radio—by right coasters.

Reed: He switched, overnight, from jazz to Top 40

Of course, there were a number of DJs who did well on both sides of the country, including Dr. Don Rose (Philadelphia, Atlanta, and San Francisco), Johnny Holliday (Cleveland and San Francisco), Dick Biondi (Chicago and Los Angeles), and Tom Donahue and Bobby Mitchell (Philadelphia, San Francisco, and L.A.).

But the most impressive of all bi-coasters may have been the man who, in his nearly thirty-year career, called himself B. Mitch Reed, B.M.R., "The Beemer," and, finally, B. Mitchel Reed; who switched from jazz to Top 40 to progressive rock, and who enjoyed the heights of success in New York, at WMCA, and in Los Angeles at KFWB, KMET, and other equally significant stations.

In a business of industrial-strength speedtalkers, B. Mitch was right up there with the fastest, to the point that he had a set line about the rapidity of his rap: "I'm not talking too fast," he'd say. "You're listening too slow."

Reed revved himself up almost overnight. A late-night jazz DJ in Baltimore and New York in the mid-fifties, the Brooklyn native moved to KFWB, where he mixed jazz with free-form raps and, as he did back East, called his show *The Boy on a Couch* because, he said, his stories were based on sessions with shrinks he was seeing.

With Chuck Blore's arrival in 1957, B. Mitch's jazz nights were over. Blore invited Reed—along with Al Jarvis, Joe Yocam, and others—to stay on, if they could adapt to Top 40. Reed swore that he couldn't. As Blore recalls: "He said, 'That's terrible. I'm a jazz fan.'" Told that, with Blore's plans for Color Radio, he could hit the top of the ratings, Reed agreed to stay.

Occupying the evening slot, Reed took the existing Top 40 formula—fast patter, horns and bells, jokes from Bob Orben—and sped to Number One.

"He was legend," said Sam Riddle. "There was no other disc jockey in the United States like him. That was why KFWB during the sixties was what it was, because of gigantic personalities like B.M.R."

After five years at KFWB, Reed got an offer from WMCA in New York, where he'd be pitted against not only powerhouse WABC, but Murray the K on WINS as well. Reed took the challenge as a personal one. A fan of Alan Freed's, he saw Murray as having wrongfully ascended to the old Moondogger's vacated seat as top dog in New York radio. "So," he said, "I decided to go back and knock off Murray...plus, I wanted to be Number One in my hometown."

Besides eclipsing the K, Reed gave him a good run for the inside track on news about the Beatles, traveling to London to hook up with the band and its associates.

Two years later, in 1965, he jumped across the country once more, returning to KFWB, where he stayed until changing times and musical interests led him to escape Top 40 altogether. He would emerge sounding like he had before the format came along. He'd sound, once again, like "a boy on a couch."

Chapter

Listen to the Music

I
t didn't take long. By the early sixties, Top 40 programmers were taking on a worried look. It was as if ASCAP and Mitch Miller's dream had come true. Rock and roll was on the ropes. At the end of its first decade, its top disc jockey, along with dozens of others, was mired in scandal. Its crown prince, Elvis, was in the Army. Jerry Lee Lewis, married to a fourteen-year-old cousin, had been effectively banished from many radio stations, and, on February 3, 1959, the music died. Buddy Holly, one of the most gifted songwriters of his generation; Ritchie Valens, who was quietly smashing racial barriers, and J.P. Richardson, "The Big Bopper," were killed when the small plane taking them to a concert in Fargo, North Dakota, crashed in a cornfield in Iowa.

By 1960, Bill Gavin was looking back at the glory days—and ratings triumphs—of Storz, McLendon, and company as "the Top 40 Revolution." "Today," he noted, "quite a few established Top 40 operations are in the midst of very serious ratings struggles against new and improved competition."

The music industry, it seemed, wasn't helping. In the early sixties, in the aftermath of the payola scandal, Top 40 radio sometimes sounded shell-shocked. There were all these surrogate teen idols—as if an Elvis could be replaced by a Frankie, a Fabian, a Bobby, or a Conway.

Although Presley would soon return, and R&B continued to spice up the radio, with Ray Charles, U.S. Bonds, Maurice Williams, and the Shirelles setting the stage for Motown, we heard all too many novelty tunes—"Please Mr. Custer," "Running Bear," "Alley-Oop," "Itsy Bitsy Teenie Weenie Yellow Polka-dot Bikini"—and pallid throwbacks to the middle of the road, with Lawrence Welk, Bert Kaemfert, and Percy Faith all reaching Number One.

In both his own publication and in a column he was writing for *Billboard*

Elvis

in early 1963, Gavin noted that sales of singles were on the decline. "I'm not shedding tears about the record business; I worry about what will happen to radio—the *total* audience that listens to pop music." He had no way of knowing that both the radio and music industries were about to explode,

courtesy of four guys from England.

In the meantime, radio didn't sit around waiting. A great deal of the fun of the Top 40 format, even after management had installed strict playlists, was in picking new records to play. Some stations actually did live up to a popular slogan of the time: "Where the hits are made—and played!" Although final decisions were in the hands of program and music directors, they often enlisted help from the DJ staff, as well

Murray the K may have been the "fifth Beatle," but he had to share them with such rivals as Cousin Brucie.

as from outside sources: national charts, tipsheets, and reports on requests and local sales.

Once a week—usually after the program managers had gathered a stack of new discs from promotion men—they'd convene a music meeting. With the right mix of people, the results could be rewarding. "One of the things that made KYA a success," said Tom Donahue about that San Francisco station in the early sixties, "was that people on the station were so involved with music. We'd have these wild meetings, these wild arguments for records."

At other stations, the mix of people might include, of all things, the promotion people. Bobby Dale was music director as well as a DJ at KFWB in Los Angeles and KEWB in Oakland. At the latter station, he says, laughing, "The jocks would come into the meeting where they would supposedly listen to the music that was selected as the best presented to the station that week. But they'd be on the phone, whatever the hell they'd be doing. So they started the deal where they allowed promotion men, one record promoter, to come in. And you'd put a record on—I would usually play the records—and, suddenly: 'That's enough!' I'd say, 'Wait until they start *singing* anyway, for chrissakes.' 'No, that's enough.' These promotion men, I mean, you had to help them out of the room, man."

Many disc jockeys couldn't care less about music. Or they cared too much about music—that is, jazz, rhythm and blues, country, classical—and didn't get the same out of Top 40. Or they tired of it. Or radio was a hopeful stepping stone to something else—acting, television, the movies. Or they'd been scared off by the payola investigations, and would no longer put up a fight for any record.

But, then and now, there is an aura about radio's ability to predict hit records. It comes with the territory, I suppose. Radio is, after all, the first exposure point for pretty much every song that does become a hit. At least it was before MTV and nightclub DJs. Top 40 stations regularly featured pick hits of the week. Early on, each DJ also had a pick hit. And every disc jockey worth his salary could point to records they broke. Hy Lit accepts the credit for "Silhouettes" by the Rays, a 1957 smash that played, repeatedly, while he was napping. "It played about thirty thousand times, and the melody stuck in my head. I went on the air and said, 'This record has really reached me.'" Dick Clark heard Gilbert O'Sullivan's "Alone Again (Naturally)" in 1972 and declared it a Number One hit. It was.

But when it came to guessing which of hundreds of new records would make it—especially those from newer artists—radio pros were no better at it than tourists picking numbers at a Vegas craps table. When the Beatles broke through, stations treated them like saviors, like long-lost sons, and smothered them with affection and airplay. They changed their call letters and became "W-A-Beatles-C" or "K-F-W-Beatles." They claimed affiliations and kinships, getting in on concert promotions and proclaiming DJs to be fifth Beatles. But when the Beatles first came along, radio couldn't hear them. Their first records came out a year before "Beatlemania." Maybe it was because Capitol, the label that had first rights to them, had passed on them, too, and those first sides were released on the indie labels Swan and VeeJay. Maybe it was the fact that they were from England, which rarely produced hits.

Bruce Morrow—Cousin Brucie—recalls sitting with five fellow DJs at WABC in early 1963 and listening to a test pressing of "I Want to Hold Your Hand": "'No way,' one of us said. 'Forget it.' 'Thumbs down.' 'Stupid name for a rock group.' Sometime in 1964, the station was calling itself W-A-Beatle-C."

Hy Lit

Morrow's details may be shaky. The Beatles didn't even record that song until the fall of 1963. Either the meeting took place in early '64, or it was an earlier Beatles release—"Please Please Me," issued by Veejay in early

1963, or "She Loves You," which Dick Clark heard in the fall of that year and shrugged off.

And Clark had reason to give the lads from England the benefit of the doubt. "She Loves You" was licensed by Swan, a label he owned part of until his post-payola hearings divestitures. His *Bandstand* producer and buddy, Tony Mamarella, had quit the TV show to stay in the record business, at Swan. Another partner at Swan, Bernie Binnick, visited Clark after returning from a trip to England. As Clark recalls in his book, *Rock, Roll & Remember*, Binnick handed over a copy of "She Loves You," and asked him to listen to it. Clark put it on his turntable and, after two minutes and eighteen seconds, shook his head at Binnick. "I don't think so, Bernie. It sounds old-fashioned, real mid-fifties, kind of hollow." Told that the Beatles were a sensation in England, Clark agreed to test it with his next panel of teen record raters. The three reviewers gave it an average score of 73, and Clark called the man from Swan.

"You saw?" asked Clark.

"Yeah," said Bernie. "I told Tony we may have a stiff."

JOE NIAGARA: "IT'S ONLY MAKE BELIEVE"

He could come across like an insurance pitchman, but there was no denying it: Joe "Rockin' Bird" Niagara loved the music he played, and the kids who tuned him in on WIBG ("Wibbage") Radio 99 in Philadelphia. He'd been on the station since 1947, long before Top 40, and he was the first to adapt to the various forms of music that coalesced into rock and roll. In his evening slot, he did simple rhymes ("We start 'em; the others chart 'em") and oozed an on-air sincerity borne of his South Philly roots. Those roots still show. Give him a simple kickoff, and he sounds like he's reading a script about the first flights of rock radio—and of the "Rockin' Bird."

The year was 1956, and you were 29.

Joe Niagara

My introduction to this thing called rock and roll was 1956. I was with WIBG in Philadelphia. At the time we were playing what was termed "middle of the road." Doris Day, Frank Sinatra, Peggy Lee, and occasional big bands. I was doing 7 P.M. to midnight. And I was hearing about this thing called rock and roll. "Rhythm and blues" was another name for it. I heard how successful this sound was with this guy, Alan Freed, in Cleveland. And slowly but surely some of the record promotion people that would come into Philly out of places like New York would drop off some of these records that I had never heard of. And I started to listen to people like Elvis Presley, Chuck Berry, Fats Domino, and the list goes on and on. And I said to myself, "Let me see what happens here if I work just one or two of these in." I drop in a Chuck Berry, drop in the Penguins, Ruth Brown, in between these other middle of the road people, and the phone didn't stop. Young people were calling—fourteen, fifteen, sixteen years old. "Who is that? Where can I buy that record?" And I figured maybe I better increase this kind of play. At night, you were able to get away with a lot of things you couldn't get away with in daytime. So I started to slip more and more of these unknown people into the format, and I shouldn't even say "format" because we had no format. In fact, we used to carry Phillies baseball, that sort of thing. And we had the record show…I started to lay more and more on this to the point where I almost stopped playing the middle of the road and started to make and break various artists and records.

There was an unknown kid named Conway Twitty. He had been strict-ly country. And I heard this thing, "It's Only Make Believe." And I said, "You know, this has an Elvis sound to it. It might happen." I started to lay on it—BOOM! The thing exploded. And this happened with quite a few others. Sam Cooke is another case in point. The distributor brought a thing in called "Summertime." I said, "*Ehh*, it's nice…what's on the other side?" He said, "Forget it. Lay on this one, I know it's going to be a hit." I played it a couple of times, frankly without a heck of a lot of reaction, and then I flipped it. And I said, "Hey, baby. This could be a hit." I started to play it. And BOOM! A genuine monster. In fact, Dick Clark called and said, "What is this thing—Sam somebody or other?" I said, "Sam Cooke?" He says, "Yeah." I said, "It's called 'You Send Me.'" He started to lay on it nationally, and it made Number One. And this happened with so many records.

Joe's greeting:
"Niagara calls!"

Joltin' Joe

May I present: Joe Niagara on "Wibbage" in Philadelphia:

"Over the Mountain" ends.

"Oo-wee! How Niagara do fall for that one, 'Over the Mountain,' Johnny and Joe. Fellas, seconds please? Hear the word from this Rockin' Bird. There is no shave like a shaving cream shave by Gillette. Who needs the noisy motor method? Besides, it's hot, too. This is a skin line, trim line shave, it's smooth, it's com-fortable, it's long-lasting. Ah, get in close.

Touch the skin of this Rockin' Bird. It's as smooth as the day I was born. Try it once and you'll be wailin' with it for life. Do it. Hear me: Bet on Gillette. There's no other way…

This is the one! At any Joe Niagara record hop, be it Camden Catholic, Roxboro High, Southern High, Collingswood, Bishop Newman—this is the one you do not get enough of. May I present the merry Mr. Chuck Berry!"

"School Days" begins.

"Rockin' Bird" was a deal where I started to realize that, hey you can talk over intros. You can really talk to the people, not like you were doing the other records where you were saying, "Here's Frank Sinatra to sing," etc. So it was a style you more or less developed. You felt it as you were going along in the process. The thing just kept growing. And we had a program director come in at the end of 1956, and he said, "With the style and the type of music you're playing, I think I've got an idea." And he played for me a record by Peggy Lee, called "Listen to the Rockin' Bird," and he said, "You know what? This would be one hell of a nickname for you." I listened to it a couple of times and I said, "You're right. Let me try it." And it stuck.

We did so many personal appearances at record hops—schools, gymnasiums, etc., where you have a thousand kids or more in there rocking and rolling, and you knew what they wanted and they knew where you were coming from. You didn't have to fool them. It was not a put-on in any way. I was not treated like, "Hey, he's my older brother," or "He's my father." I was treated like a buddy. I didn't try to act like them, but I knew where they were coming from, and they knew basically where I was going.

Other than a couple of black stations that were playing rock and roll, WIBG was pretty much alone. In fact, we had people coming in from all over the country and tape us. They would sit in a hotel room and listen for two days straight to see what was going on, jot down all kinds of notes, and then bring it back to their town. People would call and say, "Hey, I'm staying at the Ben Franklin Hotel. We're in town specifically to hear your show because we heard so much about it."

Chapter

Hey, Mr. Deejay, III: East Side, West Side

WOLFMAN JACK: HAVE MERCY, BABY!

Think raspy.

This is Wolfman Jack, skinny-dippin' in the oil of joy down here on XERB, the tower of flower power! FIFTY thousand watts of soul power! We gonna rock your soul with a steady roll and pay our dues with the BLUES! I got 'em all for ya…We have Johnny Otis, Wilson Pickett, Hank Ballard, Ritchie Valens, Clyde McPhatter, Joe Turner, Carl Perkins, the Penguins, the Platters and the Clovers! Baby, I got so much rhythm and blues up my sleeve today, I had ta staple my elbow to my armpit! Aa-WOOOOO!

It's almost spooky. In *American Graffiti*, Wolfman Jack plays himself as a mysterious nighttime disc jockey broadcasting out of a small, squat building on a remote patch of nowhere's land. You never knew where he was, but you knew where he was coming from, with that voice of his, that blend of gravel, blues, and a little old soul, slowed to a purr when he was talking about love songs or just about love; revved up to evangelical shouts when he was selling snake oil or rock and roll.

One of the lead characters in this 1973 coming-of-age movie is played by Richard Dreyfuss, a romantic who's mesmerized by a blonde he's spotted in a T-Bird. He seeks the Wolfman's help in locating her—ah, the power of radio—and finds the station's transmitter site.

The Wolfman on
The Midnight Special.

He's greeted by a guy who professes to be a lowly engineer, spinning records and playing tapes of the Wolfman's raps between them. It's only

133

when Dreyfuss makes his way out that he discovers that the low-key guy who'd been sucking on a Popsicle at the control board is, in fact, Da Wolfman.

But that's not what's spooky. It's Neil McIntyre recounting a night in Cleveland in 1957, about fifteen years before George Lucas shot *American Graffiti*:

"I was 16 and borrowed my uncle's car 'cause I heard this guy, 'Mad Daddy' Pete Myers, on the radio, and I just kept driving around the Seven

Hills area of Ohio until the signal got stronger. I went, 'Oh, must be here,' and it was the transmitter site. This man answers the door, and he's dressed in a three-piece suit with a tie on. This is Pete Myers. It's like, well, where's the black guy? We did know what an R&B disc jockey sounded like, so I figured he was just a helper there. He says, 'How can I help you?' I said, 'Well, I heard you on the radio and I like you and I'm wondering if you need any help,' and he said, 'Yeah, here's a pad, a pen. Answer the phone and write down whatever they say, and bring it to me.' As I'm doing that, I'm looking over my shoulder and I hear the 'Mad Daddy' guy. And Jesus—it's this guy, in the suit. I'm going, 'Whoa!' He sure changed colors fast."

Wolfman Jack in American Graffiti.

A couple of years later, it was Tommy Saunders' turn. Born in Buffalo, Tommy would get on the air at WKBW before he turned twenty, and find success in San Francisco in the early and mid-sixties at KYA, but he is more than willing to recall his times on the other side of the control room window.

As a kid, he said, he would hang out at the local stations, and he'd peek into the Zanzibar and see George "Hound Dog" Lorenz broadcasting live from the R&B club. At night, he and his friends would pick up the big stars on the New York stations. "I used to idolize Mad Daddy Myers at WNEW. He had a great voice. When I was in college in Ithaca, in Syracuse, all the

Get Naked!

Wolfman Jack began crafting his character on XERF in Del Rio, Texas. In his book, *Have Mercy*, he recalls a typical intro, circa 1963: "Here's Elmore James and his funky-funky slide guitar. Makes me want to get naked every time I hear it, baby. I'm runnin' around naked in the studio right now, beatin' my chest. And I wantcha ta reach over to the radio, darlin', right now, and grab my knobs. Aaa-ooooo!"

guys would listen to WNEW and WABC, and we'd try to copy them. Once, in '58 or '59, I went to visit Pete Myers in New York. I had a friend who lived there, and he took me to 'NEW. It was so damned impressive, I couldn't believe it. A huge studio and a guy sitting in the middle of it with a producer and two big 16-inch turntables, and way up in a window somewhere an engineer was running all the levels."

For those of us without such connections, there was only an imaginary studio and an often faceless voice. That's how it was for me and Wolfman Jack. Around '66, while I was a senior in college, I'd tune to 1090 and hear him ranting and raving out of some station called XERB, "Hol-lywood, Cali-*fo*-nia!" playing great sounds and pitching, constantly pitching products, from medicines to his own oldies collections, and beseeching us to send "cash, check, or money *oh*-dah" to some shop in Chula Vista. We who dug the Wolfman could swear that he was broadcasting somewhere in Mexico, stuffing envelopes and counting cash while the records played.

Many years later, I would learn that the Wolfman was actually howling out of a studio on Sunset Boulevard in Hollywood, that tapes were shipped to Tijuana—where the 50,000-watt station was licensed—and blasted back to most all of California on time delay. Wolfman Jack, it turned out, was a native of Brooklyn, a nut for Alan Freed and "Hound Dog" Lorenz, Jocko Henderson, and John R., out of WLAC in Nashville. Wolfman himself went south for some of his first gigs, including some country deejaying, before discovering the potential riches of the radio business south of the border.

It was on XERB that George Lucas, too, heard the Wolfman and wrote him into *American Graffiti*.

A few years later, writer Tom Nolan, on assignment from *Cheetah* magazine, went looking for the Wolfman. Hard as he tried—with phone calls to his P.R. company, to his manager, and, finally, to his "right-hand man," one Bob Smith—Nolan never got through. Sitting with Smith, all he got was how Wolfman only popped into the studios on occasion and taped a week's worth of intros, outros, and phone calls, and how "the guy is just so dog-gone busy, you just can't pin him down!" Nolan finally maneuvered his way into a radio talk show on which Wolfman Jack was scheduled, only to have him cancel at the last minute.

Wolfman Jack, who went on to act in more movies, host NBC-TV's *The Midnight Special*, have a show on WNBC-FM, have a radio show syndicated on seventy stations, have eighteen songs written about him, and write his memoirs, died on July 1, 1995.

It was then that many fans learned that the Wolfman's real name was Bob Smith.

The original K man: "A riot of raps."

MURRAY THE K: YOWSAH-YOWSAH!

He was Murray Kaufman; Murray the K, or, as the novelist and screenwriter Richard Price called him, "the capo di capo of undying hipness."

They called him lots of things, and the bottom line may be that of all the greats who have populated the New York airwaves, Murray the K was the truest reflection of what it was like to be rocking and rolling in and around Manhattan in the golden age of Top 40 radio.

What was he like to hear? Price, paying his respects in *Rolling Stone* magazine shortly after the K's death in 1982, was in high school when Murray was riding high. "Back then," Price wrote, "he had been a verbal hot rod, a riot of raps, riffs, war chants and 'Meusurray' talk, his own patented pig Latin. And no matter how much he babbled, chattered, loop-de-looped, spoke in tongues, he never dropped a stitch, always made sense. On my 1961 ten-dollar Jap transistor, he was awesome, a heat-seeking missile."

The Dictionary, a la Murray the K

Murray the K and his followers had their own language—think "The Name Game." In his book, *Murray the K Tells It Like It Is,* Baby, he explains the keys to "meusurray" as a second language:

1) The key to speaking Meusurray is the three letters "eus" (pronounced ee-us).

2) The "eus" follows the first letter of any word or name, then the rest of the word is pronounced after it has been inserted. For example,

"Mary" is "Meusary"

"Bob" is "Beusob"

"John" is "Jeusohn"

3) There are some exceptions to applying "eus" after the first letter. For example,

a) If a name starts with a vowel, the "eus" precedes the name or word,

"Elvis" is "Euselvis"

"And" is "eusand"

"If" is "eusif"

b) If the word or name starts with two or more consonants, the "eus" is inserted after the first group of consonants or before the first vowel.

"Frank" is "Freusank"

"String" is "streusing"

4) The final rule is if the word has three or more syllables, the "eus" is used in the first and last syllables. For example,

"Hollywood" is pronounced "Heusollyweusood"

Have fun with the language and make sure you listen to WINS. I will see you soon!

No wonder Johnny couldn't read...

In a companion obituary, Kurt Loder recalled how Kaufman's "combination of sonic blast and nonstop *yowsah-yowsah* made for electrifying radio," and explained the deejay's energy: "Murray the K was a rock & roll obsessive...he would generally buzz into the WINS studios each day, several hours before his show began, to sift through all the new singles that had arrived. Less driven jocks might have waited for someone else to break a risky record first, but not Murray. If he heard something he liked, something really boss, he would put it on the air *that night.*

In the WINS record library with Frankie Avalon

"Got this this afternoon! Sounds terrific! Take a listen!"

That, wrote Loder, "was rock & roll radio."

So was this:

"This is Murray the K on your Swingin' Soiree. The music is ready to take you there. Are you ready to go? Let me hear it, then!"

(Tape from a Fox Theater show in Brooklyn, of the audience doing Murray's pseudo-Indian chant: Ahhh-Bay! UNH! Ahh-Bay! UNH! Koo Wee Summa Summa!)

"Here's something for all the submarine race watchers in Plum Beach, New York, from Kathy Young and the Innocents...'A Thousand Stars'..." In Murray the K-nese, "submarine race watching" meant necking, since watching such a race would require going under the surface.

When rock and roll radio tightened up too much for him, he'd quit. Once, according to his own book, WINS management, tired of the battle to sell advertising to clients outside the limited teen market, tried to switch to a middle-of-the-road format. Murray quotes a couple of his listeners talking about him:

Girl's voice: "...And then remember when WINS suddenly stopped playing the rock 'n' roll, or like Murray called it, *Today's* Music. Right on the air he fought the station for us."

Boy's voice: "...Yeah, some kook made the disc jockeys play records by the big bands, some guy named Glenn Miller, Percy Faith, Artie Shaw, you know, classical music almost...Like Holy Popcorn and shades of Sammy Kate Batman. Would you believe it? Murray the K introducing Mantovani? I mean, how can you say, 'O.K., Mantovani, Baby'? It don't make it."

Murray the K: O.K., listen to me, WINSland. Up to now I felt an obligation to the management because I have a contract. However, I realize that my real obligation is to you...you and you alone are WINS. You made Murray the K and 1010 WINS and don't you let anyone forget that. Before this station started programming the music of today, its worth, some five years ago, was $400,000. Today it can't be touched for less than $10 million. Why? Because you made it the Number One rated station in New York. You increased advertising sales by buying the products we advertised. You did this because we programmed the station for you and made you a part of that programming. I don't believe in this music policy and can't accept their money, nor continue this show. I'm letting management know that, now! I think this is your station. What do you want? Come on now, you tell WINS like it is."

Boy's voice again: "Well, we sure did. I bet half of New York wrote in, petitioned, demonstrated, and they brought our music back. Yeah! Yeah! Yeah!"

In 1965, Kaufman wrote, WINS' management "forced changes in my format by having controlled music meetings. They curtailed the listener contact by cutting out my music contests and beeper phone conversations and my twelve-year habit of beginning each show with Frank Sinatra, so...I left!" And he did it with a flourish, on the air. Three months later, WINS became an all-news station, and Murray the K was gone.

For awhile.

COUSIN BRUCIE: "I NEED THE ELECTRICITY OF THE CITY"

Top 40 radio came to New York City on WINS in the fall of 1957. That's pretty early, as Top 40 goes, but the city had already seen and heard a number of raving, R&B-inclined disc jockeys, including Alan Freed, who'd been on 1010 WINS since '54; Peter Tripp, "the Curly-Headed Kid in the Third Row," on WMGM; "Dr. Jive" (Tommy Smalls) on WWRL; and "Jocko" Henderson on WOV. But it was WINS that offered the first full Top 40 format and lineup, with DJs Irv Smith, Stan Z. Burns, and Jack Lacy joining Freed. And when Freed left WINS, Murray the K was right in there.

The next year, WMCA joined in, giving Number One WINS a battle with a crew that ultimately included B. Mitch Reed, Dan Daniels, Harry Harrison, Jack Spector, Johnny Dark, and Joe O'Brien, and a Storz-trained pair, Program Director Ruth Meyer and Station Manager Steve Labunski.

Things got more crowded when WABC went into high gear, going Top 40 despite being saddled with ABC network fare like Don McNeil's "Breakfast Club." The star DJs included Herb Oscar Anderson, Bob ("Bobalu") Lewis, Jack Carney—who would be replaced by the highly

Cousin Brucie

acclaimed Dan Ingram—and Scott Muni, who would later be replaced by one "Cousin Brucie" in from WINS. Other future WABC "All-Americans" would include Charley Greer and Ron Lundy.

WABC, with 50,000 watts, soon pushed past its weaker rivals, but the war was fierce, with Murray the K scoring Beatles scoops for WINS, and "Mad Daddy" Pete Myers and Johnny Holliday on board, while WMCA had B. Mitch Reed cozying up to the Fab Four on trips to London.

Cousin Brucie at one of his hundreds of personal appearances.

"Bruce Morrow started rewriting history in favor of ABC," said former WINS program director Neil McIntyre, referring to a 1987 book by "Cousin Brucie," who thinks of WABC as a "legendary monster" that has "surpassed being a radio station and become more of a cultural phenomenon." "ABC really wasn't in it," McIntyre claimed. "It was MCA and us."

For a station that "really wasn't in it," WABC certainly has managed to maintain its legend. Along with its ABC sisters, WLS in Chicago and KQV

Putting the Jockey Into "Disc Jockey"

Cousin Brucie recalls the time he interrupted Dan Ingram's weather report:

"One afternoon I'd been shopping for underwear," he wrote, "and had bought at least three dozen pairs of jockey briefs. The salesman had stuffed them into a large crinkly bag and I had headed to the studio. I walked in during Dan's shift. He was doing the weather and he came to this line: 'There will be brief showers tonight.'

"I couldn't believe my good fortune—'brief showers'! I tossed the bag up in the air with all my might. It hit the ceiling, split open, and showered Dan with briefs. His eyes opened wide and he paused. After no more than a heartbeat, he collapsed in laughter. Every time he tried to speak, he cracked up.

"For twenty minutes the legendarily stoic Mr. Ingram could not get control of himself. He'd cue the engineer to play a song, regain his composure, and when the song had finished, lean into the open mike, only to lose it all over again.

"The brief showers episode ranks with the Beatles in Shea Stadium, the first time I broke into double-digit ratings, and the birth of my son as one of my proudest WABC memories."

in Pittsburgh, and select stations programmed or consulted by Chuck Blore and Bill Drake, WABC is remembered as one of the most influential and most often copied stations in radio history. (The station has an extensive site on the World Wide Web, complete with its famous jingles packages.) And,

Brucie in the studio.

besides Morrow's book, there was *Rockin' America*, a chronicle of the station by its late program director, Rick Sklar. In 1990, Sklar told *New York* magazine, "WABC was the most finely tuned station there ever was. The word was attack: Attack the market; attack everyone else; be on the offensive all the time." And when I spoke recently with Bruce Morrow, the Brooklyn native still had that WABC spirit.

"I don't want to sound snotty or anything," he said, "but I think the West Coast caught on later in the game, because the early Top 40 radio really started in the Midwest and really was refined in this area. Then the West Coast came around and they had their own version of Top 40, because every time I go out there and listen, I get a kick out of it. It touches what we do but yet it's unique to them, which is great."

Sure, Cousin—but what do you *really* mean?

"On the East Coast, because of the way we are, there is so much energy here, and that in-your-face attitude comes across on the air, and our audience would demand that."

And?…

"I do a lot of work in L.A. and I don't know if I would be able to handle the pace. I'm a New York guy, and I love going out to the coast to do shows, but I clamor to come home to my energy. I need the energy, the electricity of the city."

So, to Morrow, the West Coast—home of The Real Don Steele, Hunter Hancock, Red "Zorch" Blanchard, and Casey Kasem—was too laid-back. And WMCA—whose aggressive use of the "Good Guys" label for its DJs forced WABC to settle for the "All-Americans"—were nobody. Or, as he characterized that station, "It was a little guy coming after a big guy. WMCA was a 5,000-watt station that was regional in scope, it was really a local version of a WABC. They appealed generally to the boroughs, while WABC was 50,000 watts clear channel. It was really like putting poor little David up against Goliath. And [WMCA] was throwing little stones at us. WMCA appealed to the New York and nearby New Jersey person, and they gave us a run for the money, but it was really never a war between stations."

Morrow conceded the skirmish for the "Good Guys" tag to WMCA, but blamed the loss on his parent company's tight fists. "This 'Good Guys' thing started with us," he said, "but WABC in those days would really never put their money where their mouth was. In fact, we used to call WABC 'Always Be Cheap.' It was sort of our inside joke. They'd start something and never put their money up. So here's this little teapot down the street and they really did a good job, they put their money where their mouth was and they took this 'Good Guys' thing, so two weeks later we became the 'All-Americans.'"

The talk about ABC as "Always Be Cheap" reminded Morrow of the all-time biggest thorn in his side. "They were trying to grab guys who had contracts, like Dan Ingram, myself, and Herb Oscar Anderson," he said of station management, "and they said, privately, at the end of each contract, that they would like to base our compensation—this not too many people know—on rating points. In other words, there would be a base, and then if the ratings went up, compensation would go up. And if ratings went down, so be it. Well, here's after thirteen years of building a giant. [In 1973,] it wasn't the legend that it was, but it was a giant and it was the station everybody emulated and everybody wanted to get on. That was the top of your career; you wanted to be on WABC, if you were a radio guy.

Cousin Brucie

"This offended me terribly. I had another couple of months to run on my present contract. Then WNBC brings in Wolfman Jack. I didn't know anything about him. I saw him in the movie, I'd heard him on the air, and

"Terrible News" for WABC

How big was WABC? So big that, even today, a web site is devoted to the station; so big that part of the site deals with its bigness. Without getting into the specifics of the station's groundwave signal, skywave signal, and "fantastic half wave tower," here is how fan and engineer Doc Searls addressed the question, "Why Did WABC Have Such a Great Signal?":

"It did seem like you could hear WABC everywhere. During the day you could receive the station two hundred miles away without any problem. At night, it covered over thirty-eight states like a blanket. When people speak of WABC reaching eight million people a week during its peak, they're referring to only the New York City metropolitan area. But, if you take into account listeners from out of the local area, that number was even greater. There is a 1971 aircheck of Dan Ingram where he comments, "I just got some terrible news...I read the ratings, and WABC is only the thirteenth ranked station...in Pittsburgh, Pennsylvania!"

I knew he wasn't a New York guy. It just wasn't a New York act. I knew the people at NBC—they tapped me a couple of times—they said, 'Hey, when you're ready, we'd love to talk to you.' At this time, they were trying to build a radio station.

"[Wolfman Jack] came in and they did a campaign, 'Cousin Brucie's Days Are Numbered.' I have tombstones that they put out. They did this every day in the newspaper—'Only eighteen days left.' And under these it would say, 'Wolfman Jack is on the prowl.' And they issued maybe ten thousand of these, a paper weight–sized tombstone [engraved]: *Cousin Brucie is going to be buried by Wolfman Jack.* Well, they sent this out to the agencies and newspaper people and caused a big furor. NBC had a seven-foot tombstone constructed, and they left it on the stairs at ABC on Avenue of the Americas at six in the morning. It was funny, great stuff. This was a wonderful thing for me because ABC really never did much advertising, never had to. So NBC was spending a fortune. It really was amazing what it did for me.

"Wolfman comes into town, and nothing's happening. Rating period comes out, and you can check the ratings, he didn't do anything, even though his book claims he did very well. Six weeks into his tenure there, Pat Whitley, the program director at WNBC, and Perry Bascomb, the general manager/vice president, met with me in a restaurant that was out of the way, because once you're under contract and someone tries to steal you, you can be sued. We met, made a terrific deal. They wanted to get rid of Wolfman and put me on that evening in the evening slot. I told him, 'I'm going to get out of my contract.' I went back to Rick Sklar and said, 'Rick, let me out of my contract and I'll talk with you about the new deal.' The general manager was thrilled, Rick was thrilled. Two days later, I had my lawyers send him a letter that I was leaving, and I signed with NBC.

"Now, Wolfman writes a book years later. First of all, I was very nice to him, I only met the man once when he was up there. In his book he notes that he wanted to leave, which was not true, and that he then got me a great deal at triple my salary. I hear this on the air. My lawyer calls me and says, 'You'd better listen to Imus. He has Wolfman Jack on the air.'

"He was doing a book promo, he was all over the country doing this. And I was getting really furious because it is a complete lie. I never knew the man, he had nothing to do with me getting the job. I call Imus and tell him I want to go on the air—and Imus is a friend of mine, we worked together at NBC. I go on the air and I tell the true story, at which time Perry Bascomb comes on the air and completely corroborates everything I said.

"Three weeks later we have a Rock and Roll Radio Greats Reunion which we do every once in a while on CBS-FM, and they invite the old timers back. Well, Wolfman's invited to come on, we're broadcasting, I'm doing my show from the Museum of Television and Radio, and here comes Wolfman down the aisle, and I figured, well, he'd apologize, because we'd had a ballyhoo on television and radio about this war between the two of us.

"He hugged me, and then he went on the air and he proceeded to tell the story of how he got me my job. I freaked out. I mean I was inconsolable for days on my own radio station. And then the guy up and dies.

"CBS and NBC come up, and I look into the camera, and the guy says, 'How do you feel?' I said, 'Let me talk to Wolfman.' Of course, he's dead." Morrow found the center of the television camera lens and spoke. 'Wolfman, I think you were a unique man, you were a professional, but you and I are not through yet. We still have an argument.'

"And that's how it ended," said Cousin Brucie. "I'm still pissed at him, and he's dead."

"COLOR RADIO" IN BLACK AND WHITE

"In radio, I found out about a lot of things I don't like," Sly Stone once told me. He'd spent two years, off and on, at R&B stations in San Francisco and Oakland in the sixties (see Chapter 14). "Like, I think there shouldn't be 'black radio,'" he continued. "Just radio. Everybody be a part of everything. I didn't look at my job in terms of black."

That must have been what Top 40 radio programmers were thinking, too. They had to have had some reason for not hiring black disc jockeys until well into the history of the format. The first African American I could find in Top 40 was Larry McCormick, who worked at KFWB in Los Angeles between 1964—eight years after it became "Color Radio"—and 1968. Ironically, McCormick won a mention in *Billboard* magazine in 1967; he'd placed fourth in balloting for Most Popular R&B Disc Jockey, even though he was on Top 40.

Larry McCormick

On the East Coast, Chuck Leonard joined the all-star lineup at WABC in 1965 for what turned out to be a fourteen-year run, and Frankie Crocker, although much better known for his achievements in R&B and disco radio in New York and Los Angeles, logged three years as a Top 40 DJ on WMCA, beginning in 1968. "It was great," he says. "I loved the music. New York was alive with rock and roll as well as soul and R&B, and everybody went to see everybody else. The only place it was segregated was on the radio, and so that became my desire: to mix it together."

Chuck Leonard

As for the Drake stations, it'd be 1970 before Walt "Baby" Love hooked up with RKO's CKLW (out of Windsor, Ontario, just across Lake Erie from Detroit) on his way to WOR-FM and KHJ. Love also did Top 40 at KILT in Houston the year before Paul Drew hired him for CKLW.

In each case, the station had been established for five years or more before bringing on its first black disc jockey. "I don't know if we were shut out, or it was just the way radio was," says Quincy McCoy, who got a job in 1968 as a "Good Guy" at an upstate New York station. "It was like they didn't want you in there unless you could sound a certain way." McCoy, who would move on to the Miami Top 40 powerhouse, Y100, thinks of Chuck Leonard as "a big icon. He was one of the guys who opened the doors."

For Chuck Leonard, the call to join one of the most listened-to radio stations in the country—WABC, New York—was a total surprise. Life's been like that for Leonard. Born in Chicago, he studied journalism at the University of Illinois and spent some time on the campus radio station, spinning both classical music and jazz. In 1964, he was an editorial trainee at the *Washington Star* (the head copy boy, he recalls, "was a guy by the name of Carl Bernstein") when, through a college friend's recommendation, he got a part-time DJ job on a Baltimore R&B station, WEBB. It didn't take Leonard long to determine that radio paid more than newspapers, and he jumped when he got an offer from a broadcaster that landed him on WWRL in New York. He was on the evening shift, with double the salary he was earning in Baltimore and the promise of additional income for emceeing shows at the Apollo Theater. He was twenty-two, he was blessed with a rich, booming voice, and he seemed to be set. "But," he says, "I was only there for five weeks, and I got a phone call from ABC, and I began to work at ABC after being in New York for seven weeks."

WABC squeezed Leonard into a one-hour, late-evening slot. At that time, the station was still required to carry various network offerings, which resulted in a crowded and unwieldy DJ schedule. Originally offered the all-night shift, Leonard refused. He also nixed a mix of weekend and fill-in assignments. He wanted a nightly show. Just not all-nightly. The compromised, one-hour slot soon extended to three, and Chuck Leonard was on from 10 to 1 A.M.

ABC treated him so well, says Leonard, that when he got a job offer from KHJ around 1969, he turned it down. By then, he had a syndicated daily show on an ABC-affiliated network.

At WABC, Leonard doesn't recall encountering any problems that could be ascribed to race. The closest thing, he says, was being mistaken for Ron

Lundy, "a big white Southern boy from Tupelo. Ronnie and I were always mistaken for each other because he had this Southern accent. People knew that ABC had hired a black jock, so when they saw me, they called me 'Ron.' They called him 'Chuck.' Dan Ingram and I would go and do appearances, and when they would introduce us, they'd say, 'Now, ladies and gentlemen, Dan Ingram,' and I'd stand up. They'd say, 'Chuck Leonard,' and he'd stand up, and who knew? It was radio."

They'd know if they'd seen the disc jockeys' photos on the weekly Top 40 surveys. In the case of Walt "Baby" Love, listeners had to wait to see.

Love is a native of Creighton, Pennsylvania, a town of four hundred families—only five of them black—where, he claims, "I didn't know racism." After getting his first radio job, at KYOK, a Houston R&B station, he began worrying about his future. He didn't speak with any particular accent or dialect, and he was concerned that he'd have a tough time landing better jobs in black radio. What he didn't know was that tapes of his work were getting around. One day, he heard from Bill Gavin. "He said, 'You know, young man, I think more so-called 'white' stations should just give anybody the opportunity if they're good enough to make it. I don't have a job to give you, but I want to encourage you.' And I'll never forget that."

Walt Love

Gavin made note of Love in the *Gavin Report*, and, soon, Bill Young, program director at KILT in Houston and an early Gavin correspondent, gave Love his first Top 40 job. Paul Drew, then programming CKLW, was also keeping an ear on the young announcer, and, after Love had polished his act in Texas, offered him a ticket to the Windsor/Detroit area.

Love would move fast, zipping from Canada to New York to Los Angeles, then back to New York (where, incidentally, he says he was shown

Musical and Civil Rights

"What can be wrong with a rigidly controlled sound is that, eventually, its utter sameness tends to reduce listener interest. Pop music never was and never will be a segregated type of format. There are no color barriers or sound barriers to the music that people like. Integration in music, as anywhere, involves acceptance of differences. Each record should be judged on its own individual merit. True tolerance and understanding of many musical forms are essential ingredients for the music director's job. They are also great assets for the person who sets the course of the station's music policy."

—Bill Gavin, August 18, 1972

the ropes, the first time around, by one Chuck Leonard). But in his first three months at CKLW, he was a mystery man. Of all the jocks, he was the only one not pictured on the station's Top Thirty survey.

"That was part of Drew's plan," Love says. "They'd never had a black, and he explained his plan to me. He said, 'Look, we're not going to put you on the survey. We're going to wait. We're going to put up just a blank when we put up stuff about 'Listen to Walt "Baby" Love.' And we want people to like what you do. Then, as we see that they're liking what you do, we'll put your picture in there, and it ain't going to matter what color you are. Instead, they're going to go, 'Wow! I didn't know that.'"

That was all right with Love. "I didn't care," he says. "I believed in myself, and I felt the people I was working for were being not only sincere with me, but knew best how to bring me along in [a] situation that, quite frankly, was breaking open racial barriers. And I never got into the industry to do any of that. All I wanted was a chance."

Hit Me with Your Best Shot

There is no question that the life of a disc jockey can be packed with stress and uncertainty. A DJ performs live for three hours or more a day to an unseen audience, of unknown size. When the phone rings, it may be a fan or a complainer, a simple request, a contest nut, or a stalker. It could be the program director with a nit to pick because the announcer strayed ever so slightly from format, or said "the" before "Rolling Stones." And then there's that mother of all report cards. Every three months, Arbitron issues "the book," the ratings that determine advertising rates and, therefore, revenues—in short, the life or death of a station and its format, and staff. Or maybe the DJ is worried that the program director just doesn't like him. Success, stardom, power and money are no easier. Check under "Alan Freed." It comes down, ultimately, to the individual. There are the "gypsy vagabonds," as Joey Reynolds described disc jockeys, bouncing from town to town, hearing and living radio clichés ("Don't buy a house" "You're working 10 to 2 A.M.? You mean the divorce shift?"). And then there are the straight shooters, guys married to "radio wives" who understand the life and who, like a soldier's spouse, dutifully pack at the drop of a ratings book. These guys may include the ambitious young professionals, accepting transfers from one station to another within a chain, in the hopes of the ultimate link to the big time.

Elliot Field was a disc jockey in the McLendon group, which liked to move its announcers around. "I came through Gordon's swinging door in Dallas in 1956," he said. "He put you on at night. If you were any good, he sent you out to his other stations. I did three months there; he sent me to San Antonio, did five months, then seven months in Houston." Plucked by Chuck Blore to be one of the first DJs on KFWB's "Color Radio" in Los Angeles, Field recalls his feelings: "That of stepping off [into] an enormous abyss, because you don't know what's going to come up in the next place, although you've been hedgehopping. But you have to move around to move up."

Larry Lujack, who was well-traveled before finding stardom and settling in Chicago, knows that to be in radio is to be itinerant. As he

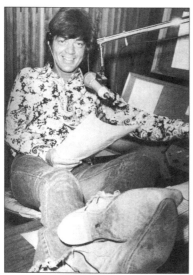

wrote in his book, *Super Jock:* "In radio, job security is zip; it simply doesn't pay worth a damn. Plus radio announcing in small cities doesn't pay worth a damn. You have to make it in the top twenty markets (cities the size of Seattle and above) to make a decent living." The best money, of course, is in the top few markets: New York, Los Angeles, Chicago. But, Lujack noted in 1975, "there isn't room for 40,000 DJs" in those three cities." And the few who make it, he added, "may not last more than three months...if you don't make it in the ratings there's too much money at stake to mess with you. They'll get somebody else."

And another DJ hits the road.

Larry Lujack, "Super Jock."

The DJ disappearances that listeners and fans remember most are the ones like Irv Smith of WINS in New York, or Don MacKinnon, Jim Washburne, and K.O. Bayley (aka "Beachin") of various stations, who died in automobile accidents. Or Pete "Mad Daddy" Myers of Cleveland and New York radio, and Bob Brannon, all-night DJ on KYA in San Francisco, or Ed Mitchell, who left a Drake station for underground radio: They all killed themselves.

Earl McDaniel, the former DJ and program director at various California stations, doesn't think radio produces any more basket cases than any other sector of the entertainment world. "It was an exciting, wonderful time," he says about his radio days. "If people were in there under an artificial situation, they may have had a problem. But my proof is that I went in and chose what I wanted to do. I picked the rock and roll, and I loved every minute of it. I loved the infighting, I loved the explosions. It was fantastic.

"Radio, being the entertainment business, attracted some people that were emotionally fragile before they ever got into radio," McDaniel says. "And radio, with its day to day pressures, is as stressful as being a standup comic, where you've got people booing you, you know? But radio does have its moments. A program director can be all over you, and when he's through with you, you feel like you don't deserve the air you breathe. But I don't think there's anything about radio itself that caused any greater stress than any [other] form of the entertainment industry. Whether it's motion pictures or standup comics or playing as a musician, it's a stressful, peculiar business in which you so much crave the adoration and the acceptance and the validation."

It may help if a DJ doesn't invest too much into the work. Tony Pigg has been in radio since the early sixties, and he's still on, at WNEW-FM in New York, although his main gig is serving as the announcer on *Live with Regis and Kathie Lee*. "I never was and still am not part of radio," he says. "I've worked in it for thirty-five years, but I never joined up with enthusiasm. I got into it because I liked music, and I like getting paid for doing a small amount of work." Pigg, then, was content to change jobs whenever someone offered something better, and to maintain a discreet distance from what he calls "the industry."

Shaw: He stayed separated, and sane.

The late Rick Shaw, whose career concluded with a 23-year run in San Francisco, at only three different stations, employed the same mental strategy. In his nearly 40 years in radio, the 53 year-old Shaw had gotten to know too many fellow disc jockeys who'd taken their own lives. He said he understood why. "You'll get screwed for no reason," he says. "When you're not very good, you'll probably be stepped on, and when you're doing very well, that's when you've *really* got to look out. Somebody will blindside you. What you have to do is step back and separate yourself from it. What I do is, I think, 'I'll get another job. There are other things I can do. I know who I am. My identity is not through a set of call letters.'" Shaw, who was also a commercial pilot and flight instructor and taught a radio announcing class at the University of San Francisco, said he knew of three disc jockeys who killed themselves, along with others "who've gone off the end of the chemical ladder, and some who are very good, but bitter, and won't try because they think the world is against them."

Norman Davis didn't get bitter, but he got very bored after being taken off his DJ show and turned into a newscaster at KYA in San Francisco, in the wake of Bill Drake's arrival as program director. At KYA news, at that time—the early sixties—meant rewriting wire copy, which Davis did quickly. He found plenty of time to play chess with a friend, and to watch a TV set he brought in. After an exchange of memos with management, Davis quit. "I think that may have been the straw that said, 'I don't want to do this Top 40 stuff any more, anyway.'"

Another KYA newscaster, by the name of Lamar Sherlock, found other ways to relieve tedium. His story is told by former program director Bob McClay, who was fired in the spring of 1965 after he allowed Sherlock to

Norman Davis at KYA and (below) with studio guest Neil Sedaka.

go on the air while inebriated. "Lamar was one-armed," McClay recalled, "and he liked to go out to the bars and have a few drinks, as we all did, and one night he came in and was feeling pretty good and went on and did a newscast. I wasn't about to argue with him, because although he had [lost] one arm, his other arm had plenty of power in it. And he went on the second time and did a newscast, the general manager came back, and my days were numbered. But I still think it was one of the great moments in radio." (See below.)

Outside the halls of KYA, the Sherlock incident didn't get much notice. But two years later, same town, different station, a disc jockey

AIR CHECK

"You Silly Thing . . ."

(Jingle: "News comes first on Radio KYA!")

"KYA temperature sixty-two degrees! Good evening, Lamar Sherlock reporting. Russia's TASS news agency has just reported that the *So*-viet probe, Luna 5, will attempt a Soviet luning on the moon…? Tomorrow! An unprecedented feat. The agen-*sa* said the rocket, weighing a ton and a half, will reach the moon at about 12 our time. Are working normally and radio communication with the station is being…maintained. More news in a moment."

Singing commercial for milk runs.

"Brought to you by the California… Dairy…Council.

"Overseas, fighting in Vietnam claimed six American lives and an envoy repr'senting Persident Johnson talked today with the leader of the rebels in Santo Domingo as part of a continuing search for a solution to the American problems.

"Here at home, the Senate defeated a proposed change in the voting rights legislation which would have banned *poll* taxes. Martin Luther King *branded* the action, quote, 'an insult and *blasphemy*'…and this…

reporter…echoes his sentiments.

(In the background, laughter is heard.)

"Also, the police chief in Demopolis, Alabama—get that name, Demop-olis, Alabama— they used tear gas to quiet about fifty civil rights demonstrators who were screaming and carrying out bunk beds in the city jail. The demonstrators had been arrested earlier after trying to stage…*(slowing and slurring now)* a march without a permit.

(More laughter)

"KYA…gives an award for every news tip used on the air. When you see NEWS, phone KYA at Exbrook 7-251…

(A jingle is punched)

"You silly thing. Wait till I'm finished. 72516. The weatherman says it'll be…who cares? Sixty-four now in San Funcisco and sixty-five in Oakland; Bobby's pad? It's about thirty-four and a half degrees. San Jose, sixty-nine? And there you are. Play the…"

(Jingle: "He's on the go! Bobby Mitchell! You're on 12-60, Radio KYA")

Over the beginning of "Help Me, Rhonda," Bobby Mitchell says: "Aren't you glad you live in the Bay Area?"

smashed up a brand-new Jaguar XKE—the grand prize of a station contest—and became an instant legend. His name was Howard Clark, and he was one of my favorites on KFRC. Possessed of a hearty voice that seemed to have a smile attached to it, he had the noon to 3 P.M. shift and came on with the greeting, "This is Howard Clark, high at noon." It turns out that he wasn't kidding.

It was always
high noon for
Howard Clark.

He started out high. He was on the air in New Orleans, doing a Saturday countdown show when a visiting Bill Drake heard him and called him up. "Bill Drake?" Clark knew better. It was one of his friends, trying to pull one over on him. He hung up. When Drake tried again, Clark hung the phone up again. Drake gave it one more shot, telling Clark which hotel he was at and which room he was in. "If and when you want to talk to me, call me back." Clark called, and the two met that night. As Clark recalled, "We were both drunk at about three in the morning, and he told me that he was going to hire me." Clark, who was accustomed to what he called "free-form" Top 40 radio, began at KFRC in San Francisco on the all-night shift for a few months while he tried to learn Drake's detailed and demanding system.

"Drake kept calling me at two or three o'clock in the morning on the Batphone—he listened all the time—and he said, "Hey, you're there, you're there. You picked up on it. There's going to be a shift change, so be ready." Soon, Clark was signing on "high at noon."

For Clark, then, the dreaded Batphone wasn't always to be feared. One night, while he was still working the graveyard shift, Drake called the KFRC studio from his car, asking Clark to play a new record, Johnny Rivers's "Poor Side of Town." "I think he had some chick in his car he wanted to impress," said Clark, who'd played the song less than an hour before. "And I told him I was sorry, I couldn't do that, and he'd have to call the request line like everybody else. I told him I didn't take requests on the Batphone—and I hung up." Clark swore that Drake got a kick out of his boldness.

Around KFRC, Clark quickly built a reputation as a wild man. "There was a lot of drugs and alcohol running around at that time," he said, "and I was heavily involved in that."

KFRC staffers knew Clark to lose track of where he'd parked his car; one night, admittedly "drunk as a skunk," he dropped a lit cigarette onto his mattress and burned down his apartment in North Beach.

In the spring of 1967, less than a year into KFRC's successful reincarnation as a Top 40 station, "The Big 610" decided to give away a fancy car.

NOON TILL THREE SIX TEN MAN
HOWARD CLARK AND FRIENDS

The Big 610

151

Clark remembered the jock meeting at which Les Turpin, the program director, ran down the rules and told the disc jockeys that they'd be taking turns driving the prize car as part of the contest. Based on information from the announcers—who'd call in reports on where they were, the XKE's odometer reading, and where they were headed next—listeners would try to call in and guess the car's exact mileage. "Turpin was saying, 'For chrissakes, guys, you've got to take care of the car, be careful out there, *da, da, da, da, da…*' and I'm looking at the floor, and there was this pregnant moment of silence. And I looked up and Turpin is looking straight at me, and the other jocks were looking at me, too. Like, 'If anybody is going to wreck this damn thing, it's gonna be Clark.'"

On the first Saturday afternoon of the contest, Clark had the car. With a female KFRC employee in the passenger seat—"one of those clandestine kind of arrangements"—he took off for Fisherman's Wharf. He encountered a four-way intersection with no stop signs. "There was a Corvair Manza, low to the ground, and I'm low to the ground, and there were cars parked everywhere. And I'm probably exceeding the speed limit, I'm accelerating the XKE, so I'm being kind of a show off, and we met at the intersection." And not in a good way.

After the collision, Clark got his companion out of the car. He remembered police officers coming onto the scene—and laughing. "They were in hysterics. The car looked like a pregnant grasshopper. It had that plastic body, or whatever. It looked awful."

Too scared to report the accident to Turpin, Clark called an engineer at the station and told him, "I wrecked it; notify Turpin." Clark, who said he was sober when the accident happened, found his way to Enrico's, a favored bar in North Beach, and got drunk. Meanwhile, Turpin, who was playing golf, got the news. In the clubhouse, he slammed his right fist through a plywood wall and broke his hand.

He also requested a meeting with Howard Clark on Monday morning.

Before Clark had to face the music, the *San Francisco Chronicle* hit the streets, and Herb Caen, the fabled columnist who regularly scooped his own paper's City Desk on local news, had the item: "KFRC, as you may have heard, has this Jaguar XKE cruising around town, and all you have to do is guess its mileage at a given time, and it's yours. Only it isn't. Not this one, anyway. Discjock Howard Clark smashed the car to smashereens at F'man's Wharf Sat., so they have to get a new one and start over."

Because of Caen, said Clark, the accident "turned into a positive, because we got publicity like we hadn't gotten before…God, it was just awesome, the response we had."

Clark survived his meeting with Turpin, who scored a replacement Jag and, even with one hand in a cast, managed to crank out a memo: "…Here we go again. For God's sake, don't take any chances when you drive the car. As much as possible, stay away from congested areas entirely. During traffic hours get out of the main traffic arteries if at all possible. Here is the driving schedule for Tuesday and Wednesday."

Five men were listed, but not Howard Clark. In his place was "Phantom Jock." That, newsman John Catchings says, was Turpin himself. Les figured that, in this case, one hand might be safer than two.

Handwritten at the bottom of the memo was this additional message:
This is God
Don't bend the merchandise. Watch Howard's hand get smaller.
I am also a student of Voodoo.

The message was signed with a drawing of a black hand.

Although Clark was thought to have been summarily fired and sent packing to a small-town station somewhere in Kentucky, he actually stayed at KFRC for another year. "Turpin hated me and wanted to fire me, and I think Drake wouldn't let him…and I was really messed up and deserved to be fired, to tell you the truth," said Clark.

"I was always protective of jocks," Drake said. "I mean, anybody can fuck up."

"Rather than fire me, they put me on the all-night show," said Clark, "and that's where I stayed until sometime during the Christmas holiday or sometime like that. I just got on a plane and left, and sobered up in Shreveport."

Shreveport, Louisiana, is Clark's hometown, and he is still there, programming a couple of stations. He is in good health, and when he thinks back to those wild days and nights in San Francisco, he does so with candor—and affection. "First day I'm in town from New Orleans," he recalled. "I had a Pepsi Cola suit on, and I'm walking down the street with Bobby Dale and I hear one of these Muni buses going *beep, beep, beep*, and I'd never heard that before, so I said to Bobby, 'What the hell is that?' And Bobby says without even hesitating, 'Don't worry, Howard, it's only a wounded bus.'"

YOU'RE FIRED!

Casual fans of Top 40 radio noted the frantic presentation, the rushed, hypoed delivery, the multi-layered mounds o' sounds the DJ wove and presided over for three or four hours. They had no idea what was going on in the studio, as the announcer, sitting in a room the size of a closet, juggled records, tapes, and pieces of advertising copy, handled phone calls for requests and contests, conducted periodic readings of transmitter meters, worked in news and sportscasts, and kept it all precisely timed. They could not know how the stress of it all built up, and the toll it could take.

More devoted listeners surely noticed the comings and goings of favorite announcers. If a disc jockey disappeared, they could call the station and get some kind of a story. They rarely got the whole story, however.

Usually, the DJ had simply been fired for low ratings or for messing up, and wound up having to slap yet another decal onto his suitcase. But, as Larry Lujack has pointed out, the DJ often was not at fault. "Even though you work your ass off and do the best you can," he wrote in his autobiography, "you may still get creamed in the ratings. No disc jockey, no matter how good he is, can carry a radio station by himself. He can't even carry his *own show* by himself." A DJ is only one of a team of six or more announcers, and even the entire on-air staff—including news and sportscasters, and the engineers who keep them on the air—is only part of a larger programming, sales, and promotion machine. A station may fail because of a poor signal, a policy of too many commercials, or the wrong music mix. But when failure comes, it's the disc jockey, more often than not, who is shown the door.

That's why Lujack, as successful a radio announcer as any you can name, will write that he pities all the young people who are drawn to what they think of as the "exciting, glamorous, high-paid field of broadcasting." Quoth Lujack: "Horse shit!"

Dr. Don Rose had spectacular successes as a DJ in Atlanta, Philadelphia, and San Francisco in the sixties and seventies. He'd rather forget the fifties. "I was fired from three jobs in one year, between '56 and '57 in Omaha and San Antonio," he says. "The first time, I could reconcile it. The guy didn't give me a chance. The next time it happens, you have more misgivings. The third time…trauma."

Rose called Bill Stewart, who was at KOWH in Omaha. There were no

Son of Radio Nightmare

Dr. Don Rose fashioned a successful career out of corny one-liners, sound effects, and wild tracks dating back to "Woo Woo" Ginsburg and Casey Kasem. But on his first show at KTSA in San Antonio in 1957, the joke was on him.

"We had a long boom mike that hung down off a piece of pipe, and somebody exhaled an enormous amount of smoke into it, and it came out around the microphone, and I lost it. I absolutely broke up."

jobs there, he was told. He got a job driving spikes for a railroad company in Nebraska. One day, there was a call from Bill. He'd found Rose a job—not at a Storz station, as Rose had hoped, but at a powerful little station in Fort Dodge, Iowa. It was there that Rose did his first morning show, took on responsibilities as a program director, and met Kae, his wife of forty years.

Lee Baby Simms

Tommy Saunders was a model of stability. In the course of a thirty-five-year residency in San Francisco, he had been at only four stations. But he'll never forget how he got fired from his first, KYA. "I was on vacation, and a couple of days before I was supposed to go back, I got a call from an engineer there. He said, 'I don't want to alarm you, but I just saw the program director in the studio erasing your jingle.'" The next day, he got a registered letter making his erasure official.

Lee "Baby" Simms has a different spin on the phenomenon of getting booted. He just doesn't see it that way—and this is a guy who, at last count, had been on twenty-seven stations in thirty-six markets over three decades, doing Top 40, Adult Contemporary, Oldies, Soul, and that rock hybrid called Adult Album Alternative, or Triple A. "I have never felt that I have bounced around," he says. "I think I have seized opportunities." While many disc jockeys might be dismayed at being forced to take jobs in smaller markets, Simms claims to have no such problems. "I've done that time and time again. I love being on the radio. If I paint a picture in Rome, so be it. If I go to Venice and paint a smaller picture, so be it. I am a working professional. I'll do it in any venue as long as I'm given the freedom to paint my picture."

When we spoke in early 1998, Simms (real name LaMar) was painting away at KISQ ("Kiss"), playing a potent blend of soul hits and enjoying high ratings. He got to the station by seizing an opportunity. The year before, in a profile in *Gavin*, programming executive Steve Rivers had listed his ten favorite disc jockeys of all time. And there, above Rick Dees, the Real Don Steele, John Records Landecker, and a half dozen others, was Simms. They'd never met. Simms moved to rectify that situation. He called Rivers to thank him and to drop a few hints about his love of painting. Soon enough, one of Rivers's programmers called with word about a possible part-time job at a new station in San Francisco. Simms needed no negotiations. He was there. "I live to be on the fuckin' radio," he says. "It is my only joy. When I'm allowed to paint that picture, using their canvas, their time, I bow down and say, 'Thank you, gentlemen.'"

BRIAN'S SONG

In extremely rare cases, a deejay is taken off the air for killing his wife.

Actually, there are two such cases. The first may be apocryphal. The way

I heard it, it sounded like a lift from a *Columbo* story: A deejay, plotting to kill his wife, recorded a segment of his show in advance and ran it while he sneaked home to kill her. But, the story goes, it was wintertime, and he slipped on some ice and was knocked out so long that by the time he got back to the station, the tape had run out, resulting in the worst sin—well, one of the worst sins—that a disc jockey can commit: dead air.

The second, more spectacular, story centers on a deejay at a top-rated station in a big city sometime in the seventies. His case, I believe, not only illustrates the personal tragedies that can beset a person in the radio profession, but it also points up the backbiting of others in the business. The way some have spread this story, with not a little glee and, in his view, with little concern for the truth, is revealing about how DJs are perceived and treated—even by their peers.

As Raechel Donahue once wrote, "Many a civilian has been left slack-jawed after hearing an exchange of endearments between two disc jockeys. No turn is left unstoned when disc jockeys lay lines upon one another…or, occasionally, upon themselves."

Here, slightly edited and with names changed, is how one disc jockey tells the story: "His wife, Mabel, was no prize…but promotion men of the day would pretty much fuck anything to get a record played. And she fucked every promotion man in town, and anybody she thought could really piss Brian off, she would screw. Sometimes in the very house in which they lived. Well, one day, he caught her in the rack with somebody and blew her face off. And Brian only did like eighteen months. This is how good his character witnesses were, and how awful Mabel was. Eighteen months, and within a fuckin' month, he was doing a radio show from his cell. He was doing a remote. I don't want to say this business is forgiving, but…"

In another account, Mabel was said to have taunted Brian by telling him she was in bed with another man, and Brian then plotted to kill her.

Brian begs—no, screams—to differ. "It was one of those things; it was a very, very, very hideous accident, and I had to do some time for it," he says. "It was a big nightmare for me…It was just a bad scene. She was very stoned, and so was I, and it was a taunting thing, and she was seeing somebody else, and I was leaving the house and everything" when whatever happened, happened.

Brian disappeared after the shooting and reportedly hid out at the home of a famous music industry figure. Police issued an all-points bulletin after investigators learned that Mabel and Brian had been quarreling. Some two weeks later, the disc jockey, with his hair dyed and his facial hair shaved off, turned himself in and was charged with first degree murder. A month later, he was in court. "I just couldn't handle everything and I just pled guilty to it," he says. Yes, he served little time, but that's because "the district attorney himself said that I should get the minimum amount of time."

As for being able to do a show from jail: "I started a radio station there. People donated old equipment, and I taught…the basics of radio to some of the guys who wanted to have something to go out to." He did not do any remote broadcasts, he says, and the prison station didn't amount to any favoritism. "That's the most bizarre thing I've ever heard. What happened was, I spent my time reading books for the blind. I did recordings for the blind. And I read and read and read and read. I mean, there was nothing but time."

And that, he says, is the truth. Even so, he pleads not to have his real name connected to the incident. After all, he is still a disc jockey, which means he's often looking for a job.

"THE WORST DJ I'VE EVER HEARD"

Bobby Dale is hardly the best known of disc jockeys. But, it seems, anyone who's heard him remembers him, and anyone who's met him professes affection for him. But I didn't choose to feature his interview because of either his on-air wit or his likeability.

He's here because, like the Real Don Steele, Robert W. Morgan, and not too many others, he spans the Chuck Blore/Crowell-Collier brand of Top 40 and the Drake-Chenault/RKO format. Like too few Top 40 DJs, he brought to his job a real affection for the best of the music he had to play. He never took his work, or himself, too seriously, so that, when a job ended, he could shrug his sloping shoulders and hang out until the next one materialized. Finally, while he freely admitted to imbibing alcohol and drugs, and to going on the air while flying high on LSD, he claimed to have a steel-trap memory of his four-decade flight through the airwaves.

And then he backed up his claim.

Your first mention in Gavin *was when you were doing the music at KFGO in Fargo, about 1957. Was that your first Top 40 experience?*

Yeah. I was 25 before I ever got into radio.

Bill Gavin said you were causing some commotion on a record, "To Know Him Is to Love Him," and that people should listen to it.

I had been arrested for drunk driving that weekend in Minneapolis, which was my home. But I used to drive there, it was about 250 miles, so you could drive it easily. And then I would go and meet all the record distributors on Monday morning, which was great because you got all the releases and you got a lot of albums.

But when I got busted, I called a guy named Bob Serempa, and he owned a distributorship with a partner, and when I said, "Man, I need $100 to bail me out," he came down and bailed me out. But his partner, who didn't care for DJs very much, said, "You stay here." And I was really sick, man. Cheap wine hangover, laying on a couch, and I hear "To Know Him Is to Love Him" coming out. I didn't even know who had the record. 'Cause I didn't know anything about records, man, living in Fargo. But I told Serempa, "Bob, that is a smash." And the first time I played it, we had calls you couldn't believe, and he said, "Really? It's so...you know..." I said, "Really, it's the kind you hate."

Bobby Dale: He had an ear for hits.

Serempa was a good friend of Bill Stewart, and Bill Stewart was the man for Todd Storz, and all the Storz stations, so I mean this guy was literally a god. He could put it on in Minneapolis/St. Paul and the new WDGY and they would add it in New Orleans, and Kansas City, and wherever else Storz had stations. 'Cause you could sit there in Fargo and play it until you died of old age and it wouldn't matter, you know. But I knew that Serempa was tight with Bill Stewart, and I said, "Hey, you're not lying to him, man." So that's what happened.

You went from Fargo to Omaha, to KOIL, replacing Gary Owens.

Yes. Are you going to get into the dark side of it at all? Okay, for instance, when I worked for Don Burden in '59 at KOIL, he opened a station in Denver, and the Top 40 station there was big, big, big, and he was not having much luck, but they had a gimmick where they had a toilet flush, and you could call up and say, "Hey I want to flush down the kids from South High." They'd say, "Hey, grab the chain," and they'd pull it, man.

So Don Burden started to tape them. He brought the tapes back to Omaha and I heard the tape and I can still remember—like they would play a record called "Boo Boo Stick Beat," and the jock would say, "You know how to do the Boo Boo Stick Beat? You take your stick out, you beat it, man."

We're all sitting in this meeting laughing. So anyway, he did all this taping, and Bill Stewart, who had blown his job with Todd Storz, now worked for Don Burden, and one Saturday, he said, "Come on, we're going out drinking, Bobby." And he had these packages of tapes. But they were addressed to the seven members of the FCC, and we went down to the Post Office, and he said, "You take these in, and you get them registered, get a receipt, and make sure that the people they are to are mailed them, blah, blah, blah." So I did it, man. I didn't pay any attention to what was going on. But that was the end of that [Top 40] station in Denver.

From KOIL, you were hired by Crowell-Collier and wound up working at all three stations they owned.

I went to KDWB in Minneapolis in January of 1960, then to KFWB in Los Angeles in '61 and '62.

Was L.A. too big a jump for you?

Well, it was not a good way [of] going in there, crossing a picket line, man. But see, here's how it was supposed to work: I was going to go do B. Mitchel Reed's show, B. Mitchel went to Minneapolis to do my show; which was just a fancy way of trying to get around it.

And then you joined KEWB in Oakland in April 1963. After you left in August of 1964, Robert W. Morgan joined. Your style reminds me of his: improvisational humor, rather than one-liners or sound effects.

I don't know Robert, but I think he's absolutely one of the top jocks I ever heard in my life.

You know, it's funny, because Don French hired me for Crowell-Collier,

Bobby Dale, the Liquidator

"Heat Wave" plays.

"That's 'Heat Wave' at Number 37 its first week on, Martha and the Vandellas from KEWB, Bobby Dale *(high-pitched tone)* at twenty-three minutes past two o'clock, and today and tomorrow will be the biggest days in appliance and furniture history, the largest liquidation sale ever held. By London Furniture Liquidators at their huge adjustment center at 5433 San Pablo Avenue in Oakland, the London Liquidators' huge center of *(begins to gag)* fire stock *(sputters a few nonsense syllables)*…that sure hurts. What's that? In retail overstock. I read this thing and I break up. Freight claims will be open *(into a W.C. Fields voice)* to the general public. *(Back to normal:)* $205,000 worth of doomed furniture, man—denied a last-minute reprieve, and it all goes today and tomorrow,

and they're open from 10 A.M. to 12 midnight. A few of the values, large lamps at $1.44, pole lamps at $3.84, odd dinette chairs at three dollars, and they're odd, I'll tell you that *(sound of getting hit by someone)*. Chests, night stands and tables from $2, living rooms $58, bedrooms $54, TVs $98, refrigerators $122, lampshades a dime *(chuckles)*. You need those for the party tonight, 'Oh, yes, you look groovy.'"

Short jingle plays.

"At twenty-four minutes now past two o'clock, we're unveiling the brand-new Fab 40 folder; this is Number 36, from Ben E. King, 29 last week. Somebody must've *returned* their records, man. *(Mutters)* Don't feel bad, Ben E. Later on, we'll play 'Spanish Harlem.'"

"I Who Have Nothing" plays.

159

"Emperor" Hudson

and like once a week, an engineer would telescope half an hour of your show and send that tape to Chuck Blore in Los Angeles. So one morning, when I came to work at KEWB, Don French called me into the office and said, "I want you to see this," and handed me this letter. And it said, "Dear Don, This man, Bobby Dale, without a doubt, is the worst disc jockey I've ever heard in my life." And I'm looking at Don, and I said, "Jesus, thanks, man." He said, "Bobby, I wouldn't have shown it to you if I didn't know the man was wrong."

So Chuck Blore came to town, and we went out to dinner, and about three months later, Don showed me a letter, again from Chuck Blore. "This guy's just fabulous. He keeps trailing off and I can't hear what he's saying, but I *want* to hear what he's saying, so I'm leaning closer to the radio."

You do sometimes mutter.

Especially when I did all-night shows. But, unfortunately, you start working it as a gimmick, and then, of course, it no longer works.

From KEWB, you went to KRLA.

KRLA was always in competition to get KFWB, and they would do pretty good. When I was there they had Charlie O'Donnell, who's [the announcer] on *Wheel of Fortune* now, Casey, "Emperor" Hudson in the morning, and Dave Hull, who I'd never even heard of, 'cause radio is such a local thing, that when I went to L.A. they said, "Oh man, wait'll you hear this. 'The Hullabalooer.'" The first night I went to work was right after the first Beatles concert, in August of '64, and there were kids everywhere trying to get in to see Hull, you know. And they're all giving me dirty looks. But Hull said, "Hey, this is one of life's truly great jocks." I said, "Jeez, I didn't know you had heard me." He said, "I haven't. But it doesn't matter."

You left in April of '65, and Don French hired you again for KEWB, which was on the ropes at the time.

They were terrible. Then, after I'd been fired, I went to KFRC, which was middle of the road then; it was a poor man's KSFO [KSFO, a sister station of KMPC in Los Angeles, was a "personality" MOR station that billed itself as "The World's Greatest Radio Station"].

And then along came Bill Drake to apply "Boss Radio" to KFRC. Did he know your work?

No, in fact, the only reason that I was kept on KFRC, I'm sure, is that [I was] the only one whose name was recognizable at that time. I was the first jock on the air when Drake started his countdown, top three hundred down to Number One. I'll never forget one thing, man. I came out of a newscast with "Tequila." He said, "I don't know." I said, "What, you don't think it's upbeat?" He said, "No, but it's an instrumental." And I said, "Oh my god, I thought it was a hit record. I mean, you think people really go buy records and say, 'Don't give me that instrumental. Call me when it gets lyrics'?"

The formatted stations all had restricted lists, things you could play only during certain dayparts. When I was doing the all-night show, and this was Thanksgiving time of the first year they were on, the Batphone rang, the 450,000-watt goddamn bulb went off like an atom bomb—*Boom*. And I pick it up and it's one of his soldiers, Bill Watson, and he wanted to know why, at twenty minutes to two, I was playing the Monkees' "I'm a Believer," because it was on our restricted list. And I said, "Well, Bill, let me refer you to memo 27893 from [KFRC program director] Tom Rounds: 'Due to the holidays, and the fact that school is closed, the restricted list has been lifted.'" And there's this long pause, and he said, "Okay, I'll get back to you." Ten minutes later, the phone rings and it's Tom Rounds saying, "What the fuck's going on, man? What happened?" And I said, "Bill Watson called and wanted to know why I was playing 'I'm a Believer' by the Monkees." He said, "Bobby, tell me you're kidding." I said, "No, man." He said, "Okay, I'm going back to bed, man, and maybe I'll never get up."

I thought you accommodated the format, yet managed to be yourself.

Yeah, but look at guys like Dr. Donald Rose, man, I mean, Jesus, just an incredible jock. I couldn't believe the guy when I heard him. I said, "Where's this guy been?" [And] Robert W. Morgan...but for me, I couldn't do it, and I don't really know why...Maybe I just got too used to doing things my own way. They'd add maybe five records a week to the Top 30, and I'd get this call from Tom Rounds: "Bobby, do you know you played all five of the new records in a half hour?" I said, "Man, I was *hungry!*"

Maybe you liked the music too much to have to fit it into the format—like when you had to do so much of your stuff over the intros.

It was like with "Reach Out I'll Be There." I said, "Man, when I hear someone talking over that goddamn record, it's all I can do to keep from driving over to the station and shooting them." Jesus, you're taking something that somebody in the studio really worked on to get this whole impact, and *blab, blab, blab, blab, blab*. My favorite is the Martha and the Vandellas song that had like a twenty-four second intro, and somebody was on there, man, and they were running out of things to say.

That policy is what started—to show you the impact the man had—the records started to come out with like 0:08, 0:12—the length of the intro—

on the label. And one day I said to him, "What happens if we have five records and they don't have any instrumental openings?" He said, "That's what I love about you, Bobby. You worry about the big things." I said, "Well, these things keep me awake nights."

One night, the Supremes were in town at the Venetian Room [at the Fairmont Hotel], and we were at a little reception or party after, and Tom Rounds came up to me and said, "Bobby, I'll give you $50 if you'll crack an amyl nitrate under Drake's nose." So there's Drake standing over there, and I said, "Bill." "Bobby"—and I went, *Bam!* and he went, "What the fuck…" and I turned around, and Tom Rounds said, "Oh, Jesus, I don't believe it, I don't believe it." And he was just praying I wouldn't say, "Tom Rounds told me to do it." I never got the $50 from that bastard.

From KFRC, you went to KSFO, where, legend has it, you were on the all-night shift in '67 or so when you did a show on LSD…

Which night?

…and had to be carried out on a stretcher…

Nah. I passed out on the air once, but that was from lack of sleep, during football season, playing cards with Tom and Raechel [Donahue] and Judy Briscoll's sister Barbara.

You had to do your own news on the all-night show, and I kept getting these calls from people saying, "Man, you're really funny tonight." And I said, "Well, I'm not trying to be." So I go in for the 3 A.M. news, and I was so out of it that when the news played, all I had was one little sports story, and I said, "Arnold Palmer shot a 69 in the L.A. Open." I said, "That's interesting," and they cut me off the air and went to music, and they called the relief man. He lived about three blocks away, and he came down and you know who was there, Norma, my current wife who I'm separated from. But she had come down to the station to see me, and she took me home to her house. I walked outside of the hotel, the Fairmont, and I fell right off the goddamn sidewalk. And Al Newman, the program director, was convinced I was drunk. He had the tape the next day. I said, "Al, believe me, I've never drunk anything on the air."

I had these diet pills, Desbutals, and they were yellow and blue. The yellow was Methedrine, and the blue was Valium. Well, the meth didn't do anything, but the Valium sure did. I would be like pouring coffee and I would like…*(He mimes missing the cup)*. I was just like a drunk. Just exactly like a drunk.

But you went back on the air there?

Oh, yeah. In fact, they moved me to 8 to midnight.

But I can tell you the craziest thing I ever did, in Omaha. They had a

Labor Day weekend safe driving promo going, and they had a crane in an empty parking lot on a busy street. Suspended from the crane was a plat-form with a car on it. And in the car was a disc jockey. He lived in this car I don't know how many days and nights, but I went out one Saturday night and I had been drinking, of course, and when I got back to my apart-ment, I wasn't tired, and I said, "Screw it, I'm going to go see Jim." So I got a cab, went down, climbed forty feet up the crane, swung over on the platform, and went up and banged on the window. And this poor guy, he jumped up so goddamn fast he smacked his head. And I said, "Jim, can you give me a ride home?"

Don MacKinnon: "Beyond belief."

And he had a six-pack. I was so out of it, he had to call the manager. He said, "I hate to tell you this, but Bobby Dale is here." He said, "What do you mean? How can he be up there?" "He climbed up there." And by then I had fallen asleep.

On Monday mornings they always had those sales meetings, and Don Burden would come and he would scream at everybody. I was on the air and I heard this roar of laughter, and then Burden opened the door and said, "You're really a fuckin' crazy motherfucker." Then he started laughing, and he said, "God, I don't believe you."

DON MACKINNON: "BEYOND BELIEF"

In 1994, Don Barrett, a veteran Southern California broadcaster and pro-grammer, compiled a book, *Los Angeles Radio People*, that profiled disc jock-eys from 1957 to date. In that book, he invited votes from readers—mainly radio industry types—for their ten favorite disc jockeys.

In volume two of the book, published in 1997, Barrett reported the results. More than 230 disc jockeys received votes, he said, and the "Top Ten Los Angeles Disc Jockeys between 1957-97" were:

1. Gary Owens
2. The Real Don Steele
3. Robert W. Morgan
4. Bill Ballance
5. B. Mitchel Reed
6. Rick Dees
7. Dick Whittington
8. Charlie Tuna

"I made a noise like an egg."

9. Emperor Bob Hudson

10. Dave Hull

I have no argument with the poll—especially since I never lived in Los Angeles—but I'm certain that the list would have included one Don MacKinnon, had he not died in 1965 at age thirty-two. And there's no telling how high in the rankings he would have landed. He had worked only four years in Los Angeles, at KABC in 1960, at KLAC from 1963 to 1964, and at KFWB until June the following year, when, one night, his sports car plunged off the road in Malibu, near his home. His brother, Doug, said he was returning from a personal appearance.

In his brief career, he impressed some of the best as one of the best. Don Imus has often said that he was inspired to get into radio "by listening to a DJ named Don MacKinnon."

"MacKinnon, to me, was beyond belief," says Robert W. Morgan. "I had never heard anything like that. I had never heard anything like Gary Owens, either, but MacKinnon had this free-form to him. You never knew where he was going."

Owens himself calls MacKinnon one of the all-time greats, and he, too, never knew where MacKinnon was going. One time, when they were still at KEWB in Oakland, they were walking just outside the station's building on Franklin Street. "All of a sudden, Don jumped into this fountain and started splashing around," Owens relates. "He was wild." (MacKinnon worked at the Chuck Blore-programmed KEWB and also logged time and temperatures at KDEO in San Diego and KROY in Sacramento.)

Born in Yonkers, New York, Don moved with his family to Des Moines when he was fifteen. He caught the radio bug from older brother Doug,

Radio Nightmare

One April Fool's Day, staffers at WIBG in Philadelphia conspired to drive star DJ Hy Lit to madness. While Lit did his show, another DJ, set up in an auxiliary studio, was actually on the air, subbing for Lit.

As Lit tells it, "I was on the air, but I wasn't really on the air...I was preempted and I was on by myself, and every few minutes somebody'd walk in and use a curse word. A record would be spinning and all of a sudden a guy would walk in and take it off and say, 'I need this record.' I had tears in my eyes! They locked me in the studio and they'd set the wastebasket on fire. And when they told me [that I wasn't on the air], I wasn't very happy about it."

Lit was apparently no stranger to near-nightmarish situations. He even began with one at one of his first radio jobs. "I walked into WHAT and the guy said, 'What're you here for?' and I said I'd like to do something around the station, and he said, 'You're on in five minutes.'" And he was.

who was an engineer at KIOA in Des Moines, and got a DJ job there in 1957. From there, he made one big leap: to Los Angeles.

"Don MacKinnon," says Chuck Blore, "was the greatest who ever, ever lived." Blore had a policy at the stations he programmed or consulted for: Air personalities not only had to do preparation for their shows, they had to write out their bits and submit them to the program director before going on the air. As Blore recalls, "After [MacKinnon] was with KEWB for three or four months, the program director, Don French, called me and said, 'We're putting handcuffs on this guy, and they don't belong. He's just too damn clever. We've got to just let him go.' And I said, 'Aw, bullshit,' and Don went ahead and told him, 'Okay, tomorrow, just go in there and wing it.' And he did this in spite of what I had said, and then he sent me two airchecks, one done my way, and one done Don MacKinnon's way, and from that moment on, he did it Don's way. But he was the only one of all the DJs at all the stations who was not required to bring in that preparation. And, boy, was he good. He was the greatest."

What made MacKinnon stand out? It's hard to say—even with the help of an aircheck. Many of the things he did—one liners, drop-ins, voices—were done by other DJs. But MacKinnon also put his heart into commercial copy, and invented jokes and bits designed to lead listeners into commercials. He had no fear; he played strange musical bits and sound bites ("Shut the cave door and back to Pygmy country!"), and, in the middle of whatever he was saying or reading, might break into song, or switch accents, or evoke Cary Grant with just one word ("Judy…") or become an ultra-bored jazzer. He clearly liked to surprise; to keep 'em guessing, laughing, and, most of all, listening.

Here's a sample. It's 1965, and MacKinnon is starting his show on KFWB with "Nowhere to Run." As it fades, he comes on, with a forceful, Slavic accent, "Goot afternoon, or, as they say in Spanish, bueno afternoon. This is the famous Don MacKinnon Program on KFW (beep) B, at one minute past 12."

A piece of music—the kind heard under a cavalry brigade in a western movie—comes on under him. He lets it play awhile, then mutters, "My theme song. Big deal, huh?"

After a song and a jingle, he announces, "I do impersonations. Yesterday I was selling eggs for Ralph's, I made a noise like an egg, a chicken; today I'm gonna sell you some choice beef, and a little while later I'll make a noise like choice beef." He does his spiel about the supermarket's meat department, then lets out a long *mooooo.*

Before KFWB, MacKinnon did mornings on sister KEWB in Oakland, California.

A stern-sounding man comes on: "That'll be quite enough." But MacKinnon continues the moo, over the beginning of "Papa-Oom-Mow-Mow" and at its conclusion.

"Those are the Rivingtons, flashing back to 19…what a year 1960 was, huh? I'll never forget that. I had a little go-cart and I drove it into a pole. That was terrible. Contusions all over the place. Eight minutes past 12…"

A dramatically read announcement about a song that the Famous Don MacKinnon predicts will make the Fabulous Forty leads into a Pepsi jingle. Another song later, MacKinnon says, "This morning, you got up early, right? And you had your breakfast cereal. Well, it's afternoon now, so it's time for our afternoon cereal."

Again, a taped voice comes on: "Oh, no, wow, oh, *no*," but MacKinnon rides over it, saying, "In the afternoon, you'll want cereal. Listen to this guy and he'll tell you about it."

It's a commercial for ABC's afternoon *serials*.

Even a simple intro for a song gets a twist. "Number 11 on the Fabulous Forty survey at KFWB, 'Little Things' by Bobby Goldsboro. Stand by for a large grunt from me."

Out of "Mrs. Brown You've Got a Lovely Daughter," he informs listeners that Mrs. Brown herself is a guest in the studio. "Mrs. Brown, can you fix me up with your daughter?"

Annoyed woman's voice: "Why don't you clam up and play a record?"

"I got a better idea. Why don't *you* clam up and *I'll* play a commercial, how's that?"

In his second hour, he plays "Go Now" by the Moody Blues, then asks, "Would you like to hear the brand-new release by the Moody Blues? Huh? It's a fantastic song…it's called 'Ding Dong! Yes, Got the Tomatoes, Lady!'" Three or four seconds of nonsense sounds ensue.

Next, he masterfully ties "Do the Freddie" by Freddie and the Dreamers into a mock offer to teach the Freddie to a group of visitors, and then, before we know it, to a commercial for slippers.

A couple of tunes later, he's recapping "Do You Love Me." "A KFWB flashback…that one goes 'way back to about 1929. That was the year of the Army leggings which, you know, didn't really do anything for your ankles…" and on into a weather forecast and, as the aircheck ends, who knows where next?

No one could ever guess. And, tragically, no one ever would.

Bill Drake:
He ordered
"more music."

Chapter

Big Boss Man

Bill Drake is doing the Twist. Or maybe he's just hiding from somebody. It's hard to tell from his photo on the cover of that classic album, *Twist to Radio KYA*. At any rate, he's crouched over, his fists are clenched, and he's smiling, knowing full well that he'll look no sillier than all the other jocks—including East Coast emigres Peter Tripp, Bobby Mitchell, and Tom Donahue—pretending to be doing the trendy dance.

Just one thing: Drake's hair is a flat-top, and, here in swingin' San Francisco in 1962, that won't do. Drake had an excuse. The young native of Donaldsville, Georgia, had just arrived from Atlanta, where he'd been program director of WAKE. When the owner, Bartell, sold the station, Drake and WAKE's Manager, Jane Swain, were transferred to big sister KYA, where Drake—real name Phil Yarborough—would double as PD and morning disc jockey.

Drake struck his new charges as a square. It wasn't just the crewcut. Norman Davis, who would soon lose his DJ shift, recalls: "We knew we were in trouble the day he walked in the door. He looked like a real hick; he had a crewcut and he wore a tweed jacket, and he was carrying books that said, 'Gimmicks,' and a formattic book, which we were not used to." Davis was shuffled off to the newsroom when Churchill Broadcasting purchased KYA in 1962 and imported a couple of DJs from its Buffalo station, WKBW. One of them was Tommy Saunders, who replaced Davis. Saunders remembers Drake keeping a collection of liners—station promotional slogans—in a recipe box.

But if Drake was less than flashy—both on and off the air—he knew what he was doing with those books and boxes. He was a student of commercial radio, and, studious as a scientist, he was preparing to change the

Drake (third from left) does the Twist in 1962.

face—and, more importantly, the sound—of Top 40 radio.

There are those who will argue that WABC in New York in the early sixties was the most influential of all Top 40 stations. Others will be just as vocal for Chuck Blore's KFWB, or Gordon McLendon's KLIF in Dallas. Over the years, WLS in Chicago, KQV in Pittsburgh, Scott Shannon's WMAK in Nashville, and Drake's KFRC in San Francisco all got radio programmers' tape recorders rolling. It's a debate that's about as easy to referee as tag-team wrestling. I will, instead, defer to Shannon, who, as a young fan of radio, listened to many stations and collected airchecks. (See Chapter Eighteen for a visit with Shannon.) As a programmer and air talent—one who, incidentally, has never been employed by Drake, but has worked for a couple of "Drake clones"—he can bring some professional objectivity to the table.

"KHJ, to me, was the finest Top 40 station of all time," he says. "Anybody who grew up in San Francisco or New York or Chicago will argue with you. But for second place I'd go with WLS in Chicago, then WABC, and then KFRC. But KHJ was the most polished. It was an incredibly disciplined, tight-fisted Top 40 station laced with high-profile personalities. Few understood how that worked; even fewer knew how to combine the two."

Ron Jacobs, KHJ's first program director, knew. "What KHJ was all about," he says, "was streamlining it down to the essentials and shifting the music-to-talk ratio, and building up an overall station image." Specifically, the streamlining meant cutting out what Drake considered clutter: extraneous talk, long jingles, and even commercials. Since KHJ wasn't selling that much time when the Drake/Jacobs crew took over, it was easy to set a limit of twelve commercial minutes an hour, six below the FCC limit. As for image: Drake aimed squarely at a demographic target of eighteen-to-thirty-four year-olds; young, active people ("The Get Set, we call them," said Gene Chenault, the station owner who helped launch Drake's career and became his business partner). If Drake had only one goal, it was to do everything he could to keep listeners from tuning out. Besides the clutter-cutting, he set newscasts away from the traditional top and bottom of the hour, or the five-minutes-before the hour trick that early Top 40 pioneers tried. His newscasts were at twenty minutes before and/or after the hour, allowing for "more music" sweeps of as long as forty minutes.

"More music" was the key promise. Drake would come to be attacked for eliminating personality.

"Bill's the guy who, along with Mr. Gene Chenault, hijacked KHJ from RKO, hired us all and let us do our thing—as long as our thing wasn't longer than six seconds."—*Robert W. Morgan, emceeing the KHJ twenty-fifth anniversary reunion dinner in Los Angeles, 1990*

Drake says he had no quarrel with personality, however. "I took the attitude, if the personality is there, fine. But there's a vast difference [between] a guy who's a personality and a guy that just talks a lot. And I said, 'If you're going to say nothing anyway, then say it in as little time as possible.'"

Contrary to popular industry belief, Drake jocks were not ordered to confine their talking—beyond the basics of time, song title, and call letters—to the instrumental introductions of records. Says Jacobs: "The main thing was, you'd better have something good to fucking say and you'd better say it in the cleanest, quickest manner.

"There were specific things. The records were played at :03, :07, :11. Every song's preceded [by] a three-second a capella jingle. If you had something to say, you could talk up to the vocal." If not, it was better to let the music play. As Jacobs noted, echoing Bobby Dale's sentiments: "Phil Spector went into the studio with nine pianos and made this great thing with the Righteous Brothers, and millions of people are buying it, and you'd better have a helluva lot to say for twenty seconds to keep up with something that's had all this talent put into it, and which has already proven itself."

Those three-second jingles were part of the revolution. Where many stations had used jingles running as long as thirty and forty-five seconds just to introduce news or weather, now listeners heard the elegant harmonies of the Johnny Mann Singers in three- to five second bursts:

"KHJ…Weather!"

The placement of a quickie KHJ jingle before each record was a key element of what Drake called "forward momentum." Bill Watson, who became one of Drake's national program directors, traveling to various stations to help install and oversee the format, said, Drake insisted on building "the firmest foundation" at each of his stations. "That means all the basics, everything tight, no dead air, everything kick-ass, perfect music. Everything perfect, perfect, perfect. A forward momentum with production, and everybody can just shut up until you do that."

In pursuit of perfect music, and the perfect rotation, or frequency of airplay per record, Drake adopted a thirty-song playlist. He was not the first. Programmers dating back to Todd Storz shortened playlists, and, according to Bill Gavin, "It was not Bill Drake or Rick Sklar or Sam Holman [the PD

Ron Jacobs

One of Jacobs' series of Cruisin' albums.

169

Ron Jacobs (right) with the King and an engineer.

at WABC in their heyday in the early sixties] who started the thing. It was around 1959 or 1960 that Clint Churchill, owner-manager of WKBW-Buffalo, cut his playlist to a Top 30 plus a very limited number of picks. Clint later bought KYA and established his tight list there. I was one of many who predicted that his system would fail, but it turned out to be a resounding success. Clint's program director when he took over KYA was Bill Drake."

Drake recalls KYA offering a "Swingin' 60" survey when he arrived, and thinking it unwieldy. "A lot of the stuff just weren't hits. It was a thing of really just tightening the damn thing up. And I took the theory too, [of] how long do people listen to the radio? I also had the idea that I'd rather be playing the thirtieth worst record than the sixtieth."

At KHJ, Drake was known to frown on songs he considered to be too long. As Boss Radio began to live up to its name, Drake exercised increasing power over the actual production of some records. "Drake was such an arrogant son of a bitch," says Robert W. Morgan. "He was so good; I liked him so much, but when the Fifth Dimension came out with 'Aquarius,' you hear that as a programmer, what are you going to do? You hear the first eight bars and say, 'Get that son of a bitch on the air!' It was 3:40 long. Drake told Bones [Howe], the producer, 'Get it under 3:00 and we'll consider it.' So Bones brought in a 2:59 version and it went on. Bones later told me it was 3:23."

Sometimes, an artist could get by the screening process. Charlie Tuna tells about the time Brian Wilson of the Beach Boys called the station late one night in 1966. He was in his studio and had just finished work on the group's "Good Vibrations." Might KHJ like to be the first to play it? "Bands would cut a record on Tuesday," says Tuna, "and Wednesday they'd give us a tape."

Boss Radio—the single most influential station in the mid-sixties—got started in Fresno, California, the raisin capital of the world. There, in this flatland town in the San Joaquin Valley, almost exactly between San

Francisco and Los Angeles, two stations waged one of the bloodiest radio wars in the history of Top 40. In the end, the victor and the vanquished teamed up in Hollywood and, together, created "Boss Radio." The combatants in Fresno were Bill Drake and Ron Jacobs.

Drake had left San Francisco, where his work at KYA had drawn the attention of Gene Chenault, the owner of KYNO in Fresno. Chenault needed help. KYNO had monopolized the region, drawing about 60 percent of the radio audience, until 1962, when Ron Jacobs roared into town. Jacobs, a native of Hawaii, was vice president of Colgreens, a small broadcasting company that had purchased KMEN in San Bernardino and KMAK in Fresno.

Jacobs, who, like Chuck Blore, has a voice that made him more suited for off-air work, combined a passion for radio with a knack for promotion. At stations in Hawaii, he'd worked with Bill Gavin on *Lucky Lager Dance Time*; he'd had occasion to talk radio formatting with Mike Joseph, the consultant, and, as a DJ in 1957, he'd met Elvis Presley and his manager, the wily Colonel Tom Parker. "I'd had the advantage of working a systemized, disciplined thing with Gavin, I'd had Mike share all the format clocks with me, and then I had Colonel Parker, who was the living extension of P.T. Barnum, who taught me a lot about how you attract a crowd."

Frank Terry

Jacobs applied that knowledge in San Bernardino, where he staged various marathons and stunts to put KMEN on top of the ratings. His next assignment was Fresno. With Robert W. Morgan and Frank Terry, both future Boss Jocks, in his stable, Jacobs and KMAK put an end to KYNO's dominance of the market. "We started out with a one [percent] share," Morgan recalls. Originally, Jacobs himself took the morning DJ shift, but after a ratings book revealed that the irascible program director had a seven share, compared to afternoon man Morgan's thirty-seven, he did the right thing. "He took himself off the air," says Morgan. "He had a tremendous ego, but he's also very practical." KYNO, he recalls, was basically copying the Blore format. "We came in and did it better, and slicker, and funner, with better promos that were more exciting, and we sounded brand new compared to them."

But Chenault was not about to give in. He called in Drake, making the move to Fresno a little sweeter by throwing in a new Cadillac and getting him a consulting job at a station in nearby Stockton.

The war was on. "In Fresno," says Morgan, who'd come in from a stint with the U.S. Army, "that's when I learned about war. That's when I learned about competition, about doing anything that's necessary—fuck 'legal'—to kill somebody." "Drake and I battled through the whole summer of '63,"

171

says Jacobs, "and I didn't have the financial support." He recalls: "KMAK started a contest with a $1,500 cash jackpot. Before I parked in my garage, KYNO was on the air with a $2,000 prize. KMAK hid a 'Golden Key' worth $2,500; KYNO scattered duplicate keys all over town. We tailed Drake in unmarked cars with radio telephones, trying to catch him doing funny stuff at motels at 3 A.M." (They never did.)

Again, Jacobs put his disc jockeys through marathons. Frank Terry, a drummer, banged away for eighty-seven hours in a discount department store. "After about fourteen hours, I started falling asleep," he recalls, "and I'd need help from the good doctor to keep going. And pretty soon the other jocks would need some help from the good doctor."

KYNO came right back, Morgan recalls, with a "thon" of its own. "So Jacobs said, 'Fuck that, go get some sleeping pills. So we went over there, and man, it took us two days, and then I slipped some downers in [the rival DJ's] coffee. Put that fucker out like a *light*."

Ultimately, Drake and KYNO prevailed. "Drake started kicking ass with brilliant, brilliant promotions," Morgan concedes. And he had some formattic ideas. It was at KYNO, says Bill Watson (whom Jacobs hired to be PD in San Bernardino) that Drake came up with the idea of placing the station ID jingle in front of a record. Watson remembers his excitement the moment Jacobs told him about it. "I'm changing it tomorrow,"

Ian Whitcomb

Ian Whitcomb: He Turned Them Off

While KHJ embraced the Beach Boys, Sonny and Cher, Tiny Tim, the Byrds, the Mamas & the Papas, and many others, there were those who wound up on the short end of the boo-boo stick.

Ian Whitcomb, the English pop artist who had the hit "You Turn Me On" in 1965, believes he was blacklisted after an incident involving KHJ's sister station in San Diego, KGB. Whitcomb was performing at a concert being presented by KGB, and, just before going on, a stranger approached him and asked him to mention one "Lord Tim Hudson," who was in the audience. Being a good Brit, Whitcomb did, and Hudson sprang up to applause, while other audience members raised a British flag. When Whitcomb completed his performance and went backstage, he was accosted by Les Turpin, then KGB's program director. Lord Tim, it turned out, was a DJ from rival station KCBQ. Turpin was livid. "He said something like, 'You son of a bitch, you stupid asshole.' I said, 'Don't you dare talk to me like that ever. If you do it again, I shall pull your beard.' Sonny Bono was there, and he said, 'Cool it, man. He's important.' I just turned on my heels and walked off."

said Watson, "because that's *it*. It's momentum. It's not stuck around some-where in the middle of commercials like Chuck Blore had it."

Giving up the fight against Drake, Jacobs returned to Hawaii. Morgan hooked up with KROY in Sacramento, where he'd be heard, and hired, by Earl McDaniel for KEWB in Oakland. Drake, meanwhile, became partners with Chenault in a consulting firm and turned KGB in San Diego into a ratings success. The owner of KGB then recommended Drake-Chenault to the owner of RKO General, whose stations in Los Angeles and San Francisco were the weakest in its chain.

KHJ would be first. Going where the talent was, Drake hired Morgan from KEWB in Oakland, and Morgan suggested his buddy, the Real Don Steele. Drake also grabbed Gary Mack, one of his Fresno DJs, from crosstown KRLA. Morgan and Watson encouraged Jacobs to go for the PD job, and, after a meeting in Los Angeles, the two former rivals were a team.

Considering how streamlined it sounded, how custom-fit it seemed for the times and the temperament of the city—the mid-sixties, Hollywood—and how exacting and disciplined the "Boss Jocks" were, with Jacobs loud-ly preaching "PCM": Preparation, Concentration, Moderation—it's ironic that when "Boss Radio" made its debut in May 1965, it was rushed onto the air, ahead of schedule.

Drake and Jacobs had entered a Los Angeles whose pop scene was ruled by two stations, KRLA and KFWB. KRLA, in the early spring of 1965, had bypassed KFWB, with an impressive DJ lineup including "Emperor" Bob Hudson, Casey Kasem, Charlie O'Donnell, Dave "The Hullabalooer" Hull, Bob Eubanks, Dick Biondi, Bobby Dale, and Gary Mack.

KFWB had lost Chuck Blore two years before, it had gone through a debilitating strike in 1961, and its music director had been the target of a highly publicized payola investigation in 1964. And, although it continued to call itself "Number One in Los Angeles," it had been passed by KRLA, with the latter station's popular disc jockeys and connections to the Beatles. (It was largely through Eubanks's efforts that KRLA presented the Beatles in concert at the Hollywood Bowl in the fall of 1964.)

Still, KFWB had its own lineup of stars: Wink Martindale in the morn-ings, followed by Sam Riddle, Joe Yocam, Gene Weed, Bill Ballance, Roger Christian, and Larry McCormick. But when KHJ beckoned, Riddle and Christian were off to become "Boss Jocks."

Nobody much cared for the phrase "Boss Radio." But, before Drake and Jacobs had assumed hands-on leadership of the station, KHJ had directed Clancy Imislund, the promotion director (who, along with Music Director Betty Breneman, was the only holdover from the old KHJ), to buy newspaper ads and put up billboards touting the new format. "I didn't know what the hell to put on it, and we were ranked about fifteenth in the market, so you couldn't say 'Number One'…So, 'Boss Radio.' Now, that *sounds* like you're Number One, but you're not," said Imislund. He recalls Jacobs responding to the phrase: "Aw, *man*, that shit's 1960, man!"

Datedness became a moot point when, on Monday, May 3, a week before the planned switchover to Top 40, Morgan heard KFWB calling itself "Boss Radio" and promising, "the Boss Jocks are coming to KFWB." It felt like Fresno all over again. Jacobs huddled with Drake and KHJ General Manager Ken DeVaney, and they decided to counter-attack by putting their "Boss Radio" on the air that day—at 3:00, with the Real Don Steele. The staff had four hours to get the format on the air. Jacobs used KRLA's "Tunedex" survey to make up KHJ's first playlist, then dispatched Betty Breneman to Wallich's Music City at Sunset and Vine to buy the records. "It was hysterical," Breneman says. "Bill sent me down in his black limousine."

At 3:00 sharp, the voice of Bill Drake, who'd voice many of his stations' spoken IDs, hit the air: "Ladies and gentlemen, presenting the *Real Don Steele Show*…with a sneak preview of the all-new Boss Radio, on…KHJ, Los Angeles." Over the intro to "Dancing in the Streets," Steele shouted, "It's three o'clock in Los Angeles!" Martha Reeves started calling out, and a station was born. KHJ, whose call letters, back in the twenties, stood for "kindness, happiness, joy," now meant "boss." And Ron Jacobs would embrace that antiquated word. In fact, three weeks into the format, he heard Dave Diamond doing the standard station ID: "KHJ, Los Angeles," and decided that, from that moment on, it'd be "Boss Angeles."

"We all tried to do a flawless execution of this format," Gary Mack (noon to 3) told the assembled crowd at the KHJ silver anniversary reunion. "Probably it was the result of the deep conversations we would have with Ron Jacobs on the hot line." He recounted a typical call:

Ring…

Jacobs: "How's it goin', man?"

Mack: "Fine."

Jacobs: "Tighten up!"

Click.

The word was that the disc jockeys lived in fear of what they called "the Batphone"; that Drake had hookups to all the stations he programmed; that he somehow managed to listen to them all, around the clock, and if something was just the eentsy-weentsiest bit off, a blinding light would go off in the offending DJ's booth, and he'd have hell to pay. "I heard one rumor," says Jacobs, "where if a jock talked more than twelve seconds, there'd be an electric jolt in his chair."

Not quite. Jacobs explains: "Drake did have a line where he could call in and listen to a station. But if he heard something he didn't like, he'd call Watson, and Watson would come down on the program directors."

Within weeks of its debut, programmers throughout the country were listening to tapes of the new KHJ, and as soon as the first ratings came out and crowned KHJ the top of the pop crop, those programmers began ordering up "Boss Radio"-styled jingles and reconfiguring their "hot clocks."

Bill Drake, who, as Morgan would note at the twenty-fifth anniversary, "was the only guy who never had to copy the Drake format," replicated the formula at one RKO station after another, in San Francisco, Boston, Detroit, and Memphis. For each station, he sought disc jockeys who could run shows under his system. "Basically," he said, "you look for voice and pacing, and that sort of stuff, and board work. Because I always felt if the guy had that, then we could add enough of a stage and a backdrop for him. And then you hoped that some personality would come out on top of that. Sometimes you were lucky…"—the quintessential Drake jocks were, of course, Steele and Morgan—"and," he added, "I always loved Bobby Mitchell…but most times you weren't."

Dave Diamond, at KHJ's anniversary bash, told about having his audition tape rejected by Drake, then traveling from Denver to Los Angeles to deliver a new tape to the man himself, and getting hired after a long day and night of drinking. Gary Mack, Howard Clark, and others have also told of job interviews conducted at various taverns. "Well," Drake reasoned, "you hang out with [a prospective DJ]. Basically, you'd already heard him, and then you wanted to get him out of a business environment or an office. People are very guarded in situations like that. So you get them out and talk and this, that, and the other, and you just sort of see where they're at. Because it also has to be a thing of compatibility. You've got to know whether a guy is going to go nuts on you or what."

Although some invariably did, Drake's jocks—and programming lieutenants—worked their magic from market to market. The only stumbling block would be New York, where AM dominated the market with an MOR format, and where WABC and WMCA had the Top 40 field locked up. Handed WOR-FM, Drake tried a mix of Top 40 and oldies and, later, album cuts, to mixed reviews. WABC's "Cousin Brucie" Morrow listened in. "To me, what's wrong with consultants is that they're strangers, they're out-of-towners. They might know their area….Where did Drake come from? Georgia? He's a very, very smart guy, but I don't think he understood

DEWAR'S PROFILES
(Pronounced Do-ers "White Label")

BILL DRAKE

HOME: Bel Air, California

AGE: 35

PROFESSION: Designs the format for pop music programs on radio stations around the country.

HOBBIES: Pool. Monitoring his radio stations.

LAST BOOK READ: "The Godfather."

LAST ACCOMPLISHMENT: Created "Solid Gold Rock and Roll" and "Hit Parade 71," two of the most successful musical formats on radio today.

QUOTE: "You can't dismiss the rock groups as 'far out'. The fact that their music succeeds, suggests that their ideas are widely circulated and probably accepted by a lot of people. I think more attention should be paid to them. Listening might give everybody a better idea about what's on young people's minds."

PROFILE: Intuitive. Shrewd. Disarmingly casual. His sometimes abrasive manner has helped make him the most powerful force in broadcast rock.

SCOTCH: Dewar's "White Label"

Authentic. There are more than a thousand ways to blend whiskies in Scotland, but few are authentic enough for Dewar's "White Label." The quality standards we set down in 1846 have never varied. Into each drop goes only the finest whiskies from the Highlands, the Lowlands, the Hebrides. *Dewar's never varies.*

Bill Drake

New York, I don't think he understood the New York mentality. Every market has its own individual spirit and feeling."

WOR-FM, Drake noted, "eventually did extremely well, but when we went in there, the penetration of FM sets in New York was about 40 percent." (By the end of 1968, WOR-FM was being counted as one of the industry's more notable ratings successes, along with WDVR in Philadelphia and KOST in Los Angeles.)

Beyond the RKO chain, Drake-Chenault were free to try their magic for other clients. But many stations chose to copy Drake without having to hire him. "Well, that's a part of the business," says Drake, who lists, as his own influences, the pioneers McLendon and Storz. "We've all been known to borrow a bit of this and a bit of that from other stations. I mean, that's what it was all about. That's how the evolution occurred."

He did find some of the copiers amusing. "A guy would come in and listen and tape us, and it was so stupid. He'd go back, and they'd put the jingles going in the commercial slots instead of in front of the records. We used to think that was hilarious. They would list all of the ingredients that we had, and then they'd put them all in the wrong place!"

At the end of 1966, Bill Gavin took note of the copying, and predicted more to come. "One of the big things in 1967 will probably be the spread of a Bill Drake type format among Top 40 operations," Gavin wrote. "Several stations in major markets are already imitating it—or trying to. KHJ-Los Angeles is probably the most monitored and air-checked station in the U.S. today.

"Imitation is a compliment, and Bill Drake deserves it. KFRC and KHJ are strong rating contenders and their gross revenues have increased sharply. But imitators all too often miss the point. The smooth sound of the Drake format sounds easy to duplicate, but it isn't. It doesn't tell you, for instance, the hours and days that each DJ has spent in the production room. It doesn't show the unrelenting monitoring and analysis of every minute detail—inflection, pauses, pace, voice tone, voice and record overlaps, cuing and segues, etc."

However, Gavin warned, "In spite of his success…we cannot agree that Bill Drake has found the way to bring Top 40 radio back into a dominant

Number One position in a major market. It is not a question of 'personality' radio versus 'time 'n' temp.' It is mainly a question of entertainment values, and the kind of a station image with which a mass audience can readily identify. In the final countdown, it could be that Bill Drake's biggest contribution will be his challenge to his competitors that their 'personalities' had better have something worth saying and know how to say it."

For more than a year, Gavin had been reporting Top 40's ratings decline in some key markets—how country, R&B, talk, and other formats were chipping away at Top 40 shares, and how the continuing "shrinkage of singles sales volume" was hurting the format. While young adults were buying albums, singles were being bought largely by teenagers. Stations using only retail information for their playlists were in danger, then, of playing records appealing only to kids, and turning off the adult listeners they needed for advertising sales.

As much as he admired programmers like Drake and Mike Joseph, Gavin was beginning to wonder about such mantras as "play the hits." He wasn't alone. "Some Top 40 operators," he noted in 1966, "are growing away from one of the format's old rules: 'If you're playing the hits, play all the hits.' Today, more programmers are discriminating. 'Which hits shall I play?' and 'When shall we play them?' Top 40's, in some cases, are ruling out R&B and country sides until they are positively confirmed as Top 20 pop sellers. A few programmers are ruling out sides that they regard as appealing exclusively to the 'teenie boppers.' Most stations restrict certain rougher sides until after

The Young Scotsman

It was a case of radio typecasting when Bill Drake was invited to appear in a scotch distillery's advertising series, "Dewar's Profiles," in the early seventies, when he, Gene Chenault, and their programming lieutenants made their march through the RKO General stations.

Age: "33."

Profession: "Designs the format for pop music programs on radio stations around the country."

Hobbies: "Pool. Monitoring his radio stations."

Last Book Read: "*The Godfather.*"

Last Accomplishment: "Created 'Solid Gold Rock and Roll' and 'Hit Parade 71,' two of the most successful musical formats on radio today."

Profile: "Intuitive. Shrewd. Disarmingly casual. His sometimes abrasive manner has helped make him the most powerful force in broadcast rock."

Scotch: "Dewar's White Label."

6 P.M., and many have a special list of 'daytime extras'—smoother sounds to please adult ears."

Those who were simply playing whatever songs the record stores were reporting as big sellers, and airing them in a high rotation, might be causing "frequency irritation," Gavin wrote in 1967, driving away teens as well as young adults. The format could be in trouble, he advised, unless it "can offer enough that is new, different, and unexpected."

While some stations struggled, Drake rolled on. By 1968, KHJ was so dominant in Los Angeles that KFWB, "Color Radio," switched to an all-news format. KRLA, whose all-star DJ roster had turned over completely, began to automate part of its programming. As Drake-Chenault rolled through the country, Bill Drake's legend grew, with articles in *Time* and other magazines. And it was inevitable: he became a lanky punching bag for critics, ranging from rival programmers to champions of personality or free-form radio.

For some disc jockeys blessed with comic gifts, the Drake format was somewhere between a challenge and an impossibility. Dave Diamond found that out the hard way. Two months after the kickoff of "Boss Radio," he was out. "I didn't understand the format," he says now. "I'd been in Denver, at KBTR, and I had been a real personality DJ. When they hired me at KHJ, they told me it was going to be tight, but I didn't know how tight it was going to be."

The late "Emperor" Bob Hudson, who parlayed his comedy into several successful albums, worked on a wide variety of stations in Los Angeles, but knew where he didn't belong. Asked by *Los Angeles Radio People* how he wanted to be remembered, he replied: "I would like to be remembered as a man…who never succumbed to Bill Drake and his disciples, who erased story-telling from radio while cutting lyrics from songs in order to play more records per hour for all the Jacks and Jills who tuned out when their attention spans became taxed."

Pat O'Day, who, at KJR in Seattle, stressed personality and entertainment, blames Drake for depleting radio of a generation of potential personalities. "I understood what Drake was doing," he says. "I understood that he could go into an undisciplined station or an undisciplined market, and, purely with discipline, would win. But I felt that what he did was, in the long run, harmful to our industry, and a cop-out. I felt that if you trained your program directors and if you really worked to create talent, that radio could be more than a tight playlist and a capella jingles and tightly controlled jocks." On Drake stations, O'Day asserts, "There was a third dimension of radio—the dimension of imagination—that was not being employed. Oh, sure, you had Robert W. Morgan and you had Don Steele, and you had some pretty funny guys on the air. But when you took those funny guys away, his format was pretty sterile." The "devaluation of the personality" is what O'Day means by the "harm" the Drake format did to the industry. Even in the nineties, he says, "We have got such a dearth of strong, belly-to-belly communicators on the air, because they don't even know what the word 'communications' means."

Drake's rise to national prominence also did not sit well with Paul Drew, who'd worked alongside Drake in Atlanta in the late fifties and became program director at several RKO stations, including CKLW in the Detroit area and KFRC in San Francisco, and would ultimately replace Drake as RKO's vice president of programming. "Bill Drake got a lot of credit for a lot of things that maybe other people were responsible for," he says. "Ron Jacobs was and is one of the greatest radio program directors of all time." Boss Radio, he says, "was the creative, nutty mind of Ron Jacobs and the mechanical understanding of formattics of Bill Watson, and two exceptionally good talents, Robert W. Morgan and the Real Don Steele."

In 1973, Paul Drew was named program director of KHJ, and, soon afterward, Drake-Chenault and RKO were history. According to Bill Watson, the company brought in a new president, Bruce Johnson: "He called Bill Drake into his office and said, 'Why do we need Gene Chenault? Why do we need Bill Watson? And why don't you fly around the country instead of Bill Watson?' He didn't understand that Bill Drake sitting in Bel Air is more powerful than anything he could ever imagine, because Bill Drake is talking to people and making people function.

Paul Drew

"And so Drake said, 'You want me to separate myself from Gene Chenault and Bill Watson?' 'Yeah.' 'Okay. Well, I'm going to think about what you said, and I'll get back to you.'

"He left. He never returned."

Actually, said Drake, it was Chenault who introduced RKO to Bruce Johnson—whose father, incidentally, was a contractor who'd worked on both Drake's and Chenault's homes.

"Bruce," said Drake, "wanted to be his own guy. So he conspired to get rid of Chenault. And he called me in and offered me more money and this, that, and the other, but he wanted Chenault out." Drake recalls leaving the office without a word, gathering his troops and calling his company's attorney. "And I never spoke to the man again. And that's how we left."

Johnson, in a 1975 interview with Woody Goulart, who operates a web site devoted to Boss Radio, says things didn't happen quite that suddenly. Drake, Chenault, and his top staffers, he said, were transformed from consultants into RKO employees, so that they could deal more effectively with program directors. Drake staffers would now work for both RKO Radio and Drake-Chenault Enterprises. When, Johnson says, ratings declined and disputes over programming ensued, he began to feel that the Drake team was putting too much energy into non-RKO projects. It was then, he says, that he gave Drake his "us or them" ultimatum.

After Drake's exit from RKO, he and Chenault bought KIQQ-FM ("K-100"), grabbing Morgan and Steele as their anchors. But, according to some in the industry who helped launch KIQQ two years before the Drake-Chenault takeover, the station sounded like the pair's attempt at revenge on RKO. K100 didn't cover the city as well as KHJ, and, Drake notes, "again, we were a little early with what we were trying to do for FM as far as market penetration of sets." However, the station did well enough that, when Drake-Chenault sold it two years later, they made a handsome profit.

Drake and his partner continued to do well with various nationally syndicated programs and specials. Drake also continued to consult for radio stations, including, in 1990, KRTH ("K-Earth"), which was once KHJ-FM and had evolved into an oldies station. It was there that, in 1992, Robert W. Morgan and the Real Don Steele would reunite.

By then, KHJ—the AM—was gone. In the early seventies, it shifted musical emphasis, recalls Guy Zapoleon, a longtime KHJ fan who wound up working for its FM sister, KRTH. Under Drew, he says, "it was very obvious that the goal was to try to get more adult numbers, and the station was playing lots of Helen Reddy and John Denver." By the time it got back to the basics, under PD Gerry Peterson, competing formats and FM were on the rise. In 1980, it went country, and in 1986, KHJ signed off and converted into a Spanish-language station. And it was not "Capataz Radio, Noventa-Tres KHJ." But Boss Radio, as hundreds of thousands had come to know it, had actually ended a dozen years before, when the Real Don Steele and Robert W. Morgan left.

At KHJ's twenty-fifth anniversary reunion, they played Morgan's first farewell to the station in 1970, when he was leaving for a job in Chicago. "The last five and a half years have been the most gratifying and important of my life," he said. "And I'd like to say thank you to a lot of people, but it's impossible because of the format." And he laughed heartily.

THE REAL DON STEELE: GETTIN' WHERE HE'S GETTIN'

It happened at Martoni's, of course. The Real Don Steele and Robert W. Morgan were drinking at the Italian restaurant that drew big and small shots from the entertainment world and served as KHJ's unofficial watering hole.

Late in the evening, Morgan recalled, Mia Farrow walked in, flanked by bodyguards, and headed through a set of curtains into a private back room. A few minutes later, Frank Sinatra, similarly flanked, strode in, looked around, and hit the private room.

"Well," says Morgan, "Steele had to use the little boys' room, which is a few steps beyond the private room. So the Real Don Steele walks back there, he's weaving a lit-

The Real Don Steele: A fun devil.

tle bit, he's bouncing from wall to wall, and one unfortunate bounce took him right into the private dining room. I thought, 'Oh, my god, they're going to shoot him,' and I ran back there, and he spun around and *sat* right in Frank Sinatra's fettuccine. There's a stunned silence. The bodyguards jumped up, and Steele stood up and went into a chorus of 'Witchcraft.' Sinatra laughed and told his bodyguards to sit down." The Chairman of the Board would let the Boss Jock live.

His listeners were "fun devils," but he was the biggest fun devil of them all. The Real Don Steele was the real deal. When I first heard him, he was in his first major market: San Francisco/Oakland. But he was already so confident (or so steeped in his shtick, honed in Yakima, Washington, Omaha, Nebraska, and Portland, Oregon), that he came on the air as "your leader" and "the cooler ruler," someone who was "in charge now," and he pounded those phrases a couple dozen times in his very first hour. I know that because someone actually kept count, and I ran an item about it in a column I wrote for a local weekly. I came to be a fan and to be influenced by Steele, but, as the years rolled by, and he went on to triumphs in his home-town, Los Angeles, I turned out to be only one of many thousands.

A ball of energy, Steele's secret was that he wasn't just a screamer, or a fast talker, or a happy, positive voice, or a hipster. He combined all those elements into a package that amounted to a perfect gift for rock and roll radio listeners in Los Angeles (make that "Boss

AND TAKE THAT SINATRA GUY WITH YOU!

At the KHJ Silver Anniversary Reunion, Boss Jock Gary Mack asked Sal, the bartender at Martoni's, to stand up and take a bow. Emcee Robert W. Morgan then returned to the podium. "Stick around for the end of the show," he said, "when the Real Don Steele throws *Sal* out."

pop *pop*

Angeles") at that time (the mid-sixties) and in that time slot (3 to 6 P.M., the three hours leading into and through the drive home from work or the bus ride home from school). The Real Don Steele spelled euphoric relief, celebration, "life as a stone breeze, baby!"

A not exactly candid photo with Sonny & Cher.

And when he himself was about to escape from work—watch out. His "Fractious Friday" sign-off became must-hear radio in B.A., a romping, stomping, excited, barely decipherable good-bye cry of jubilation that somehow came off as a partying piece of rock and roll poetry, a high-gain paean to his beloved hometown. Over the honking Philip Upchurch Combo's "You Can't Sit Down," he'd shout out, "End of the mo for the Real Don Steele Show, Humble Harve is next to entertain us in that quest for adventure on a Fractious Friday in that neon fun jungle out there, and I'll be out there shoulder to shoulder with the rest of the thrill-

Sonny, No Rain

In the summer of 1965, Sonny Bono, on the eve of releasing the second single from Sonny and Cher (the first was a bomb), was having an "A" side/"B" side disagreement with Ahmet Ertegun, the president of their record company, Atlantic. Ertegun liked a Bono song, "It's Gonna Rain." Sonny thought a more recent composition, "I Got You Babe," was "solid gold waiting to happen."

To make his case, he says, he took an acetate copy of "Babe" to KHJ. "The DJs loved it and began playing it immediately," Bono recalled in his autobiography, *And the Beat Goes On.* "It was like a rocket launch. The station's switchboard lit up instantly. Within a week, the song was tops in L.A."

seekers, baby, we're gone get it on; we're gonna get ripped but don't get ripped *off*. Kick out the jams, get good mercy, we're all gonna do it, let's get to it! Lace-bay, Andre, What'd I Say, Frances Faye, Marvin Gaye, Turhan Bey, Anita O'Day, swing and sway with Alvino Rey and Wardell Gray, Curtis LeMay, Danny Kaye, Frito-Lay, Playa Del Rey ain't Santa Fe, and what do we know and believe?"

Wild track: Tina Delgado is alive, alive!

"BYYYYYE!"

He was, said Pat Duffy, general manager of KRTH, the last station Steele worked, "the quintessential, the best DJ ever to live."

Kevin Gershan, a Boss Radio fanatic as a teenager, recalls: "We liked Robert W. best, but we all wanted to be Steele."

Donald Steele Revert was born in Hollywood. Graduating from Hollywood High, he took a DJ course at the Don Martin School of Broadcasting, where the exercises included pretending to be a DJ on the top-rated Top 40 station of the late fifties, KFWB. Steele sounded tame in the early going, but even as a student, he showed traces of what was to come. As a Peggy Lee tune ended, he came on: "Cuckoo, Peggy. Thank you very much…"

He landed his first radio job in 1960 at KBUC in the central California town of Turlock, where he hosted, rather stiffly, a one-hour jazz and pop show. Before the year was out, he'd moved to KEPR in Kennewick, Washington, and then to KIMA in Yakima, where he cranked up his deliv-ery, Top 40 style. The next stop was pivotal: KOIL in Omaha, where Gary Owens had been the morning DJ, on his way to Los Angeles. It was during his two-and-a-half-year stay here that Steele became the "Real Don Steele."

Programming Vice President Steve Brown says he came up with the idea from the television game show *To Tell the Truth*, in which a panel of three people tried to convince a celebrity panel that each of them was the person that, in fact, only one of them was. ("Would the real…please stand?" the host, Bud Collyer, would say at game's end.) When Brown suggested the nickname to Steele, he says, "he gave me this skeptical look. I said, 'Just humor me.'" Steele himself recalled (to Ian Whitcomb; see page 187) thinking, "Right. I'll take your order, you dummy." Then, "All of a sudden, people on the street no longer called me 'Bob Steele.' They called me 'The Real Don Steele.' People react to certain words."

The Boss two:
Steele and Morgan.

In Portland in 1963, at sister station KISN, he added the final touches. With Brown's encouragement, Steele lifted Los Angeles DJ "Emperor" Bob Hudson's your-highness routine, crowning himself, rather clumsily, as the "Emperor Real (the First) Don Steele."

One afternoon, the "cooler ruler," along with a band of followers, went to Portland's Steel Bridge and proclaimed it as his own. Snarling up mid-afternoon traffic, Steele shouted to passersby: "Remember our war cry: *Tina Delgado is alive, alive!*" No one knows where that line originated, but it followed Steele everywhere.

He'd sent a tape of one of his shows to Earl McDaniel, who was program director at KEWB "Color Radio" in Oakland, California. McDaniel liked what he heard and called him. "And I get this screaming phone call back: 'You crazy asshole, you dumb son of a bitch, you can't just call. We've got Don Burden at this station. If he knows I'm looking for another job...' And I thought, 'What am I talking to?'"

Steele marched, quite cockily, into Oakland, just a bridge across from the fifth-largest radio market in the country: San Francisco. Robert W. Morgan was already there, and he caught his first sight of Don Steele at a DJ meeting. "I'm in there with a pair of jeans and a sweater, and he walks in—remember now, this was 1964—he walks into his first jock meeting dressed like the fifth Beatle. He was six feet four, an imposing presence, and he had a Beatle haircut, and a Beatle suit, and he was just way ahead of the game."

Morgan found Steele's intense, brash on-air style no less intimidating. Steele did 3 to 6 P.M., Morgan, 6 to 9. Driving from his pad in North Beach over the Bay Bridge to KEWB, Morgan couldn't listen to Steele, he says, "because if you listen to him, you start to try to do him, and you can't. You sound like an idiot, because only he can do him." Succinct, yet swinging, Steele was perfect for the kind of radio Bill Drake was putting together in Los Angeles, and soon after Morgan had been hired, he recommended the fifth Beatle.

It didn't take long for Ron Jacobs, the first program director of Boss Radio, to understand Steele's qualities. "Steele is a terrific minimalist," he told Woody Goulart, originator of a web site devoted to KHJ. "Steele's thing was to kick ass in the afternoon and move it, because people had already had it during the day." The twin anchors—Morgan in the morgan; Steele driving 'em home—went on the air and showed Los Angeles just who was boss.

But, even as Steele was riding high on the airwaves in his own hometown, and began to spread out, into television and other media, he maintained a surprisingly low profile. The Real Don Steele had little use for journalists. He didn't like being simplified, and he didn't appreciate being misquoted, or quoted out of context. And, as his widow, Shaune McNamara Steele, told me, he was rarely interested in revealing his inner self: what inspired him; what motivated him; what made him what he was.

She knows of two instances when her husband let down his guard: once with a writer, Michael Laine, in 1991, and once with Ian Whitcomb, the pop musician and author, in a session in 1970 at Nickodell's, the restaurant and bar neighboring the KHJ studios.

"My two biggest influences were Elisha Cook, Jr., and Frances Faye," Steele told Laine. "In the *Falcon* series, in one of those films, Elisha Cook, Jr., plays a disc jockey, and I saw that and said, 'Jeez, what a gig.' And then years later, there was one album by Frances Faye performing live in Vegas. She had this routine, her timing and so forth—she was always a little dirty and a little risqué, the tempo was always moving—and I said, 'That's the kind of act I'd like to put on, in my own way.' And I put those two people together and created 'The Real Don Steele.'"

But not without some doubts. "I'd look at these big baritone announcers and think, how do I get to be what they are? How do I get to be popular? How do I get the fan mail? I don't have a baritone voice. I didn't have that shit. Well, how did Alan Freed get his? He was a squeaky-voiced jerk. *He played the fuckin' records!* He played the music. When you're the guy who plays the music, you become the star. It seemed real obvious to me. So that's when I said, 'Shit, I'm not gonna get into "good" music or news or anything like that. If I do, I'm not gonna have any fanatic groupies running after me. Rock and roll is what I'm gonna get into.' That's what I went for, like all DJs do—they're all trying to get laid."

Which, apparently, he did. When Whitcomb asked about his pace and drive, Steele responded, "I feel I have done a day's work after only three hours on the air."

So, Whitcomb asked, how did he relax?

"I like girls."

After Steele revealed that his college career consisted of about a month at the University of Southern California, where a journalism course left him disenchanted—"[It] trains you for absolutely nothing"—Whitcomb asked about any outside interests the disc jockey might have.

"None, unfortunately," he said. "I guess I'm pretty shallow."

Steele slowed down his speech; he didn't sound like himself at all, but he was speaking from the heart. "It's so hard to make it. I really think that my life is getting more narrow all the time. But my cop-out is that I couldn't allow any side thing, because I had to be Number One…I had this fixation—or hang-up—and I made it. But in doing so, I had to build up this armor. I'm thinking about gettin' where I'm gettin', gettin' where I'm gettin', gettin' where I'm gettin.

"Now I'm looking back and I'm seeing what I've done to myself…I'm like one little laser beam, cutting through a lot of shit. I'm very good at what I do. I've honed it and polished it, and soon I'll be out of it, like a moonshot man without moonshots."

"Did you lose many friends on the way?" Whitcomb asked.

"No," said the Real Don Steele. "I didn't *make* any."

Of course, he did. He had both friends and admirers, especially in the radio industry. Bill Watson, who served as national program director for Drake-Chenault, could barely stand to watch Steele at work. "When he hit the air, he exploded," Watson said. "And he got himself ready…he was concentrating on what he had to do, and he enjoyed doing it. He got himself ready for it mentally, but it didn't take a big effort for him, because he just couldn't wait to get on. He was in a zone, and he was in his own zone. He was an exciting disc jockey who said more in four seconds than most people say in a minute, because it was key, street, Los Angeles words."

Steele said those words, flung out those Fractious Friday signoffs, and kept Tina Delgado alive through 1973, when Drake and RKO separated. Steele joined Drake at K100, and then, after a short stint at KTNQ ("Ten-Q"), dropped off the airwaves.

He would be off the radio for seven years. The hiatus from radio, says Shaune Steele, gave her husband time to "work on spiritual growth." But, she adds, there was also a time when Steele considered the possibility that his time had passed; that, in the mid-seventies, "there was no place for a Real Don Steele on the radio." Bill Watson agreed. "At a certain point, his style became outmoded."

The time was right for this son of Tinseltown to pursue acting. He took some courses and began getting roles—mostly small ones, custom-fit to his style and image. In *Death Race 2000*, in 1975, Steele was a sportscaster whose fellow cast members included Sylvester Stallone; and in the 1977 car-crash movie, *Grand Theft Auto*, he was a radio reporter in Ron Howard's debut as a film director. He was a DJ, "Screamin' Steve Stevens," in *Rock 'N' Roll High School* in 1979. In 1982, in the black comedy classic, *Eating Raoul*, he was Howard Swine, a foul-mouthed radio announcer and the host of a swingers' party who meets his maker, so to speak, when he's electrocuted in his hot tub, along with a bevy of naked women.

Despite those connections, Steele didn't take the movie world by storm, and, in 1985, he returned to radio on a succession of oldies stations, climaxing with his joining the staff at KRTH, which, in the early nineties, was sounding a lot like the old Boss Radio. The time was right again for a Real Don Steele. "As soon as he got back on KRTH, on a station that Drake was consulting, and the good old records were back on the radio, he was immediately back in the winner's circle," says Watson.

He was rocking on KRTH when he became ill. Soon after, on August 5, 1997, the Real Don Steele died of lung cancer.

By then, he—and Morgan—had been reunited for five years. They had helped boost an oldies station to the top ranks of the ratings. They had earned stars on the Hollywood Walk of Fame. The passing of the Real Don Steele was news on all the rival stations, where reporters and disc jockeys broke format to play tribute. Steele had gone out on top.

He had reached the goal he was so fixated on, and with no apologies. As he told Ian Whitcomb, "I wanted to be Number One. Whatever ego hang-ups that shows, I'm not afraid to say it…What I'm going to have on my gravestone is this: EGO IS NOT A FOUR-LETTER WORD."

ROBERT W. MORGAN: MORGANS ONLY, PLEASE

Robert W. Morgan

"Just what is the deal? Give me some idea how long this might take, what you want from me, what lies you wanna tell…exaggerations. Talk to you later."

That was Robert W. Morgan on my answering machine. We did talk later, at his home in Tarzana, in a valley north of Hollywood, where he greeted me as "the *Rolling Stone* anti-Top 40-christ." He was saying he'd read me, and remembered the magazine's clear, hippity 'tude about Top 40. With free-form FM coming on strong in the late sixties, we had found it easy to put down "Boss Radio" and "Boss Jocks."

That explained the acidic overlay on his phone message. But Morgan soon warmed up. He wasn't the Robert W. I'd heard and admired as a college student in 1964, when he was on KEWB in Oakland, nor was he the DJ who soared to stardom at KHJ the next year, and who would soar to even greater heights at KMPC. In May 1997, months before I spoke to him, he'd announced to his audience on KRTH-FM—the oldies station that sounded so much like the old KHJ—that he had lung cancer and would be a part-time presence on the air while he fought the disease. Now, in December, it was a weakened Morgan that I met—but only in voice and physical mobility.

This wet, wintry day, he was alert and spirited, and he well understood how I could love the best of Top 40 radio—including personalities like

Robert W. Morgan—and, later, dismiss it. He knew all too well about the limitations of the format.

And he transcended them. "He had the fastest wit, and he could put phone calls on the air, and he had a great sense of timing," says Ron Jacobs, the first program director at "Boss Radio" KHJ. He made it all fit into the confines of the streamlined Bill Drake format, and, along with the Real Don Steele, he took KHJ through the ratings ceiling in "Boss Angeles." His morning show once captured 22 percent of the available audience. Today, to get a quarter of that number is to be set for life. Or, at least, another three months.

Robert W. Morgan did not tell jokes. He did not shock. He did not do voices. He did wild tracks—sound bites from the news, TV shows and movies. He'd say it was Jack Nicholson's birthday and ask, "Tell us, Jack, how old are you today? Tell us the truth," and you'd hear Jacko roaring, "You can't *handle* the truth!"

But Morgan didn't depend on tricks. About his only shtick was fulfilling listeners' entreaties to "Morganize" them. After a brief exchange and a bit of teasing, he'd say, "Zap! You're Morganized!" And another Morgan would be made.

After more than three decades in Los Angeles, the early hours did become "Morgans." While radio had its "morning mayors," superstars who dominated mornings and set the pace for the rest of their stations' days— Herb Oscar Anderson, Harry Harrison, Dick Whittinghill, Don Sherwood, Wally Phillips, and Howard Miller come to mind—only Morgan managed to change the language, so that, for many thousands of Angelenos, it became natural to say "Good Morgan."

He never wanted it any other way. "I always wanted to be a morning man," he says, "and I didn't know if I had it in me to be a morning man." He did, but it took more than his wits. It took battling alongside Jacobs in the fabled Fresno radio war against Drake to stoke his competitive fire. He recalls one day in Oakland, when he was at KEWB—then struggling against the muscular KYA, led by Tom "Big Daddy" Donahue and Bobby Mitchell—when he heard from a pal, a record promotion man. "He asked me, 'Get some night off and we can watch Donahue work.' And I said, 'Get out of this building, you fat faggot, before I knock you out.' What a thing to say. And he left. He sent some flowers and shit the next day and I sent them back. I hated him for years after that."

By 1965, Morgan had been drafted by Bill Drake to be his morning man for the new KHJ. Once again, he was with Jacobs. Once again, he would be at war—this time against KRLA, which had just surpassed KFWB when

Drake-Chenault sauntered into town. Morgan has told the story of a night at Martoni's when he approached the late "Emperor" Bob Hudson, KRLA's comic morning kingpin, with a street map he'd kept in his pocket for just such an encounter. It was a map of Omaha, Nebraska, on which he'd marked the locations of its various radio stations. At the bar, he once told *Billboard*'s Claude Hall, "I gave it to him, saying, 'You're going to need this in six months'—and he did."

Now, sitting by a crackling fire in his living room, perhaps tempered by time and other forces, and with Hudson having died this past year, Morgan pulls a retreat. "I've told that story so many times, I don't know if it's true or not," he says. "I thought Emperor Hudson was one of the most fabulous air personalities ever. Ever. In fact, when I first walked into the studio at KHJ and looked at the ratings, we had a 1.2 in the morning, and Hudson had a 29.5. People have asked me, 'To what do you attribute what success you've had?' One single thing, I've always said, is 'Emperor Hudson getting fired six months after I hit the air.' He was unbelievable."

Soon, they were saying the same about this Ohio native. Morgan got a star on the Hollywood Walk of Fame in 1993. The next year, he was one of the first inductees into the National Broadcasters Hall of Fame, along with fellow morning man Gary Owens. Along the way, he also picked up plaques as *Billboard* Air Personality of the Year and *Gavin* DJ of the Year.

Shortly after our interview, he announced his retirement from radio. In January 1998, he did his final show, from the studios of the Museum of Television & Radio in Beverly Hills. His Walk of Fame star was rededicated. Gary Owens and Joni Caryl, a longtime sidekick of Morgan's at KMPC, hosted the ceremonies. Dick Clark narrated a retrospective of his career. Casey Kasem voiced another video tribute, calling him a "jock's jock."

Morgan was also the people's jock, and five months later he succumbed to cancer. Ron Jacobs, sending the word out on the Internet, called him "the best jock I ever had the pleasure to work with." And Jacobs revealed that Morgan had supervised "every detail of his retirement" ceremony. To the end, he adhered to the lessons he'd learned at Boss Radio: Preparation, Moderation, Concentration.

CHARLIE TUNA: NICE GUYS FINISH— AND LAST LONGER

At age five, when most boys' desires revolve around food and toys, Art Ferguson wanted to be on the radio. His favorite toys, then, were the 78 r.p.m. records he played on a phonograph in his bedroom, in Kearney, Nebraska, in 1949.

Charlie Tuna: He was on the air at sixteen.

**Dick Clark and
Charlie Tuna.**

Ferguson grew up thinking of little else. When his voice changed, it became that of a radio announcer: full and melodious. It was as if he'd willed it.

By the time he was fourteen, he was spinning records in public, for dances at the Teen Center. People would hear his grown-up voice and tell him he ought to be on radio. Perhaps on KRNY, a Top 40 station where the morning star was a young man called "Dr. Don," or on KGFW, a middle-of-the-road station where Ferguson's favorite morning disc jockey liked to talk about unidentified flying objects.

After a couple of years of such encouragement, Ferguson's father approached KGFW, which agreed to put the youngster on tape and give him a listen. "Six months later," Ferguson remembers, "they called." At age sixteen, while attending high school, Ferguson became the station's announcer from 10 P.M. to 1 A.M. A few months later, the morning DJ left, and Ferguson was given his slot. Because he had classes beginning at 8:50, the station allowed him to finish his show at 8:30.

Despite his obvious head start, Ferguson maintained modest goals. To a kid in Kearney, KOMA, in Oklahoma City, just one state south, was a big station. Los Angeles or New York seemed as distant as...well, as a UFO.

But a year and a half later, Ferguson was on KOMA, where he spent a pivotal year. For one thing, the station gave him the air name "Charlie Tuna." A newsman who'd been asked to do a weekend show had been looking for a DJ name when a TV commercial for Star-Kist tuna flashed onto the air. "It got a big reaction." When the newscaster finished out his stint, and Ferguson came along, they said, "We want you to be the permanent Charlie Tuna." Ferguson, who'd been working as "Billy O'Day," didn't argue. It was, at minimum, a memorable tag.

Charlie Tuna spent only a year at KOMA. Another disc jockey, Larry Lujack, was driving through the area one day, on his way from Seattle to a new job at WMEX in Boston, when he heard Tuna. Arriving at 'MEX, he heard that the station had a DJ slot to fill, and he told his boss about the guy he'd heard on KOMA.

What was it about Tuna that propelled him into a major market at age twenty-two? "I fell in love with radio," he says, "and when you love something, you always have a lot of fun, and I've always had fun. And everybody said, 'You have a good voice. You must've had voice training.' I guess...but only in my room."

At WMEX, he did receive some training, from Lujack. "The eerie thing was, I ran into Larry in the hall and said, 'Thanks, you're responsible for me getting here.' He said, 'Aggh, I'm gettin' ready to leave!'" Tuna was shocked. "Yeah," Lujack said, "the manager's an asshole." Lujack did stick around a few months, long enough that Tuna learned his work ethic. "He'd sit there with a spiral notebook and read the papers and write notes constantly. Watching Larry work, I got inspired to prepare for a show."

In Boston, WMEX, a personality Top 40 powerhouse, was battling WRKO, which was getting the Bill Drake treatment. Within a few months, one of the Drake-Chenault forces heard Tuna and recommended him for KHJ. By 1967, Boss Radio had overwhelmed Southern California, and the Drake format was spreading around the country. Tuna himself had heard it while at KOMA in Oklahoma City. "Bill Stewart, who was the national PD for Storz, came in with what he called 'the format,' and it was tapes of KHJ," Tuna recalls. "Little did I know, ten months later, I'd be there."

Tuna, doing the midday shift, from 9 A.M. to noon, following Robert W. Morgan, took the L.A. air with confidence. Maybe a little too much, in fact. "My first morning on the air, I said, 'I'd like to thank Robert W. for warming up the audience for me.' The engineer said, 'You don't say that. He's the guy.' I didn't know about the caste system. And everybody was about seven years older than me. I was about twenty-three."

There clearly was a gap between Tuna and Morgan, and it wasn't helped any when Morgan left in 1970 for a job at WIND in Chicago, and Tuna took the morning shift. When Morgan returned in 1972, Tuna chose to leave KHJ, rather than move to another shift. "I aspired to morning drive," says Tuna. "That's where the longevity and money is."

A few years later, Morgan took a swipe at Tuna in an interview with Claude Hall of *Billboard*. Sitting with his buddy, Don Imus, at what Hall described as "a damp lunch," Morgan recoiled when the reporter called him, the Real Don Steele, and Tuna "personalities."

"Tuna and I were considered to be personalities?" he asked Hall.

"Tuna, you, and Steele," said Hall.

"Steele and I, yes," Morgan responded.

Over the years, Tuna says, the two have become friends. "As you get older, you start to understand and appreciate each other a bit more. He was brilliant; he made me laugh. But he'd see the preparation I went through, and I came from the East Coast and dressed in a suit and tie. He took me aside and said, 'Hey, you're making the rest of us look bad.'"

It was more than the suit and tie that raised his fellow Boss Jocks' eyebrows. Tuna, whose father was an alcoholic, abstained. He was married in

1965 (and still is). He was not, then, a part of the Martoni's crowd. He was, in some eyes, a square.

Tuna saw Robert W.'s former wife, Carole, not long ago. "She told me, 'When Robert and Don and Gracie [Steele's longtime girlfriend] and I were running around together, we just kept thinking, you can't be that nice. You can't be that good. It really bugged the hell out of us that you didn't swear, drink, steal, lie, like all the rest.'

"Maybe that's what prompted some of the sniping. They thought there had to be something wrong."

There was, of course, nothing wrong. Tuna, in the world of Top 40 radio, was simply a rarity, a combination of a square and a wheel, rolling through life on an even keel, picking up advice from a UFO-entranced DJ here; a Larry Lujack there.

He recalls a piece of advice from another great DJ, the late Bobby Mitchell, who worked at KHJ as Bobby Tripp. "He said to me one time, 'Just keep remembering, the wheel turns, baby. You're on top, the wheel turns, and you're on the bottom. Just stay on the wheel and you come back on top again.' I always remembered that."

British Radio: Sink the Pirates

I n the early years of rock and roll, British youth had it all: great music from America, homegrown Elvis clones like Tommy Steel, Cliff Richard, Adam Faith, Marty Wilde, and Billy Fury, and pop shows on the telly: *6.5 Special, Drumbeat, Dig This!* and *Oh Boy!*

If only they could have had Top 40 radio.

The United Kingdom's airwaves, however, were under the strict control of the British Broadcasting Corporation (BBC, also known as the "Beeb" and, later, "Auntie Beeb" or, simply, "Auntie") and off-limits to commercial operations. The BBC had been established in 1923 as a public service, a cultural oasis free from commercial concerns and constraints.

The Corporation, funded and overseen by the government, would foster the concept of a British national culture, upper middle-class values, classical education, and public service. In the twenties, the leaders of the UK had little admiration for what passed for culture in the United States. American radio was free and unfettered, bankrolled by advertising. In Great Britain, that would not do.

By the fifties, folk music, jug bands, and trad jazz had led to a sensation called skiffle—the music's biggest hit was "Rock Island Line" by Lonnie Donegan, which even crossed over to American pop charts in 1956. Donegan's "Does Your Chewing Gum Lose Its Flavor (On the Bedpost Over Night)" reached Number Five in *Billboard* in 1961. Skiffle inspired young people to begin forming their own bands, and that phenomenon helped pave the way for homegrown, British rock and roll.

But the BBC stood fixed in time. The Beeb's definition of pop music (that is, not classical) included "light music" (light opera and "light orchestral," including music for dancing), and "popular music" (military band music, musical comedy, ballads, and music by "entertainers"). Auntie Beeb was further girdled by "needle time," a strict limit on how many hours of recorded music the network could play each day. As it had in America, the recording industry initially looked at radio with suspicion, and the Musicians Union sought to protect the band and orchestra members employed by various BBC programs. If people could hear recordings for free over the air, why would they bother to buy them?

Beyond needle time, tradition, and a nationalistic paternalism, there was also the simple fact that the people in charge at the BBC just didn't *like* this noisy new music. Age, anti-Americanism, elitism—whatever it was, the result was that, as rock rolled through the United Kingdom, the Beeb tried to sweep it under its massive carpet. Pop music could only peek out, here and there, on programs like *Saturday Club* and *Talent Spot*. Those who wanted to hear more rock and roll had to turn to Radio Luxembourg, a station beaming its signal to much of Europe from the "Grand Duchy," as this tiny province was known.

It allowed what amounted to legal payola: Record companies sponsored entire programs featuring their releases, and some artists and managers even gave half the publishing rights to singles to the station as a condition of getting their record played. But most listeners only knew that Radio Luxembourg offered the kind of new music the Beeb was unwilling or unable to play, and, instead of starchy announcers reading scripted material, Lux, known as "Fabulous 208," had swinging disc jockeys, including Alan Freed—via tape recordings—and Jimmy Savile, who would become one of the most famous of all air personalities in the United Kingdom—long before he ever moved over to the BBC.

Even as the British record industry began to ape the American teen idols of the late fifties, with its Wildes and Furys, fans had to turn to television shows on BBC (*Top of the Pops* and *Juke Box Jury*) or ITV (home of *Thank Your Lucky Stars, Ready Steady Go!* and *Oh, Boy!*) to glimpse their fave raves. Or they tuned to 208 to hear them on a regular basis. And, in the early sixties, they could find another alternative to Auntie: pirate radio.

Beaming in from ships or from abandoned defense installations off the coast of the United Kingdom, the pirates—unwanted and unlicensed by the British government—sounded like rebel radio, replete with raucous, Top 40-styled disc jockeys, jingles, and promotions. In fact, they were largely commercial ventures backed by American money.

But because they bucked the British government and Auntie Beeb, and partly because of the music they played, the pirates were instantly embraced and romanticized, particularly by the underground and rock press.

In a foreword to the book *The Radio Nord Story*, Paul Harris wrote:

"There is something irresistibly romantic about a radio ship walling lazily in a light swell…and a small team of technicians and disc jockeys defying state monopolies…to take programmes into the homes of millions of people."

Yes, the very idea of pirates sounded bold and somewhat menacing. But did they reach that many listeners? Did they sell that many records? Did they push the Beeb into the modern era of broadcasting?

Opinions vary, naturally. But there's no arguing that, for a few exhilarating years in the mid-sixties, the open seas was where the radio action was.

One of the first and biggest of the pirates was Radio Caroline, launched in 1964 and named for the daughter of the late President John F. Kennedy.

Inaugurated by disc jockey Simon Dee, Caroline, employing two ships—one on the North Sea, the other transmitting from the south—operated just outside the three-mile territorial waters limits set by the British government, and estimated its peak audience at about nine million.

Radio Caroline:
Where the
action was.

Even before the *Caroline* dropped anchor, other pirates had been broadcasting into other parts of Europe, among them Radio Veronica, off the Dutch coast (it began a British service in 1961), and Radio Nord, aimed at Sweden and programmed with the help of none other than Gordon McLendon.

Among those aimed at the British ears, it was the Big L—Radio London—that's remembered as the slickest and most professional. Americans heard about this pirate station through the Who's 1967 concept album, *The Who Sell Out*. A marvelous sendup of pop culture and, in particular, of radio and consumerism, the recording includes mock commercials (for Heinz Baked Beans and body builder Charles Atlas, among others) and actual jingles for—as one of them sang so liltingly—"the highly successful sound of wonderful Radio London."

Backed by American investors, Radio London offered not only the latest, Moddest music, but also the best DJs—chief among them John Peel.

Peel, who rose to become the country's most famous champion of new music, was the voice of the underground, with a program called *The Perfumed Garden*. "[Those were] the happiest days of my life," he reflected in *Rolling Stone* in 1971. "I used to sit out there at night with just two engineers. Nobody else on the ship listened to what I was doing, and certainly none of the people in our London office knew what was going on."

Although Peel would come to be known as "the underground's public address system," most of the pirate stations broadcasted what amounted to the UK's first Top 40 radio, with high-energy DJs, echoed voices shouting "hitbound!" and, of course, jingles.

"Radio London, being American-owned, was modeled much after Top 40 radio as it was in America," said Johnny Beerling, former controller at BBC's Radio One, "and I think WABC and Cousin Brucie and disc jockeys like that had an enormous influence on the DJs that worked on those stations." And a number of the pirate DJs who would go on to become BBC institutions, such as Johnnie Walker, David "Kid" Jenson, and Peel—had honed their style on American radio stations.

By fall of 1967, Auntie Beeb had seen and heard quite enough. The Labor government enacted new laws that, along with the jamming of signals and aggressive prosecuting of anyone found delivering food or other supplies to the pirates—shut down most of the outlaws, with two stubborn exceptions, Radio Caroline and Radio Veronica.

Lawrence Diggs, an American who'd heard about Radio Caroline from members of a San Francisco commune, got a DJ job on the pirate station in 1968 despite having almost no experience. Just months before in San Francisco, he'd gone to KFRC, looking for work, and chatted with an

You're UK, You're OK

For the biggest bucket of hogwash that passes for informed comment on the current pop scene, I nominate the frequently heard observation that the popularity of British artists, songs and records is "just a fad." The plain facts are that the British musicians have achieved a level of professional maturity that very few of their American colleagues can match.

The greatest occupational disease of American music makers has always been imitation. In the past, it has taken the pioneering genius of a George Gershwin or a Cole Porter to jolt our songwriters into new paths. In pop records it is amazing how many A&R men still turn out material patterned after the hits of ten years ago.

Only in the field of rhythm and blues can our American music be considered truly creative. Producers like Berry Gordy, Burt Bacharach, and Teacho Wilshire continue to move forward with the times. As a result, more and more of the R&B entries are selling to pop record buyers.

Obviously there are new—and profitable—directions in music waiting to be discovered by Americans willing to forsake the shopworn patterns of the past. —Bill Gavin, September 11, 1964 engineer long enough to learn about the Drake format and some of the key names in the RKO chain. In Amsterdam, at Caroline's offices, he dropped a few names and, voilà, "They thought, 'This is one of Drake's guys.'" Diggs relates. "After I got out there, they discovered, 'Hey, he hardly knows how to cue up a record!'"

The pirate broadcasters, Diggs says, "were trying to copy Drake, and they thought, 'Well, we're gonna have this kinda jive guy, this black guy doing Top 40. And I'm trying to be something like Barry White. My delivery was laid-back, 'Hey, baby...' but they wanted this up thing, jumping and screaming."

Lawrence Diggs

Pirate DJs, says Diggs, boarded dinghies in Holland and stayed on the *Caroline* for six weeks at a time. "There were no more than a dozen guys running the ship, with four or six of us on-air, including the news guys. You had a bunk. Mostly, we played pool and ate and did two shifts a day. There was absolutely nothing to do but radio." Actually, there was. Every week or so, two or three prostitutes would materialize, compliments of the boss, for an overnight stay. Diggs says he did not partake in any resulting entertainment, and worked only six months before returning to San Francisco, where he eventually did join KFRC.

While it worked to shut down the pirates, the BBC knew it had to placate rock and roll fans. The Beeb tried to do so by adding a third and fourth network to the BBC lineup, including Radio One, which would offer continuous pop music from 5:30 A.M. to 7:30 P.M. and again from 10 P.M. to 2 A.M. Still based on old-fashioned block programming, Radio One featured numerous disc jockeys, many of them former pirates. The first to go on the air, on September 30, 1967, was Tony Blackburn, whose star only rose on Radio One's breakfast show. He would soon be joined by Peel, who brought along a modified version of *The Perfumed Garden*. They worked alongside BBC regulars, mostly from its Light Programme (non-classical and pop music) channel, including countdown show host Alan "Fluff" Freeman.

One prominent pundit and critic, George Melly, lent an ear, then lashed out:

"The solemnity with which the conventions evolved by the pirate stations have been plagiarized is almost Germanic in its thoroughness: the little bursts of identifying plug music, the comperes gabbling over the opening bars of the records, the fake excitement, even the deliberate amateurism and fake fear of the sack, are all there. And yet, somehow the effect is of a waxwork, absolutely lifelike but clearly lifeless."

In other words, Top 40, warts, copycat tendencies and all, had finally infiltrated the BBC itself.

Chapter

FM (No Static at All)

A funny thing happened on the way to the seventies: the sixties. The world changed. America turned topsy-turvy, and, suddenly, Top 40 began to seem irrelevant. WABC and KHJ, to name just two, were still dominating their markets, still the ones to beat (and copy). But somehow, amidst the convolutions of two wars, Vietnam and Civil Rights, and revolutions in music, the arts, fashion, and young people's views on sex and drugs, "All-Americans" and "Boss Jocks" sounded downright square. Many of the people who were creating what was called a "youthquake" began looking for something new.

Enter the underground. Radio, that is. Although its time was short, underground radio—which would become "free-form," then "progressive," then "album-oriented rock" (AOR), all within a few years—taught Top 40 that there was life on the FM band, and it scared it into making a few changes.

Tom Donahue is widely considered to be the father of free-form. It's more accurate, however, to call him one of its parents and, ultimately, its godfather. He was one of its most successful programmers and was, by far, its most articulate spokesman. But he wasn't the first to do what he later called "freak-freely" radio.

Almost a year before he took the controls at KMPX-FM in San Francisco in 1967, WOR-FM was airing rock album cuts and assorted other music to New Yorkers. After a short period of automation, Murray the K, Bill (Rosko) Mercer, and Scott Muni emerged as live voices for a new kind of radio.

At about the same time, a college student, Tom Gamache, was on the air at WTBS in Cambridge, Massachusetts. The station, owned by the Massachusetts Institute of Technology, had a modest, 30-watt signal, but

Pete Fornatale

"Uncle Tom," as Gamache called himself, would soon move to Boston University's 20,000-watt WBUR. When commercial radio stations adopted free-form, Gamache, by then a veteran of the underground, landed on WBCN in Boston.

Two years before Gamache and the WOR-FM crew hit the air, Pete Fornatale was experimenting with a show on WFUV at Fordham University in New York. Fornatale, who'd wind up on WNEW-FM a few years later, mixed album cuts into thematic sets and conducted live interviews with musicians on a show with the innocuous title *Campus Caravan*. But he was quietly breaking new ground.

Some pioneers may not have even been aware that they were setting the stage for a new form of radio. They were simply being themselves.

RUSS SYRACUSE: THE MOOSE ON THE LOOSE

Russ Syracuse's show on KYA in San Francisco made me want to stay up. And that's the highest compliment I can think of for an all-night disc jockey.

Russ the Moose

His radio nickname is "The Moose," but in the mid-sixties, he was "The Captain," pilot of the "All-Night Flight" on the "Super Freak 1260" (KYA's dial position), streaking madly toward that most frightening of destinations, "International Nowhere."

He flew directly into the headwinds of the sixties—protest, civil rights, free speech, long hair, war, drugs—with what seemed to be a perfect blend of silliness, surrealism, and cynicism. Every night, he played rock and roll and personified freedom.

If there was a record on that he didn't like, he'd have his engineer hit a sound effects cartridge of a bombing attack, and the record would soon grind to a pathetic halt. In a lilting, laughing voice, he got away with sayings like, "May the Bird of Paradise eat your face completely." He gleefully attacked sponsors. His biggest advertiser was Mayfair supermarkets, which used a jingle sung by "Bob and Penny Mayfair." One night, Syracuse bombed the bouncy couple.

When he read or heard something he didn't quite get, he'd quick-glide into a falsetto "*WHAAAT?*" that fans like me soon adapted into our daily lives. He had an imaginary crew and offered in-flight movies (he once announced *Exodus* and listed, as stars, some DJs who'd left KYA). At 4 A.M. he had his flight attendants handing out "after-crash mints," and at 5:15, doing the voices of "Barnyard Benny" and "Cy Lo," he delivered a farm report. "You could hear tractors in the background knocking down the barn," he recalls, "and ladies being seduced up in the rafters—by geese!"

A deejay at another station told Syracuse that when he turned his radio on around 2 A.M., "Everything was so bland. Then I'd hit your show, and it was like punching into a *circus*."

All this, you understand, was before FM and "underground radio." In fact, long before Tom Donahue hooked up with KMPX, Syracuse was a hero of what came to be known as the counterculture, and when some radio people talk about the true beginnings of free-form radio, they talk about the Moose.

But he wasn't what a lot of people thought he was. In 1965, when the Family Dog, the hippie commune-turned-production company, staged its first dance concert at Longshoreman's Hall, they asked Syracuse to emcee. They assumed that he was part of the drug culture. When he got the invitation, he says, "I thought it'd be a record hop. I had no idea…

"I was a family man," he continues. "I was living with my wife, and I may have had my driftwood shop in the Village Fair. They used to think I was on drugs. I had hot chocolate! I was turned on by what I was doing. I mean, a cheeseburger used to turn me on when I was hungry. It'd answer my senses."

Syracuse, a native of Rochester, New York, had been in radio since 1956, working three years at WKBW and leaving for San Francisco and KYA in 1962. When the owner asked him to be program director, he balked at the promotion. "I told him that I got into radio to be behind the mike and not behind a desk. That was a blow to his ego, so he decided, 'All

Curses from the Moose

Without forcing it, Russ "The Moose" Syracuse came across like a nice guy. His "Love Line" connected strangers; the imaginary plane he piloted featured attendants ("stewardesses," back in 1963) handing out yak fat sandwiches, and, when his mouth was up to it, he'd add a trombone to "Red Roses for a Blue Lady."

But on occasion, he'd get into a funk, as all DJs do, and he'd let fly with what he called "a terse curse from my grandfather's hearse." Over a benign pop or R&B tune, a listener might hear any of the following:

"May the wool of a thousand sheep block your nostrils while you sleep"

"May the venom of a thousand snakes replace the syrup in your chocolate shakes"

"May the waves of a thousand seas bang incessantly against your knees," and, finally,

"May the bolts of a thousand cars replace the nuts in your chocolate bars."

right, if he wants to be behind the microphone, I'll teach him. I'll put him on the all-night show.'"

The graveyard shift, says Syracuse, "was always regarded as a prison. And I figured, if I'm already in prison, they can't do anything more to me, so I'll do whatever I feel like doing…In Top 40, you have no creativity whatsoever. As soon as I got on the all-night show, it was like letting a wild lion out of a cage…and that's when I had the fun."

Syracuse concocted strange contests and characters, and, two years before *The Dating Game* went on television, he was conducting "The Love Line" over the phones at KYA, interviewing singles (typical question: "How do you like your steak done?") and connecting them with others. "There was one couple who met on 'The Love Line' at KYA, got engaged when I went to KNBR, and got married in the studio here at KSFO."

Syracuse fit perfectly with Top 40; he could talk a record up and hit the post with his ears closed, and he worked the phones with the best of them. But he also slid easily into middle-of-the-road, big band, and other formats over the years, making adjustments to his shtick as necessary, and shrugging off the uncertainties of the business. In 1986, he looked back at twenty-four years in San Francisco. He'd worked at KYA four different times, he said, at KSFO three times, at KFRC twice—just before and just after its peak Top 40 years—and at four other stations.

"As long as we're talking about radio," he reasoned, "any kind of change shouldn't come as a surprise."

SLY STONE, THE DISC JOCKEY

Five years before I interviewed Sly Stone for a *Rolling Stone* cover story in March 1970—the time of Sly & the Family Stone's third straight Number One hit, "Thank You (Falettinme Be Mice Elf Agin)"—I'd dug him as a DJ.

Sly Stone made only two stops in radio, neither of them Top 40. But if he'd chosen to continue in broadcasting, there's no doubt that he would've crossed over into any format he might have wanted to try: Top 40, freeform, jazz—even country or classical.

On the air, at KSOL in 1964 and at KDIA a couple of years later, Stone sounded smooth, his voice a blend of silk and bass. He was hip, relaxed, in control. He'd studied radio at the Chris Borden School of Modern Broadcasting in downtown San Francisco (Borden had been a DJ on KEWB a few years before), and, early on, he struck fellow DJ Johnny Morris as "a young Tom Donahue."

In fact, Stone—born Sylvester Stewart—was a protégé of Donahue's. A

dazzlingly talented multi-instrumen-
talist as well as a singer, he backed up
various musicians at concerts produced by Donahue and partner
Bobby Mitchell. When Donahue and
Mitchell formed Autumn Records in
1963, Tom appointed Stone, who was
only nineteen, as his main—actually,
his only—producer. Young Stone
worked with Bobby Freeman
("C'mon and Swim"), the Beau
Brummels ("Laugh Laugh"), the
Vejtables ("I Still Love You"), the
Mojo Men ("Dance With Me"), and a
hippie band called The Great Society,
whose lead singer was an uncertain
Grace Slick.

Sly Stone

On the air at KSOL, Stone had a wild variety of guests. They ranged
from musician pals like Billy Preston—who was working in Ray Charles's
band when he met Stone, and who cut a couple of duets with him (they
were not released, until recently)—to a hair stylist who says his shop
"catered to pimps and whores." Stone would sometimes turn commercial
copy into an improvised song. But he also executed all the formattics,
playing jingles and dutifully reading public service announcements.

KSOL (at 1450 on the dial) in 1964 was a 1,000-watt upstart, up against
the bigger, more established, 5,000-watt KDIA (at 1310 on the dial). In the
evenings, KSOL operated on only 250 watts. Stone, who'd walked into
KSOL off the streets, was an instant hit, and it wasn't long before his ratings eclipsed the competition's.

But, as much fun as he seemed to be having on the radio, he had other
ambitions. In 1964, he was also heading a band, Sly and the Stoners, at small
local clubs, joining the band when his show ended after midnight.

One night, Johnny Morris told Stone biographer Joel Selvin, "[Sly] had
a gig or something around 10:30 in the evening, and he was working until
midnight. He asked me to come and bail him out and tell the program
director that there was something wrong with the station. He signed the
station off around 10:00. Check this out. I turn the radio on and he sings
"The Star Spangled Banner" on the air and then shuts the station off and
splits...It was Sly. If you had a 40 percent share of the market, you couldn't
do any wrong."

"Sly," said Donahue in 1970, "he's got it all covered. About the only self-destructive thing about him that I could recall was a Don Quixote thing—you know, he was riding off in all directions."

In *Rolling Stone*, I described his DJ persona:

"Turn on the car radio, and you hear the big voice greeting the caller: 'Hi; Sly.' And the little voice: '*Hi-i*, Sly...I wanna dedicate to my sister Velma, to all the queens of soul in room one-oh-four, and to you and yours.' 'All right, sister,' *punch*, '*Hi-i*, Sly...' And all the time there's a tape loop, *boop, boop,* Aretha chugging 'Chain of Fools,' and Sly does three solid minutes of dedications, as musical, as tight, as produced as anything he'd air.

"At KSOL, he brought in a piano and sang happy birthday to listeners. 'Just radio,' he'd say. 'I played Dylan, Lord Buckley, the Beatles. Every night I tried something new...everything was just on instinct. You know, if there was an Ex-Lax commercial, I'd play the sound of a toilet flushing. It would've been boring otherwise.'"

By 1967, Stone, doing 6 to 9 P.M. on KDIA, had formed the Family Stone, and, after landing a gig in Las Vegas during the holidays, left radio for good.

At KDIA, General Manager Bill Doubleday hated having to say, "*Bye, Sly*"—and lose his high ratings. But he couldn't help admiring the guy. "The Family Stone always had a showmanship most other local bands couldn't muster," he said. "On the air, Sly was the same. You know how most DJs put on a whole style when they're on. Sly didn't create an air personality; that *was* Sly Stone."

MURRAY THE K: THE FIFTH BEATLE IS FIRST

When we left Murray the K, it was 1965, and WINS, which had helped launch the careers of Alan Freed, "Cousin Brucie," Jack Lacy, and Murray, among others, switched to an all-news format.

Looking for freedom and independence in an industry allowing little of either, Kaufman searched for a year before landing on the FM band, at WOR. On the AM side, the station, owned by RKO General, was doing fine, with morning DJ and Manhattan fixture John Gambling setting the pace. That explained the absence of RKO's genius consultant, Bill Drake.

Along came the Federal Communications Commission. Noting the steady growth of FM, which began stereo broadcasting in 1961, and alarmed at the crowdedness of the AM band (in 1961 there were nearly four thousand AM stations in operation; fewer than one thousand FMs), the

FCC issued an order to owners of combined AM and FM stations.

Although FM had been on the air since the forties, it was the neglected child of radio. Owners of both AM and FM operations tended to simulcast the dominant AM station's programming onto the FM. Frequency Modulation, although superior in sound to Amplitude Modulation, found more respect from independent broadcasters, noncommercial organizations, fans of classical and jazz music, and stereo experimenters.

Now the FCC told owners of AM-FM combos in markets with populations over one hundred thousand that, as of July 1965, they would no longer be able to simulcast for more than half of their broadcast hours. The deadline was later extended to January 1, 1967.

Murray the K

It was forced diversity, and RKO was one of the first to respond. On July 30, 1967, it split off the FM with new, automated programming. It began with the Troggs' "Wild Thing," and, soon, it became apparent to listeners that WOR-FM was not going to be a Top 40 station. The music leaned away from pop and toward hip. Promotional posters, by the illustrator Milton Glaser, popped up all over town. By the time the first live disc jockeys arrived, in October, WOR-FM was already getting raves from the alternative media. The *Village Voice* called it "the only place to hear vital new music, and hear it well."

Murray the K was joined by Rosko, known as "Rhymin' Bill Rosko Mercer" on the Los Angeles R&B station, KGFJ, and by Scott Muni, evening DJ on WABC until he got fired over "Hello, Dolly." The Louis Armstrong ditty had been on the charts for nearly five months in 1964, and Muni was tired of its high rotation. When he complained too loudly to Program Director Rick Sklar—and in front of station staffers—he was gone.

At WOR-FM, they found total freedom, but it lasted less than a year. In the summer of 1967, RKO decided to turn the reins over to Drake, and Kaufman responded by quitting. When he learned that Drake intended to leave the wide-ranging playlist untouched, at least for the first couple of months, he returned—only to get fired, despite reportedly having the highest ratings at WOR-FM. In the first issue of *Rolling Stone* magazine in November 1967, station manager Robert S. Smith said Kaufman was let go because of his "inability to live with direction."

"They've screwed up the most beautiful thing on the air in New

Murray the K with Gerry and the Pacemakers.

York…the music's back in the hands of the people who don't care," Kaufman told *Rolling Stone*'s reporter, who just happened to be Bob McClay, who followed Drake as PD at KYA in San Francisco in 1964. Soon after Kaufman's dismissal, fellow DJ "Rosko" Mercer quit—on the air, without management's knowledge.

"We've presented a lot of beautiful new things; we've presented a lot of new artists to you, and this has been curbed," Mercer said. "I cannot go along with the new policy here."

Mercer's goodbye lasted several minutes, and, heartfelt as it was, it would be critiqued by Bill Drake in one word—"unfortunate"—and it would remind every radio manager in the country why disc jockeys should be let go only after they've done their last show.

Murray the K would resurface at WNBC in New York, and on other stations in other markets over the years. In the late seventies, he hosted a syndicated show, *Soundtrack of the '60s*. It was already nostalgia time for the K. By then, he'd been diagnosed with lymphoid cancer. He refused to slow down. Ravaged by the disease, in the fall of 1981 he was still juggling projects and prospective gigs on radio and TV, still thinking ahead. "Are you kidding?" he told Price. "If they turned me loose in New York, I'd have the Number One ratings in a month. They *need* me."

Murray Kaufman died on February 21, 1982. He was sixty.

TOM DONAHUE FINDS THE UNDERGROUND

After one too many requisite appearances at teen fairs, "Big Daddy" Tom Donahue escaped KYA in May 1965. He had a lot of irons burning—a record label, concert promotion, a radio tipsheet—and he'd put a few more in the fire, including starting the first known psychedelic night club. Yes, the times were changing, but, no matter what he got into, Donahue had a yearning to touch and to perform the magic of radio. If only there was a way to do it without playlists, and pimple cream commercials…

He spent many a stoned evening with Raechel—a beautiful former nightclub dancer who'd become his second wife— and various friends, when, one night, he got it. As Raechel recalls: "Tom and I were sitting around with our Telegraph Hill neighbors, smashed on his birthday, playing records for each other: The Doors, Judy Collins, all kinds of records no one played on the radio. Tom said, 'Do you realize that we sit here every night and smoke dope and play records for each other? I wonder why nobody's done this on radio?'"

Not long after that revelatory night, a friend in the record business suggested that Donahue try calling some FM stations. Donahue didn't even own an FM radio at the time, and knew FM primarily as a domain for classic music and foreign language programs. Told that FM allowed for broadcasting in stereo, he decided to give it a shot. He telephoned one station after another to offer his services. One station, KMPX, had a disconnected phone.

**Tom Donohue
with Bill Gavin.**

"Ah, *ha*," he thought. "Now I've got one." He smelled trouble—the good kind. "A drowning man," he reasoned, "doesn't care who's throwing the rope." Sure enough, KMPX was a struggling station that bartered its air time to whoever would pay for it. Along with various foreign language programs, a DJ, Larry Miller, occupied the all-night shift, which he filled with blues, folk, folk-rock, and casual banter. It was the kind of radio Donahue wanted to do. On April 7, 1967, Donahue took the evening slot, adding sudden luster to the station. With the charismatic Donahue came friends and advertisers. Soon, all of KMPX was what became known as free-form radio.

KMPX was a big hit, and Donahue duplicated the formula in Los Angeles at another small FM outlet, KPPC, with another Top 40 escapee, B. Mitch Reed, along with Les Carter, by his side.

Donahue couldn't resist taking a public swipe at Top 40 radio when he had the chance. In the second issue of *Rolling Stone* magazine, in November of 1967, Donahue took up the sword. His essay has been widely quoted, primarily because of its conclusion: "Top 40 radio, as we know it today and have known it for the last ten years, is dead, and its rotting corpse is stinking up the airways." That conclusion served as the headline for the article, which, along with a half-page portrait of the long-haired, leather-fringed KMPX staff, occupied a page and a quarter of the magazine.

But Donahue did much more than name-calling. From the inside, he offered a quick history and definition of the format, then detailed how, in the way it was deciding on the music it was playing, Top 40 had fallen badly behind the times.

Donahue credited Top 40 for turning rock and roll into a boom industry. "The stations," he said, "were replete with jingles, sirens and explosions introducing the news and disc jockeys who worked at a frantic pace and never, never lost their jollity. Generally, the stations played about 100 current records, but otherwise the format was almost identical to what is heard today in every city in the nation.

"Ten years later, the biggest detriment to the progress, expansion, and success of contemporary music is that same so-called Top 40 radio."

While music has matured, Donahue argued, "radio has apparently proven to be a retarded child. Where once Top 40 radio reflected the taste of its audience, today it attempts to dictate it, and in the process has alienated its once loyal army of listeners."

No, Thanks—We'll Stick With Free-Form Radio

In May 1972, Tom Donahue observed the fifth anniversary of free-form radio with a special on KSAN. He opened with a track of Chinese music, and explained:

"That's what was going on when Raechel and I got there. The date was the 7th of April, 1967, and that's the night we went to work at KMPX, replacing a Chinese language program. And there was one lady who didn't really figure out what was happening for about three days, but…an important part of our success—with whatever this kind of radio will be known as—is that we had that foreign language audience, because those people had kids who had access to an FM radio, and foreign language was what KMPX was primarily doing at that time. Larry Miller was on from midnight to six and, as far as the audience was concerned, was also speaking a foreign language…

"Tonight's program is sort of a backward look at the year 1967 and what is sometimes called 'underground radio,' and that's a misnomer. It has been called free-form radio, and it gets too restricted for that, too, at times. I always liked what it was called by a fellow who used to play violin with Eric Burdon and the Animals—John Weider. We interviewed him one night on KMPX and he said, 'Freak 'n' roll. That's what it is. Freak 'n' roll.'"

The Beatles had changed the rules. Their dominance of the sales charts and radio airwaves, as well as their influence on making albums viable hits in their entirety rather than just packaging for a hit or two and ten tracks of filler, forced some Top 40 radio stations to change. Top 40 had never played album cuts. Now, because of the Beatles—and, soon, the Stones, Dylan, the Byrds, and others—the format had to adjust.

But most Top 40 programmers were simply ignoring albums. "To select cuts from an LP," Donahue said, "meant making independent decisions, reflecting taste and a good ear—attributes that are sadly lacking in most radio programmers and station managements."

The result, Donahue claimed, was programming designed for an audience with an "average mental age of…twelve and a half," dominated by jingles "that in their content are almost totally divorced from the kind of music the stations are playing" and "hysterical disc jockeys who are trying to cram into a ten- or fifteen-second period the inane slogans that the program director has posted on the studio wall. The tempo is Go! Go! Go!, the air is replete with such blather as, 'Here comes another twin spin sound sandwich' and 'Here's a blast from the past, a moldy oldie that'll always last.'"

Here, Donahue seemed to be letting his personal animus for his past get the better of him. His descriptions of the hyped-up DJs and of their slogans sounded five years old. But, ultimately, he was right. Despite experimenting with selected album cuts, Top 40 remained singles-minded, and the DJs rarely sounded as natural, as human as their emerging FM brethren—many of whom were trained—and drained—by Top 40.

At KMPX, KFRC's Ed Mitchell became Ed Hepp. At KSAN, where Donahue and many of his staffers moved when a labor strike at KMPX could not be resolved, Tony Bigg, formerly of of KYA, changed his surname to Pigg. In Los Angeles, B. Mitch Reed was still B. Mitch Reed. Now, he was on FM, on KPPC with Donahue. And when the action moved to KMET, Reed was there. He would move on to KRLA and to KLOS—wherever he could play his music. His delivery, now, had decelerated back to a jazz DJ tempo: laid-back and thoughtful. And, just as radio listeners accepted his switch from mellow to manic in the late fifties, so, too, they welcomed his latest—and last incarnation.

By the end of the decade, Reed was beset with health problems, and he died on March 16, 1983. He was fifty-six. At his funeral, Gary Owens recalled, "Joey Reynolds and I were driving away from the synagogue to the 405 freeway, and I spotted a camper truck with a license plate that came right out of *The Twilight Zone*: BMR 98, the numerals of which were

KFWB's frequency. The truck had nothing to do with the cortege...it was just there."

Tom Donahue died April 28, 1975, of a heart attack. He was a month shy of his forty-seventh birthday, and he was making deals to the end. After his death, it was reported that he had been in discussions with Francis Ford Coppola about taking over a station and doing free-form without corporate constraints. The station was KMPX.

Just Running Scared

Through his *Gavin Report*, Bill Gavin got to know hundreds of the top programmers and disc jockeys around the country. But he knew them only by telephone. Knowing well the problems that had beset previous gatherings of radio and music industry people, he decided to sponsor a meeting—for radio people only—in 1966 in Las Vegas, in conjunction with the National Association of Broadcasters (NAB), which was staging its annual conference there.

Gavin had next to no experience in producing such events. He'd had an informal get-together with several of his correspondents in New York in 1964, and in San Francisco the following year. Now, he'd invited a national gathering of nearly two hundred radio professionals to Vegas—and neglected to make any hotel reservations.

The guests did find places to sleep. Pat O'Day, the program director/DJ at KJR in Seattle, forgave Gavin any mistakes. "You have no idea what a unifying force Gavin was in our industry at that time," he says. "I mean, can you imagine the courage [it took] to set out and create a national radio programming convention? But Bill put the integrity and credibility of the whole *Gavin Report* on the line."

At the gathering, O'Day recalls, "the record people would check into nearby hotels and hang around—but they were excluded from the meeting itself. They'd be hanging around, hoping they could take one of the guys to dinner. And they would try and set up hospitality suites in the other hotels, much to Bill's chagrin."

For his 1967 meeting—again in Vegas—Gavin decided to welcome record company people to participate. He'd made his point. Still, he banned parties and hospitality suites hosted by record companies.

Jann Wenner, editor of *Rolling Stone*, attended the 1968 convention in Las

Vegas, where he appeared on a panel on FM radio. He checked out the Top 40 panel, and reported:

"One heard some intelligent and informed remarks—about six times in the entire panel. Joe Smith, the vice president and general manager of Warner Bros.-Seven Arts, was by far the most intelligent.

"Joe came up through the record promotion end, with a genius for talking, and engaging charm. He was once William F. Buckley's roommate at Yale. Anyway, Joe got up there and, in his totally stone blunt and totally forgivable and humorous manner, told the panelists representing the Top 40 stations and those in the audience connected with the Top 40 scene, that they were tasteless, boring, narrow-minded, ignorant, stupid, uncreative, and totally without any sense of humor. He was right and they all knew it and applauded. Unfortunately that won't change things very much."

Who're You Calling "Patty"?

In the summer of 1970, I started working weekends at KSAN-FM, where there were no hot lines, hot clocks, hot coffee, or jock critique sessions with the program director. A few months later, a friend who worked on the other side—AM radio—sent me a photocopy of a form, on which he wrote: "This is the way the PD does it at KYA."

Beneath a grid on which the boss could chart the deejay's music, there were forty-eight phrases indicating possible criticisms, with space for the PD to check off violations. Here are the best (or worst) of them

__Nothing to say

__Too patty

__Reading bad

__Screaming

__Dead air

__No topicality

__Blue material

__Too many words to get to the point

__Over use of cliché_____

__No balls

__Playing with commercials

__Not enthusiastic

__Humor not making it

__Breaking format

__Non-believable promo read

__Not selling music

__Talking over vocal

__Predictable

__Stammering

__Uninvolved

__No soul in voice

__No warmth

__Distracted.

Huh?

Oh, yes: forty-eight possible criticisms (although I'm not sure what "too patty" means), and not one positive comment. Maybe those were on another sheet.

Two years after Wenner's report, in 1970, it was my turn to cluck at all the revved-up would-be hipsters, this time at the Century Plaza in Los Angeles:

Joe Smith

"Flying around from queue to queue, here comes Sir Doug Sahm, the Texas rock and roll antelope, dressed up in football jersey, suede shirt, and jeans. 'Man, I'm just here diggin' on the people, all the different cliques,' he says in his speedy way. 'But, man, these promo people come into town for two weeks and think they can tell radio how to program themselves after fifteen years.' And so Doug seconds an emotion that's beginning to sound like an echo up and down the lobby, curving through the corridors toward the various meeting and banquet rooms. There, Bwana Johnny, cherubic music director from KYA in San Francisco, had dismissed all of Friday afternoon's meetings as 'shuck and jive.' Johnny's station is making a move towards an all-album format, following the new AM road paved by KLIV, an aggressive little station in nearby San Jose. 'Albums are the coming thing,' said Johnny."

My notes from that conference include Chuck Blore telling a crowd, "Ninety percent of radio sounds the same. There aren't many people in radio who understand the medium, beyond playing records and telling the time."

But, as Wenner had opined two years before, things were not likely to change. Everybody knew the rules and played by them.

At the awards banquet, Charlie Tuna of KHJ was named Top 40 DJ of the Year. "This is the greatest and most important moment of my life," he told the audience. "I want to say thanks to a lot of people—but it's impossible, because of the format."

If that sounds familiar, it should. Robert W. Morgan used the same joke for his first good-bye to KHJ that same year.

Who said it first? We'll let them fight it out.

TOP 40 RADIO: DEAD AND ALIVE

Despite the bad-mouthing of Tom Donahue and many others, Top 40 was not dead. It was, undeniably, on a roller coaster ride, and, sometimes, depending on one's perspective, it could be up and down at the same time. In 1968, Bill Gavin reported, Top 40 had righted itself from a recent ratings decline, with the leading performers including KHJ, KJR in Seattle, KLIF in Dallas, KILT in Houston, WTIX in New Orleans, WOKY in Milwaukee, KROY in Sacramento, and KRIZ in Phoenix. Overall, however, the format was said to be losing male listeners aged eighteen to twenty-four, as more of them moved over to free-form and album rock, on the FM side.

By 1972, when album sales were reported to be accounting for about 86 percent of record sales, and Top 40 was presumed to be near death again, it had simply shifted its target demographic, hop-scotching the hard-core rockers by aiming at the twenty-four to thirty-five year-olds with older and softer—read: "singer-songwriters"—music.

Stations were beginning to target specific age groups thanks to some major changes in audience measurement surveys. In Top 40's early years, the dominant companies were Hooper and Pulse. The former folded in the sixties; the latter would be eclipsed by the American Research Bureau, founded in Minneapolis in 1964 and later renamed Arbitron. The older companies had done their surveying by going to homes and jogging people's memories, or telephoning them and asking questions. Results were generally broken down into men, women, adults, teenagers, and children.

ARB sent out detailed diaries that listeners could (ideally) fill in while memories were fresh. The resulting ratings were broken into numerous age cells. Suddenly, the vocabulary of radio included "twelve-to-twenty-four," "eighteen-to-thirty-four," and so on.

Advertisers had never taken to the youth-based audience of Top 40. For some reason, they favored listeners known to have more money. As they searched for those listeners, radio maneuvered to accommodate them, retooling, fine-tuning, tweaking music, personalities, and formats to get the biggest share possible of the ad revenue pie.

Enter the experts; the scientists of radio: the researchers and consultants.

Actually, they'd always been around. Besides Mike Joseph, who's been advising Top 40 stations since 1956, Paul Drew, the veteran programmer for RKO and others, points to Bill Gavin, who offered programming advice, for a fee, in the first years that he published his *Record Report*. Gavin, in turn, has pointed out other pioneers, including Buzz Bennett. The former dancer on the *Buddy Deane Show* in Baltimore (see Chapter Seven) had become, at age twenty, a successful program director at WTIX in New Orleans in the mid-sixties. One reason he was winning, Gavin said, was his development of new ideas in researching music. Bennett was asking music fans at record stores not only what they were buying, but what else they liked. The information helped programmers to determine true music preferences on the local level, and to have more than sales figures on which to rely.

"Bill credited me [as] the first guy to do research where you do call outs, you tabulate all the requests, you go to the stores, and you go do focus groups. I remember him writing and saying to me, 'You're the only guy doing this, man,'" Bennett said.

As his ideas spread, Bennett found himself a wanted man. He remembers speaking at a radio conference and being frightened at the prospect of facing mostly older professionals. "These were all big guys to me, and I always thought I was nothing. Until I went to my first convention, and then I realized, 'Well, I'm not as dumb as I thought.' I got to hear everybody else talk.

"I used to have a line that I used all the time. I used to say, 'The first thing we have to do is give this station an enema.' So I was saying, 'The first thing you do to become successful is to take the shit off the air. It's not what you put on the air, it's everything that we need to get off the air that's important.' If you want to make a great radio station, you take it down to what's good about it."

As effective as they could be, conducting research and making recommendations to stations about every element of their operations, consultants didn't find a welcome mat everywhere. Program directors were naturally fearful that they were being second-guessed, that instinct was giving way to computer data, and that their jobs might be at risk. (Ironically, as the concept of consultants took hold, it almost became automatic that when a program director was out of a job, he'd declare himself to be in the consulting business.)

"Most statistics," said Ken Dowe, a longtime disc jockey and programmer in the McLendon chain, "are like the lamp post with a drunk leaning against it…the post is there more for support than illumination."

George Wilson, the Bartell Broadcasting executive who both hired and competed against Buzz Bennett, told *Billboard* columnist, Claude Hall in an interview in the mid-seventies: "In my day, everything came from my belly and the seat of my pants. Today, everything is done from research." But, he admitted, "It seems to be the successful way to go at this time. So I am certainly not going to ignore it."

As much research as it had on its side, Top 40 had plenty of battles ahead. And it didn't help when payola became public laundry once more.

In late 1972, the Washington, D.C.-based syndicated columnist, Jack Anderson, wrote that payola had returned to "the gangster-like world" of the record industry, duping "America's bop-crazy teenagers." (It was hard to believe that in the seventies, people still wrote like that.) In response, Gavin, while acknowledging that payola existed, criticized the columnist for generalizations. By singling out WABC for its care in authenticating sales reports on records it charted, said Gavin, Anderson "implies discredit to the hundreds of stations that are equally diligent in the pursuit of honesty and accuracy…mud, when indiscriminately thrown, splatters everybody." In a follow-up commentary, he added: "All of us feel righteously indignant at the implication that record promotion and the breaking of hits rests on a foundation of bribery and misrepresentation."

Investigations, Rumors Mount In Columbia 'Drugola' Scandal

NEW ROCK MUSICAL: 'SGT. PEPPER'

Promoter Kal Rudman drew national attention—including a photo in *Rolling Stone*—in the early seventies.

Gavin was fully aware that payola not only continued to fester, but had taken new forms. With most disc jockeys no longer selecting music for airplay, promotion people—both those employed by labels and a growing network of independent promo men—did their pay-for-playing with radio staffers, usually the program or music director, who reported "adds" (records being added to the playlist each week) to various trades. By getting onto a station chart that was published nationally, a record might be given additional consideration by other, perhaps more powerful, stations.

While Gavin refused to accept gifts worth more than $25, refused to take advertising in his publication, and even refused to allow artists to drop by his office in San Francisco, he knew, firsthand, about trade publications being possible conduits for record promotion. His own was a case in point.

As he recalled in 1983, he received a phone call from one Kal Rudman in 1964. Rudman had a radio show in Camden, New Jersey, and had become a Gavin correspondent. "Later, he offered to collect reports from Eastern R&B jocks, which enabled me to put together a section of our publication devoted to black radio…However, some months later, a friend told me that Kal was doing paid promotion work for some record companies. Confirming this, I immediately dropped Kal from our reporter group," Gavin said.

Gavin added that Rudman had become "one of the nation's most significant" voices in the music industry. In 1971, Rudman, who'd gone on to publish his own tipsheet, the *Friday Morning Quarterback*, was profiled in the *Wall Street Journal*, where he openly admitted to taking money from labels to hype their records in his sheet. Using the record by Jean Knight, "Mr. Big Stuff," as an example, the newspaper said that Rudman didn't seem to like the record but plugged it with enthusiasm, confessing to a "possible conflict of interest." But, Rudman told reporter Jonathan Kwitny: "I would have written exactly the same thing without the promotional fee."

For various mini-scandals, the press concocted words like "plugola" and "drugola." There was even—and I'm just coining the word here—Britola.

In England, the BBC had finally responded to the public's love of rock and roll music with a radio channel of its own: Radio One, which began operation in 1967. All well and pretty good, but, with the pirate stations shutting down and with commercial radio still a half-dozen years away, Radio One became a pop radio monopoly. Even at that, the channel offered pop music only thirty-four hours a week, according to a report by London-based DJ and writer Paul Gambaccini in *Rolling Stone* in 1971. On top of that, playlists, prepared not by disc jockeys but by program producers, leaned heavily on proven hits. Producers took few chances on new sounds. All of this made for an army of record promoters who seemed always to be on the verge of panic. And, Gambaccini noted, it was a growing army that gathered at the Beeb's studios in Egton House, London, on Tuesdays. He quoted Mark White, head of Radio One:

Yvonne Daniels

"There are so many promotion men now, it's ridiculous. Sometimes up to fifty in the building…Sometimes they're nothing more than glorified messenger boys occupying floor space."

"Rumors of attempts, successful and unsuccessful, to bribe producers and DJs have made front-page news throughout Britain," Gambaccini reported. "The *News of the World* charged that Radio One personnel had accepted call girls, expensive gifts, and free vacations. An informal BBC investigation is underway…"

What must Auntie Beeb have thought?

TOP 40 CLUBHOUSE: NO GIRLS ALOUD

The first woman to break through into major-market Top 40 radio smashed through two barriers at once. Yvonne Daniels, who came to be known as the "First Lady of Chicago Radio," was an African-American woman.

Born in Jacksonville, Florida, the daughter of the jazz singer and dancer Billy Daniels, Yvonne sang too, but by age seventeen had already landed a job at a local R&B station. After a stop in St. Louis, she joined WYNR in Chicago to host a late-night jazz show opposite the formidable Sid McCoy on WCFL. When WYNR switched formats, McCoy suggested to her that they team up. They did, with great success, until that station went Top 40 in 1964. Daniels moved to WSDM, where her early evening jazz show was Number One.

In 1973, Top 40 came calling. WLS, doing battle with WCFL, hired Daniels for all-night duties. It was a strange shift for a woman so steeped in jazz music, but she was determined to succeed." I decided that I had to make good there," she told the *Chicago Tribune*, "because if I didn't cut it, they might never hire another woman."

She cut it for nine years, and when she left in 1982, it was for a morning drive show on WVON. She was working at WNUA, a "smooth jazz" station, in 1991 when she died. Four years later, she was inducted into the Museum of Broadcast Communications' Radio Hall of Fame in Chicago.

"Before Yvonne, very few women thought about becoming disc jockeys," said a fellow DJ, Danae Alexander of WNUA. "Suddenly this new door opened for women, and it was because of Yvonne that it opened."

While Yvonne Daniels was establishing herself on Top 40, Margaret Reichl, born in North Carolina and raised just outside Detroit, was in college in Kalamazoo, working on the campus station—which had a Top 40 format—and hanging out with the "radio crowd." "WLS was like the coolest thing," she says. "I was addicted to it and followed who was doing what, and Yvonne Daniels was the only woman I knew of in any major market."

By the time she left Kalamazoo in 1974, Reichl, going by the name "Margo," had worked at a local Top 40 outlet and landed a job in Wichita, Kansas, at KWBB. It took only a few weeks before she got bored with life in the Sunflower State. For one thing, her DJ job also included cleaning the studios and emptying the trash. "I couldn't take it any more," she recalls. She telephoned the *Gavin Report*, knowing that the publication ran job listings, and spoke with Janet Gavin. "She said, 'That's really strange, because we just got a call from a Top 40 station in San Francisco saying they were looking for a female.' Three days later I was at a waterfront restaurant in Sausalito watching the sailboat races in August with Michael Spears (program director of KFRC), and got the job that weekend." Spears suggested a new air name, Shana—just Shana—and put her on the overnight shift.

"I don't think anybody made a market leap like Shana," says Dave Sholin, a DJ and music director at the station. I think KWBB was like a daytimer, and they were going bankrupt. And she was only twenty-one, and here she is in San Francisco."

Yes, she was. But it was 1974. Yvonne Daniels, the pioneer, had joined WLS just over a year before. And both women were on the all-night shift.

Also, the decision to hire a woman arose not out of any sudden jolt of feminism or equality on the management level, but out of practicality. Spears recalls that he'd heard from RKO General's national vice president of programming, Paul Drew. "He said, 'Your station is going to be kind of our laboratory, because you can do things a little ahead of the rest of us, because it's San Francisco.' He said he noticed with the EEOC and a lot of things coming down with RKO General in those days, it was just a matter of time before they were going to have to have a woman as a DJ on the major stations. He said, 'I don't know where you're going to find her. But you need to start looking around and find yourself a woman.'"

Spears put the word out—carefully—and heard from Reichl. After hearing her tape and inviting her to San Francisco, she auditioned on the air, on the all-night shift. "I remember what impressed me," says Spear. "I was standing right behind her, and she had to be scared to death. There was also an engineer behind her, helping her run the board and all this kind of stuff. And I remember she had a music bit and live commercial. She'd never seen it before, and she read it flawlessly. And we went, 'Damn.' The engineer started applauding…and I said, 'This young lady is going to be a star.'"

Shana

In an interview for *Billboard* with Claude Hall, veteran programmer George Burns declared that radio's slowness in hiring women "wasn't a case of educating management—the biggest problem was educating women listeners, because women listeners hated women on the air in 1967."

Shana had no quarrel with the statement. She, too, heard complaints about women on the radio. "In the seventies, when women were getting on the air, especially on underground FM, they would do that sexy breathy sound," she says, "and for a lot of women, when their boyfriends or husbands were commenting on how sexy that voice was, it was a threat. The [disc jockeys] weren't so much personalities as they knew they were on the air, and they knew they were on at night, and I really sensed that they were doing a very sensual type of thing as opposed to what their real personalities might be. And I think it was a little threatening to women."

On KFRC and, later, in Los Angeles at KHJ and other stations, Shana was natural, upbeat. "KFRC," she says, "was very fast-paced. I still can't believe I could do that at three in the morning. But I was so totally into it. I was working with people I totally adored. Chuck Buell; Michael Spears, who hired me, was Hal Martin on CKLW when I was a teenager and a fan of his; so I was so excited to be there, and the music was so wonderful, and I was into it. KFRC was an exciting place to work. It came out naturally. I wasn't screaming; I was just moving with the music and having a ball."

Shana had no problems blending in at KFRC. "I get along with guys really well, and I guess they sensed that easiness with me," she says. "I think they respected me for my situation and what I was doing. But I was never one to flirt or use somebody because they were a guy and I didn't think I could do it myself or whatever, so we had a real good relationship. I have nothing but great memories of it. I wasn't hit on by anybody—well, *once* in awhile, you know!—but I could take the jokes and the radio kind of goofing that you do. I was comfortable."

Today, Shana works at KPCC in Los Angeles and teaches radio at a local high school and city college. Despite the assembly-line feel of too many radio stations today, she says students still feel the potential magic of the medium. "The ones that really get excited about it won't care if they have a secure job or not," she says, "and those are the ones that I will really concentrate on, when you see that passion for it.

"I know that passion. I still have it."

MAKE-BELIEVE DISCO CLUB

Long before Top 40, dance music drove radio. Its roots, after all, moonwalk

Top 40 Funhouse Hell Toupee

Ron Jacobs, the first program director of 93/KHJ "Boss Radio," sneers at KFRC, its San Francisco sister station, as "a mere farm team."

Those farmers, Jacobs should know, managed to win seven "Radio Station of the Year" awards from *Billboard* magazine in eight years, from 1976 to 1983, beating out every other major market contemporary music station—including KHJ.

And, when it came to getting crazy, "the Big 610" was never left in the barn, either. According to DJ Frank Terry, one of the most memorable times involved Terry and fellow DJ Mike Phillips, who were having drinks and dinner one night. Enrico's, the North Beach restaurant that could have been called Martoni's North was the prime gathering spot for radio people in the Bay Area, and the setting for many a weird scene.

"Mike was bald," Terry begins. "He went out and bought himself a toupee. It was...ill-fitting. The damned thing looked like a little beanie. He'd get to drinking and it'd become askew. I always told him to get rid of the thing and be proud of himself as he was. Be real. So I started in on him about the toupee."

Phillips picks up the story: "I was fairly drunk, and I was about to take off the hairpiece and throw it at him," he recalls. "And I was sober enough to think, 'Well, taking off the hairpiece might not be a good idea.' So I grabbed the steak and I threw the steak at him. He ducked, and it ended up on the window of Enrico's."

And Terry says, "It stuck there. The place is packed, and everybody's looking at this steak. And then it slid down, leaving this track of meat juice." Phillips, says Terry, completed the performance by taking off his toupee and pitching it against the wall.

back to *Lucky Lager Dance Time* and, before that, the *Make Believe Ballroom.*

In the mid-seventies, dance exploded out of the clubs and onto radio, and by decade's end, there were stations devoted to disco music. Only a couple, but they were significant enough to add to Top 40's paranoia.

The first was WKTU, which played a mix of disco and salsa music beginning in the summer of 1978. Kent Burkhart, the veteran programmer and consultant, helped put it together. To begin with, he says that a dance format in New York City, at that time, "was really their Top 40, just playing the music that was most popular in New York."

Burkhart was on the road, consulting in Spokane, Washington, when he got a call from the owner of WKTU, then a moribund FM station in Manhattan. The owner told Burkhart about his one-share mellow-rock station, then added: 'When I walk up and down Lexington Avenue or around Central Park, all these kids have got these boom boxes up to their ears and they're listening to disco tapes. How about a disco station?' And I said, 'Great idea.'" And Burkhart wasn't just yes-sirring. He'd spent some time in Montreal and witnessed the migration of disco from Paris to Montreal to Boston to New York.

Mike Phillips

WABC, he recalls, still had big ratings, but was playing disco with caution. A week later, "we bombarded the market, and after the first 120 days, or the first four or five months, we had a ten or eleven share, and WABC went down to a five or something."

Before you could say "get down tonight," other stations were on the floor. At WBLS, a former jazz disc jockey, Frankie Crocker, who'd also done his stint as the first black Top 40 DJ in New York (at WMCA, from 1968 to 1971), got into the act.

With Crocker, however, it was no act. WBLS, he says, was "a rhythmic radio station. It always had a dance edge to it. And when disco happened, it just evolved, because I was into the clubs, into what people were doing. It was my form of research. As the clubs evolved into more places to dance, I started pulling that music out, because that was what was happening. I took the night life and the culture of those people in New York and reflected it on the radio."

He was playing disco music a few years before 'KTU made it an all-out format, he says. After a side trip to Los Angeles, where he programmed disco on WBLS' sister station, KUTE, Crocker returned to WBLS and commenced a long ride at the top of the ratings.

Disco, as a full-time format, didn't last long. But before Top 40 could take

Frankie Crocker

a breath, dance music evolved into other formats that would pose challenges to the status quo. Soon, the industry would be talking about and programming—or battling—"urban contemporary," then "Churban" (a blend of urban and CHR, which stands for "contemporary hit radio"—another way to say Top 40).

For those who thought that Top 40 was sounding dazed and confused, playing heavy metal to combat album rock radio, or going soft to cater to the adult-contemporary types, or blowing bubblegum out of desperation for a niche of its own, the funky new dance-based sub-formats were a welcome sound.

After a long and cataclysmic decade, radio was ready for the eighties.

Chapter

Video Killed the Radio Star (Reprise)

MUSIC TELEVISION®

I t took television to inspire the creation of Top 40 radio in the fifties. Nearly three decades later, it was television that would forcefully remind Top 40 of its original agenda: to find the hits, to play them, and to entertain.

The TV in question was MTV (Music Television), launched in 1981 and an immediate phenomenon wherever it could be seen, over cable television. Young people who could get it loved it: 24-7, as they say, of pop and rock videos, with video jockeys (VJs) seemingly plucked out of central casting— a black man, a blonde, a perky brunette, a white guy with an Afro— introducing the clips.

Meanwhile, radio seemed to be going through a post-disco, post-corporate rock, post-punk, spruced-up-neo-New Wave phase. Album Rock, under consultants like Kent Burkhart and his partner, Lee Abrams, was sounding mainstream and aimed directly at the Baby Boom generation. In Los Angeles, programmer Rick Carroll at KROQ-FM created a new alternative: "Rock of the Eighties," combining New Wave hits and a Top 40-styled rotation with DJs who sounded both loose and edgy. In contrast, many Top 40 programmers turned to a new tool in the consultant's box: "passive" music research. Stations called people at random, played bits of new songs to them, and calculated their responses. Instead of seeking the opinions of "actives"—listeners already interested in the calling stations and their music—these stations were playing it safe by accentuating the negative: not playing what people don't seem to like. Having jumped on various musical bandwagons, from disco to hard rock to the Urban Cowboy fad, Top 40 was sounding just plain jumpy. "Depending on your point of view, it was clever and calculated or bland and boring," wrote Dave Sholin, *Gavin's* Top 40 editor.

Stray Cats: They got a jump-start from MTV.

Now, MTV would help lead Top 40 down a new path. Even if it had wanted to, the new network couldn't play video versions of whatever was on pop radio. At that time, many established rock acts had no particular interest in making promotional video clips of singles. MTV showcased whoever gave them videos, and many of them were newer artists from overseas. Such novelties as the Buggles ("Video Killed the Radio Star"), the Stray Cats, and Duran Duran got heavy rotation.

The viewers responded. Acts that proved themselves videogenic saw their records selling—none more so than one Michael Jackson, whose work on "Billie Jean" and "Beat It" combined the power of his talent, videography, choreography, and repeated national exposure to turn him into a superpower. In the process, MTV took radio's role as the arbiter of rock and roll style—even employing promotions and contests whose inventiveness and outrageousness recalled the glory years of Top 40—and forced many radio stations to do what they should have done long ago: widen their playlists.

With MTV (and, in mid-decade VH1, featuring Scott Shannon and Frankie Crocker among its first veejays); satellite delivery of various music formats, including Top 40; the continuing growth of FM; and improvements by Arbitron in the measuring of listening by teens, young adults, and blacks; the music and radio industries began to perk up again.

With all the competition, Top 40—at least on AM—remained under siege. In New York, for example, disco remained strong at WKTU and WBLS, spelling an end to the dominance of WABC. In Los Angeles, KHJ would be switching to a country format. And in San Francisco…well, I got a look and a listen—from the inside.

ON THE AIR, ON THE "AMAZING AM"

For a column I was writing in *GQ*, and in hopes of fulfilling my teenhood fantasy of being a Top 40 disc jockey, I asked KFRC in San Francisco to give me an hour on the air—just one quick dance around the old hot clock.

At the time of my call, in the fall of 1986, KFRC, as a Top 40 station, was in decline. Still, for anyone who loved radio, those call letters were still magic. Twenty years after it'd become "The Big 610" (pronounced "sixten"), DJs seemed to get a rush from talking up the latest record, always ending, on the dime, by punching out the calls to the rhythm of the song: K! F! R!…*C!*

I wanted to do that, on the San Francisco air, just once. For journalistic purposes, I also wanted to get an idea of something I'd heard about for years—the extreme stress that comes with being a Top 40 jock. And I wanted to report on the state of the format.

The column began with a little personal history, about my fantasies and about how, when I finally reached the air in the early seventies, it was on free-form FM rock radio, the antithesis of Drake radio. Now, I wrote, the Drake era was over. I continued:

Today, AMs are littered across the radioscape. They're pinning what hopes they have on AM stereo. KFRC, "the Big 610," tried oldies and even, for a short, disastrous spell, game shows. Now it's brought back personality DJs, and it's going after the auto-bound audience (slogan: "The station worth saving a button for").

When I finally decide to feel some of the heat of that jingle-jangled format, I have only one station in mind. KFRC program director Dave Sholin, it turns out, understands all about boyhood fantasies. He sets up a guest DJ slot for me: Monday night from eleven to midnight, on Turi Ryder's show.

Through the years, I've heard about the pressures and the tolls Top 40 takes on its announcers. To get some specifics, I call on Mike Phillips, one of the original jocks on KFRC. Working for Drake, he says, "was like being in boot camp."

BIG 30

Duo record shop

MIKE PHILLIPS IS A MANY SPLENDORED THING
3 TO 6 PM ON THE BIG 610

KFRC THE BIG 610!

The result, says Phillips and other Drake alumni, was predictable. "I was drinking every night," says Phillips, "partying till midnight or three. I'd take an amphetamine at five o'clock and be on the air at six."

"It seemed to be one big party," he says. "Being a jock kinda gives you some license to be crazy because the public expects that, to some degree."

A couple of days before my appointed hour on the air, I sit in with Bobby Ocean, who's on his fourth tour of duty at KFRC. "I've been blown out a couple of times," he says. "Here at KFRC, drinking, I fell asleep on the air and had a half-hour—plus—of dead air."

Nowadays, Ocean limits his drinking to sugar-free soda pop, operates a production company, and broadcasts on KFRC as much for fun as for money. Commercial radio, however, is never just fun. Sitting under a track of lights that come on ten seconds before the end of a song, Ocean juggles dozens of tape cartridges (there is no turntable in sight) of songs, commercials, jingles and sound effects. Bobby guides me through a "stop set"—a break for commercials—and explains how he keeps listeners tuned in. "I'm always billboarding," he says. "'Coming up'—something's always coming up. That's an old Drake-ism. The curtain's always rising."

Sunday afternoon: While my wife is out of the house, I try screaming "Six-ten, KFRC" and "the amazing AM." I listen to a playback. I decide I won't scream. I try talking up a record—Madonna's "Papa Don't Preach." I've got it down—after only a dozen attempts.

I write some one-liners. Turi Ryder calls herself "the lady of the evening." I'm going to say she's charging me $100 for my hour there. Listeners will roar. The ratings will soar. I feel sick.

Monday, 10:30 P.M.: I report to the Big 610 where, at eleven, Ryder will become my engineer. I'll sit opposite her, with my own microphone controls and digital countdown clocks, so that I won't talk over the vocals.

On the air at 11:06, I deliver my opening—and immediately step on the vocal. My voice is revved up; it's high and urgent, and, it seems, it's not mine at all. Not only is my voice disembodied, the whole show is. High on adrenaline, I have no idea what song is playing or where the time clock is.

Since I don't have the added pressure of running the board, Ryder encourages me to come up with a contest. I devise a quick quiz, but lose sight of KFRC's phone numbers. No matter. Loyal listeners know. And, yes, I get to say, "We have a winner!"

From there, it's on to more commercials, more music, and more bloopers. At mid-hour, my voice drops to a conversational, almost human level, and I have to remember to get back into character.

By hour's end, I'm wiped out. I appreciate, in a different way than I did as a kid, what Top 40 DJs go through. On FM, I was cruising. Here, I'm hugging the wall. Now I understand the excesses. And, now that I'm one of them, I go right out to North Beach and have a couple of drinks with my fellow jocks. Hey, the pressure's on. Tomorrow morning, the boss is critiquing my stint.

Dave Sholin is a program director of the new school. No phone calls to the jocks; just occasional memos and a monthly meeting in which he plays a random hour and goes through it, stop set by stop set. He spots the tension in my voice, skips charitably over the mistakes (but asks how they happened), notices a missing "KFRC" after a "610" and explains why, in a contest, I should avoid saying, "If you're the winner." The word "if," he says, "implies that you could also be the loser." He laughs at my jokes and praises the way I punch out the call letters. Listening to isolated segments of the tape, to those rare seconds that are free of error, I have to agree: I do sound like a Top 40 jock—or at least as if I had been doing this, if only in my head, for twenty years.

At meeting's end, Sholin has a surprise. He asks if I want to do an occasional weekend shift. For real. My head swirls with pride, and then with visions of incessantly flashing red and white lights.

I think I need a drink.

Epilogue: A couple of weeks later, Sholin calls again. The latest ratings are in, and KFRC's dwindling numbers indicate a near total desertion by young people to FM. So the station is changing call letters and switching from Top 40 to Top Forties and Fifties: Sinatra, Cole, Fitzgerald.

The scream is over.

SCOTT SHANNON: THE MAN; THE SUPERSHAN

If Top 40 were to prosper again—on AM or FM (but probably on FM)—it would have to revert to what had worked before. While Mike Joseph was busily installing his "Hot Hits" format—"thirty records, very very tight, very very fast-moving, very very fresh"—others were rediscovering personality radio, particularly in the morning drive time slot.

Scott Shannon

One of those personalities was also a programmer, Scott Shannon of WPLJ in New York. His work at WMAQ in Nashville in the mid-seventies resulted in a four-year run at Number One in Music City. In the late eighties, he set sail on "Pirate Radio" in Los Angeles. Between those two events, there was his late seventies stint at WRBQ ("Q 105") in Tampa, where he came up with the "Morning Zoo" concept. Actually, there are arguments about that: Bobby Rich staked a claim for *The B Morning Zoo* on KFMB-FM ("B 100") in San Diego; some say the idea was conceived at KKBQ-FM in Houston. But there's no question that the Zoo concept—a raucous ensemble show usually featuring in-studio guests, phone interaction, and song parodies—swept the country, continues today, under various names, and that Scott Shannon, whose peers voted him "the most influential programmer of the past twenty years" in 1993 in *Radio & Records* magazine, was among the first in the cage.

His first cage was a self-built affair. The son of a career soldier, Shannon (born Michael Moore) traveled widely, picked up radio greats in Detroit, Chicago, St. Louis, San Diego, and Indianapolis, and became a radio and music fanatic before he was a teenager. At home, he pieced together his idea of a radio studio in the basement—with a Silvertone record player and a Revere tape recorder—and spent his allowance on records and *Billboard* magazines. The money from his first job—as a caddy—went for a transistor radio: "My first precious possession."

Having heard KFWB in Los Angeles, Shannon ran away from home at age seventeen to get a job there. Rebuffed, he hit the road until he got drafted. In the service he got into radio, and upon his discharge in 1968, at age twenty-one, he got his first professional gigs, in Columbus, Georgia, and in Mobile, Alabama. He combined the names of two favorite DJs, Tom Shannon (of CKLW in the Detroit area) and Scott Muni (of WABC), for his own air name. His first radio persona, "Supershan," was inspired by another disc jockey.

"I was driving down to Mobile," he says. "On the way, I picked up a 50,000-watt radio station out of Cleveland and I heard a fellow by the name of Jack Armstrong, who was a screaming maniac. And I said, 'You know what? I like his style,' and I had been pretty serene up until that point, but he had a certain rhythm, and I said, 'You know what? That sounds a little bit more like where radio is going,' so I adopted certain aspects of this style, the fast beat approach—the only difference is that my voice had a kind of an urban feel to it, because I've always loved R&B music, and of course listened to Wolfman Jack out of Mexico, so I kind of sounded like a black version of Jack Armstrong."—to this add a Southern accent and a fondness for a high-pitched hillbilly whoop and holler, a la Jerry Lee Lewis on "Great Balls of Fire."

After setting ratings records with his evening show at WABB in Mobile, Shannon moved on to Memphis, where he killed, and then to WMAK in Nashville, where he decided to try for the additional position of program director when the original one left. "I decided I didn't want anybody that I didn't really know or respect telling me what to do, so I said, 'How about me?'" Shannon had been a music director and/or assistant program director at his previous stations, and won the job at WMAK.

"I already knew what I was doing," he says. "I studied KHJ constantly." Shannon had a friend in California who made high-quality airchecks of Boss Radio for him, and, from some two hundred hours of tapes, he learned more than Drake formattics. "Robert W. Morgan was one of my heroes along with Don Steele, and I listened to their enunciation and articulation," he says. "It just amazed me that Don Steele was never out of control, but he was always excited. I called it suppressed dynamics. And as far as Robert W. is concerned, because I was a high school dropout I was just envious of his vocabulary and the smooth way [he talked], his word emphasis also. It was great. And I wouldn't ever actually copy these people—I would incorporate aspects of their delivery into mine, and it also served to inspire me."

I asked Shannon to keep his programming hat on for a few questions.

While you were doing the programming at WMAK in the mid-seventies, the station was widely imitated. What were they picking up from you?

Well, I've always incorporated a high-profile personality into my show and into my program and my stations, while having a very strong, tight music format. I always make sure there is a high level of integrity in our music presentation. In other words, I like to play familiar music and hit music. I'm very careful to avoid records that are hypes, and to keep a high-turnover, high-rotation approach to radio.

During the seventies, many stations that had a lot of personality were very sloppy and undisciplined with their music. Then the stations that were very disciplined with their music were also very tight and didn't have very much personality. So what I tried to do was combine the best of both worlds. My reputation is as a loose-cannon, crazy personality program director, but in reality, that was the image that the radio stations would project. The music module of the radio station was very tightly controlled, and attention to detail has always been a part of my game plan.

When I programmed a station I always put the discipline and the structure of Bill Drake [in place] and incorporated a little more looseness with the personalities.

That was Drake's thing, allowing the morning and afternoon drives to do what they wanted to.

I paid that attention to the night show, also. In the markets I was in, most of the time you couldn't afford an afternoon show like they had, so I replaced that with a night disc jockey, which was me most of the time.

The East Coast stations for the most part were a lot more undisciplined than the Drake stations on the West Coast. If you look at WFIL, which was a fantastic radio station in Philadelphia, and WIBG, another great radio station, and WABC, those were looser radio stations as far as personality goes. They were good stations, but they were just operated a little bit differently.

After Nashville, you went to WQXI in Atlanta, and then in 1976, you joined Casablanca Records as vice president of promotion. It's hard to believe that a person as passionate about radio as you were could switch over.

It's hard to imagine. It's hard to describe the emotional damage that I suffered when I was fired for the first time. I'm a very sensitive individual who just loves music and radio, and I was shell-shocked when that happened. And Bob Wilson, who is a dear friend of mine, had just gotten *Radio & Records* off the ground, and he said, "Listen, I'd like to start a radio column and maybe you could do that until you find a job." So I worked on the magazine, and I helped organize the first *Radio & Records* convention in Atlanta, and from there I got a call from Neil Bogart (the late founder of Casablanca Records), and he said, "Hey, how would you like to be a national promotion director?" He said, "I'll pay you $55,000 a year and I'll give you a brand-new Mercedes Benz and an unlimited expense account." I said, "Wow!" To a PD, a DJ that never made more than $30,000 in his life, this sounded pretty good. So I said, "Where do I sign, Neil?"

How did being a promo man sound to you?

I didn't like that because I'm not a very good salesman, I don't like to ask people for favors.

How did you do?

I did fair to good, that's about it. I found out that writing about radio and promoting radio is not the same as doing radio. There's something magical for me about walking into a radio station. And I denied myself for a couple of years that I didn't really want to go back in. Deep inside, I did and

Shannon Gets Down on It

When Scott Shannon broke into New York City in the summer of 1983, he did it in the audacious manner that would mark his marches into other stations, in Los Angeles and, again, in Manhattan. Although licensed to New Jersey, "the all new KHTZ" promised a powerful transmitter on the eighty-third floor of the Empire State Building, used jingles that evoked WABC's "I'll Take Manhattan" package of the sixties, and wasted no time getting into the faces of the big boys in the big town. Here's Scott Shannon on the debut morning. Compared with his hee-hawing nights in the South, his voice is mellow. There's a gentle, Southern lilt to his voice, and, at least this opening day, he uses his real first name:

"The all-new Z-100, New York's newest radio station, 7:12, Michael Scott Shannon and the other one, Thursday, August the fourth, 1983, the first day for that—woo!—Z-100 flame-thrower up on top of that ol' Gorilla building." (*While Shannon reads the weather forecast, we begin to hear noise in the background, of someone being ushered into the studio. Shannon introduces a special guest:*) "probably one of the greatest disc jockeys in the history of radio, and currently he is employed by WNBC—I say that right? WNBC radio. He does the morning show over there...ladies and gentlemen...(*Tympanis pounding*)...star of radio, television and recordings, welcome, please, Mr. Don Imus!"

(*A gruff, hoarse "Imus" begins a string of utterances, "Imus in the mornin'!" "Numbah one!," "Limo," and his companion, "Lisa Baby."*)

(*"Imus" offers to perform a song, "Get Down on It," using only his zipper:*) "Right on my fly...you understand, baby?...move back, Lisa!" (*He zips along a few seconds, pauses to exclaim, "Testify!" and plays a few more strokes until, suddenly, he lets out a blood-curdling scream. More screams and horrified cries of "oh, no," from Shannon and crew lead into—what else—a jingle.*)

finally admitted it to myself, and I took a job with WPGC, AM–FM in Washington. 'PGC went to Number One and we had an eleven share and [were] very successful, and then I got fired again because the general manager didn't like my style.

What was this very unlikeable style of yours?

Well, I'm not very political. To me, a radio station is a person, a living unit, a living organism, and to me, I made decisions only based on the success in that person's best interest, and sometimes you know…and I'm just basically very tough about that. I'm very emphatic about "everything must be for the good of the radio station," and sometimes I think my message was misunderstood.

Through those years, was Top 40 already going through a roller-coaster ride?

I never had any problems with it. I mean, to me it was always the same. It just…to me it was a pilot error. If Top 40 didn't work it wasn't the format's fault. It was all pilot error. And it really distresses me when you hear somebody say, "Well, this format didn't work in this city." The format works anywhere if you do it right.

Who started the Morning Zoo?

Well, the next stop was in Tampa, Florida, and I was hired to revitalize a sick puppy called Q105, and they had a really good morning man named Cleveland Wheeler and they had a pretty good staff, but they were being attacked by a station operated by Bill Tanner out of Miami, Florida. He was responsible for Y100, just an excellent, excellent program director, and he was mastermind of this whole thing across the street at 96-KIX and it was a dance-leaning female Top 40 station. So I came into the marketplace and listened to the station for about ten days and decided it needed to be a full-blown high-energy personality Top 40 radio station with a big morning show. And at that time, morning shows were just guys talking to the audience. A lot of the personality had been drained out of Top 40 radio during that particular era, in the late seventies. So I had an idea. I wanted to create a morning show that was a throwback to the days of Arthur Godfrey, the Don McNeil *Breakfast Club*, with some Johnny Carson *Tonight Show* and some *Saturday Night Live* mixed in, with a lot of skits and parody songs and heavy listener involvement.

The guy that was already on there was a pretty good writer and had a great sense of humor, a fellow named Cleveland Wheeler.

You became a team, then.

Cleveland did character voices and I wrote parody songs, and we were going to have some other members of this aggregation. And I wanted to have a concept that was different than just the *Shannon and Wheeler Show* or the

Cleveland and Scott Show, I wanted to have some sort of umbrella or title to get attention. It was WRBQ so we decided to call it the *Q Morning Zoo*, and it was an immediate success. The ratings were just humongous. And it crossed all demographic and racial lines; we had whole families. We were Number One [among listeners aged 12 to 54] in the morning. It worked fine. Then I got the offer to come to New York and form a new radio station.

Z-100 (KHTZ-FM) in 1983.

Right.

Did you bring the same formula to New York City?

Well, to be honest with you, it wasn't the same format. The morning show was the same format, but every station I do I design for that city and that situation and that environment. The Z-100 concept was what I call a salt and pepper format. Q105 was a little bit more rock and roll. This was a salt and pepper format designed to cut through the loud, hustle-bustle of New York. It was high-intensity, high-energy. When I say salt and pepper, we played one white song, one black song, one white song, one black song. And it was mostly up-tempo songs. It would be like two slow songs an hour. Nothing but hits.

Who was the power at that time?

WNBC, WPLJ was on, it was Top 40. We just blasted our way through, and in seventy-two days we went from worst to first.

And you stayed on top, you've said, for seventeen out of twenty ratings periods, or five years. Had that been a big goal for you in life, to get to New York City?

No, I wanted to go to Los Angeles. KHJ, by that time, had already been destroyed. There was no dominant Top 40 station in Los Angeles.

Enter Pirate Radio?

That was a rocket ride, boy. That was so exciting. Los Angeles didn't know what hit them. The intent was to make it sound like it was coming from a faraway place. The post office box was Catalina Island.

Was this like a nod to the pirate stations off of England?

That's exactly what it was. I had always been fascinated by Radio Caroline and oftentimes thought about trying to go out there in one of those pirate ships and do that.

Were there instant copy cats or did people wait and see?

Oh yeah, there were copy cats. We had the name trademarked because we put it up on satellite and we also had a 900 number where the radio people could call in and listen. So the first month we made more money off people listening to our station, because there were people copying all of our sweepers and our promos and everything. We had lines like, "Whatever you do, wherever you go, *don't be a dickhead*. Crank it up, Pirate Radio." Another one says, "Open your windows, crank it up, and piss off the neighbors."… "Rick Dees, bend over and kiss your ass goodbye." Our regimen was very in-your-face.

You've said that Westwood One, which owned the station(KQLZ) pulled the rug out from under you…

It took off great. We got up to Number Six, I believe, and then it started to even out, and also the music dried up, because that glam rock music just kind of dried up on us. The Guns N' Roses album was late, and a couple of the other big bands just didn't come through. And at that time the ratings had taken a dip, and the company had plenty of money invested in the radio station. There are many different theories, but it just didn't pan out. It was just under two years. That was probably the saddest moment of my career, that I didn't get to finish that. Everybody says, "Oh, was it a failure for you?" People can say it's a failure, but in my head, it was a job I didn't get to finish.

And from then on, you've been pretty much in New York.

Yeah, I went back to New York and went to 'PLJ, which was a station that we basically dismantled when I was at Z-100. We were pretty cruel.

They must have loved seeing you again.

Yeah, there were some people at 'PLJ who weren't very happy with me coming back. We poked a lot of fun at 'PLJ, we were pretty rough on them. We had running jokes on their disc jockeys and their program director, a guy named Larry Berger, was referred to as "Little Larry Booger." And we had skits about him and how inept he was and his girlfriend threw him out of the house because he couldn't make love to her, and we had him having sex with goats and various little skits, so it was a bittersweet homecoming for a lot of people.

But they were in twenty-third place.

Yeah, they needed me. Basically the station, the [advertising] billing was ridiculously low, and we managed to quadruple the billing in just four years.

RICK DEES: "HE IS… RATHER POPULAR"

Rick Dees demands more than a typical introduction. His is the interview that led me to believe that—at least in one case, and perhaps in more—readers would be better served with a full profile, by dialogue, than with selected quotes placed throughout the book.

Beyond his interview, there is his standing. Since establishing himself in the early eighties at KIIS-FM in Los Angeles, he is the poster boy of contemporary Top 40; its most vocal champion, and its greatest success story.

I told part of that story in an article in GQ magazine in 1984. To set the stage for our most recent interview, here, just slightly edited, is the way he was.

Rick Dees

He moonglides into view. He's got on his Michael Jackson shades, his Michael Jackson sequined glove and his Michael Jackson voice, which sounds faintly like his Time Fairy voice. "I wanna thank my boa constrictor," he says in a high sigh. "I wanna thank LaToya for turning me on to snakes; I wanna thank Webster even though I stepped on him last week; and I wanna thank GQ for their comments on my ep-u-lets."

This is Rick Dees, and this is how he greets me in the lobby of his radio station.

And I mean his radio station. KIIS-FM, a Top 40 outlet, dominates Los Angeles like no other station since KHJ in the heyday of Top 40 on AM. And Rick Dees dominates all of radio like a...well, like Michael Jackson.

To Dees's Jackson, there are plenty of Princes, like Scott Shannon and Don Imus in New York and Steve Dahl in Chicago; but there's no one quite like Dees. Consider: In radio these days, rock stations in large, competitive markets pop corks when their ratings hit...oh, four points—that is, four percent of the entire listening audience. In Los Angeles, home to more than forty stations (with another forty in neighboring counties), for several years KABC, with its news, talk shows and Dodgers games, had been the rarely disputed king with ratings of sevens and eights.

Then along came KIIS, which in 1981 had a disco format staggering around the bottom of the ratings ladder with a 2.7. This fall, the station zoomed to a 10.0, two points more than its nearest rival. And since one ratings point can translate into roughly an additional $1 million in annual advertising revenue, you can appreciate KIIS's new muscle.

Dees himself had an astounding 20.6 share of listeners aged eighteen to thirty-four for his 6 a.m. to 10 a.m. show. His closest competitor got 5.8. In fact, Dees's show was far and away the most popular among all adults up to age fifty-four.

Dees is beginning to look like the Eighties version of Dick Clark, Wolfman Jack and Murray the K: the deejay turned star. Since last year he has also been hosting *Rick Dees's Weekly Top 40,* a weekly nationally syndicated "countdown" radio show. It's a slightly more sedate version of his local program, and it's already said to be putting a dent into the business of the long-established king of countdowns, Casey Kasem.

"He is…rather popular," says Sue Steinberg. She says this in an understandably pained voice. Steinberg is music director of KMET, an album rock station that is well established—and well entrenched, with ratings between 3 and 4. "KIIS did an interesting thing," she continues. "They did this big campaign last year and focused only on Rick Dees. He was on every bus and billboard in town. The theory was that he'd carry the station, and it paid off. You hear him everywhere." The campaign, according to one radio insider, cost more than $1 million; in addition, the station offers a cash giveaway that can go as high as $5,000 a day, amounting to about a $750,000 annual handout.

But the bottom line justifies the expenditure. "We aren't allowed to divulge our finances," says Wally Clark, president and general manager of KIIS and its AM sister, KPRZ, "but if we're not the most profitable station in the country, we're certainly in the top five." Reliable reports have KIIS's advertising revenues for 1984 between $20 million and $25 million.

In Los Angeles, there are any number of DJs (actually, they don't spin records anymore and would rather be called personalities) who could do what Dees does. But he's the right guy at the right time. It doesn't hurt that in those posters of Dees that rode all those buses, the face was handsome, in a preppy, stylish sort of way.

His voice is basic Top 40, but on the relaxed and conversational side. There is plenty of easy chatter with a glib crew of news, sports and traffic reporters. And almost every morning Dees gets a call-in from his comedienne wife, Julie, who contributes Jane Fonda, Joan Rivers, Bo Derek and Michael Jackson imitations.

The talk is often interspersed with tapes of celebrities, usually lifted off television and always used out of context. Thanks to the ratings, Dees also has stars calling up or making voice tracks for him. Among his favorites is one from L.A. mayor Tom Bradley saying "Yes, sir, Mr. Dees." In the radio theater of the mind, Dees can have Bradley break dancing on the floor, pausing only to agree with any silly thing Dees says to him.

The show is unscripted; all Dees has is a handful of newspaper clips of human-interest stories to work from. Every break between songs is filled with breezy conversation, show-biz gossip and low-level gags. He also enjoys playing off people who wander into the studio. Announcing a quiz, he adds, on top of the regular prizes, a Black and Decker nose-hair trimmer, "and Ben Fong-Torres from *GQ* brought in tickets to *The Texas Chain Saw Vasectomy*…"

Banter with sportscaster Charleye ("Coach") Wright leads into a tape of a woman being stopped on a freeway by an officer, the punch line being: "California Highway patrolmen don't have balls." One of Dees's characters is a dirty-old flasher called Willard Wizeman; now on the phone, a San Bernardino listener offers a joke: "I hear Willard Wizeman's decided not to retire." "Oh yeah?" "He's gonna stick it out for another year." Dees howls. The listener goes on: "My wife says making love is like a ride at Magic Mountain. It's over in two minutes, and she throws up." Newscaster Liz Fulton shrieks in horror; Dees shouts, "Hang up!" and they roll into another hit record.

Sex, Dees will say later, is the one subject he's found that unifies his million and a half listeners. "Everybody's preoccupied with it."

When Dees first joined KIIS in 1981, he got yanked off the air, ostensibly for something he'd said. Quicker than you could say "more music," he was back, accompanied by radio and TV ads asking, "Did you hear what Rick Dees said this morning?" It was an old promotion stunt, but it attracted listeners—and that, of course, is what mattered.

Born in Jacksonville, Florida, thirty-four years ago, Dees made the moves all radio voices do, from market to market, hoping for a crack at the big time. Winston-Salem. Raleigh. Greensboro. Memphis. In the mid-seventies, he managed to come up with his own hit record. Remember "Disco Duck"? It sold two million copies. Then in 1977, he took a shot at Hollywood and got the morning slot at KHJ, but his timing was bad. KHJ was dying; stereo FM/album rock was taking over. KHJ went country, and after rejecting a position as a video jock on MTV in New York ("My wife and I prayed about it, and God said he didn't like video, so we stayed here"), Dees joined KIIS-FM.

By then, too many disc jockeys had been shorn of personality and reduced to time and temperature—and the station slogan of the moment. With Dees leading the way, says Wally Clark, "We're in a personality era again. Now every station would like them, but they really aren't around." Ironically, the purge of personalities, he says, left the industry with few young announcers who can be a Rick Dees.

Not that Dees is without his critics. He is often accused of shamelessly swiping ideas from other jocks. During my visit, he shows off a sound effect he says he's just recorded himself, of "the biggest zipper known to man—implying..." But that implication has been playing on radio for at least two decades.

"He rips a lot of shit off people," says one fellow announcer. "But then," he has to add, "we all do that. We're all composites."

Dees readily admits to pilferage. "I may use an idea, but I'll do it in the Rick Dees way. When something works, I say use it." Not that he is incapable of coming up with his own stuff. "Actually, I had an original joke," he says. "In 1973."

The morning of my visit, I see Dees's thievery in action. While playing "Dancing in the Dark," he shows me a newspaper clipping headlined "Bruce Springsteen loses three pounds a show."

"He's in trouble if he does more than fifty shows," I say. Dees laughs, goes back on the air, and reads the headline and part of the story about the Boss's tour. "He runs about six miles a day. Three pounds a show!" And then the punch line: "Imagine if he does fifty shows…my God!"

My line gets butted up against yet another hit record, is gone, and I don't feel used at all. A million people, I think, might have heard it; and like the guy in San Berdoo who called in the sex jokes, and like Arlene in La Puente who plays the hits on her trash can, I am pleased. Time is tight these days, but everybody can still be a star for fifteen seconds. It is radio the way I enjoyed it most—when it had personality. Rick Dees is a tradition reborn.

RICK DEES TODAY

Since the GQ article, Dees has seen numerous changes, both in the deejay lineup at KIIS and in his own morning crew. The only constants are himself, his solid ratings in a market now dominated by Hispanic stations, and his dedication to Top 40 the way he's always liked it.

Here, he tells of his initial love of radio and his success story.

Did you have the radio bug when you were in high school?

I did, I did. When I was sixteen, it just hit me. I was born in Jacksonville, Florida, I was there for eight years and then moved to my father's home, which is in Greensboro, North Carolina, and went to school there. Typical: ran for all the offices, and was the class clown. In one class, I sat behind a guy named Paul Allen, who had the world's biggest Adam's apple, and I said, "What is that used for?" And he said, "Watch this: (*He puts on an announcer's voice:*) 'The junior class of Grimsley presents *The Whole Truth*, a two-act play.'" And I said, "Wow, so you're the one who does the announcements over the intercom every morning." He said, "Not only do I do that, but I also do a radio show." I said, "Neat, how do you do that?" "Well, you have to have a third-class radio telephone license from the Federal Communications Commission with broadcast endorsement."

He said, "Come over to my house. My brother is the engineer at WGBG (a country station), and he's built a radio station that we broadcast in the neighborhood." I was just a few blocks away, on Dogwood Drive, so I rode my bike over. In a corner room, they had this radio station setup and they had a Gates board, and cartridge machines, and his hobby was collecting jingles from a company called PAMS in Dallas, and he had spliced them up and put his name in there.

I said, "Well, how do you get on the air, though? This is just your home." He said, "Well, you've got to get a license." So I got this study book, studied it, and drove my mom's light blue Comet station wagon up to Norfolk, Virginia, to this regional office of the National Association of Broadcasters, took the test and made 100. So I came back to Paul, and said, "Look, I have a license now." He said, "Well, you know what's funny is we're looking for someone to run the Sunday morning tapes at WGBG, and we'd love to have you come over and give it a shot."

I read some news copy, they liked it, so I went on Sunday mornings, and I'll never forget this guy named Tom Miller who looked like a big walrus wearing glasses, was the program director. There was one hour on the entire show where you could play records and actually act like you're on the air. And the rest of the time it was tapes of Dr. Billy Graham. I was seventeen.

I couldn't wait to turn the microphone on in the little production room, and I'd say stuff like, "Son of a bitch. Kiss my ass." We didn't have a cue speaker in the control room, so to cue up Dr. Billy Graham, you just had to look at the VU meter. Whenever it deflected, that meant he was starting, and they didn't have a lot of tape, so we had to use the same tapes for the same shows over and over again. So I taped Dr. Billy Graham from Minnesota, ran the tape back, and there was no cue speaker, so I'd come up, turned the machine up and I said, "And now, here is Dr. Billy Graham." And you hear, "Son of a bitch. Kiss my ass."

So you invented shock radio.

I did. I was the first shock jock.

But you kept your job?

Do you know what? This kind of let me know where I was in the business. I looked at the telephone for three hours, and not one light was lit. When I got home, my mom said something like, "I could've sworn I heard some weird stuff on the radio station."

Even Mom didn't call.

No, she didn't call. She still doesn't.

Besides Mom, who were your role models?

I loved Tom Miller, the program director at WGBG who started me out, and Paul Allen, at that first station. Then I went to WTOB in Winston-

Salem, then to WKIX in Raleigh, where I worked with Ken Lowe. We started listening to stations way away, like in Chicago and New York, so there's a guy named Ted Brown who was just wonderful, and Chuck Buell, who was awesome. Those are the people on radio I enjoyed, but I infused a lot of Jonathan Winters, because he's my favorite of all time, and Jackie Gleason, with his timing. And Johnny Carson; so those three from television fused with the people I mentioned from radio, plus Dan Ingram, and you've got kind of a sound.

Then there was a guy who was on mornings in Raleigh, North Carolina, that I thought, and still think, is such a great comic, named Pat Patterson. Pat Patterson, as far as a morning show, really gave me the confidence to know that if you just communicated and said what was on your mind and planned out your show, you had a fighting chance.

From Raleigh, I went to Birmingham, Alabama, and it was my first chance. I was supposed to do the afternoon show, and by the time I got there, the morning man had quit, and so Glenn Powers [who] was the program director, gave me my first shot in the morning, and he and a guy named George Williams said okay, so I've always thanked them for that.

Robert W. Morgan told me that when he first got into radio, he always wanted to do mornings. Did you ever have that feeling?

I always thought that the morning show stands apart from all other shows, because it's the only time that radio really can replace television. The radio is the first thing in the morning, so you've got a chance to get everybody. And then when you're talking about such a personal, one-on-one medium, it's dynamically powerful, so I think Robert is right. I always thought mornings, too.

How did you get to Memphis?

I was in Birmingham, and a friend, who was doing the morning show in Memphis, called, and he said, "They're getting ready to let me go because on the Fourth of July last week I blew up some fireworks in the control room on the air, and they think the station's going to get in trouble. So would you like to do the morning show? I can recommend you because I'm getting ready to leave."

So I talked to a guy named Roy Mack. I was making like peanuts in Birmingham. Roy said, "Look, we'll pay you peanuts, too." I said, "Why would I go from peanuts to peanuts?" He said, "In Memphis, you can go and make appearances that you would never be able to make in Birmingham. This city is alive with music and entertainment. You'll get out and do a lot of stuff, I'm sure, because you're an outgoing type of guy. And you love to perform in front of people." I said, "Well, that just doesn't sound right to me." He said, "I bet you make as much off the radio as you do on." He said, "We'll pay you $15,000."

What year was this?

This was last year. No, no. It was 1974. I just said, "I can't do that," and he said, "Okay, I tell you what. We'll make it $16,000, and again, like I said, you'll make a lot of money doing outside appearances."

So when I got to Memphis, I think they had cut it back to $15,000 because they knew that I was making—are you ready for this?—my first morning show in Birmingham, Alabama, I made at WSGN, this is 1973, $9,000. Nine thousand. But I never thought I wasn't making money. I had a car that I made a proper payment on, I had a small apartment, believe it or not—in Birmingham I could get a two-bedroom apartment for $110— I was single, just getting ready to make the plunge—you know, marriage—and no kids of course, so I moved to Memphis.

And then the first year on the air in Memphis, you know me, I love to market. Every night I went out somewhere and I charged a hundred bucks and I'd do a deal, a performance for seven hours if they wanted me to for $100. TGI Fridays. The place across the street, Honeywell's; you know, Chesterfield's. I had six gigs a week. So the first year I was there I made $50,000 outside the studio. The second year I made $125,000 just doing appearances.

Weren't people getting tired of seeing you everywhere?

You know what it does, they keep on seeing you, so if they've got an Arbitron diary, that's all they think about.

I was still doing kind of a hybrid style of radio people I'd heard, and tried to do some myself, and a man named Art Wonder, who was the national program director, cornered me and said, "I don't know how to tell you this, but you're so funny when you talk to the sales people and everything, I mean, you're telling these jokes and stories and doing these characters and everything. Why don't you do that on the air? And why don't you take some telephone calls and put these people on? You're trying to be Bill Drake, and although Bill Drake is very talented, just be Rick Dees."

What did he mean by "you're trying to be Bill Drake"?

Well, Bill Drake is one of the masters of all time, and he created a format which is basically "play those hits, get into them, get out of them." You could be a little clever, but don't be clever for a long time. And get in and get out, do the three major elements, do the time, the call letters, and your name. Over and over again. You know what? Drake is right, but what Bill also didn't say was, "So many of you guys in radio are so awful I have to control you this way. Because if you go on and on, you don't know how to do a monologue for three or four minutes, or you don't know how to have a beginning, a middle, and an end." Then you really don't have to go on for four or five minutes. And he didn't say exactly how to do it, he said, "But you have to do it or you're fired."

The next day is the day in Memphis that I became Rick Dees in the morning. I could go to a conversation and tell you a breaking point, when I put this guy on named Ernest Eberhart, who is an African-American who spoke for the community, and no one had ever given him a chance to get up there and talk about his frustrations and this and that, and he spoke in such a dialect that he would say, "Son of a bitch," and "kiss my ass," and everything, and no one knew what he was saying. So he was the poet laureate of Memphis, and people loved him, and he's such a great guy.

Then I went to the mayor's office—this is just before Halloween—the guy's name is Mayor Chandler, and I didn't have the ratings or anything yet, and I said, "Mayor, look. I was just told yesterday, two days ago, that I'm going to be fired if I don't come up with something, and I know that no one has shown up to tape you, talking about 'don't give razor blades to kids' and all because they're off covering other stories, so it's just basically you and I standing here. Would you be kind enough to say, 'Happy Halloween, yessir, Mr. Dees.' And then, 'Happy Halloween. Don't give that bag of candy, no, sir, Mr. Dees.' And he said, "Well, I'd be glad to do that." He had kind of a wild reputation of getting into fights and stuff.

So the next day on the air, it was like, "Well, the mayor of this entire city is here. Were you out fighting last night?" "Yessir, Mr. Dees." "Your wife like that?" "No, sir, Mr. Dees." "Get these shoes for me, would you give a little spit shine, mayor?" "Yessir, Mr. Dees." "You rub that in, Mayor, I'm going to do a little weather here. You like being down here close to the ankles?" "No, sir, Mr. Dees." In like three months, everywhere I went —"Yessir, Mr. Dees," "No, sir, Mr. Dees." It was unbelievable. And he loved it.

I went up to like a 20 share, I had the deed to the city in my back pocket, I couldn't even touch my wallet when I went into a restaurant. It was just heaven. And I got to Los Angeles—and failed. Went on KHJ, which by that time was an AM station, it was the Karen Ann Quinlan of radio, it was plugged in but nothing was going on. I did the best I could.

You must've known the heritage of the station…

I want to tell you something. I had tapes when I was at WTOB in Winston-Salem, I was nineteen years old. A guy was on the air named Wild Willie Edwards, and his wife Deanna was a flight attendant for Piedmont Airlines, and she would come out to Los Angeles, and we got her to take my little tape recorder, and tape KHJ. So she would bring back tapes of Robert W. Morgan and Charlie Tuna, and we would just marvel at how wonderfully produced their shows were. They were some of the greats. I just can't rave about them any more.

And you know what, KHJ, when I got there, still sounded great, and had some really good people on the air. Bobby Ocean was on the air and some of the real greats...I was doing morning drive, I couldn't believe it. I tell you, the start of my first day was the harbinger of things to come.

I was on the way to the radio station with my wife, Julie. It was 5:30 in the morning, on the way to KHJ. On the freeway I was stopped for speeding. Can you imagine? I got a ticket, I said, "I'm on my way to my first day at work at KHJ," and he said, "What?" And the policeman said, "KHJ? Why don't you work for KMET?" And I went, "Oooohh..."

So you were struggling along knowing most kids were listening to KMET.

I went out to an appearance the third week I was here. I didn't realize how rough it was in this city and all, but I went out to Whittier High School, and the school mascot came out, and it was a parole officer. Went to another school, they listened to KMET, and they said, "You suck! You suck!" And the front row is kids and the Home Ec teacher was knitting a gun.

They changed formats to country and let me go, so for almost a year I was begging for work. I was begging to be on the air. Nobody would take me. In the last, I remember I went out to Drake-Chenault and they said, "Well, we have a couple of recorded shows. If you come on, we can pay $28,000 a year." And I was just getting ready to take that job, when KIIS called.

KIIS-FM was a disco format, and they asked me, should we go Top 40 or A/C? I said Top 40, because my theory is that the young people of the family control the radio, so if they're in the car—and this happens to me all the time—they're in the car and they're saying, "We want to listen to KIIS," the parents are concentrating on driving or doing something else, and they say, "Oh, okay." So then all of a sudden you've got the young people and their parents listening and that's what Top 40 or contemporary radio does.

And so we went on. They had a 1.9 share, then languished there for one book, and the general manager was a guy named Jay Ray Patton, and he said, "The station sounds great, but I don't know what to do." Poor guy, he had found the secret and didn't even know it. We were kicking ass in the morning. Everybody was having so much fun, and Wally Clark came in, and he is a marketing genius, so he said, "Let's just turn up the heat some more. We're not going to go A/C, we're going to go pure Top 40." And the next book, 3 share, next book, 3.8, next book 4.7, next book 6.5, 7.5, 8, 8.5, 9.3, a 10 share with a 12 in the morning. In Los Angeles, that was something that was just unheard of.

You got into television and syndication. Did you feel that being a DJ was in some way confining or limiting?

Having been college-educated, I just recoil at that term, because it's kind of like Alan Freed, the fifties, and we don't even touch discs anymore. Well, we do touch compact discs, but if you talk to Morgan or anybody, they'll say, "Call me anything. Call me a radio host, call me a personality, call me an entertainer, call me a performer."

My favorite expression—my CPA calls me a "performing artist." But to me, it is expanding to be a radio personality, because you get a chance every day to be immediate, to be creative with the most incredible functioning organ in the world, which is the human mind.

"GOOD TIME" CHARLIE MINOR

As Top 40 splintered, and the mainstream began to flow every which way, promotion people found it increasingly difficult to pitch their product.

Russ Regan, the veteran record promoter and label executive, called pop music in the eighties "slot music." "This goes into this slot; that goes into that slot." But he wasn't complaining. Yes, he says, fragmentation made promotion more difficult—"yet in some ways it makes it easier, because you say, 'Well, here it is. We've got a hundred stations to aim at. These are our target stations.' It's not a thousand stations, so you can get answers a little quicker if you are on the ball. The one thing the program directors will do is give you answers."

Minor: A promoter to the hilt.

One promotion man who usually got the right answers was Charlie Minor. One indication of his effectiveness was his record. He was credited with convincing enough program and music directors at enough key stations to make gold out of vinyl recordings by a new wavey trio called The Police ("Roxanne"), by veteran pop and country star Kenny Rogers ("The Gambler"), by the Jacksons' little sister, Janet ("Rhythm Nation"), and by a Christian pop star hoping to go pop, Amy Grant ("Baby Baby"). Between 1986 and 1990, he was named winner of the National Top 40 Promotion Director award by Gavin three times.

An even more dramatic sign of his impact was the reaction throughout the music industry when the forty-six-year-old promo man was shot to death on March 19, 1995, by a young woman with whom he'd had an affair.

"Everything came to a halt," Dave Sholin wrote in his "Inside Top 40" column in Gavin the following week. In the obituary, Beverly Mire noted: "Everyone knew Charlie Minor. Through his seventeen years at A&M, his two years as President of Giant Records, and his short time at Hits [a Top 40-intensive trade magazine], he seemed to make an impact on everyone in the music business." Mire called Minor "a record promoter to the hilt."

What did that mean? "He enjoyed talking programmers into playing his records," Mire wrote. "His former boss, A&M co-founder Herb Alpert, used to call him 'Jaws,' because he was always on the phone to radio stations, pushing his records."

Born in Georgia, Minor had a natural flair for sales, and moved quickly through the ranks of a music company in Atlanta in the early seventies, and then into Hollywood. He mixed Southern charm with sometimes outrageous chutzpah. "He was relentless," said one former A&M promotion executive. Another promo man walked into Minor's office at A&M one day in 1976 and heard him on the phone with a Top 40 program director who, it turned out, was upset over the recent death of a girlfriend. "You know what you can do for her that would be the smartest thing in the world?" Minor said. "You take Nazareth's 'Love Hurts' and you pick it for the week, and you play it every hour, and you dedicate it to her memory. That's the smartest thing you can do."

Apparently, the mourning PD heeded Minor's advice. Regardless, "Love Hurts" went gold.

Chapter

Different Strokes…

"A sk not what's happened to Top 40 radio. Ask rather what's happened to the competition. The answer is 'diversification.' In other words, specialization: a concentrated appeal to a selected segment of the available audience."

Bill Gavin wrote that in 1966, in response to declining ratings for Top 40.

A quarter of a century later, as the nineties began, radio continued to fragment, and, as Top 40 ratings dipped, station owners looked to flip formats. The number of commercial radio stations now neared ten thousand, double the figure from 1961. Of 9,890 stations in 1993, only 441 identified themselves as Top 40, a steep, 24 percent drop from the previous year's 578. Meanwhile, news/talk stations increased by nearly 30 percent, from 641 to 841. Country stations numbered 2,612. Adult Contemporary, an umbrella term for music ranging from "lite rock" to Top 40 fare, accounted for nearly 1,900 stations. There were 734 oldies stations, and 643 had a rock format—album rock, classic rock, or alternative rock. Black radio, encompassing A/C and dance subsets, was on the increase, up to 321 stations.

What was the problem? As Gavin had said twenty-seven years before, it was diversity. Other formats, most notably country and adult contemporary, adapted Top 40 formattics; new stations created niche formats—dance, rap, urban A/C, hot A/C, alternative, classic rock, oldies, oldies of the seventies, oldies of the eighties—that chipped away at Top 40's numbers.

Top 40 had also been guilty of bandwagon-hopping, adding disco when dance was hot; turning grunge when alternative first broke through, and adding some rap when hip-hop began to prove itself commercially. Or it'd go older, softer, and sound more A/C than Top 40. Ultimately, the format confused its audience, if not itself. Ken Barnes, an astute observer of the radio scene, said in 1995 that Top 40, once a democratic jukebox, had become a "vulture" format, "picking off the choice morsels that other, more specialized formats have succeeded with, and pounding them into mass consciousness."

As the millennium approached, Top 40 regained some color. The music helped. A mini-British invasion—Spice Girls—and the reception accorded them by Top 40 in 1997 were signs of a return to pop music—with a dash of hip-hop flava, yes, but pop at its core. Hanson, the Backstreet Boys, and Savage Garden also bopped onto the radio and the charts, mixed nicely with a brewing mass taste for "rhythmic"—that is, dance—songs, and, suddenly, Top 40's ratings were up, and the format was declared alive—again.

In an interview for *Gavin* in 1994, Rick Dees said that rap music had fragmented Top 40's audience. Through his KIIS show and his syndicated Top 40 countdown program, he said, he hoped to "influence some of the urban artists to give us some more songs that you can sing to, rather than rap to."

Guy Zapoleon

"There was a self-fulfilling prophecy," he says now, "because look what has happened. There is a mainstream hip-hop—look at Mase and Will Smith. And groups like Boys II Men have become absolutely enormous, so now, finally, there's a resurgence of Top 40."

Guy Zapoleon, a longtime Los Angeles radio and music nut who works as a radio consultant, is not surprised. He has a theory, that "music trends repeat in a ten-year pattern. The pop explosion of 1997, he says, was simply the completing of the fourth cycle since the birth of rock and roll.

"The three stages of the musical cycle," he says, "are rebirth, extremes, and doldrums. In the middle of the decade is usually where music becomes very pop ("rebirth"). At the end of the decade, usually, it becomes very extreme, and at the beginning of the decade it becomes very soft ("doldrums").

During the mid-decades' "rebirth," he says, "rock, pop, and R&B move towards a mainstream sound. Top 40 regains dominance. In the eighties, this was evidenced by the rise of acts like John Mellencamp, Madonna, Michael Jackson, and Prince." Near decade's end, Zapoleon asserts, music fans tire of pop and go "extreme," for rock or black sounds. When Top 40 goes with that music, he says, it loses older listeners, then pulls back by featuring established stars and softer sounds. "Record labels react by putting out what radio wants, and pop music and Top 40 suffer."

Now, says Zapoleon, Top 40 is healthy again. With all the fragmentation, he adds, "Top 40 is the only format that I know of that reflects the best of all the genres of music today. It's the ultimate variety format plus all the basics of the great radio of the past."

Except that it still doesn't seem to like country, hard rock, and most rap music. That, says Zapoleon, is business. With 80 percent of advertisers seeking to reach consumers aged twenty-five to fifty-four, Top 40 stations don't program with teenagers in mind.

Mike Joseph, for one, thinks they should. While radio has forgotten the younger listeners, he says, "I was yelling, 'Bring back the teens.' My slogan was, 'When you blow away the teens, you blow away the future.'"

Some broadcasters, young and old, believe that Top 40, the way Zapoleon and millions of others remember it, is no more. It's part dance, part hip-hop, part urban, part A/C. "I think that's very true," says Dick Clark, "but I think it's a reflection of what happened in the radio business, not necessarily music. When we first started out, it was a melting pot of all sorts of influ-

To Everything, Turn, Turn, Turn

Here's how Guy Zapoleon defines Birth, Extremes, and Doldrums, the elements of his theory on the cycles of music. That is, "At the end of each cycle, the extreme period inadvertently gives birth to a new format, which becomes truly successful once Top 40 goes into the doldrums."

	CYCLE 1 (1956-1963)	CYCLE 2 (1964-1973)	CYCLE 3 (1974-1983)	CYCLE 4 (1984-1993)
BIRTH	1956 Pop/Rock/R&B	1964 Pop/Rock/R&B	1974 Pop/Rock/R&B	1984 Pop/Rock/R&B
	Elvis Chuck Berry Drifters	Beatles Stones Motown	Fleetwood Mac Eagles/Rolling Stones Stevie Wonder	MTV; Eurythmics/Culture Club Springsteen/Mellencamp Michael Jackson/Madonna Whitney Houston
EXTREMES	1960 Dance	1969 Acid Rock	1978 Disco	1989 Rap/Funk
	Chubby Checker Little Eva DeeDee Sharpe	Hendrix Cream Led Zeppelin	Chic Donna Summer (Punk/Alternative begins)	Hammer Tone Loc Bell Biv Devoe
DOLDRUMS	1961 Chicken Rock & Country	1971 Soft Rock & Country	1979 A/C & Country	1991 A/C & Country
	The Bobbys (Vinton/Rydell/Vee) Country Crossovers Johnny Cash/Patsy Cline	Helen Reddy/James Taylor Country Crossovers John Denver/Anne Murray	Manilow/Diamond/Streisand Country Crossovers Urban Cowboy/Kenny Rogers/Eddie Rabbitt	Elton John/Billy Joel Bolton/Estefan Country Crossovers Garth Brooks/Billy Ray Cyrus

ences, and the audience was not too discerning. As they matured and got used to new forms of music, they founds pieces that they liked and gravitated toward that segment. Well, a radio station having to sell its wares would play that segment, get that chunk of the audience, and have just enough to be able to sell. So it would be impossible to go back thirty, forty years and do what we used to do because the audience wouldn't listen. Even the youth segment is divided. Every form is divided. It doesn't particularly make me happy or sad, because if you find a favorite kind of music, you can find it on one of the multiple choices of stations."

Or, as Michael Spears puts it, "People become their own program directors. Want a little country? I'll hit this country button for two songs. If I

Jingles All the Way

In the jingles business, short did not go with sweet.

For years, Top 40 seemed content with the mini-songs being produced by companies in Dallas, New York, and Los Angeles. The Johnny Mann Singers, the Anita Kerr Singers, and far more anonymous vocalists and musicians were happily cranking out IDs and tunes, ranging from a couple of seconds to almost a couple of minutes.

Jonathan Wolfert

Then came Bill Drake. Suddenly, a station was using exclusively short jingles, where, before, brief ones were part of a larger menu. On top of that, they were a capella. The Mann Singers sounded great, the jingles worked, and the copycats got to work. And, for the jingle industry, it meant trouble.

"He removed all the personality from the jingles," says Jonathan Wolfert, president of Jam Creative Productions in Dallas. "Instead of being fun things, they were reduced and made a lot less fun, and people used less of them and changed them less often."

Wolfert, a childhood fan of such classic New York stations as WNEW and WABC, witnessed what the jingles revolution wrought. He worked at PAMS, the Dallas-based company that produced classic packages for, among others, WABC. After the Drake attrition, PAMS sought to diversify, made some mistakes, and wound up with the IRS at its doors. Wolfert formed his own company, Jam Creative, in 1974, and, partly out of loyalty, acquired PAMS and its copyrights in 1990. Along with Ken Deutsch (also known as Ken R. of Toledo, Ohio), who bought many of the PAMS master tapes at an IRS auction, Wolfert offers PAMS-based jingles as well as original work.

want a little A/C, I'll hit the A/C button for a couple. Top 40 used to do that for you."

Rick Dees wishes it still would. He'd like to see programmers open the doors to country music—as they did to LeAnn Rimes in 1998. But most of Top 40, he says, are still isolationists.

Take Dees's *Weekly Top 40* countdown. It's a bright, breezy show full of funny bits from the highest-rated DJ in Los Angeles. But the show can range from Rimes to Notorious B.I.G., with Spice Girls and Green Day in-between. For some programmers, that's too…democratic.

Dees told about trying to convince the program director of a Top 40 station in a tiny Texas town to add his show. The station, Dees said, is auto-

---

After Drake, some programmers went even further in cutting down jingles. Buzz Bennett, programming KCBQ in San Diego in the early seventies, employed the "shotgun jingle." Bennett describes it as "a blazing jingle that fired off, and then the Carpenters' record would start, almost not there." Listeners were used to slow jingles leading into ballads; bright ones introducing up-tempo songs. Bennett broke the rules and, on top of that, used only that jingle. "They played it every five minutes," says Wolfert, "and they did well, so then a whole group of other stations decided that was the way to go. When you're selling one jingle now instead of thirty, it cuts into your business."

He hadn't seen nothin' yet. Bennett then took jingles completely off the air. "I let the disc jockey do it. Because a disc jockey, if he's trained well, can never say something the same way twice, so it created repetition with variation."

Jingles took a dive. To identify themselves and drive home their positioning statements, stations sometimes hired outside voices, like those of Top 40 veterans Charlie Van Dyke and Bobby Ocean.

Ocean says he still hears jingles everywhere. But, he says, programmers' attitudes vary widely. "I know people who love jingles and want to get them updated very often; people who think the ones they have now should never be changed, and still others [who] think jingles are a dinosaur mode of delivering the message." The nay-sayers include rap-heavy stations, "because it wouldn't fit their format, at least not the jingles normally associated with radio."

"Program directors right now think of jingles as this kind of traditional thing—I heard someone describe them as Mormon Tabernacle vocals. People perceive them as very unhip," says Bob Shannon of TM Century, whose roots include TM Productions, the creator of the "shotgun" jingle. "Most Top 40 stations," he adds, "would love to have the show-biz the jingles provide, if they're hip enough to match the intensity and the attitude of the radio station."

These days, says Ocean, stations can make their own jingles. "They're in the hands of every man because of technology," he says, noting that an eight-track recorder-mixer that once cost $50,000 can be had for $1,200. All a station needs is a computer and some creativity, says Ocean. "It comes back to imagination."

Of course, a radio station creating its own jingles would be nothing new. That, after all, is how it all began, in the late forties, with Gordon McLendon and a band of imaginative musicians—and not a single computer—in Dallas, Texas.

mated for half the day. "I literally begged him to take the *Weekly Top 40*. The producer of our countdown, Melinda Allison, is from that town, so she has firsthand knowledge that there may be four hundred people in the town, and one little radio station.

"And are you ready for this? He's twenty-two years old, and I said, 'Would you play my show on the weekend? I'll do special commercials for you and do whatever it takes, because to me it's very important to get this show on, and I'd love for you to do it. Is there anything I can do to get this on?' And he said, 'I don't know. I'll have to look at the music, and if there are one or two songs that we may not play, I'm not going to play it.' And I said, 'You have to be kidding. The one or two that you wouldn't play are still in the Top 40 hottest-selling songs in the world, and maybe songs you'll play next week, and I promise you, I'll make them so alive and real and tell the story of the songs that they won't tune away.' 'I'm sorry…I'll get back to you.' That was the conversation."

Casey Kasem, for one, feels Dees's pain. The originator of the countdown show has what *Spin* magazine called a "hip-hop problem." When rap first broke into the pop charts, Kasem and his *Casey's Top 40* producers dutifully included the hits, even if it was Sir Mix-A-Lot's ode to big butts, "Baby Got Back," which charted for four months in 1992.

Charted nationally or not, many Top 40 stations shunned rap, and they protested *American Top 40's* policy of hewing to whatever was on top of *Billboard's* charts. Some stations canceled the show or went to other countdowns. In response, Kasem's company switched from *Billboard's* sales charts to another trade, *Radio & Records'* rankings of airplay on top-rated stations. And if those parameters didn't keep the hip-hop out, Kasem's producers added two other countdown shows, both tailored for adult contemporary stations, for those babyboomers.

"The mainstream used to be Top 40, but now, it's Adult Contemporary," Kasem asserted.

Actually, the mainstream is whoever does the opening number on the Grammys. Last time out, it was Will Smith "gettin' all jiggy with it." Of course, later in the show, there was Celine Dion, Aretha Franklin, Trisha Yearwood, Stevie Wonder, Bob Dylan, and Paula Cole, serving up the kind of across-the-board variety that Top 40 used to, when the charts could include Ray Charles and Dinah Washington, Patsy Cline and Jimmy Dean, Dave Brubeck and Henry Mancini—not to mention Chubby Checker—all in the same week.

But that was many yesterdays ago, and those yesterdays are as gone as those make-believe ballrooms in New York and Los Angeles, those first Top 40 dreams in Omaha and Dallas.

Maybe it's fated. All radio formats, like all friends, are bound to disappoint at one time or another. And no matter how close we got to a station or to a disc jockey, listening to them through a pillow in the dark, connected to music and to voices that seemed to be speaking only to us, they could disappear into the ether without so much as a wave good-bye or a farewell song.

Radio, after all, is a business. If a format left you, it was because, the station might say, too many of you left it. And if you left Top 40, that was okay, too. You had your reasons, and it would survive. Through forty years, it had weathered one payola scandal after another, one competing format after another, one new technology after another, and all the shifts in fortune that society, culture, politics, and the economy can bring.

When I joined *Gavin* magazine in 1993, one of the first subjects I tackled was the state of Top 40. Depending on who was talking, it was thriving, dying, or just surviving. We gathered thoughts from a hundred people in radio, and in the end I wrote, instant expert that I was, about Top 40's prospects. And it seems only appropriate that, to conclude a book about Top 40 radio, I'd wind up copying myself.

Top 40, I thought then, and now, can last forever—"especially if people realize, as the format's forefathers did, that teenagers and young adults want only a few things in life: a sense of belonging, a sense of identity, and, socially, a sense of what's new and happening. And that young people have more open and curious ears than most.

"Contemporary music responds to, reflects and entertains youth unlike any other art form, and no matter the onslaught of changing technology and the resultant myriad entertainment choices, radio remains unique in its ability to cater to the local community. Top 40 remains unique, too, in its ability to be the most democratic, the most eclectic, the most daring, the most lively of all formats—if it only chooses to be."

Top of the Pops

I n this section, we present the Number One records of Top 40 radio, as calculated by the staff of Gavin. Early on, when that staff consisted of only Bill and Janet Gavin, publication dates varied. And when they went on vacation, there were no charts for those weeks. In 1964, Bill Gavin bowed to Beatlemania and simply gave the Beatles the Number One position for a couple of issues. The numbers following artists' names indicate how many weeks their record occupied the top spot.

Left Side: Mariah Carey, Elton John, The Eagles, David Bowie,
Right Side: Johnny Mathis, Madonna, Tom Jones, Elvis Presley

1957

7/28	BYE BYE LOVE—Everly Brothers (2)
8/10	TEDDY BEAR—Elvis Presley (3)
8/31	THAT'LL BE THE DAY—Crickets (3)
9/21	MR. LEE—Bobettes
9/28	CHANCES ARE—Johnny Mathis
10/5	BE BOP BABY—Rick Nelson (3)
10/26	APRIL LOVE—Pat Boone (3)

1958

5/20	PURPLE PEOPLE EATER—Sheb Wooley (2)
6/9	HARD HEADED WOMAN—Elvis Presley (2)
7/1	SPLISH SPLASH—Bobby Darin

7/3	REBEL ROUSER—Duane Eddy
7/10	VOLARE—Domenico Modugno
7/14	KING CREOLE—Elvis Presley
7/21	VOLARE—Dean Martin/Domenico Modugno (2)
8/6	LITTLE STAR—Elegants
8/13	IT'S ALL IN THE GAME—Tommy Edwards (2)
9/17	TEARS ON MY PILLOW—Anthony & The Imperials
9/24	IT'S ONLY MAKE BELIEVE—Conway Twitty
10/1	CHANTILLY LACE—Big Bopper (2)
10/17	TOM DOOLEY—Kingston Trio
10/24	TOPSY—Cozy Cole
10/31	TO KNOW HIM IS TO LOVE HIM—Teddy Bears (3)
11/21	THE CHIPMUNK SONG—Chipmunks (5)
12/30	SMOKE GETS IN YOUR EYES—Platters

1959

1/9	DONNA—Richie Valens
1/16	STAGGER LEE—Lloyd Price (2)
1/30	PETITE FLEUR—Chris Barber's Jazz Band
2/6	TRAGEDY—Thomas Wayne
2/13	ALVIN'S HARMONICA—Chipmunks
2/20	VENUS—Frankie Avalon
2/27	IF I DIDN'T CARE—Connie Francis
3/6	COME SOFTLY TO ME—Fleetwoods
3/17	GUITAR BOOGIE SHUFFLE—Virtues
3/25	SORRY (I RAN ALL THE WAY HOME)—Impalas
4/3	HAPPY ORGAN—Dave Baby Cortez
4/10	TAKE A MESSAGE TO MARY—Everly Brothers
4/17	KOOKIE KOOKIE—Edd Byrnes
5/1	TEENAGER IN LOVE—Dion & the Belmonts
5/8	BATTLE OF NEW ORLEANS—Johnny Horton
5/15	PERSONALITY—Lloyd Price
5/22	DREAM LOVER—Bobby Darin
5/29	BATTLE OF NEW ORLEANS—Johnny Horton
6/5	LONELY BOY—Paul Anka
6/12	ALONG CAME JONES—Coasters
6/19	BOBBY SOX TO STOCKINGS—Frankie Avalon
6/26	THERE GOES MY BABY—Drifters
7/10	BIG HUNK O' LOVE—Elvis Presley
7/17	MAKIN' LOVE—Floyd Robinson
7/24	THE THREE BELLS—The Browns
8/1	BABY TALK—Jan & Dean
8/7	THE MUMMY—Bob McFadden & Dor
8/14	I'M GONNA GET MARRIED—Lloyd Price
8/21	(TIL) I KISSED YOU—Everly Brothers
8/28	PUT YOUR HEAD ON MY SHOULDER—Paul Anka
9/4	THE ANGELS LISTENED IN—Crests
9/11	MR. BLUE—Fleetwoods (2)
9/25	DECK OF CARDS—Wink Martindale
10/2	DON'T YOU KNOW—Della Reese
10/9	ENCHANTED SEA—Islanders
10/16	WE GOT THE LOVE—Bobby Rydell
10/23	BE MY GUEST—Fats Domino
10/30	SCARLET RIBBONS—The Browns
11/6	UH OH—Nutty Squirrels
11/13	EL PASO—Marty Robbins
11/20	FRIENDLY WORLD—Frankie Avalon
11/27	WAY DOWN YONDER—Freddy Cannon
12/4	WHY—Frankie Avalon
12/11	VILLAGE OF ST. BERNADETTE—Andy Williams (2)
12/23	RUNNING BEAR—Johnny Preston
12/30	TEEN ANGEL—Mark Dinning

1960

1/8	WHERE OR WHEN—Dion & The Belmonts
1/15	LET IT BE ME—Everly Brothers
1/22	TEEN ANGEL—Mark Dinning
1/29	HE'LL HAVE TO GO—Jim Reeves
2/5	MIDNIGHT SPECIAL—Paul Evans
2/12	WILD ONES—Bobby Rydell
2/19	SWEET NOTHIN'S—Brenda Lee
2/26	SINK THE BISMARCK—Johnny Horton
3/4	MAMA—Connie Francis
3/11	CLEMENTINE—Bobby Darin
3/18	FOOTSTEPS—Steve Lawrence
3/25	STEP BY STEP—Crests (2)
4/8	HITHER, THITHER & YON—Brook Benton
4/15	GOOD TIMIN'—Jimmy Jones
4/22	CATHY'S CLOWN—Everly Brothers (2)
4/29	HE'LL HAVE TO STAY—Jeanne Black
5/6	PAPER ROSES—Anita Bryant
5/13	CATHY'S CLOWN—Everly Brothers (2)
5/27	ALLEY OOP—Hollywood Argyles (3)
6/17	TELL LAURA I LOVE HER—Ray Peterson (2)
7/1	I'M SORRY—Brenda Lee
7/8	ITSY BITSY TEENIE WEENIE YELLOW POLKA DOT BIKINI—Brian Hyland (2)
7/22	ONLY THE LONELY—Roy Orbison
7/29	NOW OR NEVER—Elvis Presley (3)
8/19	VOLARE—Bobby Rydell
8/26	MR. CUSTER—Larry Verne (2)
9/9	A MILLION TO ONE—Jimmy Charles
9/16	CHAIN GANG—Sam Cooke
9/23	MY HEART HAS A MIND OF ITS OWN—Connie Francis
9/30	I WANT TO BE WANTED—Brenda Lee (2)
10/14	POETRY IN MOTION—Johnny Tillotson (2)
10/28	A THOUSAND STARS—Kathy Young (2)
11/11	ARE YOU LONESOME TONIGHT—Elvis Presley (5)
12/16	WONDERLAND BY NIGHT—Bert Kaempfert
12/28	EXODUS THEME—Ferrante & Teicher

1961

1/13	WILL YOU LOVE ME TOMORROW—Shirelles
1/20	EMOTIONS—Brenda Lee
1/27	SHOP AROUND—Miracles
2/3	EBONY EYES—Everly Brothers
2/10	WHERE THE BOYS ARE—Connie Francis
2/17	DEDICATED TO THE ONE—Shirelles
2/24	SURRENDER—Elvis Presley (2)
3/10	BLUE MOON—Marcels (2)
3/24	RUNAWAY—Del Shannon (2)

4/7   MOTHER-IN-LAW—Ernie K. Doe
4/14   I'VE TOLD EVERY LITTLE STAR—Linda Scott
4/21   YOU CAN DEPEND ON ME—Brenda Lee
4/28   DADDY'S HOME—Limelites
5/12   TRAVELIN' MAN—Rick Nelson (2)
5/26   RAINDROPS—Dee Clark
6/2   QUARTER TO THREE—Gary U.S. Bonds (2)
6/16   YELLOW BIRD—Arthur Lyman
6/23   LAST NIGHT—Mar-Keys
6/30   HATS OFF TO LARRY—Del Shannon
7/7   TOSSIN' AND TURNIN'—Bobby Lewis
7/14   DUM DUM—Brenda Lee
7/21   MICHAEL—Highwaymen (2)
8/4   GONNA KNOCK ON YOUR DOOR—Eddie Hodges
8/11   TAKE GOOD CARE OF MY BABY—Bobby Vee (2)
8/25   MORE MONEY FOR YOU AND ME—Four Preps
9/1   THE ASTRONAUT—Jose Jimenez
9/8   LET'S GET TOGETHER—Hayley Mills (2)
9/29   RUNAROUND SUE—Dion
10/6   BIG BAD JOHN—Jimmy Dean (3)
10/27   GOODBYE CRUEL WORLD—James Darren (2)
11/10   WALK ON BY—Leroy Van Dyke (2)
11/24   THE LION SLEEPS TONIGHT—Tokens (4)
12/21   CAN'T HELP FALLING IN LOVE—Elvis Presley
12/28   NORMAN—Sue Thompson (3)

1962

1/19   DUKE OF EARL—Gene Chandler (3)
2/9   HEY BABY—Bruce Channel (2)
2/23   JOHNNY ANGEL—Shelly Fabares (4)
3/23   STRANGER ON THE SHORE—Mr. Acker Bilk
3/30   SOLDIER BOY—Shirelles (5)
5/4   STRANGER ON THE SHORE—Mr. Acker Bilk (2)
5/18   I CAN'T STOP LOVING YOU—Ray Charles (4)
6/15   ROSES ARE RED—Bobby Vinton (4)
7/13   BREAKING UP IS HARD TO DO—Neil Sedaka
7/20   LOCO-MOTION—Little Eva (4)
8/17   SHEILA—Tommy Roe
8/24   SHERRY—Four Seasons (3)
9/14   MONSTER MASH—Bobby Pickett
9/21   DO YOU LOVE ME—Contours
9/28   HE'S A REBEL—Crystals (3)
10/19   ALL ALONE AM I—Brenda Lee
10/26   BIG GIRLS DON'T CRY—Four Seasons (3)
11/16   TELSTAR—Tornadoes (2)
11/30   FIRST FAMILY (album)—Vaughn Meader (4)
12/28   THE NIGHT HAS 1,000 EYES—Bobby Vee (2)

1963

1/11   HEY PAULA—Paul & Paula
1/18   WALK RIGHT IN—Rooftop Singers (2)
2/1   RHYTHM OF THE RAIN—Cascades
2/8   WALK LIKE A MAN—Four Seasons
2/15   RUBY BABY—Dion
2/22   END OF THE WORLD—Skeeter Davis (4)
3/22   PUFF THE MAGIC DRAGON—Peter, Paul & Mary
3/29   I WILL FOLLOW HIM—Little Peggy March (4)
4/26   IF YOU WANT TO BE HAPPY—Jimmy Soul (2)
5/10   IT'S MY PARTY—Lesley Gore (2)
5/24   SUKIYAKI—Kyu Sakamoto (3)
6/14   BLUE ON BLUE—Bobby Vinton
6/21   EASIER SAID THAN DONE—Essex
6/28   MEMPHIS—Lonnie Mack
7/5   FINGERTIPS PT. 2—Stevie Wonder (2)
7/19   JUDY'S TURN TO CRY—Lesley Gore
7/26   CANDY GIRL/MARLENA—Four Seasons
8/2   MY BOYFRIEND'S BACK—Angels (3)
8/23   BLUE VELVET—Bobby Vinton (3)
9/13   BE MY BABY—Ronettes (2)
9/27   SUGAR SHACK—Jimmy Gilmer (4)
10/25   I'M LEAVING IT UP TO YOU—Dale & Grace (3)
11/15   DOMINIQUE—Singing Nun (3)
12/6   LOUIE, LOUIE—Kingsmen
12/13   THERE, I'VE SAID IT AGAIN—Bobby Vinton (2)

1964

1/3   OUT OF LIMITS—Marketts
1/10   HEY LITTLE COBRA—Rip Chords
1/17   YOU DON'T OWN ME—Lesley Gore
1/24   I WANNA HOLD YOUR HAND—Beatles (2)
2/7   SHE LOVES YOU—Beatles (2)
2/21   Beatles
3/6   ALL MY LOVING—Beatles
3/13   Beatles
3/20   TWIST AND SHOUT—Beatles (2)
4/3   CAN'T BUY ME LOVE—Beatles
4/10   THANK YOU GIRL—Beatles (2)
4/24   BITS AND PIECES—Dave Clark Five
5/1   LOVE ME DO—Beatles (3)
5/22   CHAPEL OF LOVE—Dixie Cups
5/29   A WORLD WITHOUT LOVE—Peter & Gordon
6/5   DON'T LET THE SUN CATCH YOU CRYING— Gerry & the Pacemakers (2)
6/19   I GET AROUND—Beach Boys
6/26   MEMPHIS—Johnny Rivers
7/3   RAG DOLL—Four Seasons (2)
7/17   WHERE DID OUR LOVE GO—Supremes (2)

7/31	EVERYBODY LOVES SOMEBODY—Dean Martin
8/7	HOUSE OF THE RISING SUN—Animals (3)
8/28	BREAD AND BUTTER—Newbeats
9/4	OH, PRETTY WOMAN—Roy Orbison (2)
9/18	DO WAH DIDDY DIDDY—Manfred Mann (2)
10/2	WE'LL SING IN THE SUNSHINE—Gale Garnett (2)
10/16	LAST KISS—J. Frank Wilson
10/23	SHE'S NOT THERE—Zombies
10/30	LEADER OF THE PACK—Shangri-Las
11/6	RINGO—Lorne Greene (2)
11/20	MR. LONELY—Bobby Vinton (2)
12/4	I FEEL FINE—Beatles (2)
12/18	LOVE POTION #9—Searchers
12/30	YOU'VE LOST THAT LOVIN' FEELIN'—Righteous Brothers

1965

1/8	DOWNTOWN—Petula Clark (2)
1/22	THIS DIAMOND RING—Gary Lewis
2/12	GOLDFINGER—Shirley Bassey (2)
2/26	EIGHT DAYS A WEEK—Beatles
3/5	STOP! IN THE NAME OF LOVE—Supremes
3/12	CAN'T YOU HEAR MY HEART BEAT—Herman's Hermits
3/19	I'M TELLING YOU—Freddie & The Dreamers (2)
4/2	GAME OF LOVE—Mindbenders
4/9	MRS. BROWN—Herman's Hermits (3)
4/30	WOOLY BULLY—Sam the Sham
5/7	CAST YOUR FATE TO THE WIND—Sounds Orchestra
5/14	CRYING IN THE CHAPEL—Elvis Presley (2)
5/27	I CAN'T HELP MYSELF—Four Tops
6/4	MR. TAMBOURINE MAN—Byrds
6/11	SATISFACTION—Rolling Stones (4)
7/9	I'M HENRY VIII—Herman's Hermits (2)
7/23	SAVE YOUR HEART FOR ME—Gary Lewis & The Playboys
7/30	I GOT YOU BABE—Sonny & Cher (3)
8/20	LIKE A ROLLING STONE—Bob Dylan
8/27	EVE OF DESTRUCTION—Barry McGuire (3)
9/17	YESTERDAY/ACT NATURALLY—Beatles (4)
10/15	A LOVER'S CONCERTO—Toys
10/22	YOU'RE THE ONE—Vogues
10/29	GET OFF OF MY CLOUD—Rolling Stones (2)
11/12	1-2-3—Len Barry
11/19	TURN, TURN, TURN—Byrds
11/26	LET'S HANG ON—Four Seasons (2)
12/10	SOUNDS OF SILENCE—Simon & Garfunkel

1966

1/7	MICHELLE—Beatles
1/14	NO MATTER WHAT SHAPE—T-Bones
1/21	LIGHTNING STRIKES—Lou Christie
1/28	MY LOVE—Petula Clark
2/4	THESE BOOTS—Nancy Sinatra (2)
2/18	BALLAD OF THE GREEN BERETS—Sgt. Barry Sadler (2)
3/4	NOWHERE MAN—Beatles (2)
3/18	SOUL & INSPIRATION—Righteous Brothers
3/25	BANG BANG—Cher
4/1	SECRET AGENT MAN—Johnny Rivers (2)
4/15	GOOD LOVIN'—Young Rascals
4/22	MONDAY MONDAY—Mamas & the Papas (2)
5/6	WHEN A MAN LOVES A WOMAN—Percy Sledge (3)
5/27	PAINT IT BLACK—Rolling Stones (2)
6/10	PAPERBACK WRITER—Beatles
6/17	HANKY PANKY—Tommy James & the Shondells (2)
7/1	LIL' RED RIDING HOOD—Sam the Sham & the Pharoahs (2)
7/15	WILD THING—Troggs
7/22	SUMMER IN THE CITY—Lovin' Spoonful
7/29	SUNNY—Bobby Hebb (2)
8/12	SEE YOU IN SEPTEMBER—Happenings
8/19	SUNSHINE SUPERMAN—Donovan
8/26	ELEANOR RIGBY/YELLOW SUBMARINE—Beatles
9/2	YOU CAN'T HURRY LOVE—Supremes
9/9	CHERISH—The Association (4)
10/7	96 TEARS—? & the Mysterians
10/14	POOR SIDE OF TOWN—Johnny Rivers
10/21	LAST TRAIN TO CLARKSVILLE—Monkees (2)
11/4	GOOD VIBRATIONS—Beach Boys
11/11	YOU KEEP ME HANGIN' ON—Supremes
11/18	WINCHESTER CATHEDRAL—New Vaudeville Band (3)
12/9	I'M A BELIEVER—Monkees
12/16	SNOOPY & THE RED BARON—Royal Guardsmen

1967

1/6	I'M A BELIEVER—Monkees (2)
1/20	GEORGY GIRL—Seekers
1/27	KIND OF A DRAG—Buckinghams (3)
2/17	THEN YOU CAN TELL ME GOODBYE—Casinos
2/24	HAPPY TOGETHER—Turtles (3)
3/17	KIND OF A HUSH—Herman's Hermits
3/24	SOMETHIN' STUPID—Frank & Nancy Sinatra (4)
4/21	THE HAPPENING—Supremes
4/28	GROOVIN'—Young Rascals (5)

6/2	WINDY—Association (2)
6/16	SGT. PEPPER LP—Beatles
6/23	WINDY—Association
6/30	CAN'T TAKE MY EYES OFF OF YOU—Frankie Valli
7/7	I WAS MADE TO LOVE HER—Stevie Wonder (2)
7/21	LIGHT MY FIRE—Doors (2)
8/4	ALL YOU NEED IS LOVE—Beatles
8/11	ODE TO BILLIE JOE—Bobbie Gentry (2)
8/25	THE LETTER—Box Tops (3)
9/15	NEVER MY LOVE—Association (2)
9/29	TO SIR WITH LOVE—Lulu (4)
10/27	INCENSE & PEPPERMINTS—Strawberry Alarm Clock (2)
11/10	THE RAIN, THE PARK & OTHER THINGS—Cowsills
11/17	DAYDREAM BELIEVER—Monkees (3)
12/8	HELLO GOODBYE—Beatles
12/15	JUDY IN DISGUISE (WITH GLASSES)—John Fred & His Playboy Band (2)

1968

1/5	GREEN TAMBOURINE—Lemon Pipers
1/12	LOVE IS BLUE—Paul Mauriat (7)
3/1	(SITTIN' ON) THE DOCK OF THE BAY—Otis Redding (2)
3/15	YOUNG GIRL—Gary Puckett & the Union Gap (2)
3/29	HONEY—Bobby Goldsboro (4)
4/26	A BEAUTIFUL MORNING—Young Rascals
5/3	LOVE IS ALL AROUND—Troggs
5/10	THE GOOD, THE BAD & THE UGLY—Hugo Montenegro
5/17	MRS. ROBINSON—Simon & Garfunkel
5/24	THIS GUY'S IN LOVE WITH YOU—Herb Alpert (4)
6/21	JUMPIN' JACK FLASH—Rolling Stones
6/28	LADY WILLPOWER—Gary Puckett & The Union Gap (2)
7/12	GRAZIN' IN THE GRASS—Hugh Masekela
7/19	HELLO, I LOVE YOU—Doors
7/26	CLASSICAL GAS—Mason Williams
8/2	PEOPLE GOT TO BE FREE—Young Rascals (2)
8/16	LIGHT MY FIRE—Jose Feliciano
8/23	HARPER VALLEY P.T.A—Jeannie C. Riley (3)
9/13	HEY JUDE/REVOLUTION—Beatles (2)
9/27	FIRE—Arthur Brown (2)
10/11	THOSE WERE THE DAYS—Mary Hopkins (3)
11/1	LOVE CHILD—Supremes
11/8	ABRAHAM, MARTIN & JOHN—Dion (2)
11/22	STORMY—Classics IV
11/29	WICHITA LINEMAN—Glen Campbell
12/6	HEARD IT THROUGH THE GRAPEVINE—Marvin Gaye (3)

1969

1/3	CRIMSON & CLOVER—Tommy James & The Shondells (3)
1/24	TOUCH ME—Doors
1/31	BUILD ME UP BUTTERCUP—Foundations
2/7	PROUD MARY—Creedence Clearwater Revival
2/14	DIZZY—Tommy Rose (2)
2/28	TIME OF THE SEASON—Zombies (2)
3/14	YOU'VE MADE ME SO VERY HAPPY—Blood, Sweat & Tears
3/21	AQUARIUS/LET THE SUNSHINE IN—Fifth Dimension (3)
4/11	HAIR—Cowsills (2)
4/25	GUITARZAN—Ray Stevens (2)
5/9	LOVE (CAN MAKE YOU HAPPY)—Mercy
5/16	GET BACK—Beatles
5/23	ROMEO AND JULIET—Henry Mancini (2)
6/6	BAD MOON RISING—Creedence Clearwater Revival
6/13	ONE—Three Dog Night
6/20	GOOD MORNING STARSHINE—Oliver
6/27	2525—Zager & Evans (3)
7/18	A BOY NAMED SUE—Johnny Cash (3)
8/8	SUGAR SUGAR—Archies (4)
9/5	LITTLE WOMAN—Bobby Sherman (3)
9/26	JEAN—Oliver
10/3	SUSPICIOUS MINDS—Elvis Presley (2)
10/17	WEDDING BELL BLUES—Fifth Dimension (2)
10/31	COME TOGETHER/SOMETHING—Beatles (2)
11/14	LEAVING ON A JET PLANE—Peter, Paul & Mary (2)
11/28	SOMEDAY WE'LL BE TOGETHER—Supremes (3)
12/19	RAINDROPS KEEP FALLING ON MY HEAD—B.J. Thomas

1970

1/9	VENUS—Shocking Blue (2)
1/23	I WANT YOU BACK—Jackson 5
1/30	THANK YOU (FALETTIN ME BE MICE ELF AGIN)—Sly & the Family Stone (2)
2/13	BRIDGE OVER TROUBLED WATER—Simon & Garfunkel (4)
3/13	SPIRIT IN THE SKY—Norman Greenbaum
3/20	LET IT BE—Beatles (4)
4/17	ABC—Jackson 5
4/24	EVERYTHING IS BEAUTIFUL—Ray Stevens
5/1	WHICH WAY YOU GOIN' BILLY—Poppy Family (3)
5/22	GET READY—Rare Earth
5/29	LOVE ON A TWO-WAY STREET—Moments
6/5	MY BABY LOVES LOVIN'—White Plains

6/12	MAMA TOLD ME NOT TO COME— Three Dog Night (2)
6/26	CLOSE TO YOU—Carpenters (4)
7/24	MAKE IT WITH YOU—Bread (2)
8/7	IN THE SUMMERTIME—Mungo Jerry (2)
8/21	PATCHES—Clarence Carter
8/28	AIN'T NO MOUNTAIN HIGH ENOUGH— Diana Ross (2)
9/11	JULIE DO YA LOVE ME—Bobby Sherman
9/18	CRACKLIN' ROSIE—Neil Diamond
9/25	GREEN EYED LADY—Sugarloaf
10/2	I'LL BE THERE—Jackson 5(2)
10/16	WE'VE ONLY JUST BEGUN—Carpenters (2)
10/30	I THINK I LOVE YOU—Partridge Family (2)
11/13	GYPSY WOMAN—Brian Hyland
11/20	TEARS OF A CLOWN—Smokey Robinson
11/27	ONE LESS BELL TO ANSWER—Fifth Dimension
12/4	MY SWEET LORD—George Harrison (2)
12/18	KNOCK THREE TIMES—Dawn (3)

1971

1/22	ONE BAD APPLE—Osmonds (3)
2/12	SWEET MARY—Wadsworth Mansion
2/19	THEME FROM LOVE STORY—Henry Mancini (2)
3/5	SHE'S A LADY—Tom Jones
3/12	JUST MY IMAGINATION—Temptations (2)
3/26	JOY TO THE WORLD—Three Dog Night (6)
5/7	ME AND YOU AND A DOG NAMED BOO—Lobo
5/14	WANT ADS—Honey Cone
5/28	IT'S TOO LATE—Carole King (2)
6/11	RAINY DAYS & MONDAYS—Carpenters
6/18	INDIAN RESERVATION— Paul Revere & the Raiders (2)
7/9	DON'T PULL YOUR LOVE— Hamilton, Joe Frank & Reynolds
7/16	MR. BIG STUFF—Jean Knight
7/23	HOW CAN YOU MEND A BROKEN HEART— Bee Gees
7/30	SIGNS—Five Man Electrical Band
8/6	HOW CAN YOU MEND A BROKEN HEART— Bee Gees
8/13	SIGNS—Five Man Electrical Band
8/20	GO AWAY LITTLE GIRL—Donny Osmond (3)
9/10	MAGGIE MAY—Rod Stewart (3)
10/1	SUPERSTAR—Carpenters
10/8	YO-YO—Osmonds
10/15	GYPSYS, TRAMPS & THIEVES—Cher (2)
10/29	THEME FROM SHAFT—Isaac Hayes (2)
11/12	BABY I'M-A WANT YOU—Bread (2)
11/26	FAMILY AFFAIR—Sly & the Family Stone
12/3	BRAND NEW KEY—Melanie (3)

1972

1/7	AMERICAN PIE—Don McLean (3)
1/28	WITHOUT YOU—Nelson (2)
2/11	PRECIOUS AND FEW—Climax (2)
2/25	HEART OF GOLD—Neil Young (2)
3/10	A HORSE WITH NO NAME—America (3)
3/31	THE FIRST TIME EVER I SAW YOUR FACE— Roberta Flack (5)
5/5	SYLVIA'S MOTHER—Dr. Hook
5/12	CANDY MAN—Sammy Davis, Jr. (2)
5/26	OH GIRL—Chi-Lights
6/2	NICE TO BE WITH YOU—Gallery (2)
6/16	LEAN ON ME—Bill Withers (3)
7/7	BRANDY—Looking Glass (2)
7/21	ALONE AGAIN (NATURALLY)—Gilbert O'Sullivan
7/28	LONG COOL WOMAN—Hollies (3)
8/18	BABY DON'T GET HOOKED ON ME—Mac Davis (2)
9/1	GUITAR MAN—Bread
9/8	BLACK AND WHITE—Three Dog Night (2)
9/22	GARDEN PARTY—Rick Nelson
9/29	BURNING LOVE—Elvis Presley (2)
10/13	NIGHTS IN WHITE SATIN—Moody Blues
10/20	I CAN SEE CLEARLY NOW—Johnny Nash (2)
11/3	I'D LOVE YOU TO WANT ME—Lobo (2)
11/17	SUMMER BREEZE—Seals & Crafts (2)
12/1	IF YOU DON'T KNOW ME— Harold Melvin & the Bluenose
12/8	ME & MRS. JONES—Billy Paul (2)
12/27	YOU'RE SO VAIN—Carly Simon (2)

1973

1/12	CROCODILE ROCK—Elton John (2)
1/26	DON'T EXPECT ME TO BE YOUR FRIEND—Lobo
2/2	DUELING BANJOS—Deliverance soundtrack (2)
2/16	KILLING ME SOFTLY WITH HIS SONG— Roberta Flack (3)
3/9	THE NIGHT THE LIGHTS WENT OUT IN GEORGIA— Vicki Lawrence (2)
3/23	TIE A YELLOW RIBBON 'ROUND THE OLD OAK TREE—Dawn (3)
4/13	CISCO KID—War (2)
4/27	FRANKENSTEIN—Edgar Winter Group (3)
5/18	MY LOVE—Paul McCartney (2)
6/1	PLAYGROUND IN MY MIND—Clint Holmes (3)
6/22	BAD, BAD LEROY BROWN—Jim Croce (2)
7/6	SMOKE ON THE WATER—Deep Purple
7/13	MORNING AFTER—Maureen McGovern (2)
7/27	BROTHER LOUIE—Stories (2)
8/10	LIVE AND LET DIE—Paul McCartney & Wings (2)

8/24	DELTA DAWN—Helen Reddy (2)
9/7	WE'RE AN AMERICAN BAND—Grand Funk
9/14	HALF BREED—Cher
9/21	LOVES ME LIKE A ROCK—Paul Simon
9/28	RAMBLIN' MAN—Allman Brothers
10/5	ANGIE—Rolling Stones (5)
11/9	TOP OF THE WORLD—Carpenters
11/16	PHOTOGRAPH—Ringo Starr
11/23	TOP OF THE WORLD—Carpenters (2)
12/7	YELLOW BRICK WORLD—Elton John
12/14	TIME IN A BOTTLE—Jim Croce

1974

1/4	THE JOKER—The Steve Miller Band
1/11	THE WAY WE WERE—Barbara Streisand (3)
2/1	SEASONS IN THE SUN—Terry Jacks (6)
3/15	SUNSHINE ON MY SHOULDERS—John Denver
3/22	HOOKED ON A FEELING—Blue Suede (2)
4/5	BENNIE & THE JETS—Elton John
4/12	LOCO-MOTION—Grand Funk
4/19	THE STREAK—Ray Stevens (4)
5/17	BAND ON THE RUN—Paul McCartney & Wings
5/24	BILLY, DON'T BE A HERO—Heywoods
6/7	SUNDOWN—Gordon Lightfoot (2)
6/21	ROCK THE BOAT—Hues Corporation (3)
7/12	ANNIE'S SONG—John Denver
7/19	ROCK YOUR BABY—George McCrae
7/26	THE NIGHT CHICAGO DIED—Paper Lace (2)
8/9	(YOU'RE) HAVING MY BABY—Paul Anka (2)
8/23	I SHOT THE SHERIFF—Eric Clapton (2)
9/6	I HONESTLY LOVE YOU—Olivia Newton-John (3)
9/27	CAN'T GET ENOUGH—Barry White
10/4	I HONESTLY LOVE YOU—Olivia Newton-John
10/11	YOU AIN'T SEEN NOTHIN' YET—Bachman-Turner Overdrive (4)
11/8	I CAN HELP—Billy Swan (2)
11/22	WHEN WILL I SEE YOU AGAIN—Three Degrees
12/2	KUNG FU FIGHTING—Carl Douglas (4)

1975

1/3	LUCY IN THE SKY—Elton John
1/10	MANDY—Barry Manilow (3)
1/31	BLACK WATER—Doobie Brothers (2)
2/14	HAVE YOU NEVER BEEN MELLOW—Olivia Newton-John (5)
3/21	MY EYES ADORED YOU—Frankie Valli
3/28	LOVIN' YOU—Minnie Riperton
4/4	PHILADELPHIA FREEDOM—Elton John (3)
4/25	(HEY WON'T YOU PLAY) ANOTHER SOMEBODY DONE SOMEBODY WRONG SONG—B. J. Thomas

5/2	HE DON'T LOVE YOU (LIKE I LOVE YOU)—Tony Orlando & Dawn (2)
5/16	PINBALL WIZARD—Elton John
5/23	WILDFIRE—Michael Murphy (2)
6/6	LOVE WILL KEEP US TOGETHER—The Captain & Tennille (5)
7/11	LISTEN TO WHAT THE MAN SAYS—Paul McCartney & Wings (2)
7/25	JIVE TALKIN'—Bee Gees (3)
8/15	HOW SWEET IT IS—James Taylor
8/22	FALLIN' IN LOVE—Hamilton, Joe Frank & Reynolds (2)
9/5	GET DOWN TONIGHT—K.C. & the Sunshine Band (3)
9/26	FAME—David Bowie
10/3	CALYPSO/I'M SORRY—John Denver
10/10	BAD BLOOD—Neil Sedaka (4)
11/7	ISLAND GIRL—Elton John (2)
11/21	THAT'S THE WAY (I LIKE IT)—K. C. & the Sunshine Band (3)
12/12	SATURDAY NIGHT—Bay City Rollers
12/19	CONVOY—C. W. McCall (2)

1976

1/16	I WRITE THE SONGS—Barry Manilow
1/23	50 WAYS TO LEAVE YOUR LOVER—Paul Simon (2)
2/6	THEME FROM S.W.A.T.—Rhythm Heritage (2)
2/20	ALL BY MYSELF—Eric Carmen (2)
3/5	DREAM WEAVER—Gary Wright
3/12	DECEMBER 1963—Four Seasons
3/19	LONELY NIGHTS—The Captain & Tennille (2)
4/2	RIGHT BACK WHERE WE STARTED FROM—Maxine Nightingale
4/9	DISCO LADY—Johnnie Taylor (2)
4/23	BOOGIE FEVER—Sylvers (2)
5/7	WELCOME BACK—John Sebastian (2)
5/21	SILLY LOVE SONGS—Paul McCartney & Wings (3)
6/11	AFTERNOON DELIGHT—Starland Vocal Band (6)
7/23	KISS AND SAY GOODBYE—Manhattans
7/30	DON'T GO BREAKIN' MY HEART—Elton John & Kiki Dee (6)
9/10	PLAY THAT FUNKY MUSIC—Wild Cherry
9/17	IF YOU LEAVE ME NOW—Chicago (5)
10/22	ROCK 'N' ME—Steve Miller Band
10/29	MUSKRAT LOVE—The Captain & Tenille
11/5	TONIGHT'S THE NIGHT—Rod Stewart (5)
12/10	YOU MAKE ME FEEL LIKE DANCING—Leo Sayer (2)

1977

1/7	TORN BETWEEN TWO LOVERS—Mary MacGregor (3)
1/28	BLINDED BY THE LIGHT—Manfred Mann (3)
2/18	EVERGREEN—Barbara Streisand (4)
3/18	RICH GIRL—Hall & Oates (3)
4/8	HOTEL CALIFORNIA—Eagles (2)
4/22	WHEN I NEED YOU—Leo Sayer (4)
5/20	SIR DUKE—Stevie Wonder (2)
6/3	DREAMS—Fleetwood Mac (2)
6/17	UNDERCOVER ANGEL—Alan O'Day (3)
7/8	DA DOO RON RON—Shaun Cassidy
7/15	I'M IN YOU—Peter Frampton (3)
8/5	BEST OF MY LOVE—Emotions (5)
9/9	DON'T STOP—Fleetwood Mac
9/16	STAR WARS/CANTINA BAND—Meco (3)
10/7	YOU LIGHT UP MY LIFE—Debby Boone (7)
11/23	HOW DEEP IS YOUR LOVE—Bee Gees (4)
12/16	BABY COME BACK—Player

1978

1/6	YOU'RE IN MY HEART—Rod Stewart (3)
1/27	STAYIN' ALIVE—Bee Gees (6)
3/10	NIGHT FEVER—Bee Gees (7)
4/28	IF I CAN'T HAVE YOU—Yvonne Elliman
5/5	WITH A LITTLE LUCK—Paul McCartney & Wings (3)
5/26	SHADOW DANCING—Andy Gibb (4)
6/23	BAKER STREET—Gerry Rafferty (4)
7/21	MISS YOU—Rolling Stones
7/28	THREE TIMES A LADY—Commodores (6)
9/8	KISS YOU ALL OVER—Exile (4)
10/6	HOT CHILD IN THE CITY—Nick Gilder (2)
10/20	YOU NEEDED ME—Anne Murray (2)
11/3	MACARTHUR PARK—Donna Summer (3)
11/24	YOU DON'T BRING ME FLOWERS—Barbra Streisand & Neil Diamond (4)

1979

1/5	LE FREAK—Chic
1/12	TOO MUCH HEAVEN—Bee Gees (2)
1/26	DO YA THINK I'M SEXY—Rod Stewart (6)
3/9	TRAGEDY—Bee Gees (3)
4/6	WHAT A FOOL BELIEVES—Doobie Brothers
4/13	HEART OF GLASS—Blondie (2)
4/27	REUNITED—Peaches & Herb (4)
5/25	HOT STUFF—Donna Summer (3)
6/15	LOGICAL SONG—Supertramp
6/22	WE ARE FAMILY—Sister Sledge
6/29	RING MY BELL—Anita Ward (2)
7/13	BAD GIRLS—Donna Summer (3)
8/3	MY SHARONA—The Knack (5)
9/7	SAD EYES—Robert John
9/14	LONESOME LOSER—Little River Band
9/21	SAIL ON—Commodores (4)
10/19	RISE—Herb Alpert
10/26	HEARTACHE TONIGHT—Eagles (3)
11/16	BABE—Styx (3)
12/7	ESCAPE—Rupert Holmes (3)

1980

1/4	COWARD OF THE COUNTY—Kenny Rogers
1/11	ROCK WITH YOU—Michael Jackson
1/19	LONG RUN—Eagles (2)
2/1	SARA—Fleetwood Mac
2/8	LONGER—Dan Fogelberg (3)
2/29	CRAZY LITTLE THING CALLED LOVE—Queen
3/7	ANOTHER BRICK IN THE WALL—Pink Floyd (4)
4/4	CALL ME—Blondie (5)
5/9	BIGGEST PART OF ME—Ambrosia (4)
6/6	FUNKYTOWN—Lipps Inc.
6/13	COMING UP—Paul McCartney (2)
6/27	STILL ROCK 'N' ROLL TO ME—Billy Joel (4)
7/25	MAGIC—Olivia Newton-John
8/1	SAILING—Christopher Cross (3)
8/22	EMOTIONAL RESCUE—Rolling Stones
8/29	ALL OUT OF LOVE—Air Supply (2)
9/12	UPSIDE DOWN—Diana Ross (2)
9/26	ANOTHER ONE BITES THE DUST—Queen (2)
10/10	REAL LOVE—Doobie Brothers
10/17	WOMAN IN LOVE—Barbara Streisand (3)
11/7	LADY—Kenny Rogers (2)
11/21	MORE THAN I CAN SAY—Leo Sayer (3)
12/12	HUNGRY HEART—Bruce Springsteen
12/19	(JUST LIKE) STARTING OVER—John Lennon (2)

1981

1/16	THE TIDE IS HIGH—Blondie (2)
1/30	HEY NINETEEN—Steely Dan
2/6	KEEP ON LOVING YOU—REO Speedwagon (2)
2/20	WOMAN—John Lennon (2)
3/6	THE BEST OF TIMES—Styx (3)
3/27	KISS ON MY LIST—Hall & Oates (2)
4/10	JUST THE TWO OF US—Grover Washington, Jr.
4/17	MORNING TRAIN—Sheena Easton (2)
5/1	TAKE IT ON THE RUN—REO Speedwagon (2)
5/15	BETTY DAVIS EYES—Kim Carnes (4)
6/12	ALL THOSE YEARS AGO—George Harrison (3)

7/3	THE ONE THAT YOU LOVE—Air Supply (3)
7/24	GREATEST AMERICAN HERO—Joey Scarbury
7/31	SLOW HAND—Pointer Sisters (2)
8/14	ENDLESS LOVE—Diana Ross & Lionel Richie (3)
9/4	WHO'S CRYING NOW—Journey (4)
10/2	ARTHUR'S THEME—Christopher Cross (3)
10/23	PRIVATE EYES—Hall & Oates (2)
11/6	WAITING FOR A GIRL LIKE YOU—Foreigner (5)
12/11	LEATHER & LACE—Stevie Nicks (2)

1982

1/8	I CAN'T GO FOR THAT—Hall & Oates (4)
2/5	CENTERFOLD—J. Geils Band
2/12	OPEN ARMS—Journey (6)
3/26	MAKE A MOVE ON ME—Olivia Newton-John (3)
4/16	DON'T TALK TO STRANGERS—Rick Springfield (3)
5/7	EBONY & IVORY— Paul McCartney & Stevie Wonder (6)
6/18	ROSANNA—Toto (3)
7/9	EYE OF THE TIGER—Survivor (6)
8/20	HARD TO SAY I'M SORRY—Chicago (2)
9/3	JACK & DIANE—John Cougar (5)
10/8	I KEEP FORGETTIN'—Michael McDonald (3)
10/29	UP WHERE WE BELONG— Joe Cocker & Jennifer Warnes (3)
11/19	TRULY—Lionel Richie (2)
12/3	MANEATER—Hall & Oates (3)

1983

1/7	DOWN UNDER—Men At Work (4)
2/4	SHAME ON THE MOON—Bob Seger (3)
2/25	DO YOU REALLY WANT TO HURT ME—Culture Club
3/4	YOU ARE—Lionel Richie
3/11	BILLY JEAN—Michael Jackson (4)
4/8	MR. ROBOTO—Styx
4/15	JEOPARDY—Greg Kihn Band
4/22	BEAT IT—Michael Jackson (3)
5/13	OVERKILL—Men At Work (3)
6/3	FLASHDANCE—Irene Cara (2)
8/12	EVERY BREATH YOU TAKE—Police (10)
8/26	MANIAC—Michael Sembello (2)
9/9	TOTAL ECLIPSE OF THE HEART—Bonnie Tyler (5)
10/14	KING OF PAIN— Police
10/28	ALL NIGHT LONG (ALL NIGHT)—Lionel Richie (4)
11/25	SAY SAY SAY— Paul McCartney & Michael Jackson (4)

1984

1/6	OWNER OF A LONELY HEART—Yes (2)
1/20	KARMA CHAMELEON—Culture Club (3)
2/10	THRILLER—Michael Jackson (2)
2/24	JUMP—Van Halen (4)
3/23	FOOTLOOSE—Kenny Loggins (3)
4/13	AGAINST ALL ODDS (TAKE A LOOK AT ME NOW)— Phil Collins (4)
5/11	LET'S HEAR IT FOR THE BOY— Deniece Williams (3)
6/1	TIME AFTER TIME—Cyndi Lauper (3)
6/22	HEART OF ROCK 'N' ROLL— Huey Lewis & the News
6/29	DANCING IN THE DARK—Bruce Springsteen (2)
7/13	WHEN DOVES CRY—Prince (4)
8/10	GHOSTBUSTERS—Ray Parker, Jr. (2)
8/24	STUCK ON YOU—Lionel Richie
8/31	WHAT'S LOVE GOT TO DO WITH IT—Tina Turner
9/7	MISSING YOU—John Waite (2)
9/21	LET'S GO CRAZY—Prince (2)
10/5	HARD HABIT TO BREAK—Chicago
10/12	I JUST CALLED TO SAY I LOVE YOU— Stevie Wonder (3)
11/2	WAKE ME UP BEFORE YOU GO-GO—Wham! (3)
11/23	OUT OF TOUCH—Hall & Oates (2)
12/7	THE WILD BOYS—Duran Duran
12/14	LIKE A VIRGIN—Madonna (5)

1985

1/18	EASY LOVER—Philip Bailey & Phil Collins (2)
2/1	I WANT TO KNOW WHAT LOVE IS—Foreigner
2/15	CARELESS WHISPER—Wham!
2/22	CAN'T FIGHT THIS FEELING—REO Speedwagon (3)
3/15	MATERIAL GIRL—Madonna
3/22	ONE MORE NIGHT—Phil Collins (3)
4/12	WE ARE THE WORLD—USA For Africa (2)
4/26	CRAZY FOR YOU—Madonna (2)
5/10	DON'T YOU (FORGET ABOUT ME)—Simple Minds
5/17	EVERYTHING SHE WANTS—Wham! (2)
5/31	EVERYBODY WANTS TO RULE THE WORLD— Tears For Fears
6/7	HEAVEN—Bryan Adams
6/14	SUSSUDIO—Phil Collins (3)
7/5	RASPBERRY BERET—Prince
7/12	EVERY TIME YOU GO AWAY—Paul Young (3)
8/2	SHOUT—Tears For Fears
8/9	THE POWER OF LOVE— Huey Lewis & the News (3)
8/30	ST. ELMO'S FIRE (MAN IN MOTION)—John Parr (2)

9/13	MONEY FOR NOTHING—Dire Straits (3)
10/4	TAKE ON ME—A-Ha (2)
10/18	PART-TIME LOVER—Stevie Wonder (3)
11/8	WE BUILT THIS CITY—Starship (2)
11/22	SEPARATE LIVES— Phil Collins & Marilyn Martin (2)
12/6	SAY YOU, SAY ME—Lionel Richie (5)

1986

1/17	THAT'S WHAT FRIENDS ARE FOR— Dionne & Friends (2)
1/31	WHEN THE GOING GETS TOUGH, THE TOUGH GET GOING—Billy Ocean
2/7	HOW WILL I KNOW?—Whitney Houston (2)
2/21	KYRIE—Mr. Mister
2/28	SARA—Starship
3/7	THESE DREAMS—Heart (3)
3/28	ROCK ME AMADEUS—Falco
4/4	WHAT YOU NEED—INXS
4/11	ADDICTED TO LOVE—Robert Palmer (2)
4/25	WEST END GIRLS—Pet Shop Boys (2)
5/9	THE GREATEST LOVE OF ALL— Whitney Houston (2)
5/23	LIVE TO TELL—Madonna (3)
6/13	ON MY OWN—Patti LaBelle & Michael McDonald
6/20	THERE'LL BE SAD SONGS—Billy Ocean
6/27	INVISIBLE TOUCH—Genesis (3)
7/18	GLORY OF LOVE—Peter Cetera (3)
8/8	PAPA DON'T PREACH—Madonna (2)
8/22	HIGHER LOVE—Steve Winwood
8/29	DANCING ON THE CEILING—Lionel Richie
9/5	STUCK WITH YOU—Huey Lewis & the News (4)
10/3	THROWING IT ALL AWAY—Genesis (2)
10/17	TRUE COLORS—Cyndi Lauper
10/24	AMANDA—Boston (3)
11/21	HIP TO BE SQUARE—Huey Lewis & the News (2)
12/5	THE WAY IT IS—Bruce Hornsby & the Range
12/12	EVERYBODY HAVE FUN TONIGHT—Wang Chung
12/19	WALK LIKE AN EGYPTIAN— Bangles

1987

1/9	OPEN YOUR HEART—Madonna (4)
2/6	LIVIN' ON A PRAYER—Bon Jovi (3)
2/27	JACOB'S LADDER—Huey Lewis & the News
3/6	MANDOLIN RAIN—Bruce Hornsby & the Range
3/13	NOTHING'S GONNA STOP US NOW—Starship (4)
4/10	I KNEW YOU WERE WAITING (FOR ME)— Aretha Franklin & George Michael
4/17	(I JUST) DIED IN YOUR ARMS—Cutting Crew (2)
5/1	WITH OR WITHOUT YOU—U2 (4)

5/29	YOU KEEP ME HANGIN' ON-Kim Wilde
6/5	IN TOO DEEP—Genesis
6/12	I WANNA DANCE WITH SOMEBODY— Whitney Houston (3)
7/3	ALONE—Heart (3)
7/24	I STILL HAVEN'T FOUND WHAT I'M LOOKING FOR—U2 (2)
8/7	WHO'S THAT GIRL?—Madonna (2)
8/21	LA BAMBA—Los Lobos (2)
9/4	I JUST CAN'T STOP LOVING YOU— Michael Jackson (2)
9/18	DIDN'T WE ALMOST HAVE IT ALL— Whitney Houston
9/25	CARRIE—Europe (2)
10/9	LOST IN EMOTION—Lisa-Lisa & Cult Jam
10/16	BAD—Michael Jackson (2)
10/30	CAUSING A COMMOTION—Madonna
11/6	MONY MONY—Billy Idol
11/13	HEAVEN IS A PLACE ON EARTH— Belinda Carlisle (3)
12/4	FAITH—George Michael (5)

1988

1/8	THE WAY YOU MAKE ME FEEL— Michael Jackson (2)
1/22	COULD'VE BEEN—Tiffany (3)
2/12	WHAT HAVE DONE TO DESERVE THIS— Pet Shop Boys w/Dusty Springfield
2/19	FATHER FIGURE—George Michael (3)
3/11	ENDLESS SUMMER NIGHTS—Richard Marx
3/18	MAN IN THE MIRROR—Michael Jackson (2)
4/1	GET OUTTA MY DREAMS, GET INTO MY CAR— Billy Ocean (3)
4/22	WHERE DO BROKEN HEARTS GO?— Whitney Houston
4/29	ANYTHING FOR YOU— Gloria Estefan & the Miami Sound Machine (2)
5/13	ONE MORE TRY—George Michael (4)
6/10	TOGETHER FOREVER—Rick Astley
6/17	FOOLISH BEAT—Debbie Gibson (2)
7/1	NEW SENSATION—INXS (2)
7/15	ROLL WITH IT—Steve Winwood (4)
8/12	MONKEY—George Michael
9/2	PERFECT WORLD—Huey Lewis & the News
9/9	SWEET CHILD O' MINE—Guns N' Roses (2)
9/23	LOVE BITES—Def Leppard (2)
10/7	A GROOVY KIND OF LOVE—Phil Collins
10/28	KOKOMO—Beach Boys (2)
11/11	BAD MEDICINE—Bon Jovi
11/18	LOOK AWAY—Chicago (3)
12/9	EVERY ROSE HAS ITS THORN—Poison (2)

1989

1/6	TWO HEARTS—Phil Collins (2)
1/20	WHEN I'M WITH YOU—Sheriff (2)
2/3	STRAIGHT UP—Paula Abdul (2)
2/17	LOST IN YOUR EYES—Debbie Gibson (4)
3/17	ETERNAL FLAME— Bangles (2)
3/31	THE LOOK—Roxette (2)
4/13	LIKE A PRAYER—Madonna (3)
5/5	FOREVER YOUR GIRL—Paula Abdul (2)
5/19	ROCK ON—Michael Damian (2)
6/2	I'LL BE LOVING YOU—New Kids On the Block
6/9	SATISFIED—Richard Marx (2)
6/23	GOOD THING—Fine Young Cannibals (2)
7/7	EXPRESS YOURSELF—Madonna
7/14	IF YOU DON'T KNOW ME BY NOW—Simply Red
7/21	TOY SOLDIERS—Martika
7/28	BATDANCE—Prince
8/4	RIGHT HERE WAITING—Richard Marx (4)
9/1	HEAVEN—Warrant (4)
9/29	CHERISH—Madonna
10/6	MISS YOU MUCH—Janet Jackson (2)
10/22	LISTEN TO YOUR HEART—Roxette
11/2	WHEN I SEE YOU SMILE—Bad English (2)
11/17	ANGELIA—Richard Marx
11/24	WE DIDN'T START THE FIRE—Billy Joel (2)
12/8	ANOTHER DAY IN PARADISE—Phil Collins (3)

1990

1/12	HOW AM I SUPPOSED TO LIVE WITHOUT YOU—Michael Bolton
1/19	DOWNTOWN TRAIN—Rod Stewart (2)
2/2	OPPOSITES ATTRACT—Paula Abdul (3)
2/23	ESCAPADE—Janet Jackson (3)
3/16	BLACK VELVET—Alannah Myles
3/23	LOVE WILL LEAD YOU BACK—Taylor Dayne
3/30	I WISH IT WOULD RAIN DOWN—Phil Collins
4/6	DON'T WANNA FALL IN LOVE—Jane Child (2)
4/20	NOTHING COMPARES 2 U—Sinead O'Connor (4)
5/18	VOGUE—Madonna (2)
6/1	IT MUST HAVE BEEN LOVE—Roxette (3)
6/22	STEP BY STEP—New Kids on the Block (3)
7/13	SHE AIN'T WORTH IT—Glenn Medeiros & Bobby Brown
7/20	VISION OF LOVE—Mariah Carey (4)
8/17	COME BACK TO ME—Janet Jackson (2)
8/31	RELEASE ME—Wilson Phillips (2)
9/14	SOMETHING HAPPENED ON THE WAY TO HEAVEN—Phil Collins (2)
10/5	PRAYING FOR TIME—George Michael (2)

10/19	BLACK CAT—Janet Jackson (2)
11/2	LOVE TAKES TIME—Mariah Carey (3)
11/23	I'M YOUR BABY TONIGHT—Whitney Houston (3)
12/14	BECAUSE I LOVE YOU—Stevie B.

1991

1/11	LOVE WILL NEVER DO (WITHOUT YOU)—Janet Jackson (2)
1/25	THE FIRST TIME—Surface (2)
2/8	ALL THE MAN THAT I NEED—Whitney Houston
2/15	SOMEDAY—Mariah Carey (4)
3/15	COMING OUT OF THE DARK—Gloria Estefan (2)
3/29	I'VE BEEN THINKING ABOUT YOU—Londonbeat
4/5	YOU'RE IN LOVE—Wilson Phillips
4/12	BABY BABY—Amy Grant (3)
5/3	JOYRIDE—Roxette
510	I DON'T WANNA CRY—Mariah Carey (3)
5/31	LOVE IS A WONDERFUL THING—Michael Bolton (2)
6/14	RUSH, RUSH—Paula Abdul (4)
7/12	RIGHT HERE, RIGHT NOW—Jesus Jones
7/19	(EVERYTHING I DO) I DO IT FOR YOU—Bryan Adams (7)
9/6	THE PROMISE OF A NEW DAY—Paula Abdul (2)
9/20	I ADORE MI AMOR—Color Me Badd
9/27	EMOTIONS—Mariah Carey (4)
10/25	CAN'T STOP THIS THING WE STARTED—Bryan Adams (2)
11/8	CREAM—Prince & the New Power Generation
11/15	WHEN A MAN LOVES A WOMAN—Michael Bolton (3)
12/6	KEEP COMING BACK—Richard Marx (2)

1992

1/10	CAN'T LET GO—Mariah Carey (2)
1/24	DON'T LET THE SUN GO DOWN ON ME—George Michael & Elton John (2)
2/7	DIAMONDS AND PEARLS—Prince & the New Power Generation
2/14	TO BE WITH YOU—Mr. Big (3)
3/6	GOOD FOR ME—Amy Grant
3/13	MISSING YOU NOW—Michael Bolton featuring Kenny G
3/20	TEARS IN HEAVEN—Eric Clapton (3)
4/10	MAKE IT HAPPEN—Mariah Carey (2)
4/24	HUMAN TOUCH—Bruce Springsteen
5/1	ONE—U2 (2)
5/15	UNDER THE BRIDGE—Red Hot Chili Peppers (3)
6/5	DAMN, I WISH I WAS YOUR LOVER—Sophie B. Hawkins

6/12	HOLD ON MY HEART—Genesis
6/19	I'LL BE THERE—Mariah Carey (4)
7/17	LIFE IS A HIGHWAY—Tom Cochrane
7/24	FRIDAY I'M IN LOVE—The Cure (2)
8/7	THIS USED TO BE MY PLAYGROUND—Madonna (2)
8/21	THE ONE—Elton John
8/28	ALL I WANT—Toad the Wet Sprocket
9/4	END OF THE ROAD—Boyz II Men
9/11	SOMETIMES LOVE JUST AIN'T ENOUGH—Patty Smyth (6)
10/23	WALKING ON BROKEN GLASS—Annie Lennox
10/30	HOW DO YOU TALK TO AN ANGEL—The Heights (5)
12/4	I WILL ALWAYS LOVE YOU—Whitney Houston (6)

1993

1/22	DEEPER & DEEPER—Madonna (2)
2/5	A WHOLE NEW WORLD—Peabo Bryson & Regina Belle
2/12	ORDINARY WORLD—Duran Duran (5)
3/19	TWO PRINCES—Spin Doctors (2)
4/2	IF I EVER LOSE MY FAITH IN YOU—Sting (2)
4/16	I HAVE NOTHING—Whitney Houston (2)
4/30	LOOKING THROUGH PATIENT EYES—P.M. Dawn (3)
5/21	COME UNDONE—Duran Duran
5/28	THAT'S THE WAY LOVE GOES—Janet Jackson (4)
6/25	HAVE I TOLD YOU LATELY—Rod Stewart (3)
7/16	CAN'T HELP FALLING IN LOVE—UB40 (3)
8/6	RUNAWAY TRAIN—Soul Asylum (3)
8/27	DREAMLOVER—Mariah Carey (7)
10/15	NO RAIN—Blind Melon (2)
10/29	I'D DO ANYTHING FOR LOVE (BUT I WON'T DO THAT)—Meat Loaf
11/5	AGAIN—Janet Jackson (3)
11/26	HERO—Mariah Carey (4)

1994

1/7	ALL FOR LOVE—Bryan Adams, Rod Stewart, Sting (5)
2/11	THE POWER OF LOVE—Celine Dion
2/18	THE SIGN—Ace of Base (3)
3/11	WITHOUT YOU—Mariah Carey (4)
4/8	MR. JONES—Counting Crows (3)
4/29	BABY I LOVE YOUR WAY—Big Mountain
5/6	I'LL REMEMBER—Madonna (3)
5/27	I SWEAR—All-4-One (5)
7/1	DON'T TURN AROUND—Ace of Base (5)
8/5	CAN YOU FEEL THE LOVE—Elton John

8/12	STAY (I MISSED YOU)—Lisa Loeb & Nine Stories (3)
9/2	I'LL MAKE LOVE TO YOU—Boyz II Men (9)
11/4	SECRET—Madonna (4)
12/2	ALWAYS—Bon Jovi
12/9	ON BENDED KNEE—Boyz II Men (7)

1995

2/3	TAKE A BOW—Madonna (6)
3/17	I KNOW—Dionne Farris (8)
5/12	I BELIEVE—Blessid Union of the Souls (3)
6/2	LET HER CRY—Hootie & The Blowfish
6/9	WATER RUNS DRY—Boyz II Men
6/16	I'LL BE THERE FOR YOU—The Rembrandts (6)
7/28	WATERFALLS—TLC
8/4	KISS FROM A ROSE—Seal (8)
9/29	FANTASY—Mariah Carey (9)
12/1	ONE SWEET DAY—Mariah Carey with Boyz II Men (9)

1996

2/16	MISSING—Everything But the Girl (2)
3/1	NOBODY KNOWS—The Tony Rich Project (4)
3/29	IRONIC—Alanis Morissette (2)
4/12	ALWAYS BE MY BABY—Mariah Carey (3)
5/3	BECAUSE YOU LOVED ME—Celine Dion (6)
6/14	KILLING ME SOFTLY—Fugees (2)
7/5	YOU LEARN—Alanis Morissette (6)
8/16	I LOVE YOU ALWAYS FOREVER—Donna Lewis (11)
11/1	IT'S ALL COMING BACK TO ME NOW—Celine Dion (2)
11/15	MOUTH—Merril Bainbridge (3)
12/6	DON'T SPEAK—No Doubt (7)

1997

2/14	LOVEFOOL—Cardigans (9)
4/18	I WANT YOU—Savage Garden (4)
5/23	MMMBOP—Hanson (7)
7/11	DO YOU KNOW (WHAT IT TAKES)—Robyn (4)
8/8	SEMI-CHARMED LIFE—Third Eye Blind (3)
8/29	2 BECOME 1—Spice Girls (3)
9/19	FOOLISH GAMES—Jewel (3)
10/10	FLY—Sugar Ray (7)
11/28	TUBTHUMPING—Chumbawamba (4)

Bibliography

Barnard, Stephen. *On the Radio: Music Radio in Britain*. Milton Keynes: Open University Press, 1989.

Barrett, Don. *Los Angeles Radio People*. Valencia, Calif.: db Marketing Company, 1997.

Briggs, Asa. *The BBC: The First Fifty Years*. Oxford: Oxford University Press, 1985.

Brown, Les. *The New York Times Encyclopedia of Television*. New York: Times Books, 1977.

Buxton, Frank, and Bill Owen. *The Big Broadcast: 1920-1950*. New York: Viking, 1972.

Campbell, Robert. *The Golden Years of Broadcasting*. New York: Charles Scribner's Sons, 1976.

Chapple, Steve, and Reebee Garofalo. *Rock and Roll is Here to Pay: The History and Politics of the Music Industry*. Chicago: Nelson-Hall, 1977.

Clark, Dick, and Fred Bronson. *Dick Clark's American Bandstand*. New York: Collins Publishers, 1997.

Clark, Dick, and Richard Robinson. *Rock, Roll & Remember*. New York: Thomas Y. Crowell Company, 1976.

Collins, Rodney, ed. *Radio Luxembourg 1979*. London: Radio Luxembourg (London) Ltd., 1978.

Cooper, B. Lee, and Wayne S. Haney. *Rock Music in American Pop Culture*. Binghamton, New York: The Haworth Press, 1994.

DeCurtis, Anthony, and James Henke, with Holly George-Warren. *The Rolling Stone Illustrated History of Rock & Roll*. New York: Random House, 1992.

Earl, Bill. *When Radio Was Boss*. Montebello, Calif.: Research Archives, 1989.

Earl, Bill. *Dream-House*. Montebello, Calif.: Research Archives, 1991.

Eberly, Philip K. *Music in the Air: America's Changing Tastes in Popular Music, 1920-1980*. New York: Hastings House, 1982.

Fornatale, Peter, and Joshua E. Mills. *Radio in the Television Age*. New York: The Overlook Press, 1980.

Frith, Simon, ed. *Facing the Music*. New York: Pantheon, 1989.

Garay, Ronald. *Gordon McLendon: The Maverick of Radio*. New York/Westport, Connecticut/London: Greenwood Press, 1992.

George, Nelson. *The Death of Rhythm & Blues*. New York: E.P. Dutton, 1988.

Goldrosen, John, and John Beecher. *Remembering Buddy*. New York: Penguin, 1987.

Gordon, Nightingale. *WNEW: Where the Melody Lingers On*. New York: Nightingale Gordon, 1984.

Graedon, Joe. *The People's Pharmacy-2*. New York: Avon Books, 1980.

Hall, Claude, and Barbara Hall. *The Business of Radio Programming*. New York: Billboard, 1977.

Jackson, John A. *American Bandstand: Dick Clark and the Making of a Rock 'n' Roll Empire*. New York: Oxford University Press, 1997.

Jackson, John A. *Big Beat Heat: Alan Freed and the Early Years of Rock & Roll.* New York: Schirmer Books, 1991.

Kaufman, Murray. *Murray the K Tells It Like It Is, Baby.* New York, Chicago, and San Francisco:
 Holt, Rinehart, 1966.

Keith, Michael C. *Voices in the Purple Haze: Underground Radio and the Sixties.* Westport,
 Conn.: Praeger Publishers, 1997.

Lewisohn, Mark. *The Complete Beatles Chronicle.* New York: Harmony Books, 1992.

Lujack, Larry, and Daniel A. Jedlicka. *Super Jock.* Chicago: Henry Regnery Company, 1975.

Marsh, Dave. *The First Rock & Roll Confidential Report.* New York: Pantheon, 1985.

Morrow, Cousin Bruce, and Laura Baudo. *Cousin Brucie: My Life in Rock 'n' Roll Radio.* New York:
 Beech Tree Books/William Morrow, 1987.

Passman, Arnold. *The Deejays.* New York: The Macmillan Company, 1971.

Pollack, Bruce. *When Rock Was Young.* New York: Holt, Rinehart and Winston, 1981.

Rhoads, B. Eric. *A Pictorial History of Radio's First 75 Years.* West Palm Beach, Florida: Streamline Press, 1996.

Romanowski, Patricia, and Holly George-Warren, eds. *The New Rolling Stone Encyclopedia of Rock & Roll.* New
 York: Rolling Stone Press/Fireside, 1995.

Sandahl, Linda. *Encyclopedia of Rock Music on Film.* Poole: Blandsford Press, 1987.

Shaw, Arnold. *The Rockin' 50s.* New York: Hawthorn Books, 1974.

Sklar, Rick. *Rocking America.* New York: St. Martin's Press, 1984.

Smith, Joe. *Off the Record.* New York: Warner Books, 1988.

Smith, Wes. *Pied Pipers of Rock 'n' Roll.* Marietta, Georgia: Longstreet Press, 1989.

Stannard, Neville. *The Long & Winding Road: A History of the Beatles on Record.* New York: Avon Books, 1982.

Whitcomb, Ian. *After the Ball: Pop Music From Rag to Rock.* New York: Simon & Schuster, 1973.

Whitcomb, Ian. *Rock Odyssey: A Chronicle of the Sixties.* New York: Limelight Editions, 1983.

Wolfman Jack and Byron Laursen. *Have Mercy! Confessions of the Original Rock 'n' Roll Animal.*
 New York: Warner Books, Inc. 1995.

ARTICLES: MAGAZINES, NEWSPAPERS AND MISCELLANEOUS

Ahlgren, Calvin. "The Women Jockeys: Rapping With Pride and Assertion."
 San Francisco Chronicle Datebook, 29 February, 1976.

Amber, Arnie. "Porky Chedwick: Pittsburgh's Platter Pushin' Papa." *Goldmine,* February 1980.

Ball, Aimee Lee. "Rock of Ages: WCBS-FM Rides the Crest of an Oldies Revival."
 New York Magazine, 6 August, 1990.

Barnes, Ken. "Radio Wars: The Formats Duke It Out." *Gavin*, 26 May, 1995.

Blanton, Parke. "Radio in the Television Age." *Crystal Set to Satellite: The Story of California Broadcasting.*
 California Broadcasters Association, 1987.

Courtney, Ron. "Blues in the Night—The Story of WLAC Radio." *Goldmine*, February 1984.

DeLuca, David. "The Mad, Mad Daddy of Cleveland Radio." *Cleveland*, September 1984.

Donahue, Tom. "A Rotting Corpse, Stinking Up the Airways . . ." *Rolling Stone*, 23 November, 1967.

Fong-Torres, Ben. "Dick Clark: Twenty Years of Clearasil Rock." *Rolling Stone*, 16 August, 1973.

_____. "Dick Clark Gets Rocked, But Rolls On." *Gavin*, 28 January, 1994.

_____. "Did You Hear What Rick Dees Said This Morning?" *GQ*, December 1984.

_____. "DJ View." *GQ*, October 1986.

_____. "Farewell to Tom Donahue." *Rolling Stone*, 5 June, 1975.

_____. "How DJs Face Up to Life of Frequent Firings." *San Francisco Chronicle Datebook*, 7 December, 1986.

_____. "KMEL's A.M. On Top of Trend." *San Francisco Chronicle Datebook*, 18 January, 1987.

_____. "Moose on the Loose!" *BAM*, 19 May, 1978.

_____. "On the Avenue of the Stars: A Gantse Macher." *Rolling Stone*, 24 December, 1970.

_____. "Top 40 at the Crossroads . . . Again." *Gavin*, 30 July, 1993.

Gambaccini, Paul. "Radio in Britain: God Help Us All." *Rolling Stone*, 13 May, 1971.

George-Warren, Holly. "Leader of the Old School." *Rolling Stone*, 24 March, 1994.

Jacobs, Ron. "The New KHJ's First Day." *KHJ Silver Anniversary Reunion Souvenir Scrapbook*, 1990.

Kening, Dan. "Yvonne Daniels, 'First Lady of Radio.'" *Chicago Tribune*, 23 June, 1991.

"The King of the Giveaway." *Time*, 4 June, 1956.

Land, Herman. "The Storz Bombshell." *Television Magazine*, May 1957

Loder, Kurt. "Murray Kaufman 1922–1982." *Rolling Stone*, 15 April, 1982.

Marion, Jean-Charles. "The New York Disc Jockeys." *Record Exchanger*, no. 31 (1983).

McClay, Bob. "Murray the K on WOR-FM: They Screwed Things Up." *Rolling Stone*, 9 November, 1967.

Milner, Greg. "Silence of the Jams." *SPIN*, March 1998.

Orlean, Susan. "Casey at the Mike." *New York Times Magazine*, 6 May, 1990.

Patoski, Joe Nick. "Rock 'n' Roll's Wizard of Oz." *Texas Monthly*, February 1980.

Price, Richard. "Going Down with Murray the K." *Rolling Stone*, 15 April, 1982.

Puig, Claudia. "Back When Jocks Were Boss." *Los Angeles Times*, 25 April, 1993.

Reid, J.R. "Buffalo Rock Radio: The Early Years." *Goldmine*, June, 1979.

Sholin, Dave. "What Makes Steve Rivers Run." *Gavin*, 4 April, 1997.

Skurzewski, Bob. "Gone Forever: The Grand-Daddy of Rock & Roll." *Record Exchanger* (winter 1972).

Wenner, Jann. "The Blind Leading the Deaf Through a Desert." *Rolling Stone*, 4 January, 1969.

Zapoleon, Guy. "What Goes Around Comes Around." *Gavin*, 20 June, 1997.

RECORDINGS

A Child's Garden of Freberg/Stan Freberg. Capitol Records T777.

Alan Freed's Rock n' Roll Dance Party Vol. 1. WINS Records 1010.

American Graffiti. MCA Records MCA 2-8001.

Cruisin' 1955/Jumpin' George Oxford. Increase Records/Chess INCM 2000.

Cruisin' 1956/Robin Seymour. Increase Records/Chess INCM 2001.

Cruisin' 1957/Joe Niagara. Increase Records/Chess INCM 2002.

Cruisin' 1958/Jack Carney. Increase Records/Chess INCM 2003.

Cruisin' 1959/Hunter Hancock. Increase Records/Chess INCM 2004.

Cruisin' 1960/Dick Biondi. Increase Records/Chess INCM 2005.

Cruisin' 1961/Arnie Ginsburg. Increase Records/Chess INCM 2006.

Cruisin' 1962/Russ "Weird Beard" Night. Increase Records/Chess INCM 2007.

Cruisin' 1963/B. Mitchel Reed. Increase Records INCR 5-1963.

Cruisin' 1964/Johnny Holliday. Increase Records INC 1964.

Cruisin' 1965/Robert W. Morgan. Increase Records INC 1965.

Cruisin' 1966/Pat O'Day. Increase Records INC 1966.

Cruisin' 1967/Dr. Don Rose. Increase Records INCR 5-1967.

Cruisin' 1968/Johnny Dark. Increase Records INCD 1968.

Cruisin' 1970/Kris Eric Stevens. Increase Records/MCA/K-Tel International INCD 197.

Cruisin' with Porky Chedwick. Increase Records/K-Tel International INCD 3000.

KYA's Memories of the Cow Palace. Autumn Records 101.

Live From the Brooklyn Fox: Murray the K. KFM Records KFM 1001.

Programmers' Digest. (July 30, 1973). Audio Video Corp. of America AV 13-1020.

Shake, Rattle & Roll: Rock 'n' Roll in the 1950s. New World Records NW 249.

The Who. *The Who Sell Out*. Decca/MCA DL 74950.

Twist to Radio KYA/ The Bob Keene Big Band. Del-Fi Records DF 1222-SF.

INTERVIEWS

Bill Angel

Bill Ballance

Buzz Bennett

Jerry Blavat

Chuck Blore

Betty Breneman

Kent Burkhart

John Catchings

Dick Clark

Howard Clark

Frankie Crocker

Bobby Dale

David Dalton

Norman Davis

Buddy Deane

Rick Dees

Dave Diamond

Lawrence Diggs

Raechel Donahue

Ken Dowe

Bill Drake

Paul Drew

Elliot Field

Kim Fowley

Kevin Gershan

Arnie "Woo Woo" Ginsburg

John Hart

Johnny Holliday

Ron Jacobs

Mike Joseph

Casey Kasem

Larry Kent

Chuck Leonard

Walt "Baby" Love

Doug MacKinnon

Quincy McCoy

Earl McDaniel

Neil McIntyre

Robert W. Morgan

Bruce Morrow

Joe Niagara

Bobby Ocean

Pat O'Day

Gary Owens

Alec Palao

Mike Phillips

Tony Pigg

Jack Raymond

Russ Regan

Joey Reynolds

Lan Roberts

Dr. Don Rose

Tommy Saunders

Shana

Bob Shannon

Scott Shannon

Rick Shaw

Dave Sholin

Lee "Baby" Simms

Joe Smith

Michael Spears

Shaune Steele

Roger Steffens

Russ Syracuse

Frank Terry

Charlie Tuna

Bill Watson

Ian Whitcomb

Jonathan Wolfert

Don Worsham

Guy Zapoleon

Index

Credits

The author gratefully acknowledges permission from *Rolling Stone* magazine and Wenner Media for the use of the following excerpts, which are copyrighted by Straight Arrow Publishers Company:

"Murray the K on WOR-FM...," by Bob McClay, *Rolling Stone*, November 19, 1967.

"A Rotting Corpse, Stinking Up the Airways," by Tom Donahue, *Rolling Stone*, November 23, 1967.

"The Blind Leading the Blind Through a Desert," by Jann S. Wenner, *Rolling Stone*, January 4, 1969.

"Dick Clark: Twenty Years of Clearasil Rock," by Ben Fong-Torres, *Rolling Stone*, August 16, 1973.

The author is also grateful to *GQ* magazine and Conde Nast Publications Inc. for permission to use the following excerpts:

"Did You Hear What Rick Dees Said This Morning?" by Ben Fong-Torres, *GQ*, December 1984.

"DJ View," by Ben Fong-Torres, *GQ*, October 1986.

Numerous excerpts from the *Gavin Report* and *Gavin* are used with the kind permission of Gavin and the Miller Freeman Entertainment Group.

Front Cover Crowd for Alan Freed/UPI/Corbis Bettman

p. 12 Dick Clark with Fabian/Archive Photos

p. 16 TV Family/Archive Photos

p. 21 Al Jarvis/Everett Collection

p. 26 Dewey Phillips/Jim Cole/Special Collections, University of Memphis

p. 28 Freed Show Marquee/Archive Photos/Frank Diggs Collection

p. 31 Freed in Akron/Photofest

p. 32 Alan Freed-WINS/Photofest

p. 33 Alan Freed-WNEW/Everett Collection

p. 34 Freed with Everly Bros/Photofest

p. 35 Freed with Little Richard and Bill Haley/Courtesy of Roger Steffens Archive

p. 40 KLIF survey/Courtesy of Steve Eberhardt

p. 41 Gordon McLendon/Corbis-Bettman

p. 47 Chuck Blore/Courtesy of Chuck Blore private collection

p. 48 Chuck Blore with Bill Gavin/Courtesy of Chuck Blore private collection

p. 50 Chuck Blore/Courtesy of Chuck Blore private collection

p. 57 Bill Balance Mirror/Courtesy of Ben Fong-Torres private collection

p. 59 Bill Gavin/Gavin Archives

p. 60 Lucky Lager Dance Time /Gavin Archives

p. 61 Bill Gavin with Buckminster Fuller/Gavin Archives

p. 62 Bill and Janet Gavin/Gavin Archives

p. 64 Bill Gavin/Gavin Archives

p. 66 Buzz Bennett/Courtesy of Buzz Bennett private collection

p. 67 Buzz with Elton/Courtesy of Buzz Bennett private collection

p. 67 Buddy Deane/Courtesy of Buddy Deane

p. 69 Casey Kasem/Michael Ochs Archive

p. 71 Gary Owens/Gavin Archives

p. 72 Gary Owens with Crowd/ Courtesy of Norman Davis private collection

p. 75 Gary Owens cartoon/Courtesy of Gary Owens

p. 85 Bill Meeks Band/Courtesy of Don Worsham private collection

ABOUT THE AUTHOR

Ben Fong-Torres' writings first attracted widespread attention in *Rolling Stone* in 1968. He soon became the magazine's news editor, interviewing performers ranging from Bob Dylan to Diane Keaton, and in 1974 won the Deems Taylor Award for Magazine Writing for his interview with Ray Charles. During his 13-year tenure at *Rolling Stone*, Fong-Torres wrote 37 cover stories, edited several anthologies, and was a weekend DJ on the acclaimed radio station KSAN for nine years. He also wrote and narrated a syndicated radio special, "San Francisco: What a Long, Strange Trip It's Been," which won a Billboard Award for Broadcast Excellence.

Fong-Torres has been a staff feature writer and radio columnist for the *San Francisco Chronicle*, and has written for dozens of magazines, including *Esquire, GQ* (where he was pop music columnist for three years), *Playboy, American Film*, and *Harper's Bazaar*. His memoir, *The Rice Room: From Number Two Son to Rock and Roll* was published in 1994 and became a best-seller. He has updated a previous book, *Hickory Wind: The Life and Times of Gram Parsons*, for reissue in paperback.

Fong-Torres most recently served as managing editor of *Gavin*, the San Francisco-based trade weekly for the radio and recording industries—the first publication ever to chart the Top 40 hits.